D1648953

MADE IN CANADA

ECONOMICS FOR CANADIANS

THIRD EDITION

TORONTO
OXFORD UNIVERSITY PRESS

JAMES D. THEXTON

Oxford University Press
8 Sampson Mews, Suite 204, Don Mills, Ontario, M3C 0H5
www.oupcanada.com

Oxford New York
Auckland Cape Town Dar es Salaam Hong Kong Karachi
Kuala Lumpur Madrid Melbourne Mexico City Nairobi
New Delhi Shanghai Taipei Toronto

With offices in
Argentina Austria Brazil Chile Czech Republic France Greece
Guatemala Hungary Italy Japan Poland Portugal Singapore
South Korea Switzerland Thailand Turkey Ukraine Vietnam

Oxford is a trademark of Oxford University Press.

Copyright © Oxford University Press (Canada) 1996.

Canadian Cataloguing in Publication Data

Thexton, James D., 1930-
    Made in Canada : economics for Canadians

3rd ed.
Includes bibliographical references and index.

ISBN-10: 0-19-541100-5
ISBN-13: 978-0-19-541100-3

1. Economics. 2. Canada — Economic conditions.
I. Title.

HB171.5.T54   1995   330   C95-931325-7

COVER DESIGN/BOOK DESIGN: Brett Miller
COVER ILLUSTRATION: Jeff Solway
LAYOUT AND COMPOSITION: Lynda Powell
PROJECT EDITOR: Jane McNulty
PHOTO RESEARCHER: Patricia Buckley Editorial Services
MAP (PAGE 340) AND GRAPHIC ART: Lynda Powell
ILLUSTRATION (PAGE 290): Anne Stanley

This book is printed on permanent (acid-free) paper ∞

9 10 11 - 15 14 13

ACKNOWLEDGEMENTS

The publishers wish to thank the following educators
for their constructive comments in reviewing the revised manuscript:

SAM ALLISON, Centennial High School, Greenfield
    Park, Québec
LORI CRANSON, Program Director, The Learning
    Partnership, Toronto, Ontario
CHESTER FAULKNOR, Ancaster High School,
    Ancaster, Ontario
CHARLES HAWKES, David and Mary Thomson Colle-
    giate, Scarborough, Ontario
JIM HORNELL, Department Head, Social Studies,
    Grand Falls Academy High School, Grand Falls,
    Newfoundland
ANASTASIOS MAKRINOS, Mother Teresa High School,
    Scarborough, Ontario

Special thanks to STEVE OFFICER, Head of History and
Contemporary Studies, London South Secondary
School, London, Ontario.

CONTENTS

CHAPTER 1

Scarcity and Decision Making

(1)

(2)

(3)

(4)

(6)

(5)

Questions

1. What are the individuals shown in these photographs doing?

2. What problem is common to these situations?

3. If you were one of the people in these photographs, how would you decide what to buy?

1

Activity 1: Good news

AN ANNOUNCEMENT

To: Members of economics class

From: The principal

The late Marie Duval, the millionaire entrepreneur, left a large sum of money for educational purposes. By one of the terms of her will, a prize is to be awarded to the class in this school that is most likely to spend the greatest amount of time studying. After careful consideration, the staff and I have selected this class as the winner. Congratulations! Enjoy the prize — five bottles of Sparkle!

The class has a problem. More than five people would like a bottle of the new drink and yet there are only five bottles of it.

a) Some of the ways in which the problem could be solved include the following: equal shares; lottery; authority (the teacher decides). Suggest other ways of solving the problem.

b) In groups, evaluate each of the possible solutions.

c) Decide which way solves the problem best. Why was this way the best?

WANTS

USED CAR SALESPERSON: Hello, how may I help you? A recent model Chev? Volks? Honda? Fiat? Ford? Cadillac? Camaro? Toyota? Plymouth?

CUSTOMER: Yes, one of each.

An unusual reply? Certainly. The salesperson assumes that the customer can afford only one car. Many customers, probably most, would like to own a late model of one of these cars. Rarely, though, do they buy one of each. The reason is obvious. Rarely are their financial resources equal to their wants.

Wants are the need or desire for goods and/or services. Goods are visible and touchable, such as bread, audio tapes, and clothes, while services are invisible and untouchable, such as airplane trips, rock concerts, or a lesson in mathematics.

Physical wants

Physical wants are those wants or needs that are necessary to sustain human life. Such wants include the need for air, water, food, clothing, and shelter.

Because physical wants sustain life, they are the most pressing or urgent of all human wants. Physical wants are often referred to as needs.

The ways in which we satisfy these essential wants is significantly influenced by both climate and society. On a palm-fringed, sun-drenched, south sea isle, we may be able to do without clothing. Depending on custom, however, we may have to wear shorts or a skirt. In Canada for most of the year, social pressure isn't necessary to convince us to wear clothes. Canada's climate makes it necessary. Yet we are influenced by dress codes. For instance, in offices in large corporations in Canada, many people wear business suits. Few business people wear blue jeans with patches.

What we eat is also influenced by social customs. Many Canadians satisfy their appetites with thick, juicy beef steaks. We find it hard to imagine a succulent, mouth-watering horse or monkey steak. Yet, in other societies, horse or monkey meat is eaten as much as beef is in our society.

Psychological wants

Beyond strictly physical wants are a whole range of psychological wants.

Psychological wants are wants for those things that are not essential to sustain life. They include wants for exotic food, fashionable clothing, and an air-conditioned home.

When you graduate and take your first full-time job, you may think that a salary of $25 000 a year will be sufficient to meet all your wants. This could cover your physical wants. If, though, you are like most Canadians, you will soon want an additional $1000 a year and, if you get that, then another $1000 a year, and so on. You will find that you want a car, a holiday in the south, a VCR or CD player, or a larger apartment. The list of wants is probably endless.

In a sophisticated society like our own, the distinction between a physical want and a psychological want is not always clear. It is not essential for business people to wear suits to keep out the cold. They could wear overalls, but they don't. In our society, social pressure is such that people tend to dress in a similar way. The physical want, the need for clothing for warmth, has become partially a psychological want, the need to fit into society. Similarly, even though our want for food is limited by the capacity of our stomachs and we could eat porridge all the time, we continue to want new foods — a variety of meats, exotic fruits, and cuisine from other countries. We are caught, it seems, in a never-ending quest.

RESOURCES

Resources are those things used to produce goods and services. Resources include **human resources**, the skills and efforts people use in production; **capital resources**, such as factories and machinery; and **natural resources**, such as land and forests.

For a child at a candy counter, resources are limited to the coins clutched in the child's palm. The young woman who gazes longingly at the cars on a used car lot, is most acutely aware of one resource: the amount of money in her bank account. Young people have another resource available — their time. They could offer their time to work for the money needed to buy a car, but time is limited too. There are only 24 hours in a day and the more time spent working, the less time for other activities. Our resources never seem to be sufficient to meet all our wants.

SCARCITY

Scarcity is the fundamental fact of economic life: there is a limited amount of resources that can be used to produce a limited amount of goods and services to meet unlimited human wants.

To the child with only a quarter for candy, there is scarcity. To the young person on the car lot who is unable to buy a car, there is scarcity. But how can this be? There is a mini-mountain of candy in the candy store, so much that it is hard to choose. It is the same with all those cars on the lot. How can there be scarcity when neither cars nor candies are in short supply?

Generally in our everyday language, we use the word "scarcity" to mean "shortage" — a shortage of cars, a shortage of candies. *Economists use the word scarcity in a special way: scarcity is always related to our wants and our resources.* There may be little canned Mississippi mud in Manitoba — or indeed anywhere else — but there isn't scarcity because no one wants it. Scarcity does exist, though, for the child in the candy store because the child's meagre resources — the quarter — probably won't satisfy the want for candy. Scarcity also exists in the situation of the young woman in the used car lot because her resources are too limited to get what she wants, i.e., a car. Whenever our wants are greater than our resources, there is scarcity.

Economists reason that, since human wants are capable of almost infinite expansion but the Earth's resources are limited, there will never be a time when all human wants will be satisfied. Scarcity is a fact of economic life.

DECISION MAKING

Since our wants are greater than our resources and we cannot have everything we want, then we have to make decisions among various choices. If, for example, we are in a record store, we cannot have all the tapes or CDs we want. We must choose to buy this tape or that one. This necessity to make decisions is a result of scarcity. It is also in accord with our experience. We are continually faced with the necessity of making choices.

OPPORTUNITY COST

Opportunity cost is the benefit lost of doing one thing rather than another. For example, if you decide to do homework rather than watch TV, then the opportunity cost of homework is the opportunity lost of enjoying TV.

When we make decisions, we are choosing among the alternatives open to us. We select the opportunity of one choice, but we lose the opportunity of another. If you decide to go to a concert instead of buying a tape, the cost to you of going to the concert is the opportunity of having the tape. In other words, the opportunity cost is the opportunity lost.

Suppose that the next time you go into a restaurant, you would like to have a hamburger and a milkshake. You look in your wallet and find that you have enough money for one of them. If you choose the milkshake, the opportunity cost is the hamburger. If you choose the hamburger, the opportunity cost is the milkshake. The concept of opportunity cost is important in economics. Since we are continually forced to make choices, we are continually weighing the opportunity costs of tapes, concerts, hamburgers, and so on. There is an opportunity cost involved with every single purchase made.

Families (or households) are continually faced with the need to make decisions. Since the family has limited resources, it must continually choose among all its wants. The householder constantly makes purchasing decisions about whether to buy more food, clothing, appliances, or holidays away from home. Householders are aware of the opportunity costs involved in making purchasing decisions.

GOODS AND SERVICES

Goods are those concrete, visible things that satisfy human wants, that can be touched, and that last a period of time. Goods include essentials such as bread, and non-essentials such as diamonds.

Services include all those items that satisfy wants, that cannot be touched or seen, and that are consumed at the time of their production. Figure 1.2 on page 6 contrasts goods and services.

Suppose we have to choose between buying a CD and attending a concert. We would be choosing between a good (the CD) and a service (the concert). You can see and touch a CD and you can play it many times. The concert, on the other hand, cannot be touched and does not last beyond the time of its production. It is a service.

We usually think of the products of our economy as being goods only, but our economy also provides a vast number of services. In fact, about three out of four Canadians are employed in the service sector of our economy. Some examples of services are personal financial planning and medical services. Your teacher provides a service by teaching a lesson in economics.

ECONOMICS IS . . .

Economics is the study of human activity involved in using scarce resources to satisfy wants.

As we have seen, we are continually faced with scarcity because our wants are greater than our resources. As a result, we have to make decisions.

The study of economics arises out of scarcity and scarcity is the most important concern in economics. In a society, scarce resources include human resources,

BUILDING YOUR SKILLS

Making individual decisions

Elena is sixteen years old. She receives $15 a week for various jobs she does around the house. Elena is a cautious person. Only under exceptional circumstances will she borrow money. She has managed to save $20, just the amount she needs to buy a CD of her favourite group, the Rockers. The Rockers' CD is now on sale at a downtown store for a limited time only.

Elena is just about to leave one Friday evening to buy the CD when the phone rings. It's her best friend Tamara.

TAMARA: Elena, have you seen tonight's newspaper?

ELENA: No, Tamara, but I'm in a hurry now. Do you want to come downtown with me to buy the Rockers' CD that's on sale?

TAMARA: But the Rockers are coming to the Concert Bowl next week! Look in the entertainment section.

Elena drops the phone, reaches for the paper, and sees a full-page advertisement announcing the concert. In bold type at the bottom of the page is printed:

ALL SEATS: $20

Elena doesn't know what to do. She decides to seek the advice of your economics class. To help Elena solve her dilemma, go through the following five steps in your notebook.

Step 1: Define the problem.
What is Elena's dilemma? Briefly state the dilemma, preferably in a single sentence.

Step 2: List the possible alternatives.
What are the alternatives? Make a list.

Examples:
a) go to the concert
b) buy the CD
c) borrow $20 and do both
d) do neither — spend $20 on something else

Step 3: State the criteria.
The reason Elena has a dilemma is because no single alternative stands out as the best. To help her decide, list the criteria that can be used to judge the alternatives. To determine the criteria, think of all the desirable effects achieved by the alternatives.

Examples:
a) staying out of debt
b) enjoying the thrill of a live performance
c) listening to the music many times

Step 4: Weigh the criteria.
Weigh every criterion in accordance with its importance to you. For example, "staying out of debt" may be the most important criterion to you and thus you give it a weighting of 3. "Listening to the music many times" may be of more importance than "enjoying the thrill of a live performance" but still is of less importance than "staying out of debt." Thus, you give "listening to the music many times" a weighting of 2 and "enjoying the thrill of a live performance" a weighting of 1. See figure 1.1 on page 6.

Step 5: Use the criteria to evaluate each alternative.
In your notebook, draw a decision-making grid like the one in figure 1.1. List all the alternatives (step 2) down the left side of the grid. List the evaluating criteria (step 3) across the top. Place

plus or minus signs opposite each alternative, depending on whether or not the alternative fulfills the criteria, and depending on the weighting you assigned to each alternative.

Step 6: Make a decision!

The decision-making grid allows you to see clearly all your alternatives, as well as providing you with a means to weigh the alternatives. Choose from among the alternatives.

The decision-making process

Have you ever bought something on impulse? If so, you are not alone. Many of our choices are made on the spur of the moment with little consideration. Elena could have made her decision on impulse but, instead, she tried to reach her decision rationally. The advantages of using a decision-making grid are perhaps not so evident in Elena's situation, which is comparatively simple. However, the usefulness of going through a rational, step-by-step decision-making process becomes more apparent when you are faced with complex economic problems.

Figure 1.1 Decision-making grid

Alternatives	Criteria		
	stay out of debt (weighting = 3)	can listen to music many times (weighting = 2)	enjoy the thrill of a live performance (weighting = 1)
go to concert	+++	--	
buy CD	+++	++	
borrow money and do both	---	++	
do neither	+++	--	

Practise your skill

Apply the six-step decision-making process to a problem that you now have, or have had in the past, and that you are willing to share with other members of the class. Start with a brief description of the problem. Then work through the six steps you used to solve Elena's dilemma.

the skill and diligence of people, as well as natural resources and capital resources. Wants include the need for services as well as goods. While there is no generally accepted definition of economics, most express essentially the same idea: *because wants are relatively unlimited, and our resources are limited, we have to find ways of dealing with the problem of scarcity.*

REVIEW

Explain each major concept in your own words and give an example where appropriate: scarcity, physical wants, psychological wants, resources, goods, services, opportunity cost, economics.

APPLICATIONS

1. List twenty goods you would like to own. Divide the list into goods that satisfy a physical want or

Figure 1.2

GOODS

CD   candy   automobile

SERVICES

of musicians   of a teacher   of a surgeon
(concert)   (education)   (appendectomy)

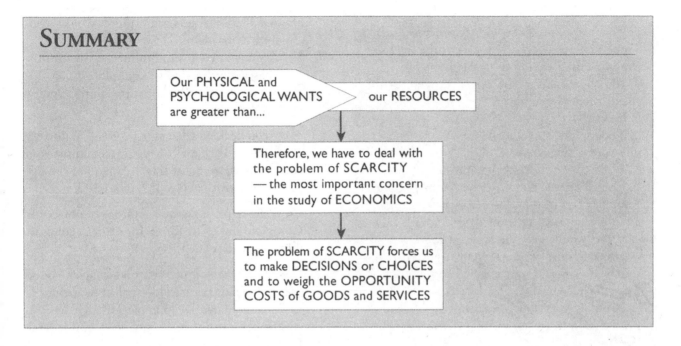

SUMMARY

Our PHYSICAL and PSYCHOLOGICAL WANTS are greater than... our RESOURCES

Therefore, we have to deal with the problem of SCARCITY — the most important concern in the study of ECONOMICS

The problem of SCARCITY forces us to make DECISIONS or CHOICES and to weigh the OPPORTUNITY COSTS of GOODS and SERVICES

need, and goods that satisfy a psychological want. Why can't you own all these goods?

2. You have just received a gift of $100 to satisfy the wants you have listed in the first application. The problem is that $100 probably will not cover the cost of all the wants on your list. You must therefore make choices. Copy the chart in Figure 1.3 into your notebook. Fill in the chart by placing your choices in the left column. Place your unsatisfied wants under costs in the right column. Why are the items in the right column "costs"?

3. According to economists, is seawater scarce in Saskatchewan? Explain.

4. As you read the newspaper article entitled "A bitter pill for Rich Marvin," consider what kind of wants Rich Marvin has and what influences his purchases.

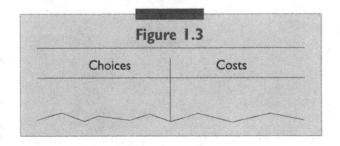

Figure 1.3

Choices	Costs

A bitter pill for Rich Marvin

For years I've considered the home of my friend Rich Marvin as the ultimate in gracious living.

However, a few days ago I saw something better.

You can imagine how difficult it was to break the news to Rich Marvin.

"I don't know how to tell you this," I began as sympathetically as possible, "but — well, your home is no longer No. 1."

The colour drained from Rich Marvin's face.

"What do you mean?" he gasped.

"I mean we've seen a home that makes my wife more envious than yours does," I replied, deciding to hold nothing back.

"That's impossible," Rich Marvin protested. "Your wife positively drools every time she sees the stone fireplace in our living room."

"This home has a blue velvet refrigerator in the kitchen," I countered.

"Velvet?"

"That's right. Not cotton, chintz, or even virgin wool — real velvet."

"What about our sunken bathtub?"

"It's still terrific but this other couple's bathroom has French doors opening onto a garden, a fantastic display of seashells — and a lifesize statue of a nude near the towel rack."

"Don't tell me your wife has forgotten how much she envied our dining room," Rich Marvin challenged.

"No, she hasn't, but these other people had a favourite dinner plate — so they built an entire bed around it."

"There's no point arguing," I added. "Your house makes my wife dissatisfied for three or four days.

"We saw this other place a week ago and my wife is still sick about it."

"Who is this other couple?" Rich Marvin demanded.

"Paul and Jeri are their names. We just met them."

"Obviously, you're a fair-weather envier," Rich Marvin said with bitterness. "The first good-looking house that comes along — pfft — you throw over a home you've envied for years."

"I'm sorry you're taking it so hard," I replied. "Look, if you think it will do any good, we'd be willing to give your home another chance. Maybe you've added something we don't know about. I'm not promising anything, mind you, but invite us over some night and perhaps we'll change our minds and put your house back on top again."

"You won't regret this," Rich Marvin assured. "By the way, how does your wife feel about mink broadloom?"

Source: Gary Lautens, *Toronto Star*.

a) Are Rich Marvin's wants physical or psychological? Explain.

b) Are any of your wants influenced by the purchases of others? Give examples.

c) What is meant by the expression "keeping up with the Joneses"?

5. Have you decided what you are going to do after graduation? Perhaps you want to continue your education, or work, or travel. What are the opportunity costs involved?

6. Copy the chart in Figure 1.4 into your notebook. Complete the chart for each of three economic decisions you made this week.

7. Describe an example of scarcity that you have heard or seen on radio or television, or in magazines or newspapers. Give an example for each level of government: municipal, provincial, and federal. For example:

Municipal: insufficient funding to community libraries, resulting in few books on economics available.

Figure 1.4

Economic decision (what you actually decided to do/buy)	Alternatives (the choices you considered)	Opportunity cost (your second best choice)
1. cheese hamburger for lunch	1. a) grilled cheese sandwich b) hot dog c) milkshake d) cheeseburger	1. hot dog
2. _____ _____	2. a) _____ b) _____ c) _____	2. _____ _____

Provincial: overcrowded classrooms due to too few classrooms and too few teachers.

Federal: cuts in Unemployment Insurance payments due to lower than expected federal government revenues.

8. Keep a record of the economic decisions you make in a week. How did scarcity influence your decisions? What was the opportunity cost of each decision?

CONTINUING PROJECT

Current events file

Economic life — of your community, your province, Canada, and the world — is continually changing. Keeping up-to-date with these changes is important. One of the best sources of information is your newspaper. In it, you will find current information and opinions on nearly every topic and issue discussed in this book.

Unemployment, taxation, government spending, the federal and provincial debt, labour unions, rising prices, and many other topics will be the subject of news columns, editorials, photos, editorial cartoons, comic strips, and letters to the editor. Information about wages, prices, and job opportunities in your area can be found in the want ads. Facts and figures about stocks and financial matters appear on the business pages.

To provide yourself with a file of information on economic events as they happen, clip out items that you find interesting and informative, and file them according to the chapter headings in this book. In this way, when you are dealing with a particular chapter, you will have clippings to supplement the information and opinions that arise in classroom work and discussion.

You may wish to develop a summary of an event from your clippings, e.g., a federal, provincial, or municipal budget, trade negotiations between countries, or variations in stock market prices. You could also use your current events file to examine a controversial issue, such as employment equity or minimum wage laws. Your file could be used to examine the economic characteristics of your local or provincial community, your local unions and cooperatives, and the problems or opportunities they face. Your file could also be used to investigate the local job market.

In addition to your local newspaper, the following publications are also useful: *The Globe and Mail, Financial Post, Financial Times, Maclean's,* and newsletters published by Canadian banks.

A MAJOR QUESTION

Does government play too large a role in the economy?

One of the questions that is debated constantly by Canadians is whether there is too much government involvement in the Canadian economy. As you study economics this year, consider this question. We shall be examining aspects of this question in many of the chapters.

CHAPTER 2

National Decision Making

(1)

(2)

(3)

(4)

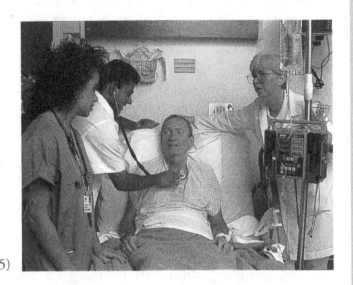

(5)

(7)

(6)

Questions

1. What goods and services are shown in these photographs?

2. What goods and services shown here are produced (a) by some level of government, (b) by private groups or institutions?

3. For three different goods and/or services, who determines which will be produced?

4. For whom are these goods and services produced?

Activity 1: Voices of Canada poll

The following questions are taken from the ninth annual *Maclean's* CTV year-end poll of Canadian opinions.

1. In groups, discuss each question to help clarify where you stand on each one and why.

2. For each question, make a note of your answer and why.

3. Survey your classmates for their answers to each of the questions. Make a note of the opinions of the class on each question. We'll return to this poll at the end of the chapter.

An opinion poll

Make a note of your response to each of the following questions.

1. In your opinion, what is the most important problem facing Canada today; in other words, the one that concerns you the most?

2. Thinking about the future, in general, would you say you are very optimistic, optimistic, pessimistic, or very pessimistic about your personal economic prospects?

3. In your view, is the economy in Canada beginning to improve, not changing, or getting worse?

4. Some people have said that they expect the economy to remain weak through most of the 1990s and that economic and job opportunities will remain limited. Other people have said that they expect the economy to become stronger over the next year or so and economic and job prospects to improve. Which point of view best reflects your own?

5. Who do you look to most to look after your best economic interests?

6. Overall, which of the following two options for government do you think is more important right now? Is it to: do everything possible to reduce the government deficit, even if it means a reduction in services; or invest in programs that give people skills for the future, even if it means deficit increases?

7. At the end of the day, we have to look to government for solutions to the major problems we face. Do you agree or disagree?

8. Canada would not be any worse off if it became part of the United States. Do you agree or disagree?

Source: *Maclean's*, January 4, 1993 and January 4, 1994.

THREE MAJOR QUESTIONS

As individuals, we are faced with the problem of scarcity and are obliged to weigh the opportunity cost of each decision we make. The problem of scarcity is not limited to individuals; all societies face it. Because a society's collective wants exceed its available resources, a society must use its resources wisely. In doing so, each society must answer three major questions.

1. What are we going to produce?
There are many different goods and services that we could produce. *What* are we going to select and in what quantities? How much and which products will we produce? How much bread and how much butter? How many airline flights and how many houses? How many flights today, to which locations, and how many next year?

2. How is it to be produced?
Since our resources are limited relative to our wants,

it follows that *how* we produce the goods and services we want is very important. Clearly, the more we can produce with a given amount of resources, the better we are able to meet the problem of scarcity. In considering how goods are to be produced, therefore, we must also examine by whom the goods are to be produced, and with what resources.

3. Who receives how much?

For whom should the goods and services be produced? How much should each person get? Should everyone receive the same amount (after all, each person has similar, basic physical wants and needs) or, should what people receive depend on a person's contribution to society based on his or her work? Does everyone contribute the same? How will we decide who gets how much?

As you can see, the resolution of these three problems — *what? how?* and *for whom?* — involves answering some very complex questions. Nonetheless, all societies manage to answer these questions. Of course, we may not all agree on the way our own society answers them. I may prefer to see a better road to my favourite beach. You may prefer more hockey arenas. Someone else may prefer more sewage treatment plants to cut down on water pollution. Others may prefer to devote more of their income to personal consumption of such things as clothes, food, or vacations. But each society answers the three major questions.

How the three major questions are answered

Each society has developed its own way of answering the three major questions. In other words, each society has developed its own economic system. There are three basic ways in which the questions are answered: by tradition or custom; by government; or by the market. Elements of all three ways exist in the economic systems of all societies today. Let's examine the major characteristics of each one of the economic systems in turn.

THREE MODEL ECONOMIES

Remember playing with toy models when you were younger? Do you remember how you used to imagine that these simplified representations of reality were actually real? In a similar way, economists use simplified representations of reality — or models — for purposes of research and explanation. Three of these are model economies: pure traditional, pure command, and pure market.

Pure traditional economy

Tradition influences our economic activity. For example, for certain special occasions and celebrations, we buy and exchange gifts. These are part of our customs and traditions. If asked why, our response is likely to be, "Because that's the way we have always done it. It is our custom or our tradition."

In a **pure traditional economy**, the custom or tradition of the society provides the answers to the three main questions: what, how, and for whom.

What are we going to produce? The answer is simple. We will produce what we have always produced. *How* will we produce it? Easy, in the same way as we have always produced it. *Who* receives how much? Again, the answer is obvious. People receive the same amount they have always received.

A pure traditional economy discourages change or growth. There is little incentive for individuals to seek better ways of doing things. This society provides economic, social, and political stability. As long as it lasts, there tend to be no upheavals and no major changes.

The economies of rural areas of developing nations in Africa, Asia, and South America, of Medieval Europe, and of traditional Native communities of North America are similar to this model.

Pure command economy

Many goods and services are provided by governments or, to put it another way, through the command aspect of the economic system. Streets, schools, sidewalks, and police and fire protection are examples of government action in our economy.

In a **pure command economy**, government, or some other central controlling body, provides the answers to the three questions. Decisions about what to produce in the pure command economy are made by government. Government decides *what* services and goods — space shuttles, consumer goods, or factories — to produce. Government also owns the land, factories, and machines, and decides *how* goods and services will be produced. Government determines who will work where, and what machines and raw materials will be available to them. Finally, by establishing the pay and benefits available, government decides *for whom* the goods and services will be produced.

In this type of economic system, logical choices are made about what, how, and for whom to produce. A fairer distribution of income may be achieved; unemployment eliminated; and the production of socially useful products assured. However, while this system seems so simple and logical, it is not without problems. The planning of an entire economy is an immensely complex task and the possibility of making many serious mistakes is high. Some of the decisions about the goals of the economy may be widely unpopular. For instance, it may be decided to produce excessive amounts of one product — space shuttles, for example — at the expense of another, such as automobiles. A totally planned economy would also not permit individual choice of occupation or of products for purchase.

In the past, the Great Wall of China and the pyramids of ancient Egypt were the result of command decision making. Until the end of the 1980s, the economies of the Soviet Union, of the countries in Eastern Europe, and of China, for example, were mainly command economies.

What, how, and for whom in a pure command economy

Suppose the government has decided to increase the country's production of steel by 10 percent. You have

been given the task of implementing the decision. You can't simply say to the steel factories: "Produce more steel." You have to arrange for the production of 10 percent more steel.

Where do you begin?

First, you have to decide how to increase the steel-making capacity of the country by 10 percent. You have to decide whether to increase the size of the existing plants by 10 percent, or to develop new plants to produce the extra 10 percent, or some combination of the two. Whatever you decide, you will have to arrange for the supply of bricks, steel girders, machinery, etc., to be sent to the sites of the new or existing mills. You will have to coordinate schedules so that these materials arrive at the same time as the construction crew.

Second, you will have to assemble new workers for the expanded steel industry. This will require the construction of new houses, shops, or even towns. The increased work force will have to be trained. You have to decide how they will be trained and by whom.

The decisions you make about the steel mills will have to be backed up with decisions about materials. Fuel and raw materials will be required. For each of these, there will have to be an increase in output that may require the opening of new mines. This raises more questions, similar to the ones you had to answer for the steel industry. Quite literally, a decision to increase productive capacity requires the answering of thousands of questions. All that has been considered here, and superficially, is the production of one good: steel. If we extend the problem to the production of all the goods of a modern industrial state with a large population and land mass, it becomes clear that the planning of a pure command economy is immensely complex. The possibilities of making significant errors are very high.

Questions

1. Suppose you are the central planner in a modern command economy. It has been decided to increase production in an industry of your choice,

e.g., automobiles, shoes, or compact discs. In small groups, brainstorm some of the questions you would have to answer.

2. Share your group's list of questions with other members of the class.

Pure market economy

In a **pure market economy**, it is the actions of the buyers and sellers of goods, services, and resources that direct the economic system.

Everyday, people in towns and cities in Canada require vast amounts of a huge number of goods and services. Many of these goods and services may have been years in the making, and may have been days or weeks in transit from the four corners of the globe. Without these goods and services, people might freeze, or go thirsty, hungry, or poorly clothed. But most people in Canada don't spend their days and nights worrying about whether the necessary goods and services will be available when, where, and in what quantities they need them. Or whether workers will be there in sufficient numbers to provide the necessary services. People *know* goods and services will be there. And they are! What is remarkable is that no one person, or group of persons, is in overall charge to ensure that all needs will be met. Rather, it is left up to the uncoordinated actions of thousands of individuals to meet these needs without a central plan. This is one example of how a market economy operates.

What, how, and for whom in a pure market economy

How, then, does a pure market economy function? The daily events in Canadian towns and cities provide the answer. *What* to produce is determined by the dollar votes of consumers. For example, by buying tapes or CDs, rather than records, consumers direct, inform, and reward those who have correctly anticipated consumer wants. Producers of tapes and CDs realize increased sales and profits. Record producers are left with unsold records, and this indicates

to them that they need to make changes to produce those things that consumers are willing to buy. In this way, consumer expenditures act to inform and direct producers of goods and services.

How does the pure market system answer the question: *how* should goods and services be produced? The "how" question is answered by the competition among producers. The market forces producers to use cheaper methods of production. Of two identical, or very similar items, consumers generally prefer the cheaper one. Again, consumers act as the driving force as they seek competitive prices.

The "for whom" question is also answered by consumers in competitive markets. Consumers reward the producers, who provide them with goods and services they want at competitive prices, by buying goods and services from them. The more producers are able to provide goods and services that others want, the greater will be their incomes and the greater the income, the more goods and services they get. Thus, who gets how much is answered by the market.

The pure market economy has a number of distinct advantages. The goods and services produced are those of a type and quality that the consumer wants and not those of some distant public servant. Individual workers are free to choose and change their jobs as they wish. Business people are free to own productive resources, to hire workers, and to decide what goods and services to produce, as well as how to produce them. The pure market economy is very flexible — it is able to adapt quickly to meet changes in the demand for goods and services.

The pure market economy has disadvantages as well. Goods and services go to those with the most money. A rich person's pet may get fed while a poor person's child goes hungry. Business people may be able to control the market for a good or a service, and thus force consumers to pay high prices or workers to accept low wages. Since business cannot always correctly anticipate the tastes of consumers, at times there will be an overproduction of some goods and services, and an underproduction of other goods and services. Consumers may be unable to recognize goods that are harmful, useless, or worthless.

The economies of Canada, the United States, Japan, and the countries of Western Europe are similar to this model.

Basic characteristics of the pure market economy

What, then, are the basic features of the pure market system? These main characteristics include private property rights, profit, consumer sovereignty, self-interest, and competition.

Private property rights

Private property is the right of individuals and corporations to own not only consumer goods, such as shoes and televisions, but also goods used in production, such as factories and machines.

One of the basic features of a pure market economy is the right to own and dispose of property as individuals think fit. People may own not only clothes and cars — consumer goods — but also goods that are used in the production of other goods, such as farmland, machines, and factories. The right to own property acts as an incentive to individuals to produce goods and services. This right is one of the major characteristics of a market economy.

Profit

Related to the right to own property is the right to earn a **profit** — the excess of revenue after expenses. Profit is the amount remaining after a business has paid all its bills. Profit is the reward for assuming risks in business and for successfully meeting the needs and wants of consumers. Profit is a vital element in our economy. Without it, few people would be willing to undertake the risks involved in business.

Consumer sovereignty

Consumer sovereignty is the dominant role of the consumer in a market economy determining what, how, and for whom to produce.

In a pure market economy, the expenditures of consumers powerfully influence the actions of business people. This power makes the consumer sovereign. Those who have correctly anticipated consumers' needs and wants benefit from the sale of their products. Those who have incorrectly anticipated these needs and wants suffer losses. Thus, consumers are sovereign — their expenditures guide, reward, and influence producers.

Self-interest

Self-interest (pursuit of your own advantage) is the major motivating force in the pure market economy. In producing goods and services to make a profit, business people are motivated by self-interest. In this, they are no different from others in the pure market economy. Workers, also motivated by self-interest, seek jobs with higher pay, better working conditions, and greater job satisfaction. Consumers look for the best products at the lowest prices.

Competition

The search for higher wages and profits and lowest prices implies **competition** among workers, business people, and consumers. Competition acts to control individual self-interest. Suppose a business person decides to sell her hamburgers at a very high price to make a larger profit. Her competitors, on the other hand, continue to sell their hamburgers at lower prices. She would be forced to lower her prices or face losses and eventual bankruptcy. In this way, competition acts to regulate individual self-interest.

Thus, in the pure market economy, private property provides a basis; profit and self-interest provide the motivation; consumer sovereignty provides the direction; and competition, the control.

TWO ECONOMIES

Canada and the former Soviet Union

So far, we have examined the major characteristics of three model economies: pure traditional, pure command, and pure market. None of these models exists in pure form in reality, but aspects of each exist in all

BUILDING YOUR SKILLS

Making comparisons

In any area of study, there is a great deal of information to remember. A useful way to recall the information is to organize and summarize it in a comparison chart. In this chapter, for example, we are comparing three different types of economies: pure traditional, pure command, and pure market. Our focus question is, then: "In what ways are the three different economic systems the same or different?" We can develop a comparison chart in which the three types are listed in columns across the top and the ways in which they are to be compared are listed in rows along the side. See figure 2.1.

Practise your skill

1. Copy the chart in figure 2.1 into your notebook. Complete your chart using information from the text.

2. What other factors might you add to the chart?

3. Complete your chart for the other factors you identified in question 2.

Figure 2.1 Comparison of economies

FACTORS		ECONOMIES		
		Pure traditional	Pure command	Pure market
How each economy answers the three questions	What to produce	what we have always produced	government decides what will be produced	
	How to produce	in the same way we have always done it	government determines how goods and services will be produced	
	For whom to produce	each person receives what they have always received	government decides the pay and benefits of individuals and therefore answers the "for whom" question	
Assessment of each economy	Advantages			
	Disadvantages			

modern economies. Let's briefly examine two economic models: one of today — Canada, and one of yesterday — the former Soviet Union.

THE ECONOMY OF CANADA

The Canadian economy is mainly a market economy, but it is influenced by tradition and, more importantly, by government. Therefore, it is called a **mixed** or a **modified market economy**. The uncoordinated actions of millions of Canadian consumers largely — but not solely — determine *what* will be produced, *how* it will be produced, and *for whom*. Cultural and family traditions influence our purchases of various goods and services. For example, we celebrate weddings and birthdays with gifts and parties. For some religious celebrations, we exchange gifts and members of families enjoy a traditional meal together.

Federal, provincial, and local governments provide the framework of laws and regulations within which the Canadian economy works. Through the police force and the courts, governments also ensure that these laws and regulations are followed. Governments also provide incomes for those in need — the old, sick, disabled, and unemployed. They provide this "social safety net" through the taxation of individuals and businesses. In addition, governments provide directly or through their agencies many of the essential goods and services in our society, such as water, electricity, education, and local transportation. Canadian governments, then, strongly influence what, how, and for whom production will take place.

Other mixed market economies that are very similar to the Canadian economy include the economies of Japan, the United States, and most Western European countries.

Objectives of the economy

If you were asked to recommend a list of economic goals for Canada, what goals would you choose? In other words, what do you want the economy to do for you?

At various times, different individuals and groups have outlined objectives for the Canadian economy. One such group was the Economic Council of Canada, a body established by Parliament in 1963 (and disbanded in 1992) to study and advise on the development of the economy in relation to the attainment of its goals. The Council identified the first five goals outlined below. Other Canadians have suggested the remaining three objectives.

1. Full employment One of the characteristics of the Canadian economy is that its development has been and continues to be uneven. It tends to fluctuate between periods of high activity or prosperity and periods of low activity or recession, that is, between periods of low and high unemployment.

With unemployment, society suffers a clear loss. We cannot regain the goods and services that unemployed workers would have produced if they were working. In addition, unemployed workers and their families suffer financially and psychologically. Some of the unemployed may resign themselves to dependence upon unemployment insurance and welfare.

But what does full employment mean? Does it mean that 100 percent of those willing and able to work are employed? In any healthy economy, there will always be some unemployed workers who have left one job and are looking for another. Thus, a percentage less than 100 — perhaps around 93 or 94 — comes close to what is meant by full employment.

2. Stable prices In the early 1990s, increases in the general level of prices tended to be low — averaging less than 2 percent a year. This low level of price increase is probably as close as many expect us to get to stable prices. At other periods during the last 50 years, inflation rates — increases in the general level of prices — have been very high. In the early 1980s, for example, price increases exceeded 10 percent a year. Notice that we refer to price increases *in general* and not to price changes in individual goods or services.

The *real* value of money is determined by what it will buy. Thus, as the general level of prices increases, or as inflation takes hold, the purchasing power (or the real value) of money decreases. This means that the amount of goods and services that can be bought by a fixed amount of money declines.

A period of generally rising prices is likely to diminish the purchasing power of the salaries of fixed income earners, the pensions of those retired, and the savings of many people. Wealth and savings in society may be redistributed to the disadvantage of those who are least able to protect themselves and in ways that we may regard as unjust. Rapid and continuous increases in prices can lead to economic, social, and political chaos and perhaps even to revolution — as occurred in Germany in the 1920s and 1930s.

3. Balance of trade We have all used products from other countries: radios, televisions, and videos from Japan; shoes, T-shirts, and socks from Taiwan; magazines and automobiles from the United States. Large numbers of workers in other countries depend on Canadians for their jobs and their pay. Similarly, Japanese, Taiwanese, and Americans enjoy the products we sell to them: wheat, aircraft, automobiles, steel, insurance and banking services, and paper. The jobs of about one-quarter of Canadian workers depend on the sale of Canadian products in other countries. In order to buy products from another country, we have to sell goods to them, and in order for them to buy goods from us, they have to sell to us. There has to be a balance of trade; or, to put it another way, what we sell to other countries has to be roughly equal to what we buy from other countries. Otherwise, trade between countries will be disrupted and its benefits lost.

4. Economic growth means an increase over a period of time —usually a year — in a country's output of goods and services. Throughout history, the Canadian economy has continued to grow, that is, to produce increasing quantities of goods and services. This growth in production has more than kept pace with the growth of population so that, today, Canadians have one of the highest standards of living in the world. In the 1980s, however, the public became even more concerned about serious environmental issues related to economics. Acid rain, ozone depletion, global warming, and soil erosion rose on the political and economic agenda as people became more aware of the impact of economic growth on the environment. Some writers stressed that economic growth and environmental protection are interdependent. The concept of "sustainable development" was introduced by a Commission of the United Nations on the environment and economic development. This means "development that meets the needs of the present without compromising [decreasing] the ability of future generations to meet their own needs."

5. Economic justice means a fair distribution of income through government intervention. Certain economically disadvantaged groups in our society, such as the disabled, the aged, and the unemployed, might receive little or no income and be deprived of adequate food, clothing, and shelter. This contradicts our ideas of what is fair or just. We have, therefore, established various schemes — welfare payments and unemployment insurance, for example — to provide some minimum level of support for those in need.

Some regions of Canada are less wealthy than others. To provide a fairer distribution of national income, the federal government provides payments to the less wealthy regions and, in various ways, encourages their economic development. With a fairer distribution of income, we have greater economic justice.

6. Economic freedom means freedom of choice for workers, for consumers, and for business people. Workers are free to choose their jobs. Business people are free to choose the type of businesses they wish to establish and to own the means of production — land, machines, factories. Consumers are free to choose whatever products they want (within certain broad limits), and thus influence what will be produced. Consumers are also free to decide how much of their income they will spend and how much they will save. They can also decide where and how they will invest their savings.

7. **Economic efficiency** means the use of economic resources to produce goods and services at a minimum cost. The more that can be produced from a fixed amount of productive resources, the better we are able to meet our needs and wants. In a mixed market economy, such as our own, we rely on competition to weed out inefficient producers and to spur others to greater efficiency. Competition promotes more and more production from a fixed amount of resources. Similarly, competition for higher profits among business people acts as a guide, incentive, and reward to produce those goods most in demand by consumers, in the most efficient way possible.

8. **A reasonable level of federal and provincial debt** means a level of debt that does not require government to cut back on essential spending in order to pay the interest on the debt. Since 1971, Canadian federal governments have had annual budget deficits — in other words, their expenditures have exceeded their incomes. The annual deficit has grown from about $600 million in 1970–71 to an estimated $45 billion in 1993–94. The total debt (the sum of all the deficits minus the surpluses) over the same period of time increased more than 14 times, from about $35 billion in 1970–71 to about $500 billion in 1994. The rapidly-growing debt and interest payments forced the federal government to consider how best to slow down or reverse the increase in the size of the federal debt. The options were to raise taxes or to cut expenditures, or some combination of the two. Canadian provincial governments in the first half of the 1990s also faced debt problems similar to those of the federal government. The provinces, too, were obliged to cut expenditures and/or raise taxes.

Conflict among economic goals

In our daily lives, we must continually make decisions regarding our competing wants. We must choose this good rather than that good, that service rather than this one, while constantly weighing the opportunity costs of our decisions.

In a similar way, in making decisions about economic goals for our society, Canadians and their governments must choose which goals are to be pursued and determine their order of importance. Policies to achieve one objective may be pursued at the expense of another objective. For example:

- Attempts to lower unemployment may result in generally higher prices.

Activity 2: Objectives of the economy

A   Individually, consider questions 1 to 3. Jot down your responses in your notebook.

B   In groups, answer questions 1 to 4.

1. In your opinion, what is the most important problem facing Canada today? In other words, which problem concerns you the most?

2. Are there any objectives that you think should be added to those listed on pages 18 to 20?

3. List the economic objectives in order of their importance to you. Base your reasoning on how you see the current situation.

4. Present and justify your decisions to the rest of the class.

C   Make a summary of what the class perceives as the most important problems. We'll return to this summary at the end of the chapter.

- Attempts to achieve a better balance of trade with other countries may involve restrictions on individual economic freedom.
- Attempts to improve economic efficiency may result in economic injustice.

In a country as large and diverse as Canada, policies to lower unemployment in one region may stoke the fires of inflation in another region. We may be obliged, therefore, to accept *trade offs* among our goals — to accept some higher level of unemployment for some lower level of price increases, or some higher level of efficiency for some lower level of economic justice; to accept some level of inflation in one region while lowering the unemployment rate in another.

Economic goals in other countries

Most of the economic goals outlined above apply to mixed market economies in other countries as well. However, the relative importance of the various goals differs from country to country. Other countries, too, experience conflicts among the goals.

THE ECONOMY OF THE FORMER SOVIET UNION

How did an economy organized differently from a mixed market economy deal with the "what," "how," and "for whom" questions? For example, how did the economy of the Soviet Union answer these questions? We know that the Soviet Union was a command economy in which the government was primarily responsible for answering the major economic questions. Let's look at this process more closely.

Public ownership

As we have seen, the basic pattern of organization in Canada is private ownership of land, factories, and machines used in production, and of private, personal goods, such as houses and clothing.

In the Soviet Union, the basic pattern of organization was that of state ownership of land, factories, and machines used in production. There were, however, some notable exceptions. Some retail businesses were privately owned. Over one third of the homes in Soviet cities were privately owned. Most of the homes on farms were privately owned. Each family working on a collective farm could use a small plot of land, and the equipment and insecticides that went with it. Personal goods such as clothing and household items were privately owned. In general, however, it was the state that owned land, factories, forests, industrial machinery, transportation, and banking facilities.

Central planning

A second way in which the Soviet economy differed from our own was that the answers to the three questions (what, how, and for whom) were made mostly by command — by some central, state planning agency — and not, as in our system, by the actions of individual producers and consumers.

What and how in the Soviet Union

Five-year plans   Between 1928 and 1991, the Soviet economy was directed by a number of five-year plans. These plans, developed at the highest levels of the Soviet government, provided a general direction for the development of the Soviet economy over the five-year period.

One-year plans   Five-year plans were translated into a number of one-year plans. The one-year plans were developed in detail so that output targets could be set for each industry, farm, and firm. These targets were set by the state planning commission (Gosplan) after extensive consultation with each factory, farm, and industry. After the targets had been set, each plant manager was given a production target and incentives to reach that goal.

Gosplan was also responsible for ensuring that all parts of the plan fitted together. If, for example, the

Summary of the economic history of the Soviet Union, 1917-1991

1917-1921 (Lenin)
Bolshevik Revolution; Communist Party in power. War communism: • forced takeover of agricultural products • state ownership of banks, industry, and transportation.

1921-1928 (Lenin-Stalin)
New Economic Policy, 1921: Market allocation of many resources.

1928-1953 (Stalin)
Abolition of market allocation of goods and productive resources. Command economic planning: • Five-year plans • Collectivization of agriculture • Emphasis on economic growth and production of capital goods and new materials.

1953-1970 (Khrushchev-Brezhnev)
Steady growth. Increasing emphasis on the production of consumer goods and services.

1970-1985 (Brezhnev-Andropov-Chernenko)
Declining productivity and slowing economic growth.

1985-1991 (Gorbachev)
Perestroika: restructuring of the Soviet economy; movement to a market system: • Decentralized decision making • Increased individual accountability.

1991
End of the Soviet Union as the constituent republics, which made up the union, declared their independence.

plan called for an increased output of trucks, it was necessary to ensure that enough steel and other materials, sufficient workers, machines, etc., were available to produce the trucks. Clearly, the need to coordinate each part of the one-year plan was of essential importance.

While profits did exist in the U.S.S.R., they did not provide the same kind of incentive as they did in the Canadian economy because they went to the state. And, since profits were calculated from prices set by government planners, profit and prices did not play the same role in allocating productive resources — land, labour, and capital — as they do in our system.

We have outlined generally how decisions about what to produce and how to produce were made by the state. Before 1985, however, there was a small but significant area of individual action in the Soviet Union. On the collective or state-owned farms, for example, individual workers had small plots of land on which they could grow what they wanted. These plots were highly productive. This privately-operated farmland in the Soviet Union produced a significant percentage of Soviet food. The produce was sold in free markets.

Under a new labour law introduced in 1987, Soviet citizens were allowed to establish businesses in twenty-four sectors of the economy, including shoe repair, interior decorating, plumbing, carpentry, auto repair, and tutoring. Workers could not be hired for these businesses; the staff was limited to family members. At the same time, business people were required to have full-time jobs unless they were homemakers, retired, or disabled. One of the reasons for the new law was the existence of many illegal services in these twenty-four sectors.

Who received how much?

The highest incomes in the Soviet Union were received by artists, scientists, professors, and government officials. In addition to wages, the use of money incentives was widespread. These were used to motivate managers to reach their production targets and workers

Summary

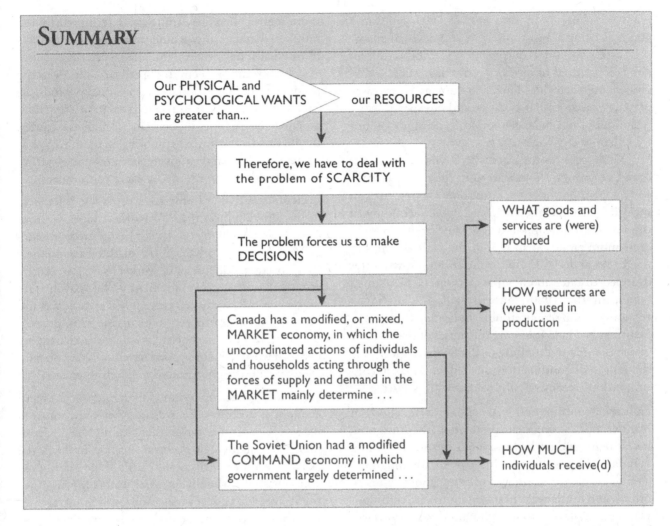

Our PHYSICAL and PSYCHOLOGICAL WANTS are greater than...   our RESOURCES

Therefore, we have to deal with the problem of SCARCITY

The problem forces us to make DECISIONS

Canada has a modified, or mixed, MARKET economy, in which the uncoordinated actions of individuals and households acting through the forces of supply and demand in the MARKET mainly determine . . .

The Soviet Union had a modified COMMAND economy in which government largely determined . . .

WHAT goods and services are (were) produced

HOW resources are (were) used in production

HOW MUCH individuals receive(d)

to increase production. Industrial workers were largely free to select their place of employment.

Soviet workers and their families received many goods and services from the state. Nurseries for children were provided. Education, and medical and hospital care were free. Most city housing was owned by the state but the rents were low, averaging only 2 to 3 percent of income.

The economy of the Soviet Union was not a pure command economy. It was a modified command economy. Individual workers did have some freedom to make economic decisions. Other countries such as Hungary, East Germany, Poland, and China had economies organized in ways that were generally similar to that of the Soviet Union. In the mid-1990s, some countries — for example, Cuba and North Korea — still had mixed command economies.

The performance of the Soviet economy

It was reasonable to expect that the Soviet economy would grow rapidly. For one thing, the economy usually operated at full employment. Second, Soviet economic planners chose economic growth over consumer goods as being a major objective and devoted a large proportion of total output to the production of goods to be used in further production, such as machines and factories. Third, the Soviet Union was playing "catch up." It is easier and cheaper to copy techniques from more economically advanced countries than to develop them yourself.

Many economists rated the Soviet economy as "good on growth" — at least until the mid-1970s — and as "poor on the efficient use of resources." Tough measures brought the backward Soviet economy of the 1920s into the modern age. The Soviet economy grew more rapidly than that of the United States in the 1950s and 1960s. But in the 1970s, growth rates dropped to rates about equal to those of the United States. In the 1980s, growth stalled. The Soviet economy was in serious trouble, indicating that central planning had failed. Among the causes of the collapse of the command economy of the Soviet Union were the failure of coordination; inadequate quality control; lack of incentives; and widespread pollution.

Failure of coordination   As we have seen, a body of planners had to coordinate production, consumption, investment, and trade throughout the Soviet Union. It became impossible to achieve this with a high degree of efficiency. Shortages of some goods, gluts of others, and bottlenecks in production were commonplace. For example, in the 1980s there were shortages of soap and toilet paper while black-and-white TV sets were readily available. In 1989 a significant part of the abundant harvest rotted on the farms because of a shortage of storage and transportation facilities.

Inadequate quality control   Control planners can monitor the number of units produced by any factory and reward those that meet their quota and punish those who fail to do so. For many years, quotas were expressed in quantitative terms — so many metres of cloth or tonnes of nails. But that led to obvious problems. If the cloth quota was measured by the metre, then the cloth was woven loosely to produce

more metres. If nail output was determined by the number, then factories would produce large numbers of tiny nails, or, if by weight, a few very large nails.

A constant problem in the Soviet Union was the production of inappropriate or poor-quality products. Factory managers were only interested in meeting their assigned quotas. Once their products left their factories, they became someone else's problem. In the case of consumer goods, shortages ensured that even low-quality items would be snapped up by eager consumers.

Lack of incentives   In market economies, differences in pay provide incentives for workers to move from job to job and the possibility of being fired provides an incentive to work hard. In planned economies, these incentives do not exist; workers have job security and there is little unemployment. While paycheques in the U.S.S.R. were guaranteed, what workers could buy with them continued to be disappointing or often unavailable. In the Soviet Union, the social contract between workers and the government was "we pretend we work and the government pretends to pay us."

Pollution   Meeting production quotas in command economies becomes the overriding objective, often to the exclusion of other concerns, including the environment. Consequently, pollution has occurred in the Soviet Union on a disastrous scale. One glaring example has been the diversion of waters flowing into the Aral Sea for cotton irrigation. As a result, the sea level has dropped more than 12 metres since 1960 and the land area has been reduced by a third. This — along with the use of fertilizers and pesticides — has polluted the waters, wiped out the fishing industry, destroyed wildlife, and increased human diseases.

The reform of the system

The continuing stagnation of the economy in the 1980s led the Soviet leader, Mikhail Gorbachev, to institute a number of reforms to restructure the economy. This restructuring was called *perestroika*. Gorbachev promoted a reduction in the central control of the economy in favour of an increase in individual and local management control and accountability. These ideas were incorporated in the Law of State Enterprises in 1987. Another law permitted the establishment of cooperative enterprises in a number of consumer goods and services industries. Laws to encourage the establishment of family farms remained largely on paper. Soviet agricultural workers were in no haste to set up their own farms, apparently preferring the security of the state and collective farms.

These first reforms of the Gorbachev years did not challenge socialism in the U.S.S.R. or state ownership of productive resources. By 1990, however, reformers began to call for the large-scale privatization of industry and agriculture and the movement to a market economy.

By 1990-91, the economy was in serious trouble. Inflation, growing budget deficits, declining output, and widespread shortages undermined the authority of the central government. Barter between regions, republics, enterprises, and farms became common.

The growing assertiveness and increasing nationalist sentiment of the republics combined with the severe economic problems faced by the Soviet Union to bring about its collapse. By the end of 1991, the Soviet Union was no more. It was replaced by a loose association of independent republics, each with its own agenda. The Soviet command system had expired.

BUILDING YOUR SKILLS

Making further comparisons

We can think of the economies of the countries of the world as appearing along a spectrum. At the pure market end of the spectrum, there is completely decentralized, economic decision making with individuals providing the answers to the three major questions. At the opposite pole — that of the pure command economy — a central authority or government provides the answers to the three questions. Along the spectrum, we can place the economies of various countries. Since the Canadian economy is a mixed market economy, it will appear toward the pure market end of the spectrum, as shown in figure 2.2.

Practise your skill

Apply your knowledge of making comparisons to the following questions.

1. Where on the spectrum would you put the United States, China, and the United Kingdom?

2. Justify your choice for each country.

Figure 2.2 Spectrum of economies

Pure command economy
(also known as pure communism or collectivism)

Pure market economy
(also known as pure capitalism, laissez-faire, or free-market economy)

Canada

Centralized authority
what, how, and for whom decisions are made by government; collective state ownership of means of production

Decentralized authority
what, how, and for whom decisions are made by individuals in free markets; private ownership of means of production

BUILDING YOUR SKILLS

Analysing political cartoons

A cartoon is a drawing designed to amuse and inform a large audience and also to express the point of view of the cartoonist (and perhaps of the newspaper in which the cartoon is published). Political cartoons are usually found on the editorial page of many Canadian newspapers. Here is a four-question model for examining political cartoons, using a cartoon by Duncan Macpherson — one of Canada's most talented cartoonists — printed on January 8, 1992 in *The Toronto Star*.

Reprinted with permission — The Toronto Star Syndicate.

Key Questions

1. What do you see?

The cartoon has no caption or title. It depicts Boris Yeltsin, president of Russia in 1992, as a poor peddler. From his cart, he is holding a bankruptcy sale of symbols of the former Soviet Union, including busts of Marx, Lenin, and Stalin and flags, rockets, rubles, etc.

2. What economic concepts or terms are implied or stated?

Monopoly, command economy, market economy, bankruptcy, money, and inflation.

3. What is the meaning of the cartoon?

The cartoon suggests that Communism and the ideas of its founders and present-day practitioners — and its command economy — are bankrupt and that inflation is rampant.

4. What is your evaluation of the effectiveness of the cartoon?

The cartoon is highly effective in expressing the point of view that Communism and its command economies are doomed to failure.

Practise your skill

Use the four key questions to analyse a political cartoon from your daily newspaper and/or analyse the following Peterson cartoon from *The Vancouver Sun*.

Roy Peterson. *Vancouver Sun.*

BUILDING YOUR SKILLS

Making social decisions: Parking at your high school

Let's suppose that at your high school, parking space is at a premium. Apart from space that is reserved for the disabled, the best spaces — those most convenient for entering the school (the "A" spaces) — are reserved for the principal, vice principal, secretarial staff, and department heads. The "B" spaces — those a little less convenient — are reserved for the other teaching and caretaking staff. The "C" spaces — the least convenient — are allocated only to senior students. However, enrollment in the school has risen considerably over the last few years. Also, well-paying part-time jobs are available, so that many students have cars. Thus, there are insufficient parking spaces for the staff and students. You and

four other students have been selected by the principal and your school's student council to resolve the problem. You and the four other students must choose for the school. In doing so, follow the 6-step decision-making process used in Chapter 1, pages 5-6, for making individual decisions. Here, though, you will be making a social, not an individual, choice.

Step 1: Define the problem.   First, we need to decide: Is there too little space? Or too many cars? Let's assume that the local school board faces budget restraints and therefore is unlikely to expand the size of the parking lot. Thus, the problem we face is not that the parking lot is too small but that there are too many cars. We can state the problem in the following way: How can we allocate the limited parking space among the staff and students?

Step 2: List the alternatives. Several major ways of handling the problem are apparent:

1. *Leave things as they are.* This option, as you can imagine, would be popular with the school staff. Staff would only rarely be made late to class because of the shortage of parking. Presumably, students could manage if they allowed themselves more time to get to class and/or used other means of transportation.

2. *First-come, first-served.* With this choice, all drivers would be treated equally and have an equal opportunity to get a parking space. Those who really want a space should be willing to get up earlier in order to get one.

3. *Markets and a price system.* In this alternative, there would be three different classes of parking: "A" stickers for the best locations; "B" stickers for the second-best locations, and "C" stickers for the remaining parking spots. Prices would be set for each location in such a way that the number of stickers bought would be roughly equal to the number of spaces available. Thus, the parking spaces would go to those who were willing to pay for them and the best spaces to those willing to pay a premium. This, of course, is the way we allocate many other things in our society, such as houses, cars, clothes, and shoes. Everyone would have the same chance of getting a good parking spot. There would be no discrimination.

4. *Allocation by need.* Students and staff who must travel long distances to reach the school or who do not have access to bus or other transportation could be given the use of a parking space because their need is greater than that of other people. This is a fair way of handling the problem. One of the difficulties, however, is that of determining precisely which persons need a space.

5. *Allocation by lottery.* Names of those wanting a parking space could be put in a box and the parking space allocated to those whose names were drawn from the box — "A" spaces first, "B's" second and "C's" third. Thus, everyone would have an equal chance of getting any one of the spaces.

Step 3: List the social goals. As we went through the choices, we outlined some of their advantages and disadvantages. Here we need some criteria to assess each alternative. On pages 18-20 are listed some of the economic goals of Canadian society. As we examine these objectives, we can see that two of them — economic justice and economic freedom — are relevant here. In addition, we should consider the cost of administering each alternative. Thus, we have three criteria — freedom, justice, and cost of administration — for evaluating each objective.

Step 4: Evaluate the criteria. From each definition of the problem, our identification of the alternatives, and our listing of the social goals, we move to a weighting of each criterion. Here we determine the relative importance to us of each one of the three criteria we have identified. Is justice more important than freedom and/or administrative cost? If so, we'll give it a greater weighting here than either of the two other criteria.

Step 5: Evaluate each of the alternatives. We can evaluate each of the five alternatives using figure 2.3. In figure 2.3 we can see that the five alternatives are listed in the first column while the criteria are listed in the first row.

Step 6: Make the best social choice. After evaluating each social choice against the social goals, we can now make a decision. As society changes, the importance we place on each social goal is also likely to reflect these changes. Thus, at different times we may reach different decisions on an issue.

Practise your skill

1. Copy the chart in figure 2.3 into your notebook.
2. Complete the chart by going through steps 4 and 5.
3. Reach a decision on the social issue.

Figure 2.3 A decision-making matrix for the school parking lot case

Alternatives	Social Goals (Criteria)		
	Economic justice	Economic freedom	Administrative cost
Leave things as they are			
First-come, first-served			
Markets and a price system			
Allocation by need			
Allocation by lottery			

REVIEW

Explain each of the following concepts in your own words, giving an example: traditional economy, market economy, command economy, private property rights, profit, consumer sovereignty.

APPLICATIONS

1. Read the statements from (a) to (m). Decide whether each statement refers to a traditional, market, or command system and which economic decision each statement reflects. Then copy the chart in figure 2.4 on page 30 into your notebook. Indicate where each statement belongs by filling in your chart with the letter for each statement.

a) Goods and services are distributed primarily according to the ability and willingness of the buyers to pay.
b) The goods produced this year are the same as those produced in the past.
c) Resources are distributed primarily by competitive bidding among producers.
d) The use to which resources are put is determined by the goals set for society.
e) Signals are sent through chains of markets indicating the pattern of consumer choices.
f) Food is distributed to members of society according to the customs of the past.
g) Decisions about whether to produce more automobiles and refrigerators rather than more factories are made by a central authority.
h) A significant number of goods and services are made available without cost to all citizens.

Figure 2.4

Economic decision	Economic system		
	Market	**Command**	**Traditional**
What to produce			
How to produce			
Who receives how much			

i) The way the crops are planted is the same way they have always been planted.

j) Competition among producers, stimulated by the desire for profit, motivates them to keep their costs as low as possible in order to attract consumers.

k) The motivation for increased productivity is the desire to reach output goals rather than to make the largest possible profit.

l) The use to which resources are put is determined by the desire for profit.

m) Consumers have choices in the market, but their choices do not act as signals in determining what will be produced.

2. List three examples of (a) traditional, (b) command, and (c) market elements in the Canadian economy today.

3. In the following article, a newspaper reporter describes how Alosha and Natasha Ivanov purchased a new car in Moscow. As you read the article, consider how their experience differs from car buying in Canada. Consider also how it reflects the characteristics of the mixed command economy of the former Soviet Union.

   a) In what ways does the Ivanovs' purchase of a new car differ from that of buying a new car in Canada?

   b) What features of a command economy are evident in the article?

Six years plus a long day to buy a car in U.S.S.R.

By Vincent J. Schodolski
Special to The Star

MOSCOW — All of you who have pressed your noses against an auto showroom window lately, or picked your way through the rebate offers, or been dazed by a fast-talking salesperson's babble on the glories of anti-lock brakes, listen to the story of Alosha and Natasha Ivanov and their new car.

Ivanov was one of the lucky ones, a war veteran, a recently retired pilot for the Soviet national airline Aeroflot, a man well-placed for quick delivery.

Only six years! Imagine, that was all, just six years between the day he applied for a new car and the morning when the little white postcard dropped through the mail slot, inviting him to come to the shop and pick up his new Zhiguli model 2104.

Wait a minute, a 2104? Ivanov had asked for a 2107. But after six years, who was going to quibble over a model number that was off by just one digit?

Ivanov had to be there at 9 a.m. the next day with a certified cheque for 8,900 rubles. (That's about $14,200 U.S.) Less than six hours remained before the banks closed. The race was on.

But Ivanov did it. With cheque in hand, he and Natasha set off at 8:30 a.m. in a taxi for the shop. The little card said he had to report to window No. 12 at 9 a.m. sharp. After six years, better not be late.

Well, what do you know, out of 20 windows in the huge reception hall of the Zhiguli shop (there is only one in Moscow), only one was open. Lo and behold, it was window No. 12.

Ivanov, the 31st person in line even though it was not yet 9 o'clock, made sure he had his passport, his little white postcard and his cheque. All was in order. All that was left was to wait.

Yes, wait. It took 90 minutes to get to window 12. Once there, Ivanov was given a ticket that entitled him to go through the next door and wait some more.

Once through the door, the Ivanovs found even more people waiting. But, after six years, they were through the second door, and nothing stood between them and their shiny new Zhiguli — a Soviet version of an Italian Fiat — but a few more windows, a few more bureaucrats, a few more bits of paper.

Two hours. Just two hours, that was all, before they heard the name "Ivanov" echo through the cavernous room and were allowed to pass through the third door and actually see their car.

Well, not just yet. There was a choice to be made. Six years earlier, Ivanov had asked for a blue car. The man in the overalls said there were only red and beige ones left.

After six years, who worries about colour? Bring on the beige, Ivanov said.

Minute after anxious minute ticked by, 30 of them to be exact, before the doors opened and six years of waiting came to an end. There it was, their car.

But wait, it was filthy. It was so dirty that Natasha did not want to get too close. Ivanov noticed that all four lugs were missing from one of the wheels. Inside, the seats were littered with bolts and screws.

The man in the overalls told Ivanov to start the car to show that the engine worked. Before Ivanov could speak, the man in the overalls told him the car would be waiting for them outside. All they had to do was sign a paper (remember window 12?) saying they would accept the car, pay their $14,200, fill out the registration papers, have the car inspected and off they could go.

Hold on, again. It was lunchtime. Everything closed for an hour.

So the Ivanovs waited for everyone to come back to work.

And, sure enough, there was the car, parked outside by the curb, along with dozens of others, all shiny and clean. They had even washed it!

Alosha and Natasha went out to inspect. Ivanov took the key from the ignition and tried to lock the door. But —what's this? — the lock didn't work. So Natasha stood guard while her husband went off to complete the formalities.

Back at window 12, all seemed to be in order. After an hour in line, Ivanov presented his cheque and agreed to take the car, the colour and model mistakes already forgotten. Things were going well.

Next stop the office where road tax was paid. Six months in advance, please. Ivanov did not even blink. It was almost over.

Then just 40 minutes to the window where the car's "technical passport" was issued, a document listing serial numbers and all the car's particulars. After 90 minutes and 5 more rubles, Ivanov, license plates in hand, rushed to his wife's side.

It was 6:30 p.m. Thirty minutes to spare before the shop's 7 p.m. closing time.

Ah, gasoline! There was none. Not even enough to turn the engine over.

So Alosha and Natasha Ivanov — and scores of other lucky new-car owners — slowly pushed their cars through the gathering dark toward the gas station around the corner.

Just one more line, and they could drive home.

Source: *The Toronto Star*, March 4, 1990.

Case study
The Ski-Doo

We have all seen these short, snub-nosed, rubber-tracked machines that provide millions of people throughout the world with outlets for their cooped-up winter energies. But few of us know the story of the snowmobile and the part played in its development by the son of a Québec farmer, the inspired tinkerer and mechanical genius, Joseph-Armand Bombardier.

During the early years of this century, many Québec villages were snow-bound during the winter. The only means of transportation was the horse and sleigh. One of the inhabitants of the tiny village of Valcourt in Québec was Joseph-Armand Bombardier.

From the age of 15, Bombardier had experimented with building motorized snow vehicles that would end the isolation imposed by winter. Then one winter years later, one of his sons died of appendicitis. This tragic loss pushed him to work even harder, and he eventually succeeded in inventing a vehicle that could be used in snow-bound emergencies. The first models produced in the 1930s were used to transport doctors, schoolchildren, hunters, and trappers.

In the winters of Bombardier's youth, it had taken a full day and three teams of horses to transport the mail 29 km from Waterloo, the nearest town of

J. Armand Bombardier.

any size. During the 1930s, Wilfred Charbonneau, one of Bombardier's boyhood friends, could cover the same distance with the mail in less than an hour using one of Bombardier's snow vehicles. By the mid-1940s, Bombardier was *the* employer in Valcourt. Some 100 workers were on the payroll and the company was earning profits of nearly $1 million a year.

By the 1950s, Bombardier's vehicles had achieved a global reputation and they were in wide use throughout North America wherever there was snow or difficult terrain.

Next, Bombardier designed a light-tracked vehicle capable of carrying one or two passengers over snow and frozen lakes. He thought that the machine would find a profitable market with trappers and game wardens, and that it could compete with dog teams in the Canadian North.

An early snowmobile (1942). J. Armand Bombardier stands beside his invention.

Montréal Métro's subway cars were manufactured by Bombardier Inc.

In 1959, Bombardier introduced the first individual snowmobile, the Ski-Doo, and contributed a new word to the English language and a new pastime to winter sports enthusiasts. By 1964, the year of Bombardier's death, over 16 000 Ski-Doos were on the market. During the next decade, the Bombardier company's sales almost doubled each year. By 1974, the company had sold over one million snowmobiles.

By the mid-1970s, however, other manufacturers had moved into the snowmobile market. New names — Skiroule, Skee-horse, Snojet, Sno-Prince and Arctic-Cat — proliferated. This fierce competition, the end of the post-war boom, and the onset of rapidly rising oil prices in the early 1970s cut into the snowmobile market. Sales of the Ski-Doo declined. Applying the philosophy of its founder, the company looked to diversify into other areas. In 1975, Bombardier purchased a majority interest in MLW-Worthington Limited, a Montréal-based manufacturer of diesel engines and diesel-electric locomotives. In preparation for the 1976 Olympic games, the city of Montréal was planning to extend its subway system. The Bombardier Company acquired the French technology for rubber-tired subway cars, and later won the contract to supply 423 cars. The snowmobile plant at La Pocatière was modified to produce them.

In the 1980s and 1990s, the Bombardier Company continued its expansion and diversification in the recreational vehicle, aerospace, and transportation industries. The Company's recreational vehicle division now produces not only the Ski-Doo but also the Sea-Doo (a marine vehicle for performance and leisure cruising); tracked equipment for snowmobile and ski hill grooming; and all-terrain vehicles for a number of new recreational markets.

Bombardier's acquisitions in the aerospace industry have included the following: Canadair (the leading Canadian manufacturer of aircraft, including

A Sea-Doo watercraft built by Bombardier Inc.

the Challenger jet) in 1986; Northern Ireland's Short Brothers PLC (a producer of civil and military aircraft and air defence systems) in 1989; the U.S. Learjet Corporation (a producer of small- and medium-sized business jets) in 1990; and, also in 1990, Toronto-based de Havilland Inc. (the producer of the Dash 8 turboprop aircraft).

In transportation equipment, Bombardier acquired a major European rail designer and manufacturer, the Belgian company BN Construction Ferroviaires et Métalliques, in 1988; ANF-Industrie — France's second-largest manufacturer of railway equipment — in 1989; Procor Engineering Ltd. (a British manufacturer of rail transportation equipment) in 1990; UTDC, an Ontario government-owned manufacturer and designer of transportation equipment, in 1992; and in 1992 as well, Constructadena Nacional de Carros de Ferrocarril (a Mexican manufacturer of transportation equipment). Bombardier produces rapid-transit vehicles, rail vehicles, shuttle-train vehicles (e.g., for the English Chunnel) and it also owns the North American manufacturing rights and technology for France's high-speed train.

Bombardier Inc. designed and manufactured the shuttle-train cars for the English Channel tunnel.

By the mid-1990s, Bombardier had grown into a multinational corporation employing over 32 000 people in nine countries with sales well over $3 billion a year.

Questions

1. Use examples from the case study to illustrate how the three major questions are answered.
2. What features of a mixed market economy appear in this case study? Give examples.

Library research

Bring the story of the Bombardier Company up to date. In your library, consult the *Financial Post*'s Corporation Service Card for Bombardier Inc., the company's recent annual reports, the vertical files for articles on Bombardier, and Canadian News Facts.

VOICES OF CANADA POLL RESULTS

The following are the results of the ninth annual *Maclean's* CTV year-end poll that you responded to at the beginning of this chapter. These results are based on telephone interviews with a random sample of 1500 Canadian residents in all provinces. The results are considered accurate 19 times out of 20 within a range of 2–6 percentage points above or below the figures given. As you survey the poll results, identify changes in responses that took place over time and suggest some reasons why these changes took place.

1. In your opinion, what is the most important problem facing Canada today; in other words, the one that concerns you the most?

	1989	1990	1991	1992	1993
Unemployment	6	9	18	39	41
Economy/recession	10	21	24	25	9
Government/deficit/spending	10	6	14	11	23
Constitution/unity	7	8	13	5	17
Taxes/GST	15	23	10	3	4
Environment	18	9	4	2	3
Other/don't know/non-answer	34	25	17	15	2

2. Thinking about the future, in general, would you say you are very optimistic, optimistic, pessimistic or very pessimistic about your personal economic prospects?

	1989	1990	1991	1992	1993*
Very pessimistic	3	3	6	4	20
Pessimistic	16	23	24	23	31
Optimistic	70	65	62	65	25
Very optimistic	10	7	7	6	7

*In the 1993 poll, 17 percent were neither more optimistic nor pessimistic. [Questions 3. to 5. were not asked in 1993.]

3. In your view, is the economy in Canada beginning to improve, not changing, or getting worse?

	1989	1990	1991	1992
Improving	17	4	9	12
Not changing	24	6	35	45
Getting worse	58	90	55	42

4. Some people have said that they expect the economy to remain weak through most of the 1990s and that economic and job opportunities will remain limited. Other people have said that they expect the economy to become stronger over the next year or so and for economic and job prospects to improve. Which point of view best reflects your own?

Remain weak	61
Become stronger	38

5. Who do you look to most to look after your best economic interests?

	1989	1990	1991	1992
Government	25	27	27	27
Business	50	45	48	53
Unions	15	16	15	13
Don't know and non-answer	10	12	9	7

6. Overall, which of the following two options for government do you think is more important right now? Is it to: do everything possible to reduce the government deficit, even if it means a reduction in services; or invest in programs that give people skills for the future, even if it means the deficit increases?

Reduce deficit, despite services	41
Invest in skills, despite deficit	57

7. At the end of the day, we have to look to government for solutions to the major problems we face.

Agree	39
Disagree	61

8. Canada would not be any worse off if it became part of the U.S.

Agree	22
Disagree	78

Source: *MacLean's*, January 4, 1993 and January 4, 1994.

Questions

1. What changes took place in the poll results between 1989 and 1992 or 1993 for questions 1 to 5 above?

2. Suggest reasons why these changes came about.

3. Compare the national poll results with those of your class and suggest reasons for the similarities and differences.

Library research

Check your library for more recent *Maclean's* CTV polls of Canada's problems and the economy. The polls are usually published each year during the first week of January.

CHAPTER 3

Productive Resources

(1)

(1) The Bassano Dam in Alberta.

(2) Inspecting a catch of fish in Caraquet, New Brunswick. The fisheries have traditionally been a primary productive resource in Canada. But with the collapse of Atlantic fish stocks in the early to mid-1990s, fishing as a productive resource has become seriously jeopardized in Eastern Canada.

(3) Agriculture is an important industry in Prince Edward Island.

(4) Thetford Mines, Québec.

(5) Forestry is a vital industry in British Columbia.

Questions

1. What resources that occur in nature and that have value are shown in photographs 1 to 5?

2. What goods used in the production of other goods and services (capital goods) — such as factories, machines, and tools — are shown in photographs 1 to 5?

(5)

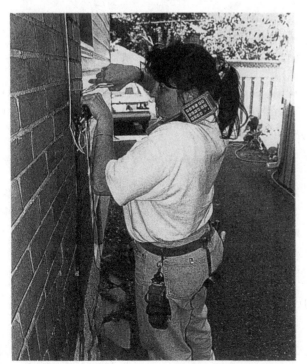

(6)

(7)

Questions

Our ability to produce goods and services is influenced not only by the natural and capital resources available, but also by the quantity and quality of the workers.

1. What knowledge, skills, and training are necessary to become (a) a telephone technician and (b) a laboratory analyst?

2. What capital resources are shown in photographs 6 and 7?

BUILDING YOUR SKILLS

Reading tables, graphs, and charts

Table 3.1 Prize money in women's tennis for the top ten (in U.S. dollars), 1993

1.	Steffi Graf	$2 821 337
2.	Arantxa Sanchez Vicario	1 938 239
3.	Conchita Martinez	1 208 795
4.	Martina Navratilova	1 036 119
5.	Gabriela Sabatini	957 680
6.	Jana Novotna	926 646
7.	Natalia Zvereva	857 160
8.	Gigi Fernandez	671 063
9.	Helena Sukova	655 573
10.	Mary Joe Fernandez	611 681

Source: *The United States Tennis Association Yearbook*, 1994.

Figure 3.1 Prize money in women's tennis for the top ten (in U.S. dollars), 1993

(in millions of U.S. dollars)

Tables

In the sports section of the daily newspaper, there is usually a listing of all the latest sports results. Often these are shown in tables because a lot of information can be presented in a small amount of space and because readers can easily find the facts they seek.

A table that you might find at the end of the tennis season is shown here (table 3.1). To extract information from a table requires some skill and practice. The following questions will help you.

1. Why was the table prepared?

The answer to this question is found in the title. This table shows the amount of prize money in U.S. dollars won by the top ten female tennis players in 1993.

2. What actual units do the figures represent?

In this table, the answer is again given in the title. The earnings are expressed in United States dollars. In other tables, the answer may be found in the column titles or in footnotes.

3. What is the source of the data presented?

Information from widely respected sources, such as *The United States Tennis Association Yearbook,* is likely to be highly accurate. Other sources may be less reliable.

4. What relationships are shown by this table?

Not enough information has been given in table 3.1 for relationships to be evident. However, relationships would become apparent if we included additional information, such as the amount of prize money won by the top

Figure 3.2 Prize money in women's tennis for the top ten (in U.S. dollars), 1993*

S. Graf	$ $ $ $ $ $ $ $ $ $ $
A. S. Vicario	$ $ $ $ $ $ $
C. Martinez	$ $ $ $ $
M. Navratilova	$ $ $ $ $
G. Sabatini	$ $ $ $
J. Novotna	$ $ $ $
N. Zvereva	$ $ $ $
G. Fernandez	$ $ $
H. Sukova	$ $ $
M. Fernandez	$ $ $

Legend $ = $0 to $124 999
$ = $125 000 to $249 999
$ = $250 000

* Note that the amounts are taken from table 3.1 on page 38.

Table 3.2 National Hockey League results for Canadian teams, 1993-94

	Wins	Losses	Ties
Québec Nordiques	34	42	8
Montréal Canadiens	41	29	14
Ottawa Senators	14	61	9
Toronto Maple Leafs	43	29	12
Vancouver Canucks	41	40	3
Calgary Flames	42	29	13
Winnipeg Jets	24	51	9
Edmonton Oilers	25	45	14

Source: The National Hockey League, *Official Guide and Record Book,* 1994-95.

ten female tennis players for the following year. This information might show an increase in the amount of prize money won, changes in the players, or shifts in the ranking of the players.

Graphs and charts

Another way to present information is in a **bar graph.** The information shown in table 3.1 is depicted in a bar graph in figure 3.1. Bar graphs or charts may be horizontal or vertical.

The **pictograph** is a kind of bar graph, but instead of showing amounts by means of a bar, quantities are shown using small, simple pictures. These small pictures may be stylized women, men, hockey pucks, or, as shown in figure 3.2, dollar signs.

If you compare the two graphs with the table, you can see some of the advantages and

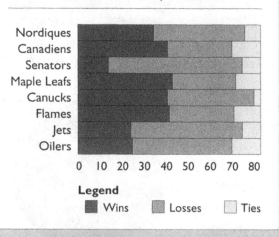

Figure 3.3 National Hockey League results for Canadian teams, 1993-94

Legend ■ Wins ▨ Losses ☐ Ties

Here, the information in table 3.2 is shown in the form of a divided bar graph. This kind of presentation helps us to compare the performance of the eight teams.

disadvantages of both. Tables are easier to construct and more accurate to read. Graphs show the main features of the information at a glance, and are easier and more interesting to read than tables.

Another way to present information is the **divided bar graph**. See how information from table 3.2 has been depicted in figure 3.3 on page 39. This way of presenting data is helpful when you want to make comparisons.

You can also make comparisons with a **pie** or **circle graph**. In a pie graph, each segment of the circle represents the total of one part. Thus, for example, in the pie graph for the Vancouver Canucks shown in figure 3.4, the solid area shows the total games won by the Canucks (41) of the total games played (84).

Time-series graphs

One of the most useful graphs in economics is the time-series graph. A **time-series graph** represents time (for example, weeks, months, or years) on the horizontal axis, and the variable

we are interested in (such as stock market prices or unemployment) on the vertical axis. Figure 3.5 shows a time-series graph. On the horizontal axis is shown time, the years from 1920 to 1995, and on the vertical axis is shown the unemployment rate — the variable we are interested in. A time-series graph can show many things; in this case, for example:

1. **When the level of unemployment is high or low.** When the line is close to the horizontal axis, the level of unemployment is low. When the line is far from the horizontal axis, the level of unemployment is high.

2. **It tells us the direction of unemployment:** whether it is increasing or decreasing.

3. **It tells us the speed at which the unemployment rate is changing** — whether it is changing quickly or slowly. For example, unemployment rose quickly between 1929 and 1931.

4. **It helps us to spot trends** — general tendencies to rise or fall. Thus, for example, we can see the general trend from 1950 onwards for the unemployment rate to rise.

5. **It helps us to compare two different time periods.** Thus, we can see that in the 1930s, unemployment was higher compared to any other time period.

Practise your skill

Use the four-question framework for examining graphs, charts, and tables (as outlined on page 38) to examine figure 3.5.

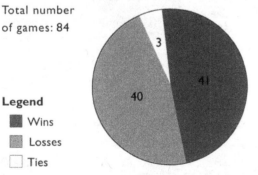

Figure 3.4 Pie graph showing National Hockey League results for the Vancouver Canucks, 1993-94

Total number of games: 84

3

41

40

Legend
■ Wins
■ Losses
□ Ties

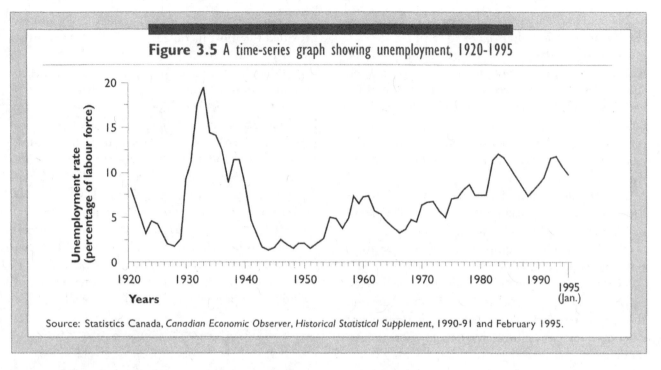

Figure 3.5 A time-series graph showing unemployment, 1920-1995

Source: Statistics Canada, *Canadian Economic Observer, Historical Statistical Supplement,* 1990-91 and February 1995.

RESOURCES AND PRODUCTION

In Canada, our ability to produce the goods and services we need depends on the quality and quantity of productive resources.

Productive resources are made up of labour or human resources (that is, workers of all kinds); natural resources or land (including forests, soil, and minerals); capital resources (such as tools, factories, and machines); and the entrepreneur (or self-employed business owner). All four resources are combined in production.

The more numerous our productive resources and the better their quality, the better we can deal with the problem of scarcity. Scarcity, as we have seen, arises because our wants are greater than our resources.

The entrepreneur as a productive resource can be included as part of labour or human resources. However, because of the special role played by entrepreneurs in our economy, we will treat this subject separately, in the next chapter. Here, we will focus on land, labour, and capital. Later in this chapter, we will examine the process of production.

NATURAL RESOURCES

Natural resources or land are all the resources that occur in nature that have value and may be used in production. These resources include minerals, forests, water, and fish. Land is considered by economists to be one of the factors of production.

Natural resources, usually called land by economists, include all the "free gifts of nature." These "free gifts" are the land in the city and on the farm, minerals in the earth, trees in natural forests, natural lakes, rivers and streams, the fish in these waters, and wild animals.

If by land we mean the total amount of dry land, then this total is fixed or limited. Additional land can be reclaimed from the sea, but in most countries such practice produces only small areas. The amount of arable land may vary greatly, however, depending on the use of irrigation, drainage, and fertilizer.

Canada is the second largest country in the world, measuring almost 10 million km². Even though only about 7 percent of the land is used for agriculture, Canada has vast areas of fertile low-lying land in the Prairies, the Great Lakes, and the St. Lawrence lowlands. The principal field crops are wheat, barley, vegetables, corn, and tobacco. Livestock and livestock products are also important.

More than a third of Canada's total land area is forested. Forestry is a major industry in British Columbia, Ontario, Québec, and Atlantic Canada. Canada is one of the world's leading producers of newsprint, pulp and paper, and lumber.

Commercial fishing in Canada dates back to the fifteenth century. The Pacific and Atlantic oceans and the inland lakes and rivers have yielded abundant catches in the past. However, overfishing off the Atlantic coast of Canada has pushed cod fishing to the verge of commercial extinction. In 1992, Canada's Minister of Fisheries ordered a two-year suspension on cod fishing along most of the Atlantic coast of Canada. Later, the Minister of Fisheries announced an indefinite suspension on cod fishing and the slashing of quotas for other species of fish as well.

The vast Canadian Shield contains a wealth of minerals. Canada also has huge reserves of coal, oil, and natural gas.

INTERPRETING STATISTICS

In economics, as in sports, much use is made of statistics. Often these statistics are presented in the form of tables and charts. Test your skills with the following tables and graphs that relate to the importance of natural resources in Canada.

Look, for example, at table 3.3. In which provinces were landings of fish and other sea products most important? least important? Suggest reasons why.

Examine table 3.4. Which agricultural products provided the most income for Canadian farmers between 1970 and 1993?

Table 3.5 shows the production of zinc, nickel, lead, and copper during selected years between 1970 and 1993. What relationships or trends are revealed by this table? As you can see, the production of nickel fell steadily between 1970 and 1980 by more than a third. Between 1980 and 1990, however, the trend was reversed and production increased. Between 1990 and 1993, nickel production again declined. What trends are evident in the production of zinc, lead, and copper?

Figures 3.6 to 3.8 on pages 43-44 show the production of other selected minerals in Canada between 1970 and 1993. Analyse these figures. In general, what trend is apparent from table 3.5 and figures 3.6 to 3.8 regarding the production of metallic minerals?

Table 3.3 Landings of sea and inland fish and other sea products, 1988 and 1989

	1988 Landed value $000	1989 Landed value $000
Newfoundland	292 096	266 359
Prince Edward Island	68 997	69 813
Nova Scotia	436 904	438 204
New Brunswick	119 469	104 935
Québec	101 485	84 686
Ontario	54 710	48 123
Manitoba	25 196	21 538
Saskatchewan	4 672	4 165
Alberta	2 842	1 912
British Columbia	533 559	416 294
Yukon and Northwest Territories	2 763	2 730
Canada	1 642 693	1 458 759

Source: Statistics Canada: *Canada Yearbook*, 1994.

Table 3.4 Sources of farm cash income (in million dollars) for selected years, 1970-1993

Year	Total cash receipts from farming operations	Total crops	Wheat	Barley	Canola	Corn	Other crops	Total livestock and products	Calves and cattle	Hogs	Dairy products	Other livestock and products	Other sources of income
1970	4 167	1 397	569	145	97	30	556	2 624	974	488	677	485	146
1975	9 998	4 802	1 699	466	261	153	2 223	4 818	1 818	886	1 419	695	378
1980	15 778	6 987	2 763	546	673	372	2 633	8 386	3 663	1403	2 065	1 255	405
1985	19 931	9 401	2 505	532	905	575	4 884	9 752	3 589	1 822	2 716	1 625	778
1990	21 616	8 539	2 694	548	793	512	1 359	11 175	4 037	2 034	3 135	1 969	2 912
1992	23 686	8 564	2 231	386	1001	509	1 647	11 324	4 459	1 776	3 089	2 000	3 798
1993	24 227	9 172	1 798	405	1 236	417	1 683	12 293	4 986	2 036	3 130	2 141	2 762

Sources: *Canada Yearbook*, 1975, 1978-79, 1985; Statistics Canada, *Canadian Statistical Review*, March 1987; Statistics Canada, *Canadian Economic Review*, January and November 1994.

Table 3.5 Production of selected minerals in Canada (in thousand tonnes) for selected years, 1970-1993

Year	Zinc	Nickel	Lead	Copper
1970	1 136	277	353	610
1975	1 229	242	349	734
1980	920	158	280	709
1985	1 049	170	268	739
1990	1 179	195	233	771
1992	1 196	181	340	746
1993	995	178	182	711

Sources: Energy, Mines and Resources Canada, *Canadian Minerals Yearbook*, 1976; Canadian Mineral Survey, 1979; Statistics Canada, *Canadian Statistical Review*, July 1982 and March 1987; *Canadian Economic Observer*, October 1992 and January and November 1994.

Figure 3.6 Production of gold in Canada (in ten-thousand kilograms) for selected years, 1970-1993

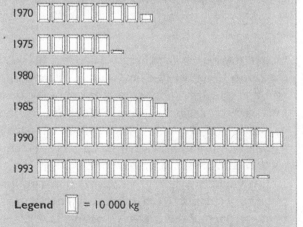

Legend ☐ = 10 000 kg

Sources: Energy, Mines and Resources Canada, *Canadian Minerals Yearbook*, 1976; *Canadian Mineral Survey*, 1979; Statistics Canada, *Canadian Statistical Review*, July 1982 and March 1987; *Canadian Economic Observer*, September 1992 and January and November 1994.

Figure 3.7 Production of iron ore in Canada (in ten-thousand tonnes) for selected years, 1970-1993

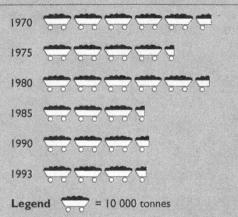

Legend = 10 000 tonnes

Sources: Energy, Mines and Resources Canada, *Canadian Minerals Yearbook*, 1976; *Canadian Mineral Survey*, 1979; Statistics Canada, *Canadian Statistical Review*, July 1982 and March 1987; *Canadian Economic Observer*, September 1992 and January and November 1994.

Figure 3.8 Production of silver in Canada (in thousand kilograms) for selected years, 1970-1993

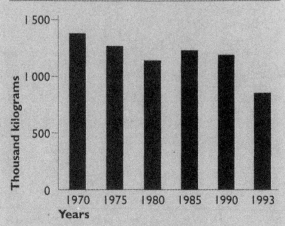

Sources: Energy, Mines and Resources Canada, *Canadian Minerals Yearbook*, 1976; *Canadian Mineral Survey*, 1978; Atlantic Canada, *Canadian Statistical Review*, July 1982 and March 1987; *Canadian Economic Observer*, September 1992 and January and August 1994.

BUILDING YOUR SKILLS

Recognizing misleading graphs

Graphs may be designed in such a way as to mislead the reader — either deliberately or unintentionally. For example, let's suppose that for some reason I wanted to exaggerate the prize money earned by Steffi Graf compared with Arantxa Sanchez Vicario. In 1993, Graf earned $2 821 337 and Vicario $1 938 239 in prize money.

As we know, figure 3.9 conveys the right impression. Figure 3.10 may be misleading, though, because part of the table is missing. The graph starts at $1 500 000 and therefore gives the impression that Vicario's earnings were approximately one third Graf's. The first thing to look at, then, is the numbers along the side of the graph.

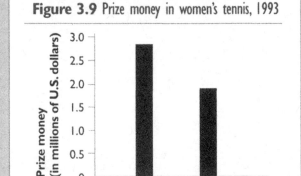

Figure 3.9 Prize money in women's tennis, 1993

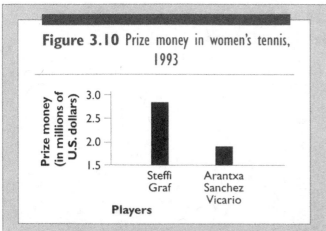

Figure 3.10 Prize money in women's tennis, 1993

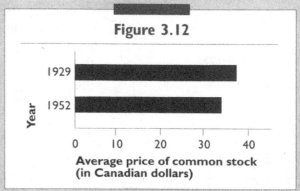

Figure 3.12

Do they start from zero? If not, the diagram may give the wrong impression.

Another way that the reader might get the wrong impression is shown in figure 3.11.

Here, the bars are replaced by dollar signs. This time, however, not only is the dollar sign one-third higher (as it should be), but it is also one-third wider, so we get the impression that it is one-third deeper. What we tend to compare is not the height but the volume — and we are left with an erroneous impression. We should, therefore, be careful when we see pictures or

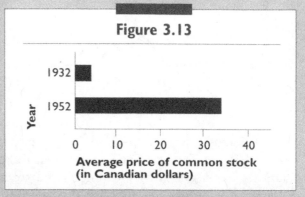

Figure 3.13

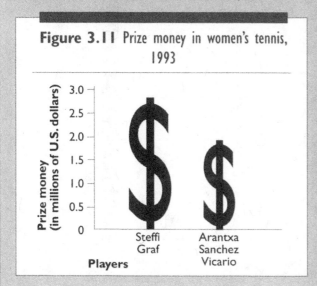

Figure 3.11 Prize money in women's tennis, 1993

silhouettes used to represent figures. Do they present an exaggerated picture?

A third way the reader can be misled is illustrated in figures 3.12 and 3.13. In both cases, the data presented are correct regarding the average price of shares. A share (or a stock) represents ownership of part of a corporation. The possession of shares entitles the owner to a share in the corporation. Shares are traded on stock exchanges, such as those in Montreal, Toronto, and Vancouver, for most large Canadian corporations.

Figure 3.12 shows that between 1929 and 1952 average share prices changed very little. Figure 3.13, on the other hand, shows that the average price nearly tripled during almost the same period. How could both these graphs be correct? The answer is that between 1929 and 1932, a calamitous stock market crash occurred.

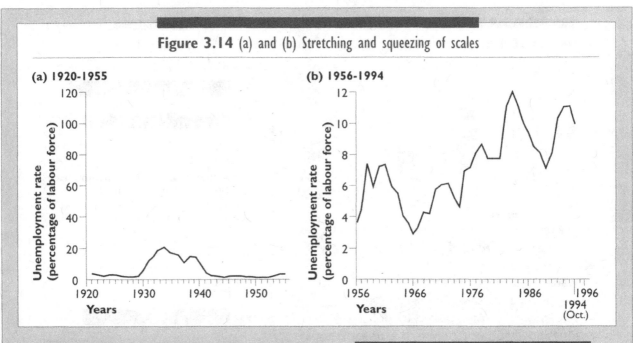

Figure 3.14 (a) and (b) Stretching and squeezing of scales

(a) 1920-1955

(b) 1956-1994

The message conveyed by the two graphs is very different. The first one suggests that there is little to be gained by investing in the stock market. The second suggests just the opposite. Thus, an author can give the reader two completely different messages, depending on the choice of the first or base year. In examining a graph or table showing how things have changed over time, we should ask ourselves, "Why has the author selected this base year?" and "Has the author selected the base year to give us a false impression?"

Misleading time-series graphs

One way of misleading the reader is to stretch and squeeze the scales on time-series graphs and to place them side by side. For example, in figure 3.14 (a), the vertical axis has been squeezed, while in figure 3.14 (b) it has been stretched. When we examine the two together, we get the wrong impression that unemployment was fairly

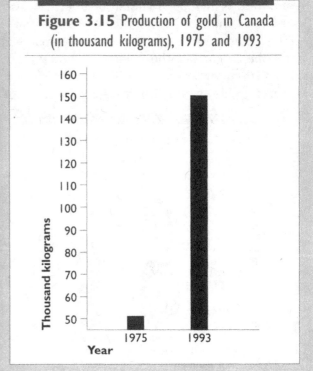

Figure 3.15 Production of gold in Canada (in thousand kilograms), 1975 and 1993

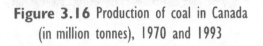

Figure 3.16 Production of coal in Canada (in million tonnes), 1970 and 1993

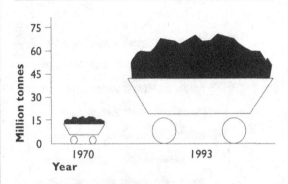

Source: Statistics Canada, *Canadian Economic Observer, Historical Statistical Supplement*, 1992-93 and November 1994.

Figure 3.17 Sales of WOW! — the new beauty product

Questions

1. Which of the graphs in figures 3.15 to 3.17 may be misleading? Give reasons for your conclusions.

2. Suggest ways in which the misleading graphs could be changed to give a more accurate impression.

3. Both graphs shown in figure 3.18 contain the same information. Which one of the two graphs is better? Why?

stable from 1920 to 1955 except for a slight blip upwards in the 1930s — and that from 1956 to 1994 by comparison, it has increased dramatically. Thus, we should be aware of the possible misconceptions that can arise by using different or inappropriate scales.

Figure 3.18

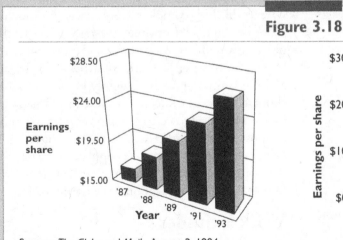

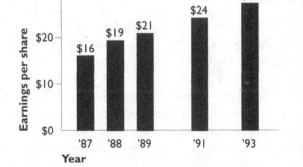

Source: *The Globe and Mail*, August 2, 1994.

HUMAN RESOURCES

Although Canada's natural resources are both rich and vast, they would be of little use in production without human resources.

Human resources, often called labour, are the services provided by workers (manual and non-manual), used in an economy or a firm to produce goods and services.

In examining human resources, we consider not only the number of workers but also their skills, knowledge, initiative, and effort. Human resources include, among many others, the services of labourers, doctors, dentists, prime ministers, computer technicians, and crane operators.

Human resources are the key element in any productive process. Production will vary in any economic community, depending on four major characteristics of human resources: health, education and skills, willingness to work, and population size.

Health

The health of workers is important to the production process. Clearly, workers who are continually sick are less productive than healthy workers. The graph in figure 3.19 shows average life expectancy in a number of countries. The longevity of Canadians indicates we are among the healthiest people in the world.

Education

The better educated a population is, the more productive the country tends to be. It is therefore appropriate to consider not only the health but also the education of Canadians.

As compared with other economically advanced Western countries, Canada has one of the most highly educated populations. In Canada in the late 1980s, nearly 60 percent of young people aged 2 to 29 years were engaged in educational programs from pre-primary to post-secondary. Only three other Western nations had higher proportions. However, young people in Canada

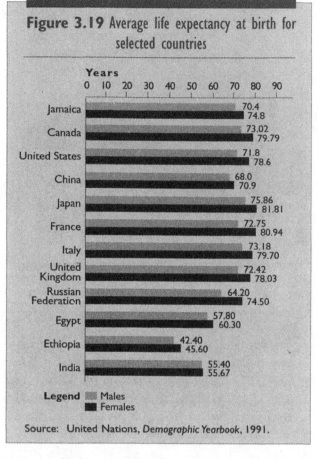

Figure 3.19 Average life expectancy at birth for selected countries

	Males	Females
Jamaica	70.4	74.8
Canada	73.02	79.79
United States	71.8	78.6
China	68.0	70.9
Japan	75.86	81.81
France	72.75	80.94
Italy	73.18	79.70
United Kingdom	72.42	78.03
Russian Federation	64.20	74.50
Egypt	57.80	60.30
Ethiopia	42.40	45.60
India	55.40	55.67

Source: United Nations, *Demographic Yearbook*, 1991.

were less likely to complete a secondary education than those in about half of other Western countries. The university graduation rate in Canada was higher than that in most other Western countries — only Japan and the United States had slightly higher rates. Only about 18 percent of degrees awarded in Canada were in science and engineering — a lower proportion than in most mixed-market countries. (See figure 3.20.) Generally, however, Canada's population aged 25 to 64 years of age has one of the highest percentages in terms of post-secondary education. (See figure 3.21.)

Work attitudes

In addition to good health and education, Canadians possess attitudes and values that make them highly

Figure 3.20 Seven countries with the largest proportion of graduates awarded science and engineering degrees and Canada, 1988

	All science and engineering	Natural sciences	Computer sciences	Engineering
	% of all graduates			
France	39.6	10.4	7.7	21.6
Belgium	32.9	5.6	2.0	25.3
Finland	32.0	6.6	5.5	19.9
Germany	29.3	7.8	2.8	18.7
Ireland	26.9	14.1	2.6	12.3
Japan	26.1	3.1	—	23.0
Denmark	25.8	5.8	1.3	18.7
Canada	**17.6**	**6.4**	**4.5**	**6.8**

Source: Statistics Canada, *Canadian Social Trends*, Autumn 1993.

Use the four-question model on pages 38-39 to analyse figures 3.20 and 3.21.

Figure 3.21 Percentage of the population aged 25-64 with a post-secondary education,* by country, 1989

United States 35%
Australia 31%
New Zealand 31%
Canada 30%
Switzerland 24%
Sweden 23%
Japan 21%
Norway 21%
Netherlands 19%
Finland 18%
Belgium 17%
Germany 17%
Denmark 17%
United Kingdom 15%
France 14%
Ireland 14%
Spain 9%
Italy 6%
Portugal 6%
Austria 5%

* Both university and non-university higher education.

Source: Statistics Canada, *Canadian Social Trends*, Autumn 1993.

productive workers. No single set of statistics would provide final evidence for this statement, but the participation rates shown in figure 3.22 give an indication of the involvement of Canadians in the workforce.

The graph in figure 3.22 on page 50 displays information differently from other graphs we have seen so far. Notice that the vertical axis starts at zero but that most of the area between zero and thirty has been omitted to save space. However, to warn the reader that part of the graph is missing, small parallel lines have been drawn across the vertical axis. Thus, the reader should not gain a wrong impression.

Population size

Another factor that obviously affects total production in any country is the size of the population. In terms of average population density — three persons per square kilometre — Canada's population density is one of the lowest in the world. The coordinate graph in figure 3.23 on page 50 shows the growth of population.

Population trends since 1945

During the 1940s, the numbers of unwed women and men declined and the age of marriage decreased significantly so that more than half the women were married by age 21 and half the men by age 22. In addition, couples increased their family size so that by the 1950s having a third and even a fourth child

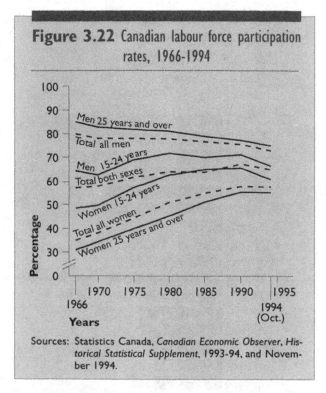

Figure 3.22 Canadian labour force participation rates, 1966-1994

Sources: Statistics Canada, *Canadian Economic Observer, Historical Statistical Supplement,* 1993-94, and November 1994.

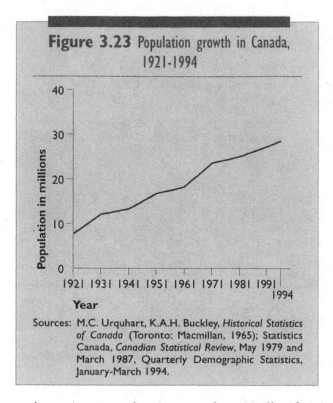

Figure 3.23 Population growth in Canada, 1921-1994

Sources: M.C. Urquhart, K.A.H. Buckley, *Historical Statistics of Canada* (Toronto: Macmillan, 1965); Statistics Canada, *Canadian Statistical Review,* May 1979 and March 1987, Quarterly Demographic Statistics, January-March 1994.

became fashionable. This increase in birth rates is called the baby boom. The total number of children born in Canada peaked in 1958. The total number of children born now is much lower, even though the population count is 50 percent higher. The number of children born for each woman of child-bearing age in 1959 was close to four. By the latter half of the 1980s, that number had declined to an average of 1.7, and that rate continued into the 1990s.

In the absence of large-scale immigration, if this rate of childbearing continues, the population of Canada will fall considerably over the next century.

Figure 3.24 shows Statistics Canada's projected population of Canada from 1992 to 2036 on the assumption that annual immigration is at 250 000 and emigration is at 86 886. We can see from the graph that population in the 0 to 14 and 15 to 44 age categories is expected to remain relatively unchanged in numbers. However, during this 45-year period the numbers and proportion of the population aged 65

and over is expected to increase dramatically. If so, this means that more services will be required for senior citizens. Pension plans will likely come under stress as more people retire, and as the age composition of the work force changes.

CAPITAL RESOURCES

Capital resources are goods that are used in the production of other goods or services. Factories, machines, and tools used in the production of automobiles, for example, are capital goods.

Canadians today have better capital resources available for the production of goods and services compared to a century ago. If you compare a modern wheat farm with a wheat farm of a century ago, you would find the modern farm a more efficient operation, owing in part to the use of modernized farm machinery. Compare how the modern dentist operates with the

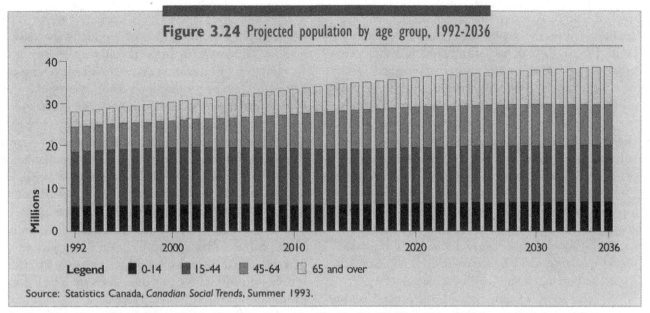

Figure 3.24 Projected population by age group, 1992-2036

Legend ■ 0-14 ■ 15-44 ■ 45-64 □ 65 and over

Source: Statistics Canada, *Canadian Social Trends*, Summer 1993.

Analyse this time-series graph using the four questions identified in the "Building Your Skills" section on page 38.

way a dentist worked a hundred years ago, and decide which one you would rather visit.

The combine is a capital good that the farmer buys in order to produce wheat. A dentist's drill is a capital good that the dentist buys in order to provide dental services. A professional musician uses a trumpet, also a capital good, to produce music at a concert. A capital good is a good purchased in order that something else can be produced or provided. It is a means to an end.

To produce capital goods, a number of conditions must be met. First, a community must "make" time to devote to the production of capital goods. Remember the concept of opportunity cost? In making capital goods, a community diverts its time from making consumption goods and services and/or from enjoying increased leisure. Thus, leisure and/or more consumption goods are the opportunity cost of the capital goods.

Second, a community has to develop the skills to produce capital goods. Third, a community must have resources to devote to the production of capital goods. If a community is producing just enough food for its survival, it is difficult to divert production to making capital goods.

There is an obvious incentive to produce capital goods. By devoting time and resources to their production now, we can increase our production in the future. Eventually, our standard of living would rise, because in devoting time in the present to making tools, we would be able to save time in the future, and the time saved could be used to produce more goods and services. This is the kind of thinking that provides communities with the incentive to allocate resources to the production of capital goods. The production of capital goods requires sacrifice because use must be made of present resources in order to gain in the future. Communities have to be confident that the investment of present resources in capital goods will bring a reasonable return in the future.

PRODUCTION

Production is any activity that serves to satisfy human wants. Thus, economists consider not only the manufacture of automobiles or the growing of crops to be production, but also the services supplied by teachers, surgeons, secretaries, and ballet dancers. Production involves the combining of economic resources (land, labour, capital, and entrepreneurial ability) to produce goods and services to meet our needs.

Generally, all productive activity can be divided into three categories: primary, secondary, and tertiary.

People who work in **primary industries** work close to the land. They are the farmers, miners, lumberjacks, oil riggers, and fishers who produce staple products of grain, iron ore, wood pulp, oil, and fish.

Secondary industries are involved in manufacturing the staple products into finished goods. A finished good could be a capital good (one that would be purchased by another manufacturer who would use it to produce other goods), or a consumer good (one that would be purchased and used by a consumer).

Once a good is manufactured, the process is not over. Take the example of a television set that has just been assembled and tested, and is now sitting in the manufacturer's warehouse. At this point, the **tertiary industries** take over. The television has to be transported to the store. It may be marketed through print or broadcast advertising across the country. A salesperson in a store sells you the television (they may deliver it, too). Then, if the television breaks down, you contact someone to repair it. Tertiary industries are the vital link between the producer and the consumer.

A large part of the production process involves workers supplying services. Service workers comprise about three-quarters of the Canadian work force. Usually when we think of production, we think of the production of goods but not services, such as education, medical care, entertainment, travel, and the people who provide those services. Production involves any activity that serves to satisfy human wants.

Production possibilities

In using our resources in the production of goods and services, we are again brought face to face with a familiar problem — that of scarcity. Even with the vast productive resources of Canada, we cannot produce all we want of everything. We have to make choices. If we are fully employing our resources, more of one good means less of another good, so we have to decide what we will produce.

One way to illustrate this need to make choices is to consider the production possibilities open to us at any time. A model will simplify the illustration. Let us suppose that, in a simple economy, only two things are produced — butter and tractors — and that the amount and quality of resources available for producing these two goods do not change. If we decided to use all our resources to produce butter only, let's assume we could make a thousand tonnes. If, however, we wanted to make some tractors, then we would have to give up some butter. If we wanted to make more tractors, we would have to give up more butter, and so on. We can then draw up a list of the production possibilities that face us.

As you look at figure 3.25, you can see that as we produce more tractors, we give up increasing amounts of butter. Not all our resources are equally able to produce butter or tractors. As resources are transferred from the production of butter, it is likely that those resources most able to work in the tractor factories and least able to work in the dairy industry will make the transfer to tractor production. As we increase tractor

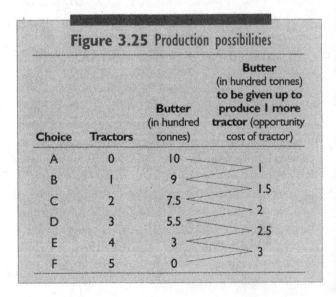

Figure 3.25 Production possibilities

Choice	Tractors	Butter (in hundred tonnes)	Butter (in hundred tonnes) to be given up to produce 1 more tractor (opportunity cost of tractor)
A	0	10	
			1
B	1	9	
			1.5
C	2	7.5	
			2
D	3	5.5	
			2.5
E	4	3	
			3
F	5	0	

production, however, the dairy industry will lose resources that are more and more capable of butter production and the tractor industry will gain more resources that are less able to produce tractors. Thus, the opportunity cost of tractors in terms of the amount of butter given up will tend to increase.

We can depict this information in the form of a graph. We can show the number of tractors along the horizontal axis and the tonnes of butter along the vertical axis.

The production possibilities curve AF in figure 3.26 shows the maximum amount that the economy is capable of producing. The maximum amount is any point along the line AF, such as A, B, C, D, E, F. In practice, the production of goods and services may be less than the full capability of the economy. At point X, for example, the economy could produce more butter (and the same amount of tractors) by moving to C; more tractors and the same amount of butter — as at E; or more of both, by moving to D. Any point to the left of the curve or within the curve (AF) can be achieved by the economy. Any point to the right of or outside the curve (such as Y), cannot be achieved. In order to reach Y we would need more resources.

The production possibilities curve gives us a boundary or a limit to the choices open to us. With the full employment of our productive resources, we can select any point along AF as being within the range of choice available to us. If, however, some of our productive resources are not employed, then our range of choice is inside the production possibilities curve.

The production possibilities curve illustrates some of the major concepts of economics. Resources are scarce and we have to make choices from among the goods and services available to us. We cannot have an infinite number of tractors or tonnes of butter. We have to choose some combination of the available products. In choosing to have three tractors rather than two, we should be aware of the opportunity cost of the additional tractors, of what we have to do without in order to get the additional tractor. In other words, we have to make trade offs. In this case, we have to trade off butter for tractors.

But does the production possibilities curve have any connection to a real economy? Any real economy is infinitely more complex than our simple model. There are many more thousands of goods and services and a vast number of combinations of resources. Yet,

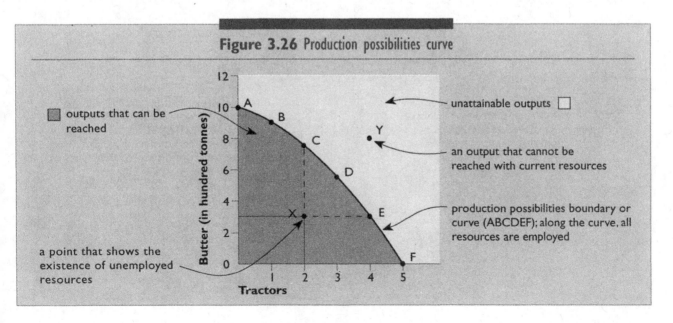

Figure 3.26 Production possibilities curve

even though very much more complex, real economies still face the same problem.

Circular flow between businesses and households

The production possibilities curve represents one model of an economy. Here, we begin to develop another model — the **circular flow** diagram. We can view our entire economy as a flow of goods and services and money between and among the four main actors in our economy: governments, businesses, households, and other countries. We'll start our development of the circular flow diagram by describing the flow of goods and services and productive resources between households and businesses.

Who are households? All workers and all consumers are part of the household sector. Households include all families and unattached individuals living on their own. Households include all of us.

What kinds of economic activity do households engage in? We have examined two of them: the consumption of goods and services and the supply of productive resources (land, labour, capital, and entrepreneurial skills).

Who are businesses? Businesses include all kinds of organizations engaged in economic activity, for example, your corner store, your local gas station, and huge enterprises such as General Motors of Canada and the Steel Company of Canada. Businesses hire productive resources from householders and provide households with goods and services. We can show the relationship between households and businesses in a circular flow diagram. (See figure 3.27.)

We can view our entire economy as being a great circular flow of goods, services, and productive resources. Businesses produce goods and services that flow to households where they are consumed. In return, households provide businesses with productive

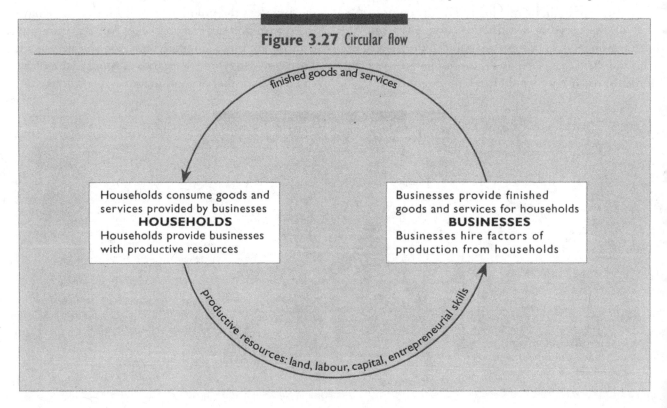

Figure 3.27 Circular flow

finished goods and services

Households consume goods and services provided by businesses
HOUSEHOLDS
Households provide businesses with productive resources

Businesses provide finished goods and services for households
BUSINESSES
Businesses hire factors of production from households

productive resources: land, labour, capital, entrepreneurial skills

BUILDING YOUR SKILLS

Drawing graphs

As we know, much information in economics (and elsewhere) can be displayed in the form of graphs. So far in this chapter, our focus has been on reading graphs. Now we turn our attention to drawing line graphs. The simplest form of graph shows just one variable. We'll start there.

In Figure 3.28 (a) and (b), we can see two examples of graphing a single variable. Figure 3.28 (a) shows the price of hot dogs measured in dollars and cents. The point (A) indicates that hot dogs sell at $1.00 each; at point (B) they sell at $1.25; at (C), $1.50; and at (D), $1.75. As we move to the left along the scale, prices diminish; as we move to the right, prices increase.

Figure 3.28 (b) shows quantities. As we move along the scale to the right, the quantity of hot dogs bought increases at (W), 50 hot dogs; at (X), 75; at (Y), 100; and at (Z), 125.

The graphs in figure 3.28 (a) and (b) represent only a single variable each, and graphing a single variable doesn't tell us very much. Graphs become much more useful, however, when they show how two variables are related.

A graph with two variables

In a graph with two variables, we put one variable at right angles to the other variable. For example, we can set the price scale at a right angle to the quantity scale, so that price is measured along the vertical line and quantity along the horizontal. These two lines are called axes: the vertical line is called the **y-axis** and the horizontal, the **x-axis**. Each of the two axes has a zero point common to both. This point is called the **origin**.

Figure 3.28 Graphing one variable

(a) Price of hot dogs

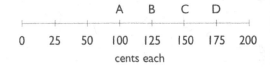

(b) Quantity of hot dogs bought

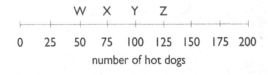

Graphs measure quantity as a distance. The graph in (a) measures price, and in (b) quantity bought. Quantity and price increase as we move to the right.

To construct a two-variable graph, we need to know two pieces of information. For example, let's assume that at a price of $1.00 each, 125 hot dogs are bought; at $1.25, 100 hot dogs; at $1.50, 75 hot dogs; and at $1.75, 50 hot dogs. We can show this data on a graph. See figure 3.29 on page 56.

The basic steps in constructing a graph are quite straightforward:

1. **Select a title for your graph.** For figure 3.29, the title is: "The demand for hot dogs."

2. **Select a suitable scale.** There are no firm rules for selecting a suitable scale. The scale depends on the range of the variables being

graphed — here, to $1.75 on one axis and to 125 on the other. The scale also depends on the amount of space available.

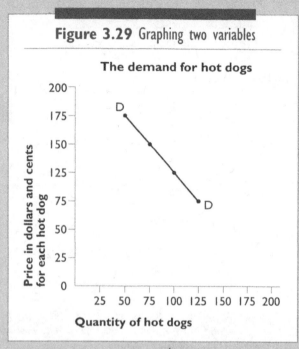

Figure 3.29 Graphing two variables

The demand for hot dogs

The points on the graph are joined to give the line DD. Although the line is straight in this case, it is generally referred to as a curve.

3. **Decide what each graph will measure on each of the two axes, then draw and label them.** When drawing graphs in economics, we always measure price along the vertical axis, and quantity along the horizontal axis.

4. **Plot the points on the graph and join them.**

Practise your skill

Draw a production possibilities curve using the following information.

Production possibilities of Country Q

Production possibility	Tractors	Wheat (in hundreds of tonnes)
A	0	20
B	1	18
C	2	15
D	3	11
E	4	6
F	5	0

Write a title for the graph, and label the horizontal and vertical axes and the origin 0.

resources: land, labour, capital, and the skills of the entrepreneur. Businesses use the resources to produce the consumer goods and services that they provide to households.

REVIEW

Explain each major concept in your own words with an example: natural resources, human resources, capital resources, productive resources.

APPLICATIONS

1. What conditions must be met for a capital good to be produced?

2. At current immigration and birth rates, some experts have predicted that, in the next century, Canada's population will start to decline.

   a) What effects might a declining population have on the economy of Canada?

   b) What effects might a large increase in immigration of, say, twice the rate of 1994 of

SUMMARY

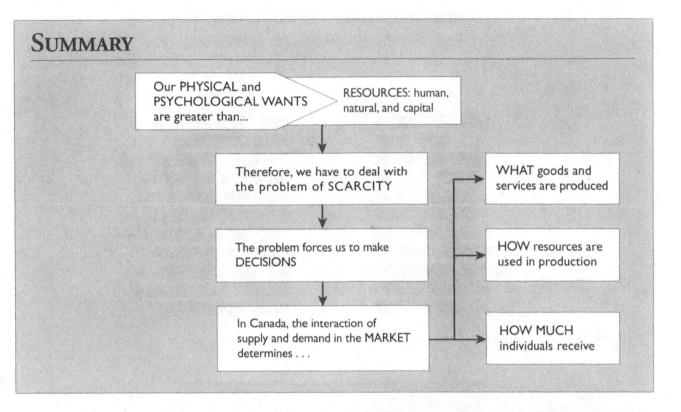

Our PHYSICAL and PSYCHOLOGICAL WANTS are greater than...

RESOURCES: human, natural, and capital

Therefore, we have to deal with the problem of SCARCITY

WHAT goods and services are produced

The problem forces us to make DECISIONS

HOW resources are used in production

In Canada, the interaction of supply and demand in the MARKET determines . . .

HOW MUCH individuals receive

250 000 per year have on the Canadian economy? Suggest reasons for your conclusions.

3. Figure 3.30 displays the production possibilities for the land of Nowhere.
   a) How much wheat and how much wool will be produced at A and at B?
   b) Which point(s) (A, B, Y, Z) show(s) production possibilities that can be achieved by the people of Nowhere?
   c) Which point(s) indicate(s) that Nowhere has unemployed resources?

4. Analyse figures 3.31 and 3.32 on page 58.
   a) What is meant by the participation rate?
   b) Explain why there are different participation rates among the four categories.
   c) In what ways do the participation rates for your province differ from those of other provinces and with Canada as a whole?

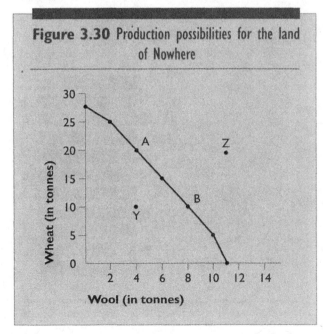

Figure 3.30 Production possibilities for the land of Nowhere

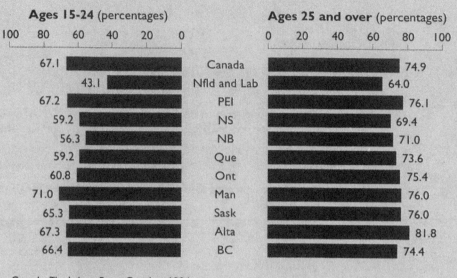

Figure 3.31 Male participation rates in Canada, 1994

Ages 15-24 (percentages)   **Ages 25 and over** (percentages)

	Ages 15-24	Ages 25 and over
Canada	67.1	74.9
Nfld and Lab	43.1	64.0
PEI	67.2	76.1
NS	59.2	69.4
NB	56.3	71.0
Que	59.2	73.6
Ont	60.8	75.4
Man	71.0	76.0
Sask	65.3	76.0
Alta	67.3	81.8
BC	66.4	74.4

Source: Statistics Canada, *The Labour Force*, October 1994.

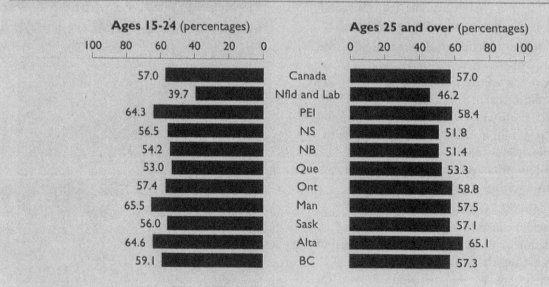

Figure 3.32 Female participation rates in Canada, 1994

Ages 15-24 (percentages)   **Ages 25 and over** (percentages)

	Ages 15-24	Ages 25 and over
Canada	57.0	57.0
Nfld and Lab	39.7	46.2
PEI	64.3	58.4
NS	56.5	51.8
NB	54.2	51.4
Que	53.0	53.3
Ont	57.4	58.8
Man	65.5	57.5
Sask	56.0	57.1
Alta	64.6	65.1
BC	59.1	57.3

Source: Statistics Canada, *The Labour Force*, October 1994.

d) Suggest possible reasons for the differences you identified.

5. Refer to Fig. 3.33 to answer questions a) to e).
    a) Calculate the opportunity cost of each additional combine.
    b) Draw a production possibilities curve. Give it a title, and label the vertical and the horizontal axes and the origin 0.
    c) Indicate two points R and S, which cannot be achieved by country Q's economy.
    d) Indicate a point U, which shows widespread unemployment in country Q.
    e) Suppose that country Q has no unemployed resources and produces its maximum output. Indicate a point X where this is so.

6. The Consumer Price Index shows the changes in price of a group of goods and services bought by Canadians. It is often used as an indicator of the rate of inflation — the rate at which prices of goods and services increase over a period of time.

Draw and label a time-series graph using the data in figure 3.34. Use the graph to answer the following questions:
a) In which year was inflation highest?
b) In which year was inflation lowest?
c) What have been the main trends in inflation?

Figure 3.33 Production possibilities for country Q

	1	2	3	4
Production possibility	Combines	Bushels of wheat	Opportunity cost of each combine	
A	0	17	
B	1	15	
C	2	12	
D	3	9	
E	4	5	
F	5	0	

Figure 3.34 Inflation 1980-1994

Year	Annual increase in the Consumer Price Index
1980	10.2
1981	12.4
1982	10.9
1983	5.7
1984	4.4
1985	3.9
1986	4.2
1987	4.4
1988	4.0
1989	5.0
1990	4.8
1991	5.6
1992	1.5
1993	1.8
1994 (June annual rate)	0.0

Source: Statistics Canada, *Canadian Economic Observer*, 1992-93 and August 1994.

CHAPTER 4

The Entrepreneur

(1) Lick's Burger & Ice Cream Shops is renowned for tasty food and an upbeat, friendly atmosphere. The young staff energetically sings out their orders, and customers' first names, to the beat of 1960s rock-and-roll tunes. In 1979, founder Denise Meehan used $2000 of her own and $2000 from the bank to open a tiny burger outlet on Queen Street East in Toronto's popular Beaches area. This first Lick's is now 10 times its original size. The company has expanded into eight other Southern Ontario locations. By 1993, sales had reached almost $14 million. (Read more about Lick's on pages 72-73.)

(2) These four young men — from left to right, Ash Modha, Raj Bahl, Amit Bahl, and Prashant Modha — started a business selling beachwear at Grand Beach on Lake Winnipeg in the summer of 1986. They called their company Mondetta, meaning "small world." But a chance observation by Ash Modha in 1988 led to big sales for the tiny company. While driving down a Winnipeg side street, he noticed a Volkswagen Jetta with a German flag on the licence plate. He thought: Why not market a line of T-shirts and sweatshirts with national flags embroidered on them?

He persuaded his partners to borrow $30 000 from their parents to design and market high-quality cotton sweatshirts called "FlagTops." Retailers cautiously ordered a few, and customers snapped them up — at $80 each! Today, buyers can choose from among 45 national flags. (For the full Mondetta Clothing story, see pages 63-64.)

Kaaydah Schatten-Forrest is co-founder of Ceiling Doctor International Inc., a leading cleaner of ceilings and industrial surfaces. Established in Toronto in 1984, the company has expanded into the United States, Southeast Asia, the Far East, Mexico, and Eastern Europe.

A Native Canadian, Kaaydah Schatten started working part-time in a real estate office in Nanaimo, B.C. at the age of twelve, typing offers and learning about mortgages. Eventually, her experiences renovating and reselling properties led her to ceiling cleaning. Until 1968, there was no efficient way to clean acoustic ceiling tiles. When dirty, they had to be replaced. Schatten examined several cleaning methods and decided they could be improved upon. She spent a year mixing chemicals with the help of a local chemist and searching for a suitable high-pressure pump to spray them in a mist.

Ceiling Doctor's co-founder Rob Forrest says their services brighten a company's appearance for a fraction of the cost of replacing or painting a ceiling. Plus, Ceiling Doctor's method is not abrasive and does not degrade ceiling material. Nor does the finely atomized spray drop to the floor and stain carpets. When companies see how much this type of cleaning can save them on their bottom line, they become solid repeat customers.

Adapted from Gordon Donaldson, "Vaulting ambition," *Canadian Business*, January 1989, and *Income Opportunities*, "The Platinum 200: Reaching For the Top," February 1995.

(3)

Questions

1. What is an entrepreneur?

2. What are some of the characteristics of a successful entrepreneur?

PART 1: ENTREPRENEURSHIP

The role of the entrepreneur

Entrepreneurs are individuals who start their own businesses or who aggressively expand existing ones. They organize the other productive factors (land, labour, and capital) for the purpose of producing goods or services, and assume the risks involved in running the business.

What qualities is an entrepreneur likely to possess? How do entrepreneurs establish their businesses? What role do they play in our economic system?

Think about these questions as you read the following case studies. Consider, also, the problems each entrepreneur faced, and how they overcame or attempted to overcome these problems.

Discreet moves

By Ann Gibbon
Québec Bureau, Montréal

Speed is the name of a hot Hollywood action flick. It also describes the breathtaking growth pace of the Montréal company whose software stars in the movie.

Discreet Logic Inc. was born in 1992 in a modest space on Montréal's trendy Boulevard St-Laurent. Armed with just $27,000 in seed [start-up] money, its founders — former employees of its better-known rival down the street, Softimage Inc. — planned to generate high-end computer graphics software that the film and video industry would snap up.

Those plans have come to life dramatically. Discreet's annual sales ... hit a staggering $22-million by the end of July, 1994.

Its open-concept offices, decked out with modern art and an espresso bar, now accommodate 30 employees. Fifty more will be hired in Montréal in 1994-95. Add in sales reps, and total employment will reach 100 in 1995.

But chief executive Richard Szalwinski knows he can't revel forever in dazzling sales, steady profits (the company will make up to $3.5-million in 1994) and rising celebrity from hit movie roles.

"We're concerned about growing too fast and repeating the mistakes other companies have made," says Mr. Szalwinski, 45, the laid-back former Softimage sales and marketing expert who founded Discreet with Diana Shearwood and Simon Mowbray.

Discreet must work to avoid what Mr. Szalwinski calls "hitting the wall" — the all-too-common plight of companies that can't sustain growth and support all the overhead they've added.

He also knows that while the sales surge may seem surprising, it only reflects the software mania in the entertainment market. "It's exploding," says David Wright, who follows software firms for Montréal brokerage Marleau Lemire. "Movies, television, video games are all using this technology."

By garnering [gaining] coverage in trade magazines and appearances at crucial trade shows, Discreet has cracked markets like Moscow, Paris and, of course, Hollywood. Buyers pay $300,000 to $900,000 for a "solution" — jargon for the package of Discreet's Flame software that runs on powerful supercomputers it buys from California-based Silicon Graphics Inc.

Sitting at a terminal, movie makers can generate digital images such as the outer-space pictures for the movie *Coneheads* or the highway hole that confronts the racing bus in *Speed*. They can add them to film or video pictures for a realistic, seamless total effect.

Customers, such as Centre de Montage Électronique of Montréal, which creates special effects for commercials and TV shows, like Flame software because it integrates all the functions they need to perform. "This is really the equipment of the future," says executive director Muriel Kearney.

All very nice, but what does Discreet do now? "You get to a size where you have to put in controls, such as on costs, so you can manage your business properly," says Mr. Wright of Marleau Lemire. "Some companies do it well, others don't."

Discreet is working on several strategies. First, it wants to evolve from a single-product company. That is why it has set up a company in Boston, a high-tech hot spot with an abundance of skilled engineers.

The U.S. branch has five employees who are developing a software-based product to be launched in April, 1995, destined for a market broader than entertainment. Beyond those details, Mr. Szalwinski is, well, discreet [noncommittal].

Discreet also plans to protect itself by prowling for that essential element of a young firm: capital. It hopes to align with a strategic partner in the industry or find an outside financier. It could also sell shares to the public to raise money, although that's the least desirable option.

New capital would go to building its own distribution network in Europe and Asia, instead of working through third-party agents who sell not only Flame but also products of other companies. An international sales force would consume precious management time and resources, but the reps would focus exclusively on Discreet.

Source: *The Globe and Mail*, June 27, 1994.

Sweat equity

By David Roberts
Manitoba Bureau, Winnipeg

The directors of **Mondetta Clothing** are locked in deep debate about a new product line. Suddenly, the talk shifts to another pressing issue: the coming ball hockey game against the warehouse staff.

Such mixed priorities are to be expected in a company run by four young men in their mid-20s. "This is like a high-school project gone wrong," jokes one partner, Raj Bahl, describing Mondetta's overnight rise as a merchandiser of upscale youth-oriented sportswear.

Mr. Bahl and his brother Amit joined forces with another pair of brothers, Ash and Prashant Modha, as teen-aged university students in the mid-1980s. The company has grown to annual sales of $8.5-million, and the Mondetta label has found its way into some of the flashiest boutiques in the world.

It's a success built on youthful energy, aggressiveness and a bright idea — embroidering country flags on sweatshirts. But Mondetta is in a tough business, going up against such names as The Gap and Benetton. The founders realize they have to continually leap ahead of their fickle young consumers.

"The rag trade is the easiest to get into and the easiest to fall flat on your face with," says Ash Modha, the 25-year-old president. "We really didn't know what we were doing. But you have to be aggressive."

The four partners have grown up together in business. Their families have known each other since moving to Winnipeg from East Africa (the Modhas from Uganda, the Bahls from Kenya) in the 1970s. The boys hung out together at the University of Winnipeg and flogged [sold] beachwear at Grand Beach on Lake Winnipeg in the summer of 1986.

They called their fledging company Mondetta, coined from the French *monde*, or world, and the suffix *etta*, which suggests small. Hence, small world.

In the beginning, it was small — until a chance observation by Ash Modha in 1988. Driving down a Winnipeg side street, he spotted a Volkswagen Jetta with a German flag on the licence plate. Why not put national flags on T-shirts and sweatshirts? Why not sell them for $80? He convinced his partners.

Retailers initially scoffed at the upstarts. "We saw their sweatshirts with flags on them," says Vancouver retailer Christian Toth. "But at 40 bucks wholesale we said forget it. After a while, we kept looking at them. They're so nice. Unbelievable quality."

Mr. Toth took a chance and ordered a handful of Mondetta's "FlagTops" for each of his six Off The Wall outlets in British Columbia. "They were gone in basically a day at $80 a pop. We said, 'Holy cow, something's happening here.'"

Sensing a market, the partners took a $30,000 loan from their parents to design and market the FlagTops on 18-ounce Egyptian cotton with detailed non-shrink embroidery. The first big sellers were flags of Canada, the United States and Italy.

Today, Mondetta sells 80 products: belts, ball caps, wristwatches, jackets, ski accessories, rugby shirts, sweat-tops, outdoor camping gear. Seventy-five percent of its sales are in Canada, mainly to 15- to 25-year-olds. But the FlagTop, still the big seller at $80 (your choice of 45 nations), is beginning to take hold in Europe and the United States. Licencing agreements are in the works for Singapore, Japan and Australia.

The challenge now is to sustain the momentum of the past two years and ensure the company's long-term survival. What happens, for example, when the flag shirts become uncool?

"We had great concerns about that issue," Mondetta's general manager, Ron Yager, admits. The company is trying to widen its demographics to older consumers. It has drawn up licencing agreements with NHL and CFL sports teams, several dozen U.S. colleges, and organizers of World Cup Soccer to produce high-quality jackets and sport tops. This diversification is combined with a new up-market [high quality] product line which shows only the Mondetta name.

Retailers say the strategy seems to be working.

Ash Modha recognizes that shifting tastes will be a continuing challenge. "We decided that as soon as a product matures, we're going to have to move on to something else."

Source: *The Globe and Mail*, February 28, 1994.

When style is a state of mind

By Cathryn Motherwell
Regina

The sign in the window says "Shoplifting is bad karma [destiny]." The curtains in the change room are thick, purple fake fur with pompoms. The merchandise is decidedly alternative — if you are looking for a ring to wear in your pierced navel, **World of Trout** has a nice selection.

This is Cornelia Biegler's creation, an independent design, manufacturing and retail business selling hip garments to cool young people. It's located on the main floor of an old warehouse, across the street from an industrial rail yard — in Regina.

Ms. Biegler sells her wares through a handful of independent shops in the four western provinces, plus her own local outlet. "We just think she's brilliant," said Hielkje Sandoval, who has sold Ms. Biegler's designs at Velvet Dread, her Calgary clothing store, for three years. "We're dealing with a person who obviously has very good design sense."

World of Trout's route to success is as unusual as its garments. Ms. Biegler got her start in retailing with the stylish Le Château chain, but wanted to break out on her own. When family matters called her back to Regina, she set up shop in her basement making basketball uniforms for school teams in Saskatchewan and Manitoba.

The uniforms paid the rent, but her real inspiration was the designs she cooked up on the side — hats in the style of joker's caps, slinky knit scoop-neck dresses, and vests like the ones your grandfather may have worn on Sundays. In 1991 she decided to turn her dream into reality.

First, there was the name. It was originally to be "Trout," which she liked because of the graphic possibilities of a word with two t's. One-word companies weren't permitted by the province, however, and so the name was expanded to World of Trout, or just WOT.

Sales have climbed to $250,000 from $40,000 in three years, which she attributes to hard work, common sense and listening to customers. In the beginning, her Regina shop was only open on Saturdays, but shoppers started showing up in the workroom during the week. Ms. Biegler expanded the hours. New retail outlets were added only when they demonstrated they could sell the stuff.

She's done it all without bank financing. Bankers suggested the presence of a husband or father in the business might help get a loan. Instead, Ms. Biegler's mother supplied the seed [start-up] capital and came on board as the accountant.

So far, Ms. Biegler has built her business through intuition. She purchases a bolt of fabric if it catches her eye; she undertakes to supply a store only if the relationship feels right.

"I'm very selective in who I deal with," she says. "No malls. People come up to us and say, 'Could we sell some of your clothes in our store?' And I say I want to keep it limited. I don't want it to be mass produced."

The trouble is her company has grown so fast that it's getting hard to maintain that personal touch. She wants to continue to be designer, retailer and manufacturer, but the demands are considerable. Like many entrepreneurs, she is starting to wrestle with how the company — and her role in it — should evolve.

For a fashion pioneer, Ms. Biegler's business goals are still conservative — to supply 12 to 15 outlets, up from the current nine. She has targeted Vancouver and Victoria for the next push.

Marketing is still limited to sponsoring local bands and selling their tickets and independently produced CDs in the shop. There are no end-of-season clearouts advertised in newspapers, and no commercials on television.

This helps keep prices moderate — the most expensive garment in the shop is about $75. That will be bumped up a notch to about $100 over the next year as Ms. Biegler expands the range of clothing she designs.

"The prices are really, really, really good," said Ms. Sandoval, the Calgary retailer. "And the stuff is totally original."

Source: *The Globe and Mail*, July 25, 1994.

ENTERING THE MARKET

Each of these people — like all entrepreneurs — was taking a risk. There was and is no guarantee that after the expenditure of a great deal of effort, care, thought, and money, they would be able to sell enough of their clothing and accessories or computer graphics software to exceed or even meet their expenditures.

Each of the entrepreneurs saw a market for a product, and each one moved to fill that need. Richard Szalwinski, Diana Shearwood, and Simon Mowbray saw a market for computer graphics software in the film and video industries; the Bahl and Modha brothers saw they could supply high-quality sweatshirts and accessories; and Cornelia Biegler saw an opportunity to sell "hip garments to cool young people."

Each entrepreneur was able to find the financing necessary for the operation of the firm, to find the money necessary to buy the raw materials, to buy, rent, or construct the necessary buildings and equipment, and to hire workers. Cornelia Biegler did it without a bank loan — her mother provided the seed capital. The Bahl and Modha brothers took a $30,000 loan from their parents. Discreet Logic Inc. was started with just $27,000.

These entrepreneurs decided on the level of demand for their own products and organized supply to meet that demand. Richard Szalwinski, Diana Shearwood, and Simon Mowbray, for example, found that there was a large and increasing market for computer graphics software in Canada and the United States. They organized the factors of production to produce the software: capital in the form of office space and computers, and labour in the form of 30 employees. They also decided how much of each of the factors of production was necessary and how best to organize the factors to produce the software.

Often, entrepreneurs have considerable knowledge of the business they choose to enter. As former employees of another computer graphics software firm, Softimage Inc., the founders of Discreet Logic Inc. had a firm grasp of computer graphics software.

Cornelia Biegler gained knowledge and experience of the fashion industry from her work at the Le Château chain of stores.

In our economy, entrepreneurs play a key role. They are the ones who identify a need for a new good or service. They are the innovators. They organize the factors of production. They arrange to finance the business. And they assume the risks.

The financial rewards for successful entrepreneurs may be substantial if, after paying the total costs of the business or enterprise from the total amount of money earned from the goods and services sold, there is still money left over. This money is the payment to entrepreneurs: their profit. Similarly, their losses may be substantial, if they misjudge the demand for the goods and services they provide.

We are all familiar with the entrepreneurs in our own communities, for example, the local business people who open their own convenience stores or household services. Many young people are entrepreneurs in such businesses as window washing, snow shovelling, lawn cutting, and child care.

CHARACTERISTICS OF SUCCESSFUL ENTREPRENEURS

Anyone can open a business. Therefore, anyone can be an entrepreneur. Here are outlined some of the major characteristics of successful entrepreneurs.

1. A "go-getter" attitude

Entrepreneurs are individuals who recognize the opportunities that exist in situations. They seek to turn disasters into challenges to be met and resolved. With this attitude comes an optimistic frame of mind — a cup is seen as half-full rather than half-empty. In a situation in which it rained for forty days and forty nights, the entrepreneur would be the one who would hire

Activity 1: Entrepreneur quiz

We have examined a number of cases of entrepreneurs and we have considered the role they play in our economy. Here, by means of a questionnaire, we will examine some of the characteristics of entrepreneurs. In your notebook, indicate what you think is the best response to each of the following questions. Briefly give reasons for your chosen response.

1. Suppose we learn that it is going to rain for forty days and forty nights. Which of the following are entrepreneurs most likely to do?
   A Move their possessions, themselves, and their immediate family to higher ground.
   B Hire trucks and workers to move people and their possessions to higher ground.
   C Assist in moving people and their possessions to higher ground.

2. In which one of the following would entrepreneurs be most likely to invest?
   A A savings account with a return of 6 percent with the amount invested guaranteed by the government.
   B Speculative mining shares with a possible return of 30 percent.
   C After careful study of the market, in shares with a very good chance of return at 10 percent.

3. Which of the following best describes the work habits of entrepreneurs?
   A They keep watching the clock.
   B They work a regular 9-to-5 day.
   C They don't notice the passage of time.

4. Which of the following conditions would entrepreneurs favour in working on a task?
   A Working with a friend.
   B Working with a stranger who is an expert.
   C Working alone.

5. Which of the following is the most important reason entrepreneurs set up their own businesses?
   A To make a lot of money.
   B To become well known.
   C To work for themselves.

6. Entrepreneurs believe that the success or failure of a new business venture depends mainly on
   A Good luck.
   B The strength and abilities of others.
   C Their own strength and abilities.

Adapted from Joseph B. Mancuse, *How to Start, Finance and Manage Your Own Small Business* Rev. ed. (Prentice-Hall); Arthur H. Kuriloff and John Hemphill, *Starting and Managing the Small Business* (McGraw-Hill); William E. Jennings, *Entrepreneurship, A Primer for Canadians* (Canadian Foundation for Economic Education).

workers, rent trucks, move people to higher ground, and house them in rented tents. Entrepreneurs seize whatever opportunities may be available.

2. Risk taking

Entrepreneurs are moderate risk takers. They are not likely to get involved in a pure gamble with excessive risks (such as purchasing speculative mining shares). They are more likely to invest in a venture involving moderate risk and the probability of reward, in which

their abilities can have a definite impact on the outcome (such as shares with a significantly above-average return). Entrepreneurs are likely to avoid the safe and guaranteed low-interest savings account.

3. Hard work

Establishing a business involves the expenditure of much time, energy, effort, and ingenuity on the part of entrepreneurs. They need good health to get them through the pressures and long hours of establishing a business. They are creative and energetic self-starters who, when working on a task, don't notice the passage of time.

4. Motivation

Money is a major motivation for obvious reasons. It also serves as an indicator of how well entrepreneurs are doing. The main reason entrepreneurs establish a business in the first place is to work for themselves rather than for someone else. Entrepreneurs can control and direct the business in the way they wish. Entrepreneurs must also be able to motivate their employees by setting a good example, making sound decisions, and being fair.

5. Self-confidence

Entrepreneurs have sufficient faith in themselves to believe that they can make a reasonable success of their business — otherwise they would not start it in the first place. While there may be problems, there are always solutions and entrepreneurs are adept at finding them. Successful entrepreneurs are unlikely to rely on luck or friends but rather on themselves to make a success of their businesses.

6. Objectivity

Self-reliance and self-confidence are two attributes of entrepreneurs. However, in any business there is a huge array of specialized tasks to perform. Therefore,

---

Activity 2: Entrepreneurial problem-solving

Suppose you and the other members of your group are partners in a business you own. It is often stated that entrepreneurs are people who can turn problems into opportunities. For each of the five problems outlined below, suggest ways in which it can be turned into an opportunity.

1. You have been making heavy-duty work pants from canvas, but your supply of fabric runs out. You can't find any place to buy more canvas. What could you do to solve this problem?

2. You own a firm that produces corks for bottles. Your best customer is a winemaker who buys thousands of corks each year. In tonight's paper you read that the government plans to pass a law making the production of wine illegal. If that happened, you would lose your best customer. What could you do to solve your problem?

3. You own a firm that manufactures posters. You have just finished printing thousands of posters

of a political candidate showing him without a beard, only to discover he has recently grown a beard. Now no one wants to buy your posters. What could you do to solve your problem?

4. For several years, you and your sister have owned a business that produces and markets pants. You ran the factory while your sister sold the pants. Last week your sister died, and you don't feel confident in marketing your product. What could you do to solve your problem?

5. You have developed a new frozen-food product. Although it is of good quality and is well liked by customers, you lack the money and training to mass-produce and market the product. What could you do to solve your problem?

Source: *Entrepreneurship in the U.S. Economy*, © National Council on Economic Education, New York, N.Y., 1994.

while working on a task, entrepreneurs recognize the need for skilled help. What is important is to solve the problem. Thus, entrepreneurs will seek out expert help, rather than go it alone. In analysing any problem, skilled assistance is often necessary.

WHY DO BUSINESSES FAIL?

The rate of failure among newly established businesses is very high. Studies have indicated that as many as four out of five new businesses are likely to fail in the first five years. Hard work alone is not sufficient to ensure success.

Businesses may fail because of the personal characteristics of the entrepreneurs. They may not be able or willing to devote the immense amount of time and effort necessary to maintain the business. They may have too little knowledge of the business and how to run it. They may have failed to devise an adequate financial plan for the business and to assess its ability to return a profit.

Entrepreneurs may fail to understand the market in which they are selling their goods and services. The competition from other businesses may be too severe. Their own prices may be too high. The market may be too small for the products they have to offer.

Businesses may take months or even years to build up sufficient customers. If there is insufficient cash in the interim, the business may fail.

In establishing a business, it is easy for an individual's judgment to become clouded. The desire to go into business may encourage entrepreneurs to plunge into the first business that they can afford, without stopping to consider its potential earning power.

One response to the high rate of failure among newly established businesses has been the development of industrial incubators.

An Industrial Incubator

The Venture Centre is a place to start for new entrepreneurs. Located in Pasadena near Corner Brook on the west coast of Newfoundland, this industrial incubator provides a favourable environment in which new businesses can take root and grow. It is a practical way to promote and support the skills and ideas of entrepreneurs.

The activities of the centre have focused on increasing public awareness of small business opportunities, as well as exposing potential entrepreneurs to the business prospects of worthwhile industries. The Venture Centre also helps budding entrepreneurs in the following ways.

1. Low rent

One of the hurdles faced by entrepreneurs is the difficulty of finding affordable accommodation for the business. During the first two years, the Venture Centre provides space for the business at 25 percent of the industrial rents in the Pasadena area. In year three, the rent increases to 50 percent, and in year four to 75 percent.

If the business is still in the centre during its fifth year, rent increases to 110 percent of industrial rents in the area. In this way, businesses are encouraged to leave the centre once they are fully established.

2. Development officer

A development officer is available at the Venture Centre to guide and assist entrepreneurs. This service includes arranging financing, reviewing business plans, and setting up cash-flow forecasts.

The Venture Centre in Pasadena, Newfoundland.

3. Cost sharing of services

The Venture Centre provides opportunities for businesses to share common costs that would be expensive individually. Such services include secretarial help, photocopying, telephone answering, and access to computer information.

4. Business advisory committee

A lawyer, a banker, an accountant, and three other business people provide business advice.

Established in 1986, the Venture Centre is Newfoundland's first industrial incubator. Funding for the project was provided by the federal government. In the spring of 1994, ten of the twelve units in the Venture Centre were occupied. Since 1986, ten companies have graduated from the Venture Centre. Similar incubators have been established in other parts of Canada, the United States, Britain, and Europe. There are now a number of Venture Centres for students where they can earn credits and start a business, e.g., the Enterprise Centre in Dawson Creek, British Columbia, and Scarborough Ventures in Ontario.

Questions

1. What are some of the problems faced by entrepreneurs?

2. How does the Venture Centre help new entrepreneurs overcome these problems?

PART 2: FRANCHISES

Tim Hortons (Oakville, Ontario).

Depanneur Couche-Tard Inc. (Laval, Québec).

Mark's Work Wearhouse (North Bay, Ontario).

Uniglobe Travel (International) Inc. (Vancouver).

Century 21 (Vancouver, British Columbia).

P.S. Paint Shop Inc. (Mount Pearl, Newfoundland).

A **franchise** is a licence or privilege granted by a corporation (the franchiser) to another corporation or individual (the franchisee) to sell a particular product or service with an advertised trade name.

Questions

1. Name some franchised businesses in your area.
2. In what industries are there franchises?
3. Why is franchising appropriate in these industries?
4. What are some of the advantages to (a) the franchisor, (b) the franchisee, and (c) the consumer of franchises?

Suppose that you like a certain kind of hamburger — say, the one sold in the restaurant beneath the golden arch. You can be fairly sure that you will find an identical hamburger in the same kind of restaurant served by someone wearing the same type of uniform in any major city in Canada, or in the world — providing, of course, that the restaurant has the familiar golden arch. We take this for granted. Given that many of these restaurants are operated by local entrepreneurs, it's somewhat surprising that they are so similar. The reason for their similarity? They are franchises. In Canada today, many goods and services — ice cream, pizzas, mufflers, haircuts, fried chicken, and others — are sold by franchises. Literally thousands of goods and services are franchised.

So far, as we have seen, individual entrepreneurs who wished to go into business for themselves had only two options: either to establish their own business from scratch or to buy an existing one. Franchising provides a third option. Typically, the franchiser pays a fee (ranging from a few hundred to half-a-million dollars) plus a percentage of sales of the product or service. The franchiser also signs an agreement to maintain the franchiser's operating standards in the provision of the good or service. In return, the franchisee often gets business advice, financial advice, training programs, and permission to use a widely recognized name, image, and product. The franchisee purchases a "packaged" business that must be operated in cooperation with the franchiser.

Rates of failure among franchised businesses are much lower than the estimated 70 to 80 percent rate in the first five years among businesses established by individual entrepreneurs. A franchisee can be described as a "semi-entrepreneur," because a franchise demands somewhat less risk, less innovation, and less self-reliance, compared to an independently-launched small business.

Trials and triumphs in a far-out franchise

By Ellen Roseman
Kingston, Ont.

With the mercury touching 30 below, few customers are venturing out to Lick's, a fast- food restaurant on downtown Princess Street. But franchise owner Heather Priestley has her hands full.

The heating system is acting up, the toilet water has a yellowish tinge, and the truck used to cook burgers for Queen's University students is grounded because it can't handle the cold.

Meanwhile, Ms. Priestley sports a bandage on her middle finger. A moment of inattention while cleaning a French-fry machine last week left her with a second-degree burn. A few months ago, she lost a patch of hair on her scalp after a propane gas accident in the truck.

"You can never really relax in this business," she says, taking time between stints at the grill and the cash register. "There's always something breaking down."

For some entrepreneurs, buying a franchise means buying someone else's expertise. You read the training manual, hire the right people and sit back — you hope — to watch the money flow in.

At **Lick's Burger & Ice Cream Shops**, a franchise owner is not a passive investor, but someone active in all aspects of day-to-day operation. "Lick's does not believe in absentee ownership," the franchise package states in bold print.

Founded in 1979 in east-end Toronto, Lick's is known for fresh food and friendly vibes. The young staff is trained to use customers' first names and sing out their orders to the beat of 1960s rock-and-roll tunes.

Founder Denise Meehan, 42, grew up in Sturgeon Falls, Ontario, where her parents owned a hotel. A Grade 11 dropout, she traipsed across North America, bunking in hostels and picking up bartending and waitress jobs.

"I always enjoyed being with the public and after working in so many restaurants, I thought, 'Hey, I can do that.'"

With $2,000 of her money and $2,000 from the bank, Ms. Meehan opened a tiny burger outlet on Queen Street East in Toronto's Beaches area, known for its dense summer crowds.

The first Lick's, now 10 times its original size, is still going strong and has been joined by eight other Southern Ontario locations, some company-owned and some franchised. Sales last year reached almost $14-million.

Franchisees pay about $375,000 to open a restaurant, including a franchise fee of $35,000, and hand over 6 percent of sales to head office, plus 3 percent for advertising. Franchise director Frank Peruzzi says they can expect to hit $1-million in annual sales within two years and earn a 10- to 20-percent return.

Ms. Meehan planned to open three to four franchises in 1994 and five in 1995 (possibly one in Florida). In no hurry to expand, she has strong ideas about who should run her restaurants.

"I'm looking for owner-operators who are prepared to invest time and energy using motivational skills with employees.

"Business for me is twofold — not only making money but feeling good, encouraging growth in the people I've met."

Once Lick's was a going concern, Ms. Meehan began thinking about franchising. She knew her success depended on attracting people who would work hard — "no job is beneath you," she insists — and share her values.

Heather Priestley seemed an ideal candidate. Although lacking fast-food experience, "she had a tremendous amount of energy and could hardly wait to get going," Ms. Meehan says.

Unable to come up with financing herself, Ms. Priestley enlisted a partner, Carol Harris, a clinical psychologist at Queen's University and a successful real estate investor. "We agreed I would never work behind the counter," says Ms. Harris, who prefers a background role.

At first, Ms. Priestley worried about entering the franchise arrangement, where every detail was spelled out with little room to manoeuvre. "Personally, I need a high level of autonomy."

But Lick's turned out to be a motherly, touchy-feely environment, with a franchise network small enough to accommodate frequent communication. Head office is in touch with Kingston at least once a week.

Ms. Priestley works 55 to 60 hours a week — down from 80 — and her family helps out.

Heather Priestley's proudest moment came last November when Lick's won the Golden Broom Award, honouring a local business for cleanliness and customer service.

Source: *The Globe and Mail*, February 7, 1994.

Questions

1. What qualities of a successful entrepreneur does Denise Meehan have?

2. Why did she franchise Lick's?

3. What kind of people was Ms. Meehan looking for as franchisees?

4. What are the costs to Heather Priestley of being a franchisee? What are the benefits? What is Carol Harris's role in the business?

5. Is Heather Priestley an entrepreneur? Explain your answer.

6. Are franchisees entrepreneurs? Explain your answer.

Pros and cons of the franchise

Franchisers sometimes have problems selecting good franchisees and in controlling them, since both are, after all, independent business persons. But the advantages to the franchiser of granting franchises are obvious. By having others finance the establishment of the stores or outlets, the franchiser's total sales can grow very quickly. And franchisees are highly motivated to run their businesses efficiently, because their money is tied up in the franchise.

For the franchisee, too, there are advantages and disadvantages. The franchisee must follow the operating procedures of the parent firm, pay a fee for the franchise, and usually pay the franchiser a percentage of sales. But the franchisee gets a proven business with proven expertise, and ongoing assistance to keep it running.

BUILDING YOUR SKILLS

Developing a business plan

Before establishing a business, successful entrepreneurs spend time developing a written plan outlining how to organize, finance, and operate the business. Some business plans run to hundreds of pages of print. Here, however, we will consider only some of the major questions that are included in a plan.

Why do entrepreneurs go to all the trouble of drawing up a business plan? The plan obliges entrepreneurs to think their way through their project in a logical, objective, and critical way. The plan forms a valuable tool or blueprint in helping the entrepreneur manage the business. The plan is also useful for communicating with others, for example, possible partners and possible sources of finance (such as bank loan officers). The entrepreneur can show them the plan to persuade them to join the business or to lend money to the project.

Let's examine some of the main questions in a business plan and apply them to a highly successful haircutting firm called First Choice Haircutters Ltd. Brian Tucker, Jim Tucker, and Bud Cowan opened their first haircutting salon in June 1980. The franchise fee was $25 000 with a royalty of 6 percent of sales in the U.S. and 7 percent in Canada. The total investment price was $80 000 (which includes the franchise fee).

The plan

1. Business information
Name of business: First Choice Haircutters Ltd.
Type of business organization
Will the business operate as:

a) a sole proprietorship   _____
b) a partnership   _____
c) a corporation   ✓‾‾‾‾

Is the business:
a) retail   _____
b) wholesale   _____
c) manufacturing   _____
d) agricultural   _____
e) a service   ✓‾‾‾‾

Is the business a franchise?
a) yes   _____
b) no   ✓‾‾‾‾

2. What is the big idea?

To apply big business techniques to an often poorly-run industry by means of the mass marketing of a cost-priced, standardized haircutting service in a no-frills, unisex haircutting salon.

3. Operation

a) Business

What good or service will be provided?

No-frills, unisex haircutting. Salon will have extended hours, no appointments, money-back guarantee. Unpretentious decor. A la carte menu of services: customers can choose what they want and pay for only what they choose. Staff will wear company T-shirts and matching skirts or pants, and will be trained to deal with customers courteously.

b) Management

i)   What are the names of all the partners?
ii) What work will each perform in the business?
iii) What is the experience and skill of each partner?

Brian Tucker
Work in the business: finance
Experience: entrepreneur
Skills: chartered accountant

Jim Tucker (brother of Brian)
Work in the business: marketing and real estate
Experience: seven years in sales
Skills: mechanical engineer

Bud Cowan
Work in the business: equipment, floor layout, and training
Experience: entrepreneur and hairstylist
Skills: hairstylist

c) Marketing plan

i)   What prices will be charged for the good or service?
ii) How much will it cost you to produce the good or service?

> $6 haircut
> $3 shampoo
> $3 brush and blow dry
> $1 reservation of a particular haircutter

The amount not stated, but the claim is that the return on money invested in the business will be above the average in the business

d) Promotion and advertising

i) How will potential customers be informed of the business? When will advertising begin? How much will be spent on it?

$80 000 will be spent on a year's air time for a TV commercial in the local area

e) Customers

i) How many potential customers are there?

The number of potential customers is large — everyone is a potential customer. The value of the total Canadian haircutting industry is estimated at $1.2 billion a year.

f) Competition

i) Who are the competitors?
ii) What are their strengths and weaknesses?

Many individual owners are usually hairstylists, not business people.

The industry lacks organization and management.

There are only 15 chains in Canada with more than four salons each; possibility for growth is tremendous.

g) Financing

i) How will the business be financed?

The three partners managed to raise $150 000. (Banks turned them down.)

h) Regulations

i) Has the need for permits for the business from the government been met?

yes ✓

no _____

i) Insurance

i) Has the necessary insurance been acquired?

yes ✓

no _____

The growth of First Choice

Since opening its first haircutting salon in June 1980, First Choice has been highly successful. The number of company-owned units reached 73 in 1994. By 1994, First Choice Haircutters Ltd. had grown to 136 franchise outlets in all provinces in Canada (except Saskatchewan) and had expanded into the U.S.

Practise your skill

Many high school and university students have set up their own businesses, for example, garden maintenance, odd jobs, painting, and babysitting. Jennifer McGowan, a seventeen-year-old high school student, set up her own Rent-A-Clown business; twenty-year-old Mark Brokloff, a university student, set up a clothing store specializing in casual and beach wear; eighteen-year-old Donald Hyette set up his own boat-rental business; seventeen-year-old Lisa Chanyi set up her own business painting designs on T-shirts and sweat shirts; Laurie Nagus, sixteen, Suzie Chung, eighteen, and Heidi Suiger, sixteen, set up their own flyer-distribution company.

Test your knowledge of a business plan. Suppose that instead of working for someone else next summer, you have decided to be your own boss.

With two or three other members of your class, select an idea for a business and develop a business plan for the project. Use the headings and questions that were used in the plan for First Choice Haircutters Ltd. For now, do not include your estimate of the cash flow.

BUILDING YOUR SKILLS

Preparing a simple cash-flow forecast

As part of their business plan, entrepreneurs also include a cash-flow forecast to enable them to see if the plan is a sensible one financially. Here we will examine some of the main elements of the forecast.

We will assume that Olivia Dias, a seventeen-year-old student, has decided to go into the house-painting business during the months of July and August. One of her relatives has agreed to loan Olivia her pick-up truck for her business.

Olivia Dias Painting

Here is how Olivia did the calculations for her cash-flow forecast.

Money she gets (cash receipts)

Total sales: she charges $10 an hour. She expects to work 8 hours a day and 6 days a week. Total sales per day will be $8 \times \$10 = \$80$ per month (26 days): $\$80 \times 26 = \$2\ 080$

Loan from a relative: $500

Other: she is investing her savings of $200

Money she pays out (cash disbursements)

Purchase of equipment

ladders	$200
miscellaneous (brushes, scrapers, etc.)	$300
Total	$500

Rental of equipment: extension ladder, sprayer, total $30 per month

Labour expenses: Olivia's sole labour expense is her own pay of $5 an hour

Materials: used in painting — paint, thinner, turpentine, etc., $80 per month

Business fees and licences: the expense of registering Olivia's company, $20 monthly

Advertising: cost of lawn signs, flyers, advertisements in local newspaper, $75 monthly

Insurance: for the business and the truck, $500 bimonthly

Office expenses: rental of answering service, stationery, stamps, etc., $25 monthly

Other: oil, gas, and truck repairs, $150 monthly

Olivia Dias Painting: Cash-flow forecast

Cash receipts (the money Olivia gets)

	July	August	Total
Estimated sales	2 080	2 080	4 160
Loan from relative	500		500
Other (her savings)	200		200
Total	2 780	2 080	4 860

Cash disbursements (the money Olivia pays out)

	July	August	Total
Purchase of equipment	500		500
Rental of equipment	30	30	60
Labour expenses	1 040	1 040	2 080
Materials	80	80	160
Business fees and licences	20	20	40
Advertising	75	75	150
Insurance	500		500
Office expenses	25	25	50
Other	150	150	300
Total	2 420	1 420	3 840

Net cash (Total cash receipts minus cash disbursements)

	July	August	Total
Monthly surplus		360	660
Monthly deficit			
Cumulative total		360	1020

Practise your skill

For the business plan you developed in the previous "Building Your Skills" section, develop a simple cash-flow forecast. Use the headings of Olivia's cash-flow forecast.

REVIEW

Explain each major concept in your own words and give an example: franchise, franchisee, franchiser, entrepreneur.

APPLICATIONS

1. Do you think you have the qualities and skills of a good entrepreneur? Explain. To what activities, other than starting up a small business, could you apply your entrepreneurial skills?

2. Invite a local entrepreneur to class to explain how she or he established the business. Before the entrepreneur visits you, review this chapter to see what kinds of questions you might ask.

3. Arrange to interview a local entrepreneur. Before doing so, draw up a list of key questions.

4. Check the Yellow Pages of your telephone directory for franchised businesses in your area. Find out details about the franchise program of a business in your area.

CASE STUDY
A failed venture

As you read the following case study, consider why Lynn Choromanskis' shoe outlet failed.

Lynn Choromanskis was laid off from her job as a management-information specialist at Canada Packers Inc. in Toronto with a $37 000 severance package and a desire to do something different. In 1991, she paid $140 000, most of it borrowed, to Moneysworth & Best Quality Shoe Repair for a franchised shoe-repair outlet in downtown

Toronto. The money covered store fixtures, equipment, site selection and training, as well as a franchise fee. "I wanted something small, where I wouldn't have a lot of employees," she said at the time, "where I'd meet the public, and provide a service they'd need. Even in a recession, people always get their shoes repaired."

Unfortunately, Choromanskis relied on the assurances of the franchiser rather than her own investigations when she signed up. Opening her shop in a downtown skyscraper, she soon discovered that the building's tenants were less optimistic than she was about their prospects in the recession. They began moving out in droves. Meanwhile, in nearby underground malls, Choromanskis counted at least 10 shoe repair shops competing with hers, some of them independently owned. Since 1991, she has managed to pay her store's bills and meet her royalty and loan payments, but she has not paid herself a penny.

In June, 1992, Choromanskis hired a manager to run the store while she returned to the world of the employed, working 12-hour shifts as a computer operator at a Toronto hospital. "I need a job," she says. "But the job market's the pits, even worse than my business. So I took what I could get."

Last March, when her manager said the store had not generated enough money to pay its bills, Choromanskis closed the door. "I had two choices," she says. "I could have stuck it out and asked [the franchiser] to let me get behind on my payments, which I would have been responsible for paying, or I could get out while I didn't owe any more money." Choromanskis chose the second option, breaking her 10-year agreement with her franchiser.

Choromanskis now is all-too-well acquainted with the substantial differences between buying a franchise and running your own business. A franchise offers little of the flexibility and none of the independence of her self-employed competitors. As a franchisee, she had to buy her supplies from the franchiser, for example, even if she could get them more cheaply elsewhere. She could not negotiate another lease. She could not independently cut prices or pursue any of the other options available to cash-strapped entrepreneurs. And she had to continue paying the franchiser 12% of her sales in royalties and advertising fees, whether she could afford it or not.

Choromanskis does not blame Moneysworth & Best for her predicament, even though the company did suggest verbally at the outset that her sales would be satisfactory. But even if she did complain, she would find no legal remedy for her predicament other than an expensive and time-consuming lawsuit. "Except in Alberta, there's little protection for a franchisee," observes Toronto franchise lawyer John Sotos. "Franchisees don't benefit from consumer legislation, because they're considered to be sophisticated investors and businesspeople."

Source: *Report on Business Magazine*, August 1993.

Question

Why did Lynn Choromanskis' store fail?

CHAPTER 5

Business Organization and Finance

(1)

(1) Many small stores, like the vegetable store shown here, are owned by one person and are therefore called single or sole proprietorships.

(2) Partnerships are common in such professions as law, accounting, medicine, and, as shown here, architecture.

(3) Alcan Aluminium Ltd., a large Canadian corporation, owns and operates the Laterrière smelter in Chicoutimi, Québec.

Question

What might be some ways in which corporations differ from sole proprietorships and partnerships?

(5)

(4) Via Rail Canada is a Crown corporation.

(5) This is one of the new grain elevators being built by Alberta Wheat Pool, which is an example of a cooperative.

(6) The Chinatown branch of the Vancouver City Savings Credit Union.

Questions

1. How does a cooperative such as Alberta Wheat Pool or Vancouver City Savings Credit Union differ from a corporation?

2. How do Crown corporations differ from corporations?

Activity 1: Types of businesses

In Chapter 2, we used a comparison organizer to answer this focus question: what are the similarities and differences among three main types of economic systems? To answer this question, we summarized information about pure traditional, pure command, and pure market economies in chart form. We can also use a comparison organizer in chart form to help us summarize information to answer this focus question: what are the similarities and differences between each of the different types of business organizations?

Each business can be categorized into one of the following five types: single proprietorship, partnership, corporation, public enterprise, or cooperative. Aspects of each type will include (among others) the business's name, date of foundation, current capital assets, net earnings, industry, number of employees, location, and ownership.

May's Corner Store, a sole proprietorship, has been owned by May Chung since 1971. She has three employees. The retail grocery has capital assets of $100 000 and net earnings of $10 000. Stores like May's are found throughout Canada.*

Tina's Taxi, a sole proprietorship, is operated and owned by Tina Smith, who runs the business herself. Tina's Taxi, founded in 1976, has capital assets of $80 000 and net earnings of $24 000. Tina's Taxi is located in Halifax, Nova Scotia.*

Fishwick, Snelgrove, and Associates, founded in 1978, is a partnership of five people. The partnership has twenty employees, net earnings of $200 000, and capital assets of $1 million. The partnership of accountants is located in St. John's, Newfoundland.*

Van Graff's Holsteins, a sole proprietorship founded in 1975, has capital assets of $500 000, and net earnings of $50 000. Nicholas Van Graff is the owner and operator of this southern Ontario farm.*

Victor's Taxi, a partnership of three people, was founded in 1978. The capital assets of the firm are over $800 000. The net earnings are $60 000. The firm has thirty employees and is located in Montréal, Québec.*

Jeanne La Chance's Farm, a partnership of two people, was founded in 1970. The current capital assets are $1.2 million, and net earnings are $60 000. This beef cattle farm is located in southern Québec.*

Bell Canada Enterprises Inc., a corporation with its headquarters in Montréal, had almost $37 billion in assets, a net loss of over $650 million, and about 118 000 employees, as of 1993. Founded in 1880, Bell has a very large number of shareholders (98 percent Canadian) who own the company. Bell is in the communications industry.**

Alcan Aluminium Ltd. has its headquarters in Montréal. Alcan employs 44 000 workers and has net assets of over $13 billion. It lost over $134 million in 1993. The company was founded in 1928. Alcan is in the mining and metal processing industries. It has a large number of shareholders, both in Canada and in the United States.**

Stelco Inc., founded in 1910, has capital assets of nearly $2.4 billion. The company, owned by its many shareholders, is in the steel industry. It lost $36 million in 1993. Stelco employs nearly 12 000 workers and has its headquarters in Toronto.**

Toronto Transit Commission, founded in 1921, is in the urban commuter transit business. Capital assets totaled nearly $2.3 billion in 1992. It has an operating subsidy of $227.6 million. The Commission employed 10 051 workers (on average) in 1992 and is 100 percent owned by the government of Metropolitan Toronto.***

Hydro-Québec, which is in the electricity generating and distribution business, has its headquarters in Montréal. Founded in 1944, the corporation has assets of almost $48 billion and profits (in 1993) of almost $761 million. The 100 percent provincially-owned Crown corporation has about 27 000 employees.**

Newfoundland and Labrador Hydro Electric Corporation has its headquarters in St. John's, Newfoundland. Founded in 1954, the 100 percent provincially-owned Crown corporation has assets of over $2 billion. In 1993 the corporation reported a profit of $24.9 million. The work force totals about 1000. In 1994 the provincial government announced plans to sell the corporation to the public.**

Canada Post Corporation has assets of about $2.5 billion and over 52 000 employees. Founded in 1981, the 100 percent federally-owned Crown corporation has its headquarters in Ottawa. The corporation had a profit of $26 million in 1993.**

Desjardins Life Assurance, founded in 1959, has its headquarters in Québec City. This cooperative has over 1500 employees, assets of nearly $4 billion, and an annual profit of nearly $44 million. As its name suggests, the cooperative is in the life insurance business. It is owned by its 3.2 million members.**

Co-op Atlantic, a grocery wholesaler founded in 1927, has its headquarters in Moncton, New Brunswick. The cooperative is owned by its

approximately 1000 members. The net assets of the cooperative were over $100 million and its profits were over $6 million in 1993.**

Alberta Wheat Pool was founded in 1923 and has its headquarters in Calgary. Its assets were nearly $380 million and its profits over $12 million in 1992. This grain marketing cooperative, owned by its members, has approximately 1500 employees.**

*Source: Actual or typical examples. With the actual examples, the names have been changed to preserve confidentiality.

**Source: *Canadian Business, The Corporate 500*, June 1994; *The Financial Post 500* (Summer 1994); *The Globe and Mail, Report on Business Magazine*, "1000 Ranking Corporate Performance in Canada," (July 1994); and the *Financial Post* Corporation Service Cards.

***Source: Toronto Transit Commission, *Annual Report 1992*.

Organize the information about the firms in chart form. Then use your chart to answer the following questions.

1. What are the common characteristics of the firms listed under each type of business organization?

2. What is the major difference between sole proprietorships and partnerships?

3. In what ways are sole proprietorships and partnerships similar?

4. In what ways do corporations differ from sole proprietorships and partnerships? In what ways are they the same?

5. In what ways do public enterprises and cooperatives differ from corporations?

6. From your own knowledge, give other examples of each type of business organization.

ORGANIZATION OF BUSINESS

Businesses are established and financed in five ways: sole proprietorships, partnerships, corporations, cooperatives, and public or government enterprises. Let's begin with the sole proprietorship — the most simple and popular form of business organization.

SOLE PROPRIETORSHIPS

The **sole proprietorship** is a form of business organization in which one person owns and operates the business.

Of the more than 600 000 firms in Canada, there are more sole proprietorships than any other type of organization. They are easy to establish. There are no general laws governing the establishment of a proprietorship; each province has its own regulations. All you need to say is, "Today I am in business," and you are. You are the one who makes all the decisions about what, where, when, and how much to produce. You establish the prices. You decide if you should hire workers. You supply the finances (capital) necessary. You do what you like and you collect all the profits. The sole proprietor is the only one who can say, "I am the company." In short, you are an entrepreneur.

Sounds perfect? Many people who establish their own business think so, at least at first. Soon, however, they become aware of the problems that beset sole proprietors. The size of the operation — the number of workers employed, the amount of capital invested, and the size of the output produced — is severely limited by proprietors' financial resources and their ability to borrow money. Proprietors are obliged to oversee the entire operation and frequently perform all the various tasks themselves. For some of these tasks, the sole proprietor may not be particularly well-suited. A sole proprietorship will probably require the owner's continuous presence. Any prolonged absence on the owner's part could lead to serious losses or even bankruptcy for the firm.

Sole proprietors also face severe financial risks. Legally, proprietors are entirely liable for the losses of their business. This liability is unlimited. Not only might they lose the capital they invested in the business, but they might also lose their homes and general belongings. Often, too, sole proprietors find it difficult to sell their businesses. People with the necessary knowledge, skills, and capital to take over the firm may be hard to find.

If the proprietor dies, goes to prison, or becomes insane, the proprietorship is ended. If the business is passed on to a daughter or son, a new proprietorship must be formed. The impermanence of the proprietorship might make it hard to attract workers looking for a permanent job. It might also make it difficult for the firm to grow and prosper.

Despite these problems, sole proprietorships are especially appropriate in the production of goods and services where the total market is small, where large-scale production is out of the question, and where the operations are not routine.

Sole proprietorships are common in professional services such as accounting, dentistry, and engineering. They are also common in farming, in stores and restaurants, and in house construction and appliance repair.

PARTNERSHIPS

A **partnership** is a business organization in which two or more individuals enter a business as owners, and share the profits and losses.

One way the sole proprietor can raise more capital is to bring one or more partners into the business. A partnership involves an oral or written agreement specifying the money, skills, and participation to be provided by each partner, as well as each partner's authority. There is no standard formula regarding how profits and losses will be shared. The procedure for the withdrawal of a partner and how the partnership will be ended is negotiated by the partners.

The partnership has clear advantages over the sole proprietorship. It can raise more capital, so it is better able to undertake operations on a larger scale. Responsibilities can be divided and therefore handled more efficiently. Shared expertise allows each partner to specialize in different parts of the business. Business decisions arrived at by discussions between or among partners may be much sounder than the decisions made by a sole proprietor. If one member of the partnership is absent for an extended period of time, due to illness, for example, the business can continue to run under the control of one or more of the other partners.

But the partnership also has its problems. Partners may find it difficult to reach agreement on certain issues. They may disagree, for example, over how long they plan to stay in business, their salaries, how profits and losses will be shared, whom to admit into the firm, and how hiring is to be done. Each partner is legally liable for the debts of the entire firm. This liability is unlimited in that it extends beyond the original amount invested in the business by the partners and can include their personal property. The problems posed by unlimited liability are compounded in a partnership. Each partner usually has full power to sign contracts that bind the firm in the ordinary activities of the business. Each partner's property is, therefore, at the mercy of the judgment of each of the other partners.

A partner cannot simply withdraw from the business. She or he must find someone (or a present partner) who is willing to buy into the firm and who is acceptable to the other partners. A further disadvantage of the partnership is that each time a partner resigns, or dies, a new agreement must be drawn up. Because partnerships are subject to dissolution at any time, they are unsuitable organizations for industries that require the acquisition of extensive and durable businesses and properties. Partnerships, like sole proprietorships, are common in farming, the professions, restaurants, construction, and repair work.

CORPORATIONS

The **corporation** is a form of business organization that has an existence of its own separate from those who created it or own it. There are two main types of corporations: Crown corporations and business corporations. Crown corporations are owned and controlled by some level of government, such as the Canadian Broadcasting Corporation (CBC) or Hydro-Québec. We will examine this type of corporation later in the chapter. Here, our focus is on the business corporation, which is owned and controlled by private individuals.

The weaknesses of the partnership and the sole proprietorship led to the formation of the corporation. The corporation is regarded in law as a legal personality. It has all the legal rights and responsibilities of an adult person. It can hold property in its name, enter into contracts, and sue or be sued in a court of law. Officials of a corporation act as its agents to fulfill its obligations and exercise its legal rights.

The two most common ways of establishing a corporation are federal incorporation under the Canada Business Corporations Act, and provincial incorporation under provincial laws. If the corporation is going to operate in more than one province, the business is incorporated under federal laws. If the founders intend to operate in only one province, the business is incorporated under provincial laws.

One great advantage of a corporation over partnerships and sole proprietorships is the legal right of **limited liability**. People who have invested in the stocks of a corporation are not personally liable for all its debts. Their liability is limited to the value of their investment in the business and that investment is all they can lose. Companies attach the word Limited (Ltd.) or Incorporated (Inc.) to their name to indicate to suppliers and customers that the owners have limited liability for corporate debts.

When a corporation wants to grow, it needs funds, or capital. One way to raise capital is to retain the earnings of the corporation rather than distributing them in the form of dividends to the owners. A second way to raise capital is by issuing securities. There are three main types of securities that corporations offer to the public today: the common share, the preferred share, and the bond.

Each of these three types is significantly different from the others, as we shall see.

An investment opportunity

Suppose that a relative left you $1000 in her will to invest in her favourite business, Hens' Teeth Manufacturing Company. Like many Canadian corporations, Hens' Teeth has three main types of securities that it has offered for sale to the general public: the common share, the preferred share, and the bond.

Common shares

If you purchase one or more **common shares** in Hens' Teeth, you will become a part-owner of the corporation with a right to vote in the affairs of the corporation and a right to share in its distributed profits. Your voting power and share of the profits will depend on the number of shares you hold compared with the total number that have been issued. It is not a case of "one person, one vote" but of "one share, one vote."

Suppose you bought 100 shares at $10 each and that 100 000 shares had been issued in total. You would have a claim to one thousandth of the voting power and the distributed profits. If you wish to recover your investment in the corporation, you may do so quickly and easily by selling your shares on the stock market. Common share prices, however, are likely to vary considerably over time, depending on the supply and demand for the shares.

Investment in common shares sounds attractive, but there is no certainty that you will receive any particular return on your investment. All depends on the profitability of the corporation, and what the corporation decides to do with its profits. If Hens' Teeth decided to distribute its profits in a given year rather than "plough them back" (or invest them to expand the business), then you will receive your portion — your dividend.

If Hens' Teeth comes to an end, you will receive your share of the assets only after all other financial obligations of the business have been met.

Preferred shares

Preferred shares are stock issued by a corporation that shows ownership of the company. Preferred shares have a preference over the common stock in the payment of dividends, and, in the event of the corporation's bankruptcy, in the distribution of the corporation's assets. Preferred shareholders usually don't have a right to vote in the affairs of the corporation.

If you are a cautious person who decided that you would prefer something more secure than common stock, the preferred share may be more to your liking. It is true that you may not have the right to vote in the election of company officers. You are, however, promised a fixed return or dividend on your investment, but the dividend is not owed until declared by the directors of the corporation. Should the company be terminated, your claim must be paid before that of the common shareholder.

Bonds

A **bond** is a written promise to pay a stated sum of money at some time in the future. Until that time, interest is paid on stated dates.

If you want the maximum security for your $1000 investment in Hens' Teeth, then the bond is your best bet. As a bondholder, you are not a part-owner of the corporation: you are its creditor. At a specified date, the corporation must repay you the money it borrowed from you. Until then, you are entitled to interest payments on your loan. If the company is terminated, the debt owed to you must be repaid before those of the common and preferred shareholders.

Why the variety of securities?

A moment's reflection will reveal that the various types of securities meet differing needs on the part of investors and corporations. In general, bonds are a safer investment than either the common or preferred shares because interest on them is paid before profits are distributed to shareholders. Also, in the case of bankruptcy, bondholders' claims must be satisfied before those of shareholders. Generally, however, bonds give a lower return than either of the two types of shares. Thus, investors can choose to purchase bonds if they want a relatively safe investment with lower return; or stocks, if they want a higher return and are willing to face higher risk.

While all corporations must issue common stock, it is not obligatory to issue preferred shares or bonds. It is likely, then, that the corporation will issue preferred shares or bonds only when such an issue is in its best interests. If the company is highly profitable, it may find that it is in its best interests to raise additional capital by the sale of bonds rather than shares. On bonds, only relatively low interest needs to be paid. If the additional capital were raised through the issuing of more shares, the new shareholders would participate in the firm's profits equally with the old shareholders. Thus, the share of profit by the older shareholders would be proportionately diminished.

Control of the corporation

The common shareholders, the owners, ultimately control the corporation. However, in many corporations there are thousands of shareholders, too many to administer the company effectively. A board of directors is elected by the shareholders of the corporation at an annual shareholders' meeting. In the election, each shareholder receives one vote for each share owned. Voters who expect to be absent at the time of the meeting may arrange to vote by proxy, i.e., by transferring their voting right to someone else who will be present.

The board of directors, in turn, elects the chairperson, vice-chairperson, secretary, and other officers of the board. The board of directors appoints officers of the corporation, its top managers such as the president, vice-presidents, and treasurer to administer the affairs of the corporation on a day-to-day basis. The directors meet from time to time to give general guidance to management, to consider the affairs of the company, and to make decisions on corporate policy. The board of directors performs a "watchdog" role — it is responsible to the shareholders for the actions of the officers of the corporation. For each shareholders' meeting, the directors will prepare a statement of the financial affairs of the company.

Advantages of the corporation

By now, some of the advantages of the corporation over the sole proprietorship and partnership are apparent. For the shareholders, their liability is limited solely to the amount of money put into the firm. They usually have no difficulty in selling their shares on the stock market. They do not need to consult other owners before selling their stock. Investors have a range of different securities in which they may invest with different degrees of risk and return.

The major advantage of the corporation is that it can raise very large amounts of capital from a large number of individuals. See figure 5.1 on page 88, showing the top 20 Canadian corporations by sales. (They could be ranked in other ways, e.g., by profit or by assets, in which case we would have a very different ranking.) Far better than the sole proprietorship or the partnership, the corporation can take advantage of the possibilities presented by mass production, marketing, and automation. This, in turn, can offer an advantage to consumers — all of us — in lower prices per unit.

The corporation, too, may last a long time. The Hudson's Bay Company was incorporated under royal charter on May 2, 1670, and is still flourishing. Partnerships and proprietorships may

Figure 5.1 The top 20 Canadian corporations by sales

Sales rank '92 '91			Sales ($MIL)	Profit -(loss) ($MIL)	Assets ($MIL)	Number of Employees	Ownership
1	1	BCE Inc. (management holding company)	20 784.0	1 390.0	48 312.0	124 000	widely held
2	2	General Motors of Canada Ltd. (automobiles)	18 347.8	-(72.0)	6 230.9	39 237	General Motors Corp. (Michigan) (100%)
3	3	Ford Motor Co. of Canada Ltd. (automobiles)	14 443.1	-(363.8)	3 881.9	19 784	Ford Motor Co. (Michigan) (94%)
4	4	George Weston Ltd. (grocery stores, bakeries)	11 599.0	48.0	3 965.0	62 000	Wittington Investments Ltd. (Toronto) (57%)
5	6	Imasco Ltd. (tobacco, restaurants, drug stores)	9 957.2	380.4	48 519.0	75 000	BAT Industries PLC (UK) (41%)
6	7	Alcan Aluminium Ltd. (mining and processing)	9 654.0	-(142.3)	12 894.6	46 000	widely held
7	11	Chrysler Canada Ltd. (automobiles)	9 453.8	-(48.6)	3 141.7	13 800	Chrysler Corp. (Michigan) (100%)
8	9	Loblaw Cos. Ltd. (grocery stores)	9 261.6	79.8	2 474.1	47 000	Weston Food Distribution Inc. (Toronto) (71%)
9	8	Imperial Oil Ltd. (oil and gas)	9 127.0	195.0	13 192.0	10 152	Exxon Corp. (Texas) (70%)
10	5	Canadian Pacific Ltd. (management holding company)	8 963.6	-(487.3)	20 223.8	63 300	widely held
11	10	Noranda Inc. (mining, pulp and paper, oil and gas)	8 643.0	79.0	14 370.0	48 000	Brascan Ltd. (Toronto) (49%)
12	12	Northern Telecom Ltd. (telecommunications equipment)	8 408.9	548.3	9 379.3	57 955	BCE Inc. (Montréal) (52%)
13	14	Brascan Ltd. (management holding company)	8 094.0	-(113.4)	4 920.3	20	Brascan Holdings (Toronto) (49%)
14	15	Bell Canada (telecommunications)	7 862.8	1 006.1	18 414.4	52 897	BCE Inc. (Montréal) (100%)
15	13	Seagram Co. Ltd. (spirits, wine, juice)	7 734.8	-(1 141.0)	12 809.9	15 800	Edgar Miles Bronfman Trust (New York) (17%)
16	16	Thomson Corp. (newspaper publishing)	7 600.0	211.0	10 049.0	45 700	Woodbridge Co. Ltd. (Toronto) (71%)
17	18	Ontario Hydro (electric utility)	7 143.0	204.0	38 170.0	28 000	Province of Ontario (Toronto) (100%)
18	20	Hydro-Québec (electric utility)	6 807.0	724.0	44 864.0	25 000	Province of Québec (Montréal) (100%)
19	19	IBM Canada Ltd. (information systems)	6 759.0	1.0	3 110.0	10 000	IBM World Trade Corp. (New York) (100%)
20	17	Univa Inc. (food distribution)	6 701.6	32.5	1 465.6	18 700	Unigesco Inc. (Montréal) (26%)

Source: *Canadian Business*, June 1993.

come to a quick end owing to the death or dissatisfaction of participants. Stockholders and bondholders, it seems, may come and go, but the corporation may go on forever — provided the management is competent.

Disadvantages of the corporation

While in theory the corporation may appear to be under the democratic control of the shareholders, in practice a small group may control it. Many small shareholders do not bother to appear at the annual meetings. Other shareholders may be willing to sign proxies — documents that give their voting power to the officers of the company. Thus, effective control may rest in the hands of a minority that may use this power for their own selfish advantage, to the detriment of the shareholders in general.

In sole proprietorships and partnerships, the manager is likely to be the owner or part-owner, and the motivation and the willingness to assume reasonable risk are likely to be high. In a large corporation, on the other hand, hired managers are likely to be simply corporate employees with less motivation and less willingness to accept risk — even when it is in the corporation's interest. Separation of ownership and control may also reduce personal contact between owners and managers.

Corporations are more expensive to establish than sole proprietorships or partnerships. Fees have to be paid to acquire a federal or provincial incorporation. Costs of auditors, accountants, and lawyers also have to be met. These costs are likely to be higher than for the two other forms of business organization we have examined so far. One of the major disadvantages of the corporation is that it is subject to double taxation. As a firm, it pays federal and provincial taxes on its profits. After-tax profits paid to its shareholders are also subject to federal and provincial income tax on dividend income. A corporation's profits are therefore taxed twice.

The stock exchange

> Gold stocks lead losers in Toronto
>
> Montréal market up in heavy trading
>
> Dow marches toward a new record
>
> Vancouver stock prices shed their early gains

The **stock exchange** is an organized market where listed stocks can be bought and sold.

On one occasion or another, you have probably seen headlines such as these in your local newspaper.

The headlines tell us what is happening on the Montréal, Toronto, New York, and Vancouver stock exchanges or stock markets. A stock exchange is an actual building that provides a marketplace for the buying and selling of stocks. Every day on the floor of the exchange, traders execute their clients' orders to buy or sell listed shares. The stock exchange doesn't buy, sell, or set the price of stock. Trading is done at prices that reflect the public opinion of the worth and potential of the company.

The first exchanges opened in Canada in the mid-nineteenth century. Today, there are four main ones in the country, located in Montréal (founded in 1832), Toronto (1852), Calgary (1913), and Vancouver (1907). The Toronto Stock Exchange is the fifth largest in the world, after the New York and American Exchange in New York and those in Tokyo and London. The Toronto exchange has the greatest percentage of the total value of shares traded (approximately 75 percent), followed by Montréal (approximately 21 percent) and Vancouver (approximately 3 percent). Total dollar value of stocks traded on the Toronto Stock Exchange reached a record of almost $150 billion in 1993.

Canadian stock exchanges are mainly secondary markets. That is, the shares traded are ones that have already been sold to the public by stockbrokers acting on behalf of corporations that wish to raise money.

The stock exchanges provide a marketplace for these publicly-held shares. On any business day, Canadians can find the value and quantity of the stocks traded either by checking their local newspaper or by calling their stockbroker for the latest quotations. They can also buy and sell stocks easily and quickly on any business day. Canadian laws and stock exchange rules control the activities of corporations and stockbrokers to ensure as fair and honest dealings as possible, as well as full disclosure of information.

Stock trading

Buying	Selling

Buying

1. You decide you would like to invest in the stock market
   a) after examining your financial situation and deciding you can afford to risk some money;
   b) after finding out what you can about the market from newspapers, books, annual reports of businesses, etc.

2. You select a stockbroker (an individual who buys and sells stocks on your behalf) after talking with several of them. The stockbroker may be a full-service broker who will provide you with advice on what to buy and will keep an eye on your investment. For his or her services you will be charged a commission of about 2 to 3 percent — depending mainly on the total dollar amount of your purchase. Alternatively, you may select a discount broker whose fees are lower — often 1 to 1 1/2 percent of the value of your purchase or sale. However, discount brokers typically don't give advice to individual investors.

3. You meet your broker, to whom you outline your investment objectives. Your broker gives you advice on your investment.

4. You place an order with your broker for 100 shares of the ABC company at the market price. At this point, your order may go one of two ways. The *conventional way* is used on most of the big stock exchanges of the world (e.g., the New York Stock Exchange) and for many of the orders for large companies (e.g., Bell Telephone) on the Toronto Stock Exchange. The alternative is the *computer way*, which is used for stocks on the Vancouver, Montréal, and, as of 1995, Alberta stock exchanges. An increasing number of stocks have been traded this way on the Toronto Stock Exchange since 1977. There are plans to conduct all of the trading on the Toronto exchange through computer terminals. But there is considerable opposition from those who prefer the conventional way.

Selling

1. I need money to pay for a trip.

2. I decide to sell some shares — perhaps in ABC company.

3. I ask my broker for a quote on ABC (or I check the stock market quotations in my newspaper).

4. I decide to sell 100 shares of ABC at the market price.

5. In the computer way, the orders are relayed directly by your broker and mine to the stock exchange's computer. The computer matches the buy and sell orders. Confirmation of the transaction is transmitted to the two brokers involved. In the conventional way, the orders — yours and mine — are relayed to one of the brokerage firms' telephone clerks, who relays it to one of each firm's traders on the floor of the stock exchange.

6. Your trader calls out your order to attract the attention of my trader, who has my order to sell the stock. When the traders agree on a price, the selling trader makes out a floor ticket in triplicate. The traders initial it and keep a copy for their records.

7. The transaction is then recorded on the electronic ticker.

8. You are informed of the price of the trade and you pay for the shares and the broker's commission.

8. I surrender my 100 shares in ABC and collect the proceeds from the sale minus the broker's commission.

BUILDING YOUR SKILLS

Reading newspaper stock market pages

If you turn to the business section of the newspaper, you will see the latest quotations from Canadian stock markets and from the New York Stock Exchange. You will also see many references to the Dow Jones industrial average and to the Toronto Stock Exchange composite 300 index.

The following are quotations for five Canadian stocks taken from one newspaper. Beneath the quotations are explanations for the terms used. Test your ability to read newspaper stock market pages by answering the questions that follow the explanations.

Montréal stock market quotations

Friday, February 25, 1994

52-week							Friday	
High	Low	Stock	Symbol	Div	High	Low	Change	Vol
$7^1/_4$	280	Air Canada	AC		$6^3/_4$	$6^1/_2$		6 026
$17^1/_4$	$15^1/_8$	B.C. Gas	BCG	0.90	$15^6/_8$	$15^1/_2$		104
$30^3/_4$	$21^7/_8$	Bank of Montréal	BMO	1.20	$29^1/_8$	$28^1/_2$	$+^6/_8$	1 531
$33^1/_4$	$22^7/_8$	Bank of Nova Scotia	BNS	1.16	$30^7/_8$	$30^1/_4$	$+^1/_2$	438
$24^3/_4$	$16^1/_2$	Canadian Pacific	CP	0.32	$23^1/_8$	$22^7/_8$	$+^1/_2$	1 150

52-week high and low The highest and lowest prices paid for the stock during the past 52 weeks. Prices for the same stock on different exchanges are usually the same. Stocks are listed in dollars with fractions indicating partial dollars; thus, for Canadian Pacific, $24^3/_4$ = $24.75, $16^1/_2$ = $16.50, $22^7/_8$ = $22.88. Stocks less than $5 are listed in cents; Air Canada's 52-week low was 280 = $2.80.

Stock The name of the company.

Symbol The company's name is followed by the company's stock exchange trading symbol, which is used by many brokers and computerized information services. Canadian Pacific's symbol is CP.

Div The annual dividend (in dollars) paid by the company. Canadian Pacific paid a dividend of 32 cents.

High The highest price paid for the stock on Friday, February 25, 1994. The highest price paid for Canadian Pacific was $23.125.

Low The lowest price paid for the stock on this day. The lowest price for Canadian Pacific was $22.88.

Change The change in the price of the stock (if any) between the end of today's trading session and the previous session. The difference in price for Canadian Pacific stock between this day's closing price and that of the previous session was $1/_2$ or 50 cents.

Vol Total number of shares traded on this day in hundreds of shares on the Montréal Stock Exchange. On this day, 115 000 shares of Canadian Pacific changed hands.

Source: The quotations on the Montréal Stock Exchange for Friday, February 25, 1994, were given in *The Globe and Mail* on Saturday, February 26, 1994.

Practise your skill

1. What was the highest price paid for Bank of Montréal stock over the past year? the lowest price paid?

2. What was the highest price paid for B.C. Gas shares on this trading day? the lowest?

3. How many Bank of Montréal shares were traded?

4. What was the range in prices paid for Bank of Nova Scotia shares on this trading day?

5. What was the closing price of Bank of Montréal shares on the previous trading day?

6. If you bought 100 shares of Air Canada stock at the lowest price that they were traded in the previous 52 weeks, how much would they cost you? Assume that you have to pay your stockbroker a commission of 2 percent.

7. Yesterday's stock market prices are available in many local daily newspapers in Canada and in *The Globe and Mail* and *Financial Post*. Check one of these sources for the most recent quotations for the stocks listed above.

BUILDING YOUR SKILLS

Reading stock market indicators

Suppose that in your economics course, marks are only awarded for examinations and that there are three examinations. Your final mark is the average of the total marks you achieved on the three exams. You achieved 50 percent on the first exam; 60 percent on the second; and 70 percent on the third. Your average is the total of the marks on the three exams divided by the number of exams — the division being three in this case. In other words, your average would be calculated as follows:

$$50 + 60 + 70 = \frac{180}{3} = 60 \text{ percent}$$

If someone asks you how you did in the economics course, your response is likely to be "I got 60 percent" rather than detailing every mark on every exam. The 60 percent summarizes your achievement.

In a similar way, if we want to know what general price changes are taking place on the stock market, a recounting of the changes of prices of every stock would not be very helpful. What we need is some way of summarizing the price changes that are taking place.

The Dow Jones industrial average is probably the best-known and most widely quoted indicator of the general trend of stock market prices in the United States. You will see the Dow (as it is often called) quoted daily on TV and in your local newspaper. This average was begun in 1884 by Charles Dow, who, along with Eddie Jones, modified it in 1896. Since 1928, the Dow has been based on the closing prices of the stock of thirty major U.S. corporations from sectors considered most representative of the U.S. economy. These corporations include General Motors, IBM,

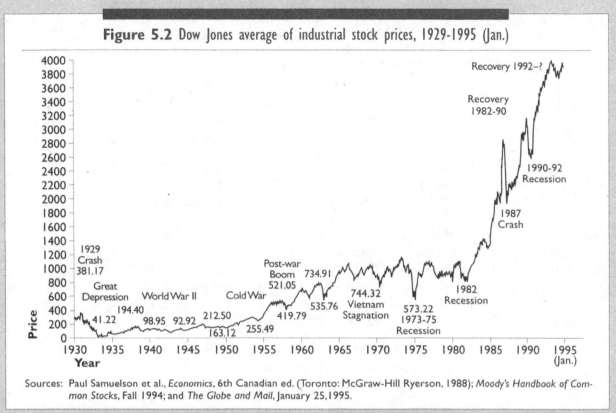

Figure 5.2 Dow Jones average of industrial stock prices, 1929-1995 (Jan.)

Sources: Paul Samuelson et al., *Economics*, 6th Canadian ed. (Toronto: McGraw-Hill Ryerson, 1988); *Moody's Handbook of Common Stocks*, Fall 1994; and *The Globe and Mail*, January 25, 1995.

The Dow Jones industrial average is the most widely quoted stock price indicator. It tracks the weighted average prices of 30 blue chip stocks on the New York Stock Exchange.

Exxon, McDonald's, Texaco, Boeing, Coca Cola, and American Express. Until 1928, the Dow was, as its full name implies, simply an average of the closing prices of the selected stocks. It was calculated in a way similar to that by which we arrived at your mark of 60 percent. Since 1928, however, the divisor has been continually adjusted to take account of the effect of dividends and the substitution of new companies for old ones. In this way, despite the changes, the Dow is widely used over a period of time to track the movement of stock prices on the New York Stock Exchange.

Canadian stock exchanges also publish indicators of the general trend in stock prices. The one that is most widely known and commonly quoted is the Toronto Stock Exchange's 300 composite index. The TSE 300 (as it is commonly called) is constructed in a way that is somewhat different from the Dow.

To get an idea of how it is calculated, let's return to the example of the economics course in which you get 50, 60, and 70 percent on exams one, two, and three. Let's suppose, however, that exam numbers two and three each count for twice as much as exam number one. In other words, we have weighted exams numbered two and three. These are judged to be much more important than the first exam. Now your final mark would be calculated as shown on the following page.

$$\frac{50 + 2 \times 60 + 2 \times 70}{5} = \frac{310}{5} = 62 \text{ percent}$$

The TSE 300 uses a similar process to arrive at the index.

The TSE 300, introduced at the beginning of 1977, measures changes in the prices of 300 leading and representative Canadian stocks. Each stock is given a weighting in the index roughly according to its number of shares. It is subdivided into 14 major industrial groups, such as oil and gas; metals and minerals; communications and media; and merchandising. Each group contains a number of stocks of individual companies. In November 1993, the Royal Bank — Canada's largest bank — had a weighting of 3.32 while the very much smaller Maritime Telegraph and Telephone's weighting was 0.18. Small changes in Royal Bank stock would have a greater impact

on the TSE 300 than much bigger changes in the price of Maritime Telegraph and Telephone.

Reading the market index

Figure 5.3 shows variations in the TSE 300 composite index, 1978-1994. The trading days are shown along the horizontal axis, as well as the high, low, and close of the index. Thus, for example, in October 1994, the index stood between 4243 and 4355.

Practise your skill

1. Use figure 5.3 to answer the following questions:

a) What was the approximate level of the index for the last trading month shown?

b) What was the highest price reached during the period shown? What was the month on which this occurred?

Figure 5.3 TSE composite index, 1978-1994

Sources: J.D. Thexton, *Economics: A Canadian Perspective* (Toronto: Oxford, 1991) and the *TSE Review*, October, 1994.

Note that the two parallel lines drawn between 0 and 1000 indicate that part of the graph has been omitted.

c) Check your local newspaper. What is the present level of the TSE 300?

d) Plot changes in the TSE 300 over the next three months. Check your newspaper for the reasons given for the changes.

2. Use figure 5.2 to answer these questions:

a) What was the highest point that the Dow reached before the 1950s?

b) What was the lowest point the Dow reached after 1920? In which year did this happen?

c) What has been the general trend in New York stock market prices?

d) In general, which would have been the better year to invest in the New York stock market: 1972 or 1974?

e) Check your newspaper for the most recent figure for the Dow. How has the Dow changed since the last recorded level on the graph?

f) Plot changes in the Dow over the next three months. Check your newspaper for the reasons given for the changes.

Black Monday, October 19, 1987

Following the record one-day drop in the Dow Jones industrial average of 108.35 points on Friday, October 16, nervous Japanese investors began to flood the Tokyo Stock Exchange when it opened Monday, October 19 (late Sunday night New York time) with orders to sell their stock. This sell-off was contagious. Opening about five hours before New York, the London Stock Exchange's financial times index plunged 250 points, cutting $108 billion worth of stock market values.

A wave of panic swept the New York stock market when it opened. Prices plunged lower and lower. Some called it a market meltdown. One trader exclaimed, "This is going to make 1929 look like a kiddie party." At the end of trading that day, the Dow Jones industrial average had dropped 508 points to 1739 — a record drop of 22.62 percent, shattering the benchmark of fear established on Black Thursday, October 28, 1929. In that stock market crash, the Dow fell 12.9 percent. Black Monday also shattered another record. The volume of shares traded on that day reached 605

Figure 5.4 Newspapers report on the stock market, October 19, 1987

The stock market crash of October 19, 1987, was headline news around the world — in the U.S., Canada, Japan, France, Italy, and Germany.

million. The average volume on the exchange was less than a third of that amount.

On Canadian stock exchanges, records were broken as well. The Toronto Stock Exchange index lost 407 points. Similar losses were sustained on the Vancouver and Montréal exchanges. See figure 5.5.

Crowds of people lined up in the stock markets to gain a glimpse of the events on the floor of the exchanges. Others watched price movements inside brokerage houses. In one such crowd a viewer was heard to gasp and then exclaim, "I've just lost a million!" The collapse was headline news around the world (see figure 5.4 on page 95). In the week that followed Black Monday, stock prices bounced up and down.

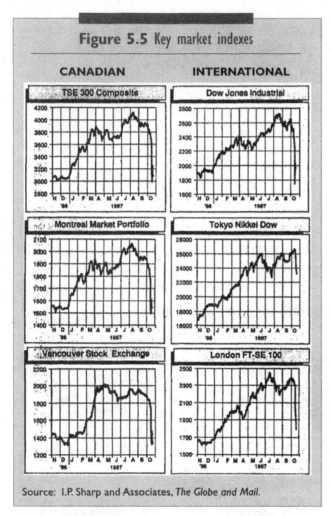

The price of stocks on the New York Stock Exchange collapsed on October 19, 1987. So, too, did stock prices on the Toronto, Montréal, and Vancouver exchanges. Prices on the second and third largest exchanges in the world — Tokyo and London — also plummeted.

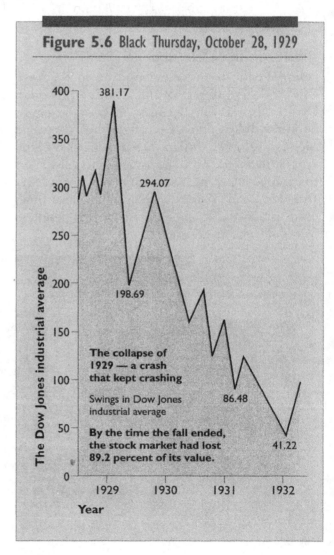

BUILDING YOUR SKILLS

Reading financial statements

The success or failure of any investment you make in a company depends on how well the business will do in the future. Although it is impossible to predict the future with any accuracy, clues to the future performance of a corporation can be found in annual financial statements. The report of the president or board of directors to the shareholders also highlights the corporation's past performance and outlines future plans.

In the report are found at least four financial statements. Here, we will examine two of them: the balance sheet and the statement of income. For the investor, these are the most important.

Not Your Average Company

Balance sheet
The balance sheet shows the company's financial position on a specific date, usually the last day of the company's fiscal year.

This is the name of the company

The **balance sheet** is one of the basic financial statements in an annual report. As its name suggests, the three main parts — **assets, liabilities,** and **shareholders' equity** — always balance. Two years are usually shown in an annual report so that a comparison can be made of the corporation's performance over two years.

I Assets include all those things that the corporation owns or is owed. There are three types of assets: current, fixed, and intangible.

Current assets include cash and anything that can be turned into cash in a year, such as inventories (which include raw materials, parts, bonds, etc.).

Fixed assets include land, buildings, machinery, trucks, with allowance being made for depreciation.

Intangible assets include such assets as patents.

Not Your Average Company
Balance Sheet
as of December 31, 1995
(in thousand dollars)

Assets	1995	1994
Current assets Item 1	6 865	6 410
Fixed assets Item 2	3 700	3 745
Intangible assets Item 3	200	200
	10 765	10 355

Liabilities
Item 4 ← **II Liabilities** are all the debts of the corporation. They include current and long-term liabilities.

1995	1994		
2 800	2 830	**Current liabilities Item 5**	← **Current liabilities** include such things as bank loans, and income taxes that are payable.
2 500	2 500	**Long-term liabilities Item 6**	← **Long-term liabilities** include bonds issued by the corporation.
5 300	5 330	**Total liabilities Item 7**	

Shareholders' equity ← **III Shareholders' equity** is the interest of the shareholders in a corporation if all its liabilities were paid off. It can consist of two main parts: capital stock and retained earnings.

1995	1994		
2 265	2 265	**Capital stock Item 8**	← **Capital stock** is money raised by the sale of shares in the corporation. Number of shares issued is 2 200 000.
3 200	2 760	**Retained earnings Item 9**	← **Retained earnings** are profits of the firm that have been reinvested in the business.
5 465	5 025	**Total shareholders' equity Item 10**	

1995	1994		
10 765	10 355	**Total liabilities and total shareholders' equity Item 11**	

Statement of income

The income statement is the financial report that shows how much the company earns and how much it spends on wages, salaries, materials, and so on. What remains after taxes is profit from which dividends are paid. All earnings statements provide these four main elements.

Depreciation

One important factor to keep in mind when calculating the fixed assets and operating expenses of a corporation is **depreciation**. Depreciation may be viewed as the decline in the value of assets — such as machinery and vehicles — due to new technology, or to wear and tear. Rather than deducting the entire cost of the machine or vehicle in the year of its purchase, it makes more sense to allocate a certain amount of the cost of each year of the life of the machine. One method of doing this is declining balance depreciation. Each year's depreciation is calculated as a percentage of the total cost of the machine, after depreciation of previous years has been deducted.

Not Your Average Company

Statement of income (in thousands of dollars) for the year ending December 31, 1995.

Income Statement	1995	1994
Net sales Item 12	11 500	10 200
Cost of sales and operating expenses Item 13	9 500	9 000
Operating profit Item 14	2 000	1 200
Payments to creditors Item 15	1 150	732
Net profit for year Item 16	850	468

Income (on earnings) statement is that part of the annual report that shows the source of the company's income and its expenditures.

Net sales is the total amount the company earns from the sales of goods and services.

Cost of sales includes the cost of labour, raw materials, parts, depreciation, etc., that are used to produce the company's goods and services.

Operating profit (or loss) is the amount that is left over after expenditures have been deducted from income. If expenditures exceed income, the company has a loss. If income exceeds expenditures, the company has a profit.

Payments to creditors include interest on bank loans and income taxes.

Net profit (or loss) for year.

Interpreting financial statements

Having examined what financial statements tell us about the condition of the company, our next step is to use that knowledge to test how worthwhile an investment in the company would be. Examining ratios and examining trends are two general ways of assessing a corporation.

Ratios

A ratio is a relationship between two numbers. Thus, if there are ten males in your class and twenty females, we would say that the ratio of males to females is one to two (1:2). In the case of Not Your Average Company, we can compare numbers in the balance sheet or earnings statement to give us a number of ratios.

Trends

Ratios calculated for one (or even two) years are of limited value. They become more useful if we can compare them over a period of several years. In this way, we can examine trends in the company and see which way the company is heading, that is, whether profits, earnings, etc., are generally increasing or decreasing. It is also useful to compare the ratios of our company with those of other companies in the same kind of business. The ratios can thus help us make decisions about which company is likely to be the best investment.

Types of ratios

There are many ratios we could examine that are widely used. Here, however, we will consider only some of the most widely known ones.

1. Balance sheet ratios

Here we will examine those ratios that can be calculated from the numbers in the balance sheet alone.

a) The working capital ratio

This ratio is one of two that are used to measure how readily the corporation can pay off its debts and thus avoid bankruptcy. The other ratio is the quick ratio. It is examined next.

Formula:

$$\text{Working capital ratio} = \frac{\text{Current assets}}{\text{Current liabilities}}$$

$$\text{Example for 1995} = \frac{\text{Item 1}}{\text{Item 5}} = \frac{6\ 865\ 000}{2\ 800\ 000}$$

$$= \frac{2.45}{1} \text{ or 2.45 to 1}$$

On December 31, 1995 the company had $2.45 or its equivalent for each $1 of current debt.

Evaluation How good a ratio is this? Depending on the company's type of business, many financial analysts believe that a minimum level of safety requires that the corporation should have a ratio of 2:1. The ratio of Not Your Average Company at 2.45:1 is good.

b) Quick ratio (acid test)

The second and more rigorous test of the corporation's ability to pay off its debts readily is the quick ratio. This ratio is often called the "acid test." Quick assets are assets that can be converted readily into cash. Inventories are not part of quick assets.

Formula:

$$\text{Quick ratio} = \frac{\text{Current assets} - \text{inventories}}{\text{Current liabilities}}$$

Example:

$$\frac{\text{Item 1} - \text{inventories*}}{\text{Item 5}}$$

$$= \frac{6\ 865\ 000 - 2\ 800\ 000*}{2\ 800\ 000} = 1.45{:}1$$

*We assume inventories = $2 800 000

The company had $1.45 of quick assets for every $1 in current liabilities.

Evaluation Analysts generally agree that a ratio of 1:1 or better suggests that the corporation has good ability to meet its current debts. On this basis, Not Your Average Company is well situated to pay its debts.

2. Earnings statement ratio

Here we examine one of the ratios that can be calculated from the second financial statement we examined — the earnings statement. The major purpose of a corporation is to make a profit and it is in the earnings statement that we have a measure of that ability.

Net profit or earnings margin ratio

This ratio is the end result of the business's activities for the year. It summarizes in one ratio the ability of management to run the company.

Formula: Net profit margin $= \dfrac{\text{Net profit}}{\text{Net sales}}$

Example: $\dfrac{\text{Item 12}}{\text{Item 16}} = \dfrac{850\ 000}{11\ 500\ 000} = 7.4$ percent

Evaluation The profit margin on every $1 of sales was 7.4 cents. It is useful to compare the net profit margin with other years, and with other companies in the same business, to see how well the company is performing.

3. Combined ratios

Since the following ratios use figures from the balance sheet and the earnings statement, they are called combined ratios. These ratios allow analysts to see how well the company's assets are being used.

a) Earnings per common share

For those who have invested in a corporation, one of the key ratios is earnings per common share.

Formula: Earnings per common share $=$

$$\dfrac{\text{Profit for the year}}{\text{Number of common shares}}$$

Example: $\dfrac{\text{Item 16}}{\text{Item 8}} = \dfrac{\$850\ 000}{2\ 200\ 000} = 38$ cents

Evaluation The corporation's earnings per share for the year equalled 38 cents. This ratio is one that is widely used and reported in the press. It is easy to calculate and can be used to compare performance among different companies.

b) Price-earnings ratio (or PE multiple)

The price-earnings (PE) ratio is widely quoted in the financial pages of many newspapers.

Formula:

$$\text{PE ratio} = \dfrac{\substack{\text{Current market price} \\ \text{of common share}}}{\substack{\text{Earnings per share} \\ \text{(in latest 12-month period)}}}$$

Example: Let's assume that the current market price of Not Your Average Company is $8.95. Earlier, we calculated the earnings per common share to be 38 cents.

The PE ratio, then, equals $\dfrac{\$8.95}{\$0.38} = 23.6$

Evaluation PE ratios can be used to compare the performance of one company with another, in the same industry. The ratio is the most widely quoted of all financial ratios because it summarizes in one figure all the other ratios. It summarizes the evaluation of a company by investors.

Practise your skill

1. For the Not Your Average Company for the year 1995, calculate the following ratios.
a) The working capital ratio
b) The quick ratio (assume inventories equal $3 million)
c) The net profit margin
d) The earnings per common share
e) The price-earnings ratio (assume the price of the stock is $9)

2. Compare the company's performance in 1994 and in 1995. What is the trend? In which year did the company perform better? Explain.

Why did the market crash?

In the days that followed Black Monday, many reasons were suggested for the collapse.

For some time, market analysts had been waiting for a "market correction," that is, a significant fall in prices, in the stock market. The market had continued to rise, almost without interruption, since August 1982 so that a fall was to be expected. However, only very few analysts predicted approximately when it would occur and most were stunned by the extent of the fall.

The crash was fuelled by doubts about the United States' economy. Three areas were of special concern: the budget deficit, the trade deficit, and interest rates. The United States' government's budget deficit was $160 billion in 1986. In other words, in 1986 the government spent $160 billion more than it received. Continual squabbling between the President and Congress made it seem that the deficit would not or could not be cut far and fast enough.

In 1986, the United States bought $156 billion more goods and services from other countries than it sold to them. The United States' trade deficit for August 1987 was $15.7 billion. Thus it seemed that the United States — by then the world's biggest debtor nation — might be forced to continue lowering the value of its dollar. For foreigners who had invested heavily in the United States' stock market, a decline in the value of the dollar would lower the value of their investments. A decline in the value of the dollar also increased concern in the United States that it would bring about another round of generally rising prices.

Rising interest rates also increased concern about the United States' economy and stock market. Rising interest rates would likely slow consumer and business borrowing and spending, and bring about a slowdown in the economy — a recession. Rising interest rates would make bonds more attractive than stocks. Thus some people would be encouraged to make the switch. Stock prices therefore would tend to fall as demand fell.

Some analysts have suggested looking for explanations not only in fundamental economic factors, but also in market psychology, especially the twin emotions that drive the market — fear and greed. Greed drives the market higher and higher. Fear, as we saw on Black Monday, drives the market lower and lower.

Others have suggested that the reason for the collapse in stock market prices was computerized trading in stocks. There are now computer programs that track market prices and that will buy or sell huge blocks of stock under certain conditions. If stocks start to decline, computer programs may dictate the sale of stocks. This results in the programs feeding on themselves, and causes stock prices to spiral downwards.

What next?

Some analysts suggested that the stock market crash of 1987 would follow the path of the 1929 crash — into a prolonged and deep depression. Others suggested that, while 1987 was very different from 1929 in that we were better able to prevent prolonged depression, there was a likelihood of a recession. Let's briefly examine their arguments.

The stock market index is often an indicator of where the economy is likely to be in six months' or a year's time. For example, the rise in stock market prices in August 1982 was a signal of the end of the 1981–82 recession and of the beginning of the recovery of 1983. If the economy followed the lead of the stock market after Black Monday, then we would have undergone a depression in the economy in 1988 or 1989.

Some of the reasons why a downturn in the economy occurs are clear. A stock market collapse is likely to affect the future outlook of consumers and business people. They are likely to change from being optimistic or "bullish," as they were before the crash, to being pessimistic or "bearish." This change in outlook, coupled with stock market losses, is likely to make both consumers and business people more conservative in their future spending plans. Less spending is likely to mean a slowdown in the economy.

Despite the economic slowdown, depression — a deep and very prolonged downturn in the economy

— is far from certain. Governments, for example, may be able to implement appropriate policies to avoid a depression.

The worst fears of investors and most other people in capitalist countries — that the stock market would continue crashing — were not borne out after the 1987 crash. Though there were large variations in stock market prices in the week following Black Monday, stock market prices did not continue collapsing (see figure 5.2, which shows the Dow Jones industrial average, and figure 5.3, which shows the TSE composite index). Though the rate of economic growth did begin to slow after 1987, it was not until 1990 that the recession began. Again in the bull market in stocks starting in 1991 and continuing to early 1994, some investors were jittery over the prospect of another crash —like that in 1987 and 1929. Others feared a "creeping crash," in which the stock market undergoes a gradual, but persistent, decline in stock market prices.

COOPERATIVES

A **cooperative** is a form of business organization with the aim of benefiting its owners through lower prices and/or distribution of surpluses at the end of the year. Like a corporation, a cooperative issues shares to the public. Unlike the corporation common shareholder, the shareholder (or member) of the cooperative has only one vote. This is a primary feature of cooperatives: they are democratically run.

Although a member is restricted to one vote, each member may purchase more than one share in a cooperative. Each member receives a fixed rate of return on invested capital.

Membership in a cooperative implies responsibilities. Members vote on how the cooperative is to be administered and on what should be done with savings arising from its operation. Members vote on whether these should be invested to develop the cooperative or distributed among the members. If savings are distributed among the members, this is done on a patronage basis. This means that the more business a member has transacted with the society, the greater the patronage dividend the member receives.

The first successful cooperative society was established in 1844 in Rochdale, England. This society operated a store and was a **consumers' cooperative**. In Canada, the first cooperative store was established in Nova Scotia in 1861. Today, cooperative stores exist in all provinces in Canada. See figure 5.7 on page 104. This figure lists (by assets) the top five financial cooperatives and the top five non-financial cooperatives. Both kinds of cooperatives operate throughout Canada. Financial cooperatives operate mainly in the credit union and insurance areas, while the largest non-financial cooperatives are wholesalers and farmers' cooperatives.

Producers' cooperatives have become very common in Canada, especially in the marketing of agricultural products. Farmers have established cooperatives to market their produce and to provide them with such things as fertilizer, seed, and insurance, believing that they can get better prices through their own organization than if they relied on corporations. Producers' cooperatives operate in the same way as consumers' cooperatives. Members supply the capital on which they receive a fixed rate of interest; each member has only one vote; and each shares in the surpluses according to the amount she or he has sold to, or bought from, the cooperative.

Credit unions are also cooperatives that are quite common in Canada. Usually, they are established by people in the same industry or occupation. Members make deposits with their credit union which, in turn, loans out these funds to other members.

Strengths and weaknesses of cooperatives

The strengths of a cooperative stem from the basic principles on which it is organized. The ideas of

Figure 5.7 The top ten cooperatives

Company	Group	Profit $000	Revenue $000	Assets $000	Employees	Members	Provinces of Operations
Top Five Financial Cooperatives							
Caisse Centrale Desjardins	services	4 259	429 671	6 440 169	154	5 095 237	PQ
Desjardins Life Assurance Co.	life insurance	21 925	834 109	3 360 573	1 461	3 100 000	All
Vancouver City Savings C.U.	services	23 276	323 025	3 324 482	897	194 000	BC
Co-operators Group	property and casualty insurance	-9 437	1 425 823	2 833 527	5 182	35	Not PQ
B.C. Central Credit Union	services	7 112	167 268	2 086 887	210	1 167 506	BC
Top Five Non-Financial Cooperatives							
Federated Co-operatives	wholesalers	92 026	1 717 507	713 347	2 480	750 000	ON, W. CAN.
Saskatchewan Wheat Pool	farmers' cooperatives	39 946	1 877 433	677 254	2 702	85 000	SK
Alberta Wheat Pool	farmers' cooperatives	12 263	995 489	378 808	1 461	60 000	AB
Agropur Co-operative Agro-Al.	farmers' cooperatives	6 313	1 007 122	321 702	2 980	4 158	PQ, ON
Manitoba Pool Elevators	farmers' cooperatives	10 668	146 731	186 784	870	18 000	MB

Source: *Report on Business Magazine,* July 1993.

democratic control and the patronage dividend act as a magnet to many people, making them loyal members. However, cooperatives do have difficulty in remaining competitive with private firms. Their democratic structure makes it hard for them to hire and work with aggressive managers and staff without losing something of the ideals on which they are founded.

PUBLIC ENTERPRISES

The greatest proportion of goods and services in Canada is produced by privately owned firms. Today, however, governments (federal, provincial, and municipal) also supply us with a large number of goods and services.

We rely on government for provision of — among other things — water, electricity, public transportation, education, defence, and fire protection. A number of these services are provided by departments that are under the direct control of elected representatives. Defence is provided by the (federal) department of defence, for example, and education by provincial departments of education and locally elected school boards. Other services are provided by organizations that, though owned by government, have been given a certain degree of autonomy to operate without government interference and to operate in a manner similar to a corporation. Such semi-independent bodies at the federal and provincial levels are called **Crown corporations** (examples include Canadian National Railways, Hydro-Québec, New Brunswick Power Commission and B.C. Hydro and Power). There are well over 250 federal and provincial Crown corporations in Canada. See figure 5.8, which lists the top twenty federal and provincial Crown corporations by revenue. The top ten federal Crown corporations are concentrated mainly in transportation and service industries. The top ten provincial Crown corporations are concentrated mainly in hydroelectricity, finance, and insurance.

An appraisal

In a modern mixed market economy, government plays an important role. It must provide those services that cannot be produced at a profit but that are essential to a community. It must perform a great number of regulatory tasks to ensure that private enterprise operates in the best interests of the community. Whether gas, electricity, and telephone services are best provided by a Crown corporation or a private corporation is open to debate. All major political parties when in office have at different times supported the extension of government ownership. Debate on government ownership in the past has tended to focus on the merits and demerits of particular instances, such as ownership in aircraft and petroleum industries, rather than on the general principle of government involvement in the industrial process.

Figure 5.8 The top 20 Crown corporations

Revenue Rank	Company	Group	Revenue $000	Profit -(loss)	Assets $000	Employees
Top 10 Federal						
1	Canadian National Railway	transportation	4 069 550	-(1 005 242)	7 051 580	37 255
2	Canada Post Corp.	services	3 872 759	-(127 529)	2 461 915	56 000
3	Canada Mortgage and Housing	services	1 115 352	-(369)	10 338 426	2 955
4	Canadian Commercial Corp.	services	761 629	-(11 345)	677 508	80
5	Export Development Corp.	services	660 314	44 178	8 107 153	525
6	Via Rail Canada	transportation	546 056	141	866 436	4 500
7	Farm Credit Corp.	trust company	423 358	21 566	3 688 405	754
8	Atomic Energy of Canada	industrial products	395 832	1 973	855 206	4 503
·9	Canadian Broadcasting Corp.	radio broadcasting	392 440	-(83 303)	1 072 811	10 131
10	Royal Canadian Mint	metal fabrication	377 971	8 958	102 682	763
Top 10 Provincial						
1	Ontario Hydro	utility	7 900 000	312 000	46 671 000	33 339
2	Hydro-Québec	utility	7 002 000	724 000	44 864 000	18 933
3	Caisse de Dépôt et Placement	finance	3 290 000	2 930 000	40 598 000	302
4	B.C. Hydro and Power	utility	2 371 000	220 000	9 608 000	5 498
5	Insurance Corp. of B.C.	insurance	2 104 326	-(64 186)	3 396 851	3 800
6	Alberta Heritage Savings	finance	1 483 236	1 381 589	12 039 098	0
7	N.B. Power Commission	utility	991 077	25 079	3 776 481	3 158
8	Manitoba Hydro-Electric Board	utility	833 200	17 700	5 934 700	4 321
9	Alberta Treasury Branches	banking	791 043	12 663	7 323 376	3 204
10	Saskatchewan Power Corp.	utility	762 000	107 000	3 237 000	2 392

Source: *Report on Business Magazine*, July 1993.

Selling the crowns

Since the early 1980s, Canadian governments — federal and provincial — have explored ways to "privatize" the industries they own. Privatization means that the business is sold to individuals through the stock market (as in the case of Air Canada) or to a business corporation (as in the case of Canadair Corporation to Bombardier). The federal government has privatized a number of Crown corporations, including Air Canada, Fishery Products International Ltd., and Teleglobe Canada. Petro-Canada has been partially privatized. The federal government has also considered privatizing other Crown corporations such as Canada Post and Canadian National Railways and to complete the privatization of Petro-Canada. Provincial governments have also sold provincially-owned businesses to private groups. The government of Alberta sold the provincial liquor board outlets and the Ontario government sold de Havilland Aircraft Company to Boeing Corporation.

In November 1993, the Nova Scotia government announced that it had reached an agreement to sell the provincially-owned Sydney Steel Corporation to China Minmetals. In 1994 the government of New Brunswick announced plans to privatize provincial liquor stores. The Québec government sold Sidbec-Dosco, a provincial steel-making Crown corporation, to Ispat Mexicana SA in 1994. The government of Newfoundland and Labrador announced plans to privatize the Newfoundland and Labrador Hydro-Electric Corporation in 1994 as well. Throughout the 1980s, governments in Britain, France, Brazil, Mexico, and Japan implemented programs to transfer ownership from the government to the public. With the collapse of the command economies in Eastern Europe and the Soviet Union, many of the state-owned industries were sold to private interests.

Privatization

In some cases, the original reason for the establishment of a Crown corporation may have vanished. The unprofitable firm that was teetering on the verge of bankruptcy may be back on firm financial footing and the jobs in the firm no longer in danger. There may also be ways in which government can achieve its objectives through private business.

Some people would argue that, in some cases, Crown corporations are not as effective in meeting the needs of their customers compared to private businesses. They reason that privatizing them and subjecting them to competition in the market will improve the corporations' efficiency and flexibility. Corporations would have, therefore, greater ability and incentive to respond to signals from the market. It has also been argued that it is hard for governments to exercise adequate control over so many different and complex corporations, as well as performing all the other tasks that the government has to perform.

As you would expect, however, the case is not all one-sided. Workers in Crown corporations slated for privatization are concerned about what will happen to them and their jobs. Some are concerned, too, that in the pursuit of profit the quality of service of the privatized corporation will decline. There are difficulties in deciding the price at which to sell the corporation and to whom and when. For example, should foreign corporations be permitted to buy them? It has also been suggested that there is never a right time to sell a Crown corporation. If it is losing money, buyers are scarce. If it is making money, taxpayers want to hang on to it to benefit from the profits.

REVIEW

Explain each of the following concepts in your own words with an example: sole proprietorship, partnership, cooperative, corporation, stock market (stock exchange), public enterprise, stock, bond, preferred stock, board of directors, limited liability, credit union, privatization.

SUMMARY

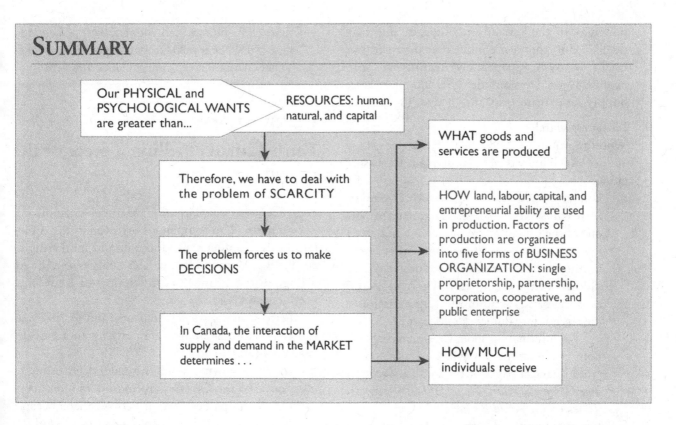

Our PHYSICAL and PSYCHOLOGICAL WANTS are greater than...

RESOURCES: human, natural, and capital

Therefore, we have to deal with the problem of SCARCITY

The problem forces us to make DECISIONS

In Canada, the interaction of supply and demand in the MARKET determines . . .

WHAT goods and services are produced

HOW land, labour, capital, and entrepreneurial ability are used in production. Factors of production are organized into five forms of BUSINESS ORGANIZATION: single proprietorship, partnership, corporation, cooperative, and public enterprise

HOW MUCH individuals receive

APPLICATIONS

1. What are the advantages and disadvantages of a corporation compared with (a) a sole proprietorship and (b) a partnership?

2. Describe what happens after you ask your broker to buy XYZ stock at the market price.

3. In what ways does a cooperative differ from a corporation?

4. What is a Crown corporation? Give some examples, including at least one from your province.

5. What arguments are there (a) for and (b) against the privatization of Crown corporations?

6. A consumer cooperative of which you are a member has sold $100 000 worth of goods and

has a surplus of $1000 to distribute to its members. You own one-fifth of the capital of the cooperative and you have bought $100 worth of goods. What is your patronage dividend?

7. You have decided to go into the hairstyling business with two friends. Among you, you have managed to raise $30 000.
   a) What form of business organization will you use? Explain your choice.
   b) What skills should you have to run the business?
   c) What capital goods will you need to buy?
   d) Would you buy a franchise? Explain why or why not.

8. **Library research**
   Use the newspapers in your library to graph the changes in *either* the Dow or the Montréal market

portfolio, or the Vancouver composite index or the TSE 300 composite index over the next two weeks. Many newspapers give reasons why the changes in the Dow and the TSE 300 take place. Supply some reasons for the changes in the two.

9. **Library research**

Work in groups or individually. Follow the steps and see which individual or group made the wisest choice.

a) You have $5000 to invest. Select a Canadian firm whose common shares are traded on one of the Canadian stock exchanges. Before investing, use your library and other community resources to find out as much as possible about the corporation. Describe to the class the background of the corporation and the reasons for your stock selection.

For information about Canadian corporations, examine the following:
• the financial pages of the local newspaper, *The Globe and Mail, Financial Post, Financial Times,* or *Canadian Business;*
• annual reports of corporations that can be found in business libraries or obtained by writing to particular corporations;
• the *Financial Post* Corporation Service Cards. You could also contact a stockbroker to get his or her analysis of the stock.

b) Draw a graph showing the variations in the price of your stock over three months. You can do this by monitoring your stock every two weeks in the financial pages of a newspaper. Give possible reasons for variations in price.

c) After three months, calculate the value of your stock. See how much you would gain (or lose!) if you sold your stock.

10. **Library research**

Use the most recent available copy of *Canadian Business, The Corporate 500* to update figure 5.1, The top 20 Canadian corporations by sales, p. 88;

figure 5.7, The top ten cooperatives, p. 104; and figure 5.8, The top 20 Crown corporations, p. 105. What changes have occurred since 1991-92?

CASE STUDY
Petro-Canada: Selling a piece of the crown

Petro-Canada is the largest Canadian-owned oil and gas company. The company is involved in the exploration, development, production, and marketing of crude oil and natural gas. It is also engaged in the refining, distribution, and marketing of petroleum products and related services.

Petro-Canada was created on July 30, 1975, as Canada's national energy company by an act of the Parliament of Canada.

In the following year, the federal government transferred to the Crown corporation its interests in various oil companies, so that Petro-Canada became involved in the northern exploration of oil and gas and in the development of the Alberta tar sands. Later acquisitions of Panarctic Oils Ltd. in 1976 (for $350 million), Pacific Petroleums in 1978 (for $1.5 billion), Petrofina in 1981 ($1.6 billion), and Gulf Canada in 1985 (for $600 million) moved Petro-Canada into the exploration, production, refining, and marketing of oil and gas in Western Canada and Ontario. In 1989, the corporation acquired a 44 percent interest in Jiffy Lube — a chain of fast-lubrication stations. In 1990, the company completed the purchase of a retail propane business. In 1990 as well, the company (along with others) signed agreements with the governments of Canada and Newfoundland and Labrador to begin the development of the Hibernia offshore oil development project.

The following year, an act of Parliament authorized the company to proceed with an initial public offering of shares. In June 1991, the company raised about $500 million from the sale of $42.8 million shares at $13 a share or about 20 percent of the total. A second share sale of about 10 percent of the company's stock netted the company a further $25 million. The 30 million shares were sold for $8.25 each. The decline in the price of the share — $8.25 down from $13 — reflects the oil industry's prolonged slump.

Since 1991, the company has continued its program of rationalization by closing or selling off unprofitable refineries in Ontario and British Columbia, by selling off some oil and gas properties, and by launching an internal reorganization and staff reduction program. From a profit of $176 million in 1990, the company suffered a loss in 1991 — its first part-year of post-privatization — of almost $600 million, followed by a profit of $9 million in 1992.

Questions

1. Do you think that, as a general rule, governments should privatize Crown corporations whenever possible?

2. Under what conditions — if any — should governments (a) nationalize corporations and (b) privatize corporations?

CHAPTER 6

Demand, Supply, and Markets

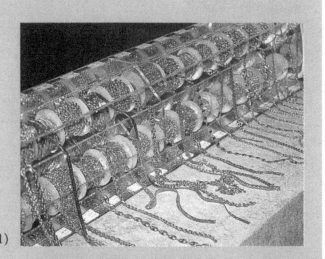

(1)

(3)

A music store in the West Edmonton Mall, Edmonton, Alberta.

(5)

Kitchener Farmers' Market, Kitchener, Ontario.

The Montreal Stock Exchange.

Questions

1. Why does a gold chain cost so much more than a litre of milk or a loaf of bread — both of which are essentials?

2. What prevents a seller from raising prices sky high?

3. How are prices determined in a market?

WHAT IS A MARKET?

A **market** is any network that brings buyers and sellers into contact with one another so they can exchange goods and services.

As we have seen, markets play a central role in our economy. It is through markets that our economy answers the three major questions: what to produce, how to produce, and for whom to produce.

Around sunrise on Saturday mornings, farmers drive their trucks to a central location in many cities and towns across Canada. They set up their stalls and stock them with produce. They may also post prices. Then they wait for customers to arrive.

With all the produce on display, customers can inspect the tomatoes for bruises and the chickens for plumpness. They can compare the price of asparagus at one stall with the price of asparagus farther on down the row. This is a farmers' market where the farmers sell directly to the consumer.

A market, however, doesn't have to have a physical setting. For many products, business may be done by phone, fax, computer modem, or written communication. Face-to-face contact is unnecessary. A wholesaler in Regina might order dresses without seeing or talking to a Montreal manufacturer.

In some cases, buyers don't even have to see the product they are purchasing. A good example of this is the highly organized international grain market. A description of the kind and quality of the grain purchased is often all that is necessary. In Canada, the Winnipeg Grain Exchange handles orders from around the world. Trading is accomplished through the Exchange's member dealers, who buy and sell grain for future delivery for their clients.

A market exists wherever the forces of supply and demand meet to effect an exchange. In any given market at any given time, the total number of sellers constitute the supply and the total number of buyers constitute the demand. In this chapter, we will find out how supply and demand interact to determine the price and quantity of goods and services supplied and demanded.

DEMAND

Demand is the quantities of a good or service that buyers are willing and able to buy at various prices in a particular period of time.

Consider for a moment your last purchase of apples. If the price were higher, you might buy less, and if the price were lower, you might buy more. You could think of a schedule (or list) of prices and the number of apples you would buy at each of the prices. This price and quantity relationship would be your personal **demand schedule** for the apples on the day you purchased them. We could put together a list of the prices and number of apples each person in the class would buy at each price on a particular day. By adding all the individual student's quantities at each of the prices, we arrive at a price-quantity relationship that is the class demand schedule for that day. In a similar way we could construct class demand schedules for soft drinks, hamburgers, or any other good or service.

The class demand schedule for apples represents the number of apples the class is willing and able to buy at various market prices during a particular period of time. If the apples were actually for sale, you might find that you would be willing to buy an apple for 50 cents. However, if you didn't have 50 cents, you couldn't afford one. Ability to pay is the ultimate determining factor.

A possible class demand schedule for apples is shown in figure 6.2 on page 114. Notice that the schedule refers to a particular group of people (the class) for a particular period of time (that class period).

Graphing demand curves

Another way of showing the information in a demand schedule is to draw a graph.

Activity 1: An apple from the teacher

From a basket, your economics teacher takes a large, Red Delicious apple. Your teacher announces that she is offering apples like this one for sale to the class. Naturally, everyone in the class wants to know the price of the apples. Your teacher does not state the price. Instead, she distributes purchase agreement forms, and asks each student to complete one. When completing your form, follow the instructions carefully.

1. Write your name at the top of your form. Assess your finances and then start at the top with the 50-cent price and indicate, under "quantity," the number of apples you would be willing to buy at that price. If you are not willing to buy any apples at the price of 50 cents per apple, enter a zero under "quantity."

2. If you wish to buy one or more apples at 50 cents each, enter the desired number under "quantity." If you decide you would buy one apple at 50 cents, it follows that you are willing to buy at least one apple at any price lower than 50 cents. Similarly, if you are willing to buy two apples at

40 cents, then you must be willing to buy at least two apples at any price lower than 40 cents. Complete your form for all prices downwards from 50 cents to 10 cents.

3. Return your completed form to your teacher.

From the completed forms, the teacher will calculate the total class demand schedule for apples by adding the quantities that all the students are willing to pay under each price.

Questions

1. Why did we assume that if a buyer is willing to buy one apple at 50 cents, the buyer will also be willing to buy at least one apple at all prices below 50 cents? Does this assumption always hold true? Explain and give examples.

2. What was the opportunity cost of the first apple you were willing to buy? Explain.

3. Why were some people willing to pay a higher price than others for the same quantity of apples?

4. What is the relationship between price and quantity demanded?

5. What would be the effect on quantity demanded if:
    a) two enterprising members of the class produced a crate of oranges, two others a crate of pears, two others a crate of peaches, and these six students began to sell fruit at the same time as your teacher?
    b) the apples were sold during the first period of the day rather than just before lunch?
    c) the apples were sold the day after the students in the class got their pay or allowance rather than the day before?

Figure 6.1

Purchase agreement form

Name:_____ Class:_____

Price per apple (in cents)	Quantity
50	
40	
30	
20	
10	

We know from figure 6.2 that at a price of 50 cents the class is only able and willing to buy one apple. Find 50 cents on the vertical price axis in figure 6.3 and 1 on the horizontal quantity axis. As you can see, lines run across from 50 cents and up from 1. The point at which the lines intersect is labelled A. It corresponds with row A in the class-demand schedule. The remaining rows are plotted in a similar way.

When all the intersection points are joined, the price-quantity relationship forms a curve. The curve is called a **demand curve** — a graph showing the relationship between price and quantity. Like the demand schedule, it shows us that as price increases, quantity demanded decreases; and as price decreases, quantity demanded increases. Or, to put it another way, there is an inverse relationship between quantity demanded and price. Notice that the graph has a title, and that the two axes are also labelled. The vertical axis always measures price; the horizontal axis always measures quantity.

A demand curve — just like a demand schedule — shows the quantities of a good or service that buyers would be willing and able to buy at various times.

Downward-sloping demand

It seems reasonable to think that the more limited in quantity a product is, the higher its price will be and the higher the price is, the fewer the consumers who will be able to afford the product. Price thus serves as a means of rationing the good. Suppose, for example, the price of Red Delicious apples rose to $5 each. Only those people who really enjoy Red Delicious apples would buy them. The high price would serve to ration apples among consumers. If, conversely, the price of these apples fell to 1 cent each, we would assume that the apples were plentiful and that more people would buy more of them. This, then, brings us to the law of downward-sloping demand.

The **law of downward-sloping demand** states that when the price of a good is raised (and there are no other changes), less of it will be demanded. If the price of a good is lowered (and there are no other changes), then the quantity demanded will increase.

Demand and utility

Suppose that it's a cold winter day and you have been outside for a while. A cup of hot chocolate would taste great, so you buy and drink one. Now suppose in

Figure 6.2 Class demand schedule for apples

Row	Price per apple (in cents)	Quantity the class is able and willing to buy
A	50	1
B	40	4
C	30	10
D	20	22
E	10	40

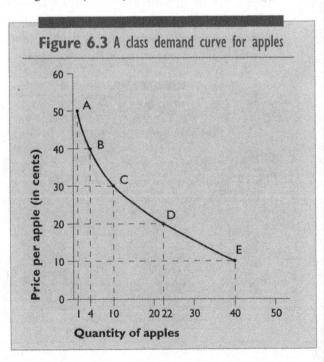

Figure 6.3 A class demand curve for apples

addition to the first one you buy a second cup of hot chocolate. How does the satisfaction you get from it compare to the first cup? It is probably less. As you buy successive cups of hot chocolate — a third, a fourth, and even a fifth — you will find your satisfaction diminishing from the previous cup you consumed. By the time you drink the fifth cup, you probably would prefer not to drink any more. You have come into contact with the economist's law of diminishing marginal utility. The **law of diminishing marginal utility** states that each additional unit of a good consumed at any given time yields less satisfaction than the one previously consumed.

The law of diminishing marginal utility helps explain why the demand curve slopes down to the right. Since the marginal utility of a good diminishes as more is consumed, people would only be willing to buy more if the price were reduced.

Elasticity of demand

Elasticity of demand means the responsiveness of the quantity demanded to a change in price.

Elastic demand

If McDonald's were to cut the price of their hamburgers by 10 percent, it's likely that the total amount of money spent on McDonald's hamburgers would be greater after this decrease in price than before. Some of the people who might have bought hamburgers from Wendy's, Burger King, or another hamburger restaurant, would be more likely to buy at McDonald's. Similarly, people who usually ate hot dogs, pizza or fried chicken might buy a McDonald's hamburger. Those who usually ate McDonald's hamburgers might buy more because the price would be lower. In the case of McDonald's hamburgers, then, quantity demanded is very likely to be responsive to change in price. Or, to put it another way, the amount of money spent on McDonald's hamburgers is likely to be greater after a 10 percent price cut than before. Similarly, if McDonald's were to raise the price of hamburgers by 10 percent, it is

likely that the total amount of money spent on their hamburgers would decrease. Economists would say that the demand for McDonald's hamburgers is **elastic**.

Inelastic demand

Examine figure 6.4. Here the elasticity of demand for apples is shown. The total amount spent on the apples is calculated by multiplying the price per apple (column 1) by the quantity demanded (column 2). The total amount spent on apples at one price is compared with that at a higher price. For example, at the price of 50 cents, only one apple is demanded ($50 \times 1 = 50$). At the price of 45 cents each, two apples are demanded. The total spent when each apple costs 45 cents equals 90 cents ($45 \times 2 = 90$). Since the total amount spent on apples is greater when the price of each apple is 45 cents, then demand at this price is said to be elastic (column 4). However, at low prices, 10 and 5 cents each, the total amount spent on apples declines. The demand for apples is then said to be **inelastic**.

Figure 6.4 Elasticity of demand for apples

1 Price ($)	2 Quantity demanded	3 Total amount spent ($)	4 Elasticity
.50	1	.50	
.45	2	.90	Elastic
.40	7	1.60	Elastic
.35	7	2.45	Elastic
.30	10	3.00	Elastic
.25	15	3.75	Elastic
.20	22	4.40	Elastic
.15	30	4.50	Elastic
.10	40	4.00	Inelastic
.05	50	2.50	Inelastic

Unitary elasticity of demand

With **unitary elasticity of demand**, a change in price brings about an exactly proportionate change in quantity demanded. For example, with unitary elasticity, an increase in price of 1 percent will bring about a decrease in demand of 1 percent.

Factors determining elasticity of demand

What factors determine the elasticity of demand for products? One factor has already been noted. There are lots of substitutes for McDonald's hamburgers, such as those produced by other restaurants, and lots of other food products that can be substituted for hamburgers, such as hot dogs, pizza, chicken, and submarine sandwiches. Thus, products that have lots of substitutes will have an elastic demand.

Small items in a budget tend to be unaffected by price changes. For example, a percent increase (or decrease) in the price of a car is more likely to influence sales than a 5 percent change in the price of pepper. Big items in a budget are likely to be elastic; small items, inelastic.

Essential items, such as bread and electrical energy, tend to have inelastic demand because consumers cannot readily avoid using them. We cannot easily do without electricity — we need it for light, power, and heat. Luxury goods, such as holidays on tropical islands, tend to have elastic demand because consumers can easily stop buying them if prices rise.

Over time, goods tend to be more elastic. For example, the demand for gasoline is inelastic over a short period of time because it is an essential good with few substitutes. With a large increase in the price of gasoline, there is relatively little that motorists can do immediately. Through time, however, they can switch to more fuel-efficient vehicles or to other sources of energy such as natural gas and electricity. Thus, over a period of time, demand is likely to be more elastic.

Applications of elasticity of demand

The concept of elasticity of demand is useful in understanding some of the events taking place around us. Why are there such heavy taxes on alcoholic beverages and tobacco? One of the reasons is that people will not stop buying a product simply because of price increases caused by taxes. In other words, the demand for alcohol and tobacco is inelastic.

Health groups argue that even though cigarette consumption may be price inelastic overall, it is price elastic where it counts — for young Canadians. According to the 1991 federal budget, a 10 percent increase in the price of cigarettes will reduce consumption among young Canadians by about 14 percent. Studies have shown that relatively few Canadians start smoking after age 20. Thus, increased taxes on cigarettes by federal and provincial governments have the effect of discouraging those from smoking who are most likely to start. This positive view of tobacco sales prevailed generally until, in 1991, the federal finance minister levied a $6 tax increase on a 200-cigarette carton. This action led to a huge increase in smuggled cigarettes. By 1992 it was estimated that 18 percent of cigarettes were contraband; a year later this figure had jumped to 40 percent. The federal government's economic response was twofold. It slashed taxes by up to $22 a carton, thereby lowering the price of legal cigarettes. It imposed an export tax on Canadian cigarettes. This had the effect of raising the price of smuggled cigarettes, since most of the smuggled cigarettes were Canadian-made brands.

The demand for bread and milk is also inelastic, but to tax them would likely be very unpopular.

The concept of elasticity of demand also helps explain one reason why governments have closely controlled the prices of products of certain industries. The demand for local telephone service, electricity, and natural gas is highly inelastic. Thus, corporations could raise the prices of these products considerably — especially since they are supplied by one or only a few companies — without suffering a loss in the quantity demanded.

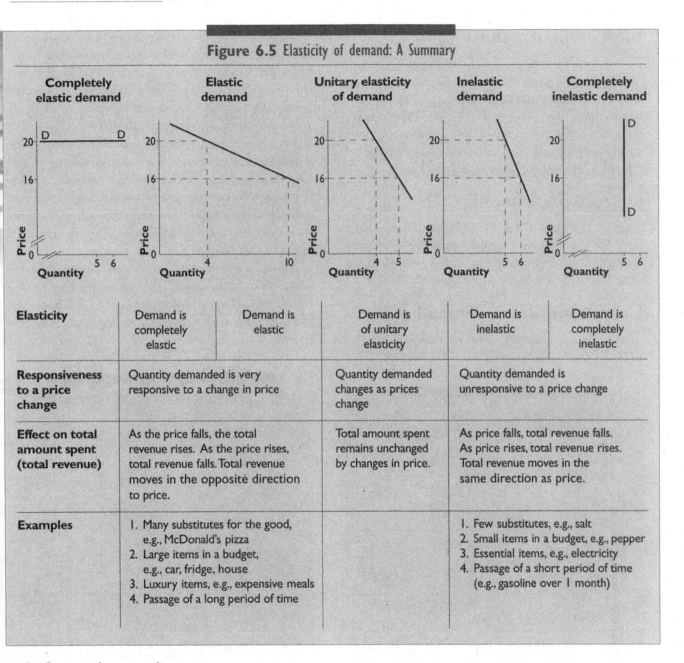

Figure 6.5 Elasticity of demand: A Summary

Elasticity	Demand is completely elastic	Demand is elastic	Demand is of unitary elasticity	Demand is inelastic	Demand is completely inelastic
Responsiveness to a price change	Quantity demanded is very responsive to a change in price		Quantity demanded changes as prices change	Quantity demanded is unresponsive to a price change	
Effect on total amount spent (total revenue)	As the price falls, the total revenue rises. As the price rises, total revenue falls. Total revenue moves in the opposite direction to price.		Total amount spent remains unchanged by changes in price.	As price falls, total revenue falls. As price rises, total revenue rises. Total revenue moves in the same direction as price.	
Examples	1. Many substitutes for the good, e.g., McDonald's pizza 2. Large items in a budget, e.g., car, fridge, house 3. Luxury items, e.g., expensive meals 4. Passage of a long period of time			1. Few substitutes, e.g., salt 2. Small items in a budget, e.g., pepper 3. Essential items, e.g., electricity 4. Passage of a short period of time (e.g., gasoline over 1 month)	

Shifts in demand

Changes or **shifts in demand** occur when there is a change in the quantity of a product demanded for reasons other than a price change.

As we have seen, a demand schedule shows the relationship between price and quantity of a product: as the price changes, so does the quantity demanded.

Increase in demand

The curve DD in figure 6.6 shows the class demand for apples. If twenty students were added to your class, the class demand curve for apples would shift to the right, from DD to D₁D₁. With the original class, there was a demand for ten apples at 30 cents. With the additional students, the class demand increased to twenty apples at 30 cents each.

Decrease in demand

Suppose the class was reduced by ten students. Instead of a demand for ten apples at 30 cents, only five are demanded. There would be a decrease in demand, from DD to D₂D₂ as shown in figure 6.7.

Causes of shifts in demand

As the previous example shows, a change in market size can cause a change (shift) in demand. Also, increases in the allowances (or pay) of students in your class, increases in the cost of substitutes (e.g., pears and oranges), or a change in student tastes (more students preferring more apples) would increase the demand for apples. Thus, the demand curve for apples would shift to the right. Similar factors could cause a shift in the national demand curve for apples. Increases in the income of Canadians, in the Canadian population, or in the cost of substitutes for apples, and changes in Canadian preference for apples would shift the demand curve to the right. Decreases in each of the above factors would shift the demand curve to the left.

Finally, a change in the price of "complementary products" will also cause a shift in demand for certain items. As one example, the price of gasoline can affect the number of big cars that consumers decide to buy.

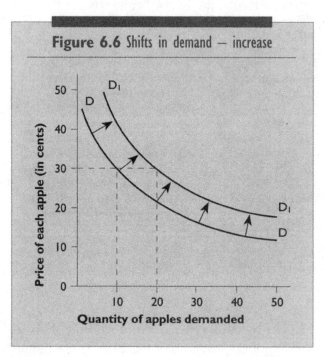

The demand curve shifts to the right with an increase in demand from DD to D₁D₁.

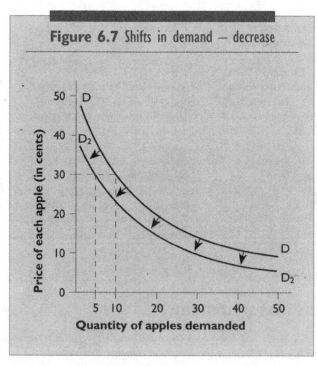

The demand curve shifts to the left from DD to D₂D₂ with a decrease in demand.

REVIEW

Explain each major concept in your own words with an example: demand, elasticity of demand, demand curve, increase or decrease in quantity demanded.

APPLICATIONS

1. Figure 6.8 represents the demand schedule for hot dogs in your school cafeteria. Draw a demand curve from the schedule. Label each axis and give your graph a title.

2. Make up your own hypothetical demand schedule for a product or service you buy. Plot the price and quantity relationships on a graph, showing the demand curve. Remember to label the axes and give your graph a title.

3. Using the figures from activity 1 on page 113, complete the following.
   a) Draw the class demand curve.
   b) Calculate the amount spent by the class at each price level.
   c) Indicate whether the demand was elastic or inelastic at each price level.

4. For which of the following products is the demand likely to be elastic? Explain why.
   a) Corvette "Sting Ray"   f) gasoline
   b) silk shirt   g) salt
   c) milk   h) bread
   d) rock music CD   i) electricity
   e) designer jeans

5. Figure 6.9 shows the demand schedule for cartons of milk in your school cafeteria at lunchtime. Draw a demand curve from the schedule.
   a) Label the axes of your graph.
   b) Show a shift in the demand curve to the left and a shift in the demand curve to the right.
   c) What effects would the following probably have on the demand curve for cartons of milk in your school?

Figure 6.8 Demand schedule for hot dogs

Price (in cents each)	Quantity demanded
.80	150
.90	130
1.00	120
1.10	110
1.20	100

Figure 6.9 Demand schedule for milk

Price per carton (in cents)	Numbers of cartons students will buy
100	100
90	200
80	300
70	400
60	500

• an increase in the allowances of students in your school
• a reduction in the price of soft drinks in your cafeteria
• an increase in the price of a carton of milk

6. As you read the following article, note those products that the author identifies as having elastic and inelastic demand and the reasons why. Note also why he says that government is addicted to sin. Then answer questions a) to e) on page 121.

Governments, too, are addicted to sin

You should know something about the elasticity of our demand for various goods and services.

It's not a dry-as-dust idea from an economist's ivory tower. It affects you every day.

Differing degrees of elasticity for different products help explain the way they're priced and taxed. And the way they're seen by governments and those passionate reformers always trying to change our ways and the ways of the economic system.

Among other things there's probably an inelastic demand for:

Lottery tickets.

Alcoholic beverages.

Cigarettes.

It means the prices of these things can be set very high compared with the cost of production without losing much in the way of sales.

Take cigarettes. If the price rose 30 percent, we'd probably buy almost as many. The number sold might drop only 5 or 10 percent, maybe less.

That's an inelastic demand and it's typical of such things. A jump in prices may cause an initial "shock" decline in sales. After a while, though, buyers come back. In the end, there's little reduction.

Contrast that with, say, baseball games or pizzas. If their prices went stratospherically high, many people probably would quickly find other things to do with their money.

That's an elastic demand. A higher price causes a comparatively large reduction in sales. There's an ability and desire to find substitute satisfaction at less cost.

Of course, that's if other things are equal. A hot, pennant-contending ball club — the Toronto Blue Jays or the New York Yankees — could keep its customers in greater numbers than an average one. But in the longer run, suppliers of such products know that price changes can swing their sales by quite a bit.

You'll have tumbled onto the fact that so-called "sin" products frequently have an inelastic demand.

That's precisely why governments can't resist them. It almost seems that any activity felt suggestive of bad habits will end up being run by government.

Rather than becoming the finest flower of civilization, government will sit atop society's trash heap; at least, atop those products many of us see as temptations to be less than wise.

The great growth of governments in this area rests on several impulses. It's argued that they should have close control of products related to bad habits; that private business really shouldn't make profits from such things or might actively encourage the habits; and, besides, that the prices should be kept very high to discourage consumption.

Right there — to the delight of the governments — you run into inelastic demand.

Governments can and do take increasing revenues from tobacco and alcohol, shoving up prices endlessly, comforted by the thought that we'll keep right on buying. The result: they keep raking in more and more money — something they couldn't do if an elastic demand wrecked sales as prices rose.

By now, governments are at least as hooked as we are. They can no longer afford to be without the revenues — somewhere above $4 billion annually.

They tell us piously to sharply reduce our consumption. But they're mighty careful to avoid anything — direct controls, for example — that might have dramatic effect.

And why can lotteries pay out a lot less money in prizes than they collect from ticket-buyers? Because the customer's impulse is a gambler's greed, not a tough shopper's judgment of what's a fair price.

High-priced tickets won't reduce buying much — as long as there aren't a bunch of better-priced alternatives. Thus governments want two things: to control a great little money-maker and to eliminate any competition that might force lower prices for lottery tickets or higher payouts in prizes.

Even in the oil business, there's something similar. The tax-take and amount of government controls are very high, right down to the gas pump. Sure enough, it's felt vaguely — and the feeling is encouraged by governments — that the industry itself is a bit sinful and gas-guzzling car-drivers more so.

Governments just can't resist jackpots of inelastic demand.

Here we reach the dreamworld of the federal health minister, who is fuming because Canadians smoke too much.

But the idea of a tax-created 30 percent price increase for cigarettes probably wouldn't cut sales much in the long run. And if it did, the governments wouldn't do it.

Source: Jack McArthur, *Toronto Star.*

a) According to Jack McArthur, what goods have an inelastic demand? Explain why.
b) According to Jack McArthur, what goods or services have an elastic demand? Explain why.
c) Why is it, according to the author, that "any activity felt suggestive of bad habits will end up being run by government"?
d) Why is the author dubious about a tax-created 30 percent increase in the price of cigarettes as a means of cutting cigarette consumption?
e) What effect do you think the 1993 tax cut on cigarettes has had on consumption? In what way is elasticity involved in your response?

7. Suppose average Canadian consumption of turkey is 5 kg per year as compared to 16 kg for chicken and 55 kg for beef, and that 35 percent of turkeys consumed are sold during the holidays in December and 15 percent at Thanksgiving.
   a) How would you expect demand curves for turkey to differ for each of the five months from September to January?

b) When would you expect the price of turkey to be highest?
c) If you especially liked turkey, when would be the best time to stock your freezer with it?

SUPPLY

Supply is the quantities of a good or service that sellers are willing and able to sell at various prices in a particular period of time.

As you know, demand can be illustrated in a schedule that shows a price-quantity relationship. A **supply schedule** shows a similar price-quantity relationship.

Suppose a supply schedule for melons was like that shown in figure 6.10. This tabular information can be shown graphically as a **supply curve**, as in figure 6.11 on page 122. Note that the supply curve slopes up and to the right — showing that as prices rise, suppliers are willing and able to supply more melons.

A glance at either the supply schedule or supply curve reveals that as prices diminish, fewer melons

Figure 6.10 Supply schedule for melons

Row	Price per melon ($)	Quantity supplied
A	1.00	40
B	.90	35
C	.80	30
D	.70	25
E	.60	20
F	.50	15
G	.40	10
H	.30	5

Note that, as the price of melons increases, producers are willing and able to supply more melons. For example, as the price increases from 30 to 40 cents a melon, 5 more melons will be supplied.

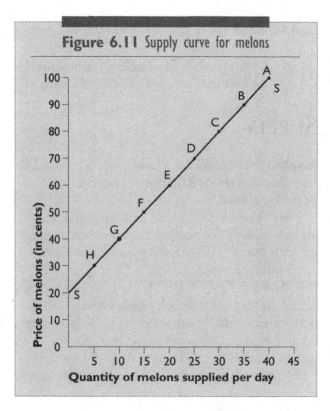

Figure 6.11 Supply curve for melons

will be supplied and, as prices increase, more will be supplied. Or, to put it another way, there is a **direct relationship** between price and the quantity supplied.

This price-quantity relationship makes sense because, as prices increase, more and more farmers see the chance for greater profits and are willing to switch over to melon production. In the same way, as the prices of melons decline, farmers will tend to switch from producing melons to producing carrots, beans, or other fruits or vegetables.

Buyers and sellers look at high (and low) prices in different ways. Buyers are discouraged by high prices; they buy less and look for substitute products. Sellers, on the other hand, are encouraged by high prices; they seek to produce more and to sell more. Lower prices, on the other hand, have the opposite effect. Buyers are encouraged to buy more and sellers are discouraged: they sell less at lower prices.

SUPPLY, DEMAND, AND EQUILIBRIUM

Assuming no other changes take place, we know that as the price of melons falls, more melons will be demanded and fewer supplied. Conversely, as the price rises, more will be supplied and fewer demanded. At some price,

Figure 6.12 Supply and demand schedule for melons

Quantity supplied	Price per melon ($)	Quantity demanded	Surplus (+) or shortage (−)	Pressure on price	
40	1.00	—	+40	Downward	↓
35	.90	5	+30	Downward	↓
30	.80	10	+20	Downward	↓
25	.70	15	+10	Downward	↓
20	**.60**	**20**	**0**	**Equilibrium none**	
15	.50	25	−10	Upward	↑
10	.40	30	−20	Upward	↑
5	.30	35	−30	Upward	↑
—	.20	40	−40	Upward	↑

then, the quantity supplied and the quantity demanded will be equal. Here supply and demand are in **equilibrium**.

As we can see by the supply and demand schedule in figure 6.12, supply equals demand at the price of 60 cents. At this price, twenty melons are supplied and twenty melons are demanded. Sixty cents is the equilibrium price and twenty melons is the equilibrium quantity.

As the price declines from $1.00 per melon, the quantity supplied diminishes, the quantity demanded increases, and the surplus diminishes. When the price falls to 60 cents per melon, the quantity supplied equals the quantity demanded — equilibrium; there is no shortage and no surplus. At prices lower than 60 cents, the quantity demanded is greater than the quantity supplied — there is a shortage. Here the pressure on price is upward.

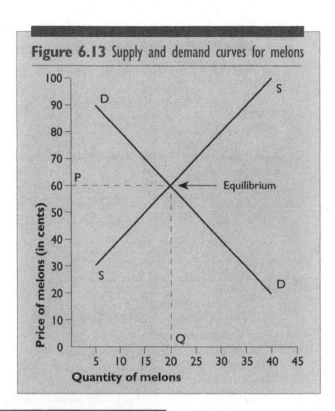

Figure 6.13 Supply and demand curves for melons

Activity 2: The Marvellous Melon Market

This market activity simulates a competitive market for one commodity — melons.

Materials

Buyer and seller cards should be made up according to the distribution chart in figure 6.14. A buyer card should read: **Buy a melon for *not more* than $_____**. A seller card should read: **Sell a melon for *not less* than $_____**.

An **armband** should be worn on buyers' left arms so that they are easily identified. An **individual score sheet**, like the one in figure 6.15 on page 124, should be prepared by each buyer/seller.

A **master transaction chart** (see figure 6.16 on page 124), should be drawn on the chalkboard on which a record of the market transactions may be kept.

Figure 6.14 Distribution chart

Price	Buyers (*not more than the price*)	Sellers (*not less than the price*)
$1.00	4	—
.90	4	4
.80	4	4
.70	4	4
.60	4	4
.50	4	4
.40	4	4
.30	4	4
.20	4	4
.10	—	4

Figure 6.15 Individual score sheet

Name: _____

Buyer: _____

Seller: _____

Transaction number	Price on card	Transaction price	Gains	Losses
1				
2				
3				
4				
5				
6				
7				

Total number of transactions   _____

Total gains   _____

Total losses   _____

Net gain or loss   _____

Figure 6.16 Master transaction chart

Distribution of transactions

Price ($)	1st five minutes	2nd five minutes	3rd five minutes	4th five minutes
1.00				
.95				
.90				
.85				
.80				
.75				
.70				
.65				
.60				
.55				
.50				
.45				
.40				
.35				
.30				
.25				
.20				
.15				
.10				

Instructions to buyers and sellers

You are about to participate in the operation of a competitive market. The class is divided into two groups — buyers and sellers. You are either a buyer or a seller for the duration of the activity. Think of yourself as an agent representing clients who have given you instructions to follow. Try to get the best deal for your clients but be sure to follow their instructions (designated on the cards).

When the market opens at the signal of your instructor, you may enter the market. When a buyer and seller agree on the terms of a sale, they should report the transaction to the instructor who will record it on the master transaction table, and announce it to the class. Remember to record your transactions on your own individual score sheet as well. As soon as the transaction is reported, you turn in your buyer/seller card and receive a new one of the same kind.

If you are having trouble making a transaction within five minutes, turn in your card and obtain another.

Play the game

1. Push desks to walls to provide space in the middle of the room for the Marvellous Melon Market.

2. Two students should be assigned, one to handle the buyer cards and one to handle the seller cards. Each student should shuffle the cards and place them on a desk away from the other, at the front of the room.

3. The class should be divided into buyers and sellers and each student should obtain the appropriate card.

4. When everyone is sure they understand the activity, the instructor should signal the opening of the market.

5. After twenty minutes, the market closes.

6. After the market closes, the class can figure out whether the buyers or sellers have been more successful. This can be determined by tallying up the net gains or losses on the individual score sheets.

7. The class can also figure out who was the most brilliant buyer and who was the super seller by surveying the class to find out who had the greatest gains (or smallest losses!) in each of the two categories.

As a class

1. Copy the demand schedule shown in figure 6.17 into your notebook. Complete the schedule using the figures listed under "price on card" from all the individual score sheets of the buyers.

    As you can see from figure 6.14 on page 123, four people are each willing to pay $1 for one melon, and four other people are willing to pay 90 cents. It is reasonable to assume that, if four people are willing to buy one melon at $1 each, they will also be willing to buy melons at lower prices. Therefore, the total demand for melons at 90 cents each would be 8 (4 + 4). Using the same kind of reasoning, we can see that the demand for melons at 80 cents would be 12 (4 + 4 + 4), and so on.

2. Draw a graph plotting the demand curve for melons.

3. Copy the supply schedule shown in figure 6.18 into your notebook. Complete the schedule, using the figures listed under "price on card" from all the individual score sheets of the sellers.

Figure 6.17 Demand schedule for melons

	Price per melon ($)	Quantity demanded
A	1.00	4
B	.90	8
C	.80	12
D	.70	
E	.60	
F	.50	
G	.40	
H	.30	
I	.20	
J	.10	

As you can see from figure 6.14, four people are each willing to sell one melon at 10 cents, and four people are willing to sell one melon at 20 cents. It is reasonable to assume that, if four people are willing to sell one melon at 10 cents, they will also be willing to sell their melons at 20

Figure 6.18 Supply schedule for melons

Price per melon ($)	Quantity supplied
1.00	
.90	
.80	
.70	
.60	
.50	
.40	
.30	12
.20	8
.10	4

cents each. Therefore, the total number of melons for sale at 20 cents each would be 8 (4 + 4).

4. How does the supply schedule differ from the demand schedule?

5. Draw a graph plotting the supply curve for melons.

6. In the Marvellous Melon Market, melons sold at a number of different prices. The master transaction chart was divided into four five-minute periods. What happened to the prices the longer the game was played?

7. In many markets, there tends to be one price for products of the same or very similar quality. What is that one price likely to be in the Marvellous Melon Market? Explain how you reached your conclusion.

8. In what ways was this market simulation (a) the same as and (b) different from the markets you know? Explain.

If we were to illustrate the same information about equilibrium price in a graph, it would look like figure 6.13 on page 123. In reading this graph, we say that at the price of 60 cents per melon (OP), the quantity of melons supplied and demanded, 20 (OQ), is at equilibrium. At this price, the quantity of melons coming onto the market is equal to the quantity of melons taken off the market by consumers. At equilibrium price, the market is cleared of melons. Another way to describe equilibrium price is to call it the **market clearing price**. At 60 cents, the quantity supplied equals the quantity demanded. The market is cleared.

Let's look at what happens at a *higher* price (see figure 6.19). At the price of 70 cents per melon, for example, 15 melons (OQ_3) are demanded and 25 (OQ_1) supplied. There is a surplus of melons.

At a price of 70 cents a melon, 15 melons are demanded while 25 melons are supplied. Competition among melon suppliers pushes the price down. As the price declines, more melons are demanded and fewer supplied, until supply and demand are in equilibrium at E at a price of 60 cents.

Let's look at a *lower* price. At a price of 40 cents a melon, 10 are supplied and 30 demanded. There is a shortage of 20 melons. Competition among melon buyers forces the price up toward the equilibrium. Higher prices for melons encourages the production of more melons. Supply and demand reach equilibrium at E at a price of 60 cents.

Thus, surpluses result in competition among suppliers to sell their products, and prices fall. As the price falls, more consumers buy the products until the price falls to the point where supply and demand are in equilibrium. Here the market is cleared. Similarly, if the price for a product is below equilibrium, then

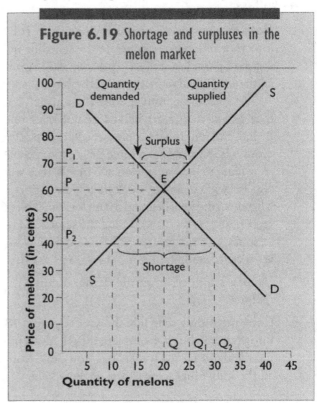

Figure 6.19 Shortage and surpluses in the melon market

more would be demanded than supplied. There would be a shortage. Sellers would notice the shortage as all of the product is bought up by eager buyers, and sellers would see that they could charge more and supply more of their goods. Buyers would be willing to pay more to get more. The price would rise. When the price reaches equilibrium, the market would be cleared. Thus, when the price is above equilibrium and there is a surplus and when the price is below equilibrium and there is a shortage, the forces of supply and demand automatically bring the market back to equilibrium.

Market equilibrium

In markets, equilibrium is seldom reached. A large number of factors continuously influence the supply and demand of goods and services. However, when there is freedom of competition among and between buyers and sellers, the forces of supply and demand move toward equilibrium to resolve the problems of shortages and surpluses.

Shifts in supply and demand

The quantity that consumers demand is based on the price of the good or service. The demand curve illustrates the relationship between quantity and price. It shows how quantity demanded is influenced by changes in price and only price. However, as we have seen, demand may be affected by other factors such as changes in income, changes in price and availability of substitutes, and changes in tastes.

Let's consider one factor: income. If incomes generally increase, then it is likely that people will be able and willing to buy more melons at every price, or to put it another way, the entire demand curve shifts to the right. On the other hand, if incomes generally decrease, then fewer melons will be demanded at every price; thus, the entire demand curve will shift to the left. What we have suggested about demand applies also to supply. It, too, represents a relationship between quantity and price and we have so far ignored any influence on

quantity supplied other than price. Many other factors also influence the quantity supplied.

We have ignored the influence of things other than price in order to make the explanation simple. *We assumed that all these factors remained unchanged.* This assumption is frequently referred to in economic texts by the Latin term *ceteris paribus,* meaning "other things being equal." You may have come across forms of these two words before: *ceteris* in *et cetera,* meaning "and other things," and *par* from the word *paribus,* meaning "being equal."

Increase in demand and the equilibrium

Suppose it was discovered that melons promote good health and appearance. Melons would be featured in magazine articles and on the menus of fashionable restaurants. The demand for melons would increase, as shown in figure 6.20. The increase in demand shifts the demand curve from DD to the right at D_1D_1. With the

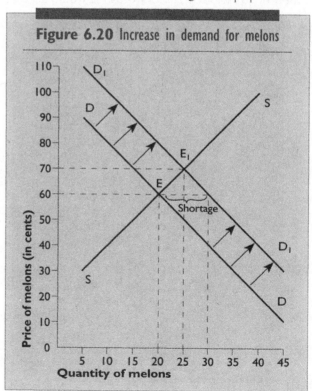

Figure 6.20 Increase in demand for melons

new demand curve, at the price of 60 cents per melon, there would be a demand for 30 melons while the supply was only 20 melons. There would be a shortage and the price would increase. Competition among melon buyers would bring increases in price. As price increased, more melons would be supplied and fewer demanded. A new equilibrium price would be reached where the price was 70 cents, and the quantity supplied and demanded would be equal at 25 melons.

Decrease in demand and the equilibrium

Suppose it was discovered that eating melons results in a purple skin rash and causes people to gain weight. With this news, there would be a decrease in the demand for melons. As you can see in figure 6.21, the demand curve shifts to the left, from DD to D_2D_2. At a price of 60 cents a melon, there is now a demand for only 10 melons but a supply of 20 melons. In other words, we would have a

surplus of 10 melons. Competition among sellers would force the price down. As the price declined, fewer melons would be supplied and more melons demanded until we reached the new equilibrium at E_2 where 15 melons are supplied and demanded at 50 cents each.

Shifts in supply

Not only does the demand curve shift to the left or right, but so, too, does the supply curve. Shifts in the supply curve also produce changes in equilibrium price and quantity.

As shown in figure 6.22, a decrease in supply occurs when the curve shifts to the left (from SS to S_1S_1). This means that, at any price, fewer melons will be supplied. Formerly (on supply curve SS), 20 melons were supplied at 60 cents each. Now (on supply curve S_1S_1), only 15 melons are supplied at that price. A decrease in supply can be caused by adverse weather conditions, or by increases in the prices of resources used to produce melons (e.g., fertilizers and machinery).

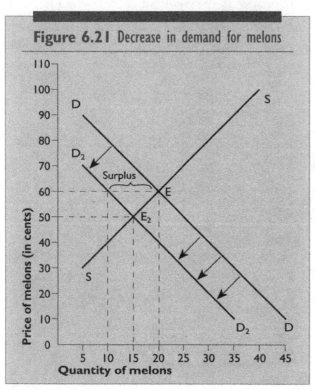

Figure 6.21 Decrease in demand for melons

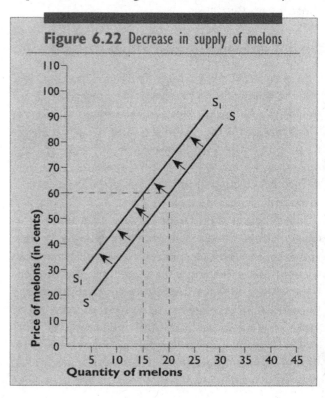

Figure 6.22 Decrease in supply of melons

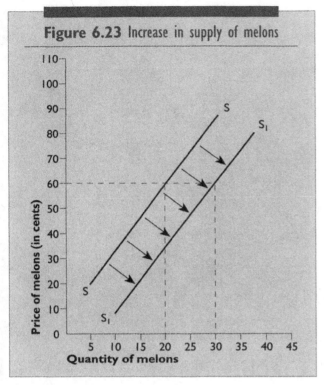

Figure 6.23 Increase in supply of melons

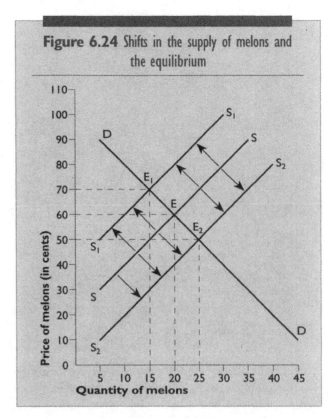

Figure 6.24 Shifts in the supply of melons and the equilibrium

With an increase in supply, the supply curve shifts to the right, as in figure 6.23. This shift from SS to S_1S_1 means that more melons will be supplied at any price. For example, 20 melons were supplied at 60 cents each. Now 30 melons are supplied at that price. An increase in supply can result from very favourable weather conditions, from decreases in prices of resources used to produce melons, and from improvements in the technology used in melon production.

Shifts in supply and the equilibrium

Shifts in supply will cause changes in the equilibrium price and quantity, as shown in figure 6.24. Suppose that bad weather destroyed much of the melon crop. This change is represented by the shift of the supply curve from SS to the left to S_1S_1. The equilibrium price would increase from 60 cents (E) to 70 cents (E_1). At this price, the quantity of melons supplied would decrease from 20 to 15 melons.

Improvements in machines for planting or harvesting melons, the development of better or cheaper fertilizers, or an improvement in the skills of agricultural workers would all cause the supply of melons to increase. As illustrated, the supply curve would shift to the right (S_2S_2), and the equilibrium would shift from E to E_2. The new equilibrium price would be 50 cents and the new quantity 25 melons.

Elasticity of supply

Like demand, supply can be elastic or inelastic depending on the product and circumstances. In a farmers' market on a Saturday, the supply of fresh tomatoes is relatively fixed and thus inelastic. A 10 percent increase in price is not going to increase the supply of tomatoes much. For many perishable articles, such as fruits and vegetables, the supply on a particular day is likely to be inelastic. As shown in figure 6.25 on page 130, the increase in price from OP to OP_1, brings a tiny increase in supply from OQ to OQ_1.

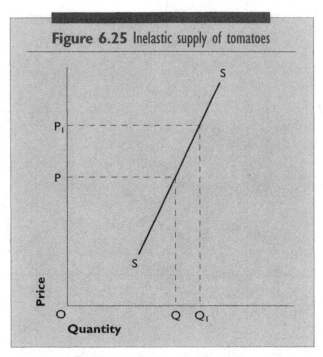

Figure 6.25 Inelastic supply of tomatoes

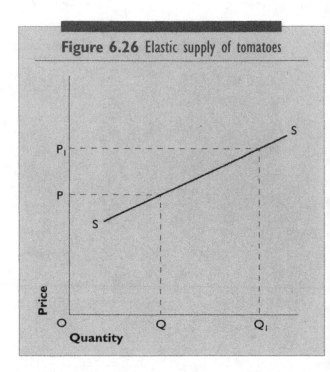

Figure 6.26 Elastic supply of tomatoes

Over a period of time, however, businesses can adapt so that supply is more responsive to price change. For example, the amount of tomatoes brought to market can be increased by augmenting the number of hectares devoted to tomato production, by taking on additional farm workers, and by increasing the amount of fertilizer and pesticides. Figure 6.26 shows that, given time, the supply of tomatoes can be highly elastic. Over a period of time, the rise in the price of tomatoes (from OP to OP_1) will produce a substantial increase in the supply of tomatoes.

Over a long period of time, the supply of many goods, including tomatoes, is likely to be highly responsive to changes in price.

The responsiveness of producers to price changes in their products — **elasticity of supply** — depends on a number of factors, of which time is one of the most important. Given enough time, the supply of most products can be highly elastic.

The supply of goods that can be stored easily, inexpensively, and for a long period of time will be more elastic than products that spoil easily and that are difficult to store (e.g., tomatoes).

CIRCULAR FLOW

We saw in Chapter 3 that the entire economy can be viewed as a circular flow of resources, goods, and services between businesses and households. Goods and services flow from business to households. In return, productive resources flow from households to business. Here we add the consumer goods and services market to the flow. See figure 6.27.

In this chapter, we have focussed on three economic concepts: demand, supply, and markets. How do they relate to our circular flow diagram? In our model, households represent the demand for goods and services which is represented by a flow of expenditures for goods and services. Businesses supply the goods and services. The household demand for goods and services represented by the flow of expenditures and the business supply of goods and services are exchanged in the product market. Thus, households receive the goods and services they want and businesses receive money in exchange for supplying goods and services.

Figure 6.27 Circular flow

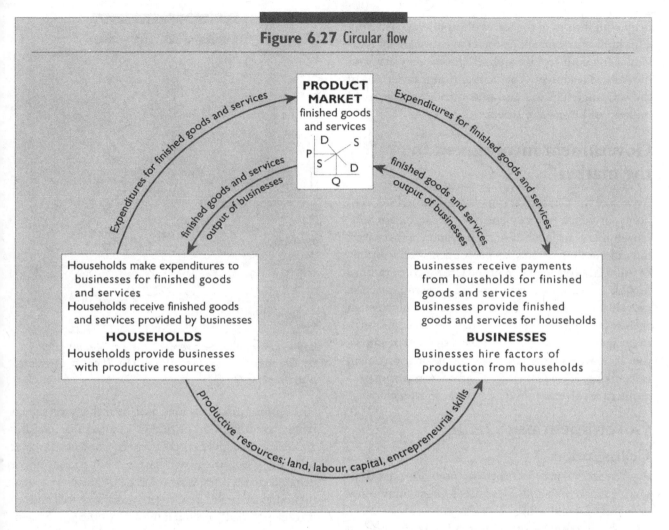

The lower loop in the circular flow diagram represents the flow of productive resources from households to businesses. We will return to it in Chapter 8.

THE ROLE OF THE MARKET IN OUR ECONOMIC SYSTEM

As we have seen, the market acts in our mixed market economic system to provide answers to the three main questions — what to produce, how to produce, and for whom to produce — and it does so largely without the need of a central agency to control it or direct it. It takes place automatically through the price system.

Prices act as guides to owners of resources and indicate where they can get the best deal for their labour, land, or capital. Prices signal opportunities to entrepreneurs. Prices also provide entrepreneurs with the incentive to adjust production to meet these opportunities. Prices also provide the information and incentive that consumers need to allocate their scarce resources to meet their needs and wants. Also, as we have seen, prices signal shortages and surpluses, and, in turn, set in motion the economic forces that in free markets automatically lead to an equilibrium of the forces of supply and demand. This kind of system allows for a large measure of individual freedom to buy and sell goods, services, and productive resources. The market brings order out of the seemingly chaotic and uncontrolled activities of millions of buyers and sellers.

Government involvement in the market

As we saw in Chapter 2, ours is a mixed market economy in which government plays a significant role. Governments are involved in the operation of the market in a variety of ways. Canadian governments either directly or indirectly (through one of the Crown corporations) provide us with goods and services. Governments also provide the framework of laws (and the law enforcement agencies) within which the market operates. Government spending and taxation have a significant impact too. Here we will examine one example of government price-fixing. We will investigate other examples of government involvement in the economy in later chapters.

Government price fixing

Ceiling prices

A government may feel that the price for a good or service is too high and, therefore, it fixes a maximum or ceiling price for it.

The **maximum** or **ceiling price** is the highest price that may be charged legally for a good or service. Rent controls are an example. The graph in figure 6.28 shows the establishment of a ceiling price.

In figure 6.28, the equilibrium price is set at OP and the equilibrium quantity at OQ. The government believes that the price of OP is too high and enforces the maximum price of OP_1. At a price of OP_1, only OQ_1 is supplied while the amount of OQ_2 is demanded. Thus, there is a shortage represented by the difference between OQ_2 and OQ_1.

In a competitive market, we know that a shortage would be met by increases in the price until the

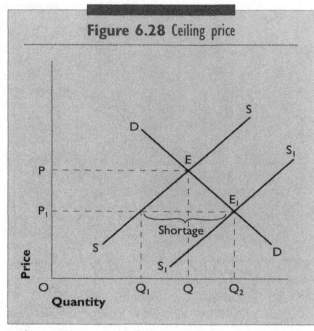

Figure 6.28 Ceiling price

Before government involvement, the equilibrium price is OP. Government fixes the price at OP_1. There is, therefore, a shortage of Q_1, Q_2.

equilibrium price was met. But with the government fixing the equilibrium price at OP_1, such price increases are illegal. To establish the new equilibrium price at OP_1, the government will have to shift the supply or demand curves. One way would be for the government to produce the good in sufficient quantities itself and sell it at the price OP_1, even if it meant that the government would lose money. Another way would be to provide suppliers with financial assistance (subsidies) so that the supply curve shifts to the right to S_1S_1.

As mentioned above, one example of a price ceiling currently in effect is the controls on rents in many Canadian provinces. Rent controls exist in many other countries as well.

Floor prices

With ceiling prices we get shortages. We may then reasonably expect to get surpluses from floor prices. If the government believes that the price of a good or a service is too low, it may impose a floor price.

A **floor price** is the minimum price below which it is illegal to buy or sell a good or a service. The minimum wage is an example.

Here again a graph is useful to show us what is happening. The equilibrium is at E in figure 6.29, where the price is OP and the quantity OQ. However, the government intervenes to fix the legal minimum or floor price above the equilibrium price at OP_1. At OP_1, only OQ_1 is demanded, while OQ_2 is supplied. In this situation, there is a surplus of the good.

As we have seen, in a competitive market the surplus would be eliminated by a decline in price. With a floor price in effect, however, a lowering of price is illegal. The only way to establish a new equilibrium at OP_1 is by shifting the demand and/or supply curves. Advertising may induce consumers to buy more, thus shifting the demand curve to the right. The government may curtail the amount produced by restricting the amount each business may sell.

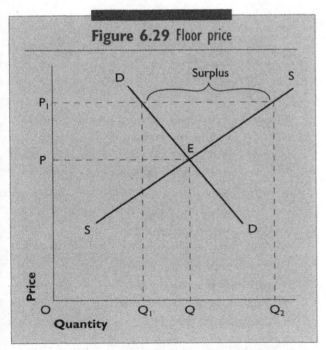

Figure 6.29 Floor price

The equilibrium price is at E. Government imposes a floor price at OP_1. As a result, there is a surplus of Q_1, Q_2.

One example of a floor price is the minimum wage. Canadian provinces and the federal government have fixed certain wages as being the rate below which workers may not be employed. Governments have introduced minimum wages into the labour market in an effort to cut the amount of poverty and raise living standards.

Analyse the cartoon

Schwadron. Cartoonists & Writers Syndicate.

REVIEW

Explain each major concept in your own words with an example: supply schedule, price, equilibrium, market, surplus, shortage, increase in supply, decrease in supply, inelastic supply, elastic supply.

APPLICATIONS

You are a buyer of corn for the Corny Corn Company. Anticipate what will happen to the price of corn in each of the following situations. Will the price rise, fall, or remain the same? Explain why in each situation.

1. a) Corn farmers meet and agree to grow less corn next year.
   b) Farmers plant more hectares of corn.

Summary

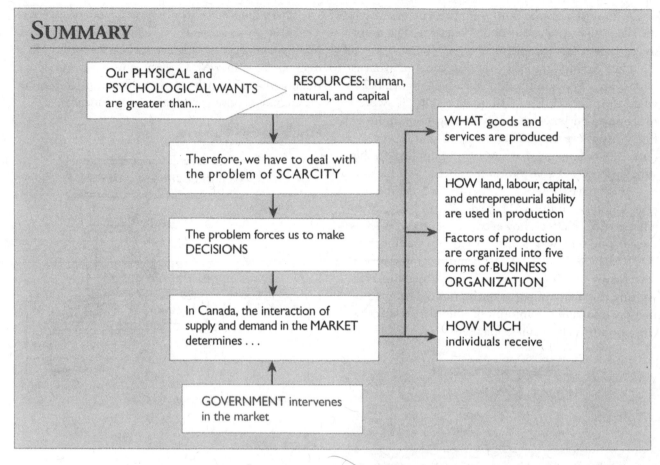

Our PHYSICAL and PSYCHOLOGICAL WANTS are greater than...

RESOURCES: human, natural, and capital

Therefore, we have to deal with the problem of SCARCITY

The problem forces us to make DECISIONS

In Canada, the interaction of supply and demand in the MARKET determines . . .

GOVERNMENT intervenes in the market

WHAT goods and services are produced

HOW land, labour, capital, and entrepreneurial ability are used in production

Factors of production are organized into five forms of BUSINESS ORGANIZATION

HOW MUCH individuals receive

c) Corn growers run an advertising campaign promoting corn as an essential part of a well-balanced diet.

d) Agricultural scientists develop a much tastier kind of corn.

e) Blight strikes the corn fields.

f) The price of wheat increases by 50 percent.

g) Medical researchers discover that people who consume large quantities of corn become fat and dumpy.

h) Popcorn is replaced in North American movie theatres by popwheat.

i) Medical researchers discover that the popcorn served in North American movie theatres has very high cholesterol levels.

2. What effect will each of the following probably have on the demand for hamburgers? Will the demand curve shift to the left or to the right? Will the quantity demanded increase or decrease?

a) Incomes of teenagers increase by 10 percent.

b) The prices of hot dogs and fried chicken increase by 10 percent.

c) It is discovered that hamburgers are good for people's health and complexions.

d) Incomes of teenagers decrease by 10 percent.

e) The prices of hot dogs and fried chicken decrease by 10 percent.

3. What effect will each of the following probably have on the supply of hamburgers? Will the supply

curve shift to the left or to the right? Will the supply increase or decrease?

a) The price of beef falls by 10 percent.

b) The wages of workers in hamburger restaurants increase by 20 percent.

c) The price of hamburger buns increases by 20 percent.

d) A new machine enables restaurant workers to produce hamburgers in half the time.

4. a) Cuba is the second-largest sugar producer in the world. In March 1993, a fierce winter storm seriously disrupted the sugar cane harvest in eight of Cuba's 14 provinces. What effect did the storm probably have on the price and quantity of sugar supplied and demanded? Use a graph to illustrate your answer.

b) Florida (one of Canada's principal suppliers of orange juice) was also hard hit by the same storm. What effect do you think the storm had on the orange juice market in Canada?

5. Describe the shift in supply or demand that would produce each of the following results — assuming that only one of the curves has shifted. For each one, draw a graph to show the change.

a) The price of transistor radios has fallen greatly over the last 25 years and the quantity bought has increased considerably.

b) The failure of the Florida orange crop is expected to increase the cost of orange juice in Canada.

c) As North American and European standards of living have increased over the past 25 years, the number of tourists crossing the North Atlantic has increased considerably.

d) With the onset of a recession, automobile sales have dropped considerably.

e) Hotel prices in Bridgetown, Barbados, are much higher in January than in July.

ISSUE 1
A shortage problem

Your nearest university has received 500 applications from students who wish to enroll in its computer engineering program. The university has space for only 200 applicants in this program. All 500 applicants have the necessary academic requirements and all have sent in their $5000 tuition fee cheques. Individually at first, and then in groups, decide how the university should admit the students.

ISSUE 2
Rent controls

As you read the following text, decide where you stand on the issue of rent controls and consider the reasons why you take that position.

During the 1970s, many Canadian provinces introduced laws (or rent controls) to limit maximum rents. In the early 1990s, many of these controls were still in existence. A lively debate developed in various parts of Canada about what provincial governments should do. Where there were rent controls, governments were urged to abolish them. Where there were no rent controls, governments were being asked to impose them.

Arguments against rent controls

Those opposing rent controls argue that the setting of rents should be left to the operation of the market. Let's outline the arguments they make. Since there are many forms that rent controls may take, we will consider only the simplest: government imposition of a maximum rent.

The immediate effects of the imposition of rent controls can be seen in figure 6.30 on page 136. Before rent controls, the equilibrium price was OP, and the equilibrium quantity OQ. With the imposition of rent controls, a shortage appears: only OQ_1 is supplied and OQ$_2$ is demanded. AB represents the shortage. Apartments become difficult to find.

Critics of rent controls argue that there is a better way than rent controls — a voucher system. With this system, rent controls would be eliminated and replaced by vouchers — which would provide the poor with rent supplements and which landlords could redeem for cash from government. How much each family would receive in vouchers would depend on family size, income, and general level of rents.

While being more expensive in the beginning, the voucher system has distinct advantages. The incentives for private investors to supply more accommodation are left intact. It doesn't require as expensive a bureaucracy to administer it. It helps the poor according to their needs and does not subsidize those who don't need it.

After a period of time, however, things get worse. With rent controls, fewer new apartments are constructed because people can find more profitable places to invest their money. If rents are controlled at low levels, owners may let their buildings fall into

disrepair and, eventually, apartments may reach the point where they cannot be rented. Old apartment buildings are not replaced. The stock of rental accommodation diminishes.

During the first years of rent controls, tenants benefit. Rents are below equilibrium and there is only a slight decrease in the stock of housing. However, as time passes, and the quantity of rental housing diminishes, tenants find it harder and harder to find accommodation. In the long run, rent controls may not be of general benefit to those who rent. Landlords who own rental buildings are clearly worse off: their income from rents has fallen. If both tenants and owners suffer from rent controls, there can be no good argument for these controls.

Arguments in favour of rent controls

The basic argument of those who favour the removal of rent controls is that those who rent should be subjected to the full rigour of the operation of the market. This is argued, even though in many sectors of our economy, e.g., in transportation, energy, and public utilities, we have significant controls on prices that businesses may charge. In the provision of health services, for example, we have decided that the market is not a useful mechanism for determining who gets what health care. In some cases, then, we do not trust the market to distribute benefits fairly. Housing, like health care, is a basic human need. Homes are not like warehouses where, when the rent increases, the user can simply move elsewhere.

Homes are different in that moving means a considerable disruption in the lives and relationships of many people.

Rent controls permit low income families to continue living in areas where richer families live. Thus controls help prevent the stratification of neighbourhoods.

Rent controls are seen by some as being a means of redistributing income in favour of the poor. Keeping rents low is a way of subsidizing the income of the poor.

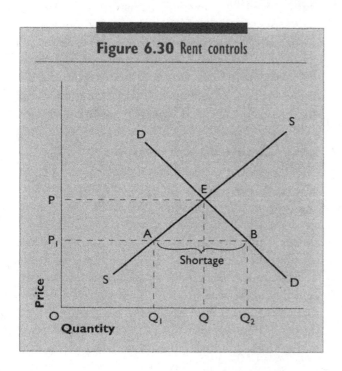

Figure 6.30 Rent controls

Controls are also an essential part of ensuring tenant security. Without them, to get rid of a tenant, all a landlord has to do is simply raise the rent by an amount that is unacceptably high to the tenant.

Rent controls help maintain the affordability of housing for those with low or fixed incomes, such as the poor and those on pensions. These are the people who are especially affected by rent increases and therefore should be protected by government.

Finally, to remove rent controls in a situation where few rental units have been constructed and vacancy rates are low is to invite serious problems. In this situation, rents are likely to rise dramatically. Many people, and most especially the poor and those on fixed incomes, are likely to experience severe hardship.

Questions

Either

1. What is your province's policy on rent controls?

2. Do you agree with your province's policy? Why or why not?

Or

Read the text carefully and prepare to debate the motion, "Be it resolved that rent controls be abolished."

CHAPTER 7

A Spectrum of Markets

(1)

(2)

The markets shown in photographs 1 and 2 — a farmers' market and a stock exchange — illustrate perfect competition.

Economists refer to businesses such as these as monopolistic competition.

Industries that supply goods such as gasoline and steel are called homogeneous oligopolies by economists.

(7)

Industries that supply local telephone service, water service, and electrical service are called monopolies.

Industries that produce goods such as automobiles and breakfast cereals are called differentiated oligopolies by economists.

Questions

1. What characteristics do the markets in photographs (1) and (2) have in common?

2. What do the businesses in photograph (3) have in common?

3. How do homogeneous oligopolies (such as oil or steel companies) differ from differentiated oligopolies (such as manufacturers of breakfast cereals)?

4. What do monopolies such as telephone companies and hydro companies have in common?

A SPECTRUM OF MARKETS

In the previous chapter, we examined how the forces of supply and demand interact in markets. In this chapter, we will compare and contrast four different kinds of markets, how prices vary among them, and how governments act in markets to promote the public interest. Of the four kinds of markets, two models — perfect or pure competition and pure monopoly — represent opposite poles along a spectrum of markets. See figure 7.1. Two other models represent the actual conditions faced by most firms —monopolistic competition and oligopoly. We'll look at each model in turn, starting with perfect competition.

PERFECT COMPETITION

The supply and demand curves we examined in Chapter 6 mainly apply to perfectly competitive markets. **Perfectly competitive markets** are ones in which uniform goods are bought and sold, and where prices are generally known; where there is competition in the market between many buyers and sellers; and where no group of buyers or sellers attempts to fix prices. In our economy, perfectly competitive markets

are rare. However, one example of a purely competitive market is a stock exchange.

If we wish to buy shares of the common stock of Canadian Pacific, we do not care from whom we buy the shares or which shares we buy. One share of the common stock of Canadian Pacific is identical to any other. The prices of the stock are generally known and no one person or small group of persons controls the price. If we wish to sell our stock later, similar conditions exist for us as sellers.

The characteristics of the Marvellous Melon Market in Chapter 6 are those of a perfectly competitive market. There are many buyers and sellers, no single one of whom is able to influence the price of the product. Thus firms in purely competitive markets are known as "price-takers." They have to accept the prevailing price; they cannot change it by their actions. Each firm produces the same product, so buyers have no reason to buy from one seller rather than another. Buyers and sellers know the prices at which the goods are sold in the market. Workers are able to move into the industry easily. There are no barriers preventing firms from entering a perfectly competitive market. Business people can easily set up new firms.

These ideal conditions, however, rarely exist in any market — the stock market and farmers' markets

Analyse the comic strip

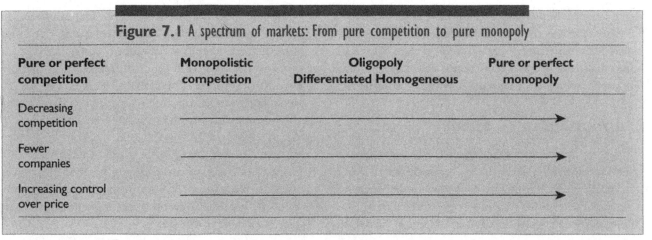

Figure 7.1 A spectrum of markets: From pure competition to pure monopoly

Pure or perfect competition	Monopolistic competition	Oligopoly Differentiated Homogeneous	Pure or perfect monopoly
Decreasing competition			
Fewer companies			
Increasing control over price			

As we move from left to right along the spectrum of markets from pure or perfect competition through monopolistic competition and oligopoly to pure monopoly, the amount of competition decreases, the number of companies in an industry decreases, and the ability of each company to influence the price it charges for its products increases.

which are not controlled by the government come closest to attaining them. Despite its rarity, perfect competition is examined here because it is one pole of the market spectrum.

MONOPOLY

Monopoly is a market situation in which there is only one producer of a good or service and many buyers. Examples include local telephone service, natural gas supply, and electricity supply. Monopoly is at the opposite end of the market spectrum from pure competition.

Kinds of monopolies

Various suppliers provide electricity in Canada. But if you wish to have *local* electrical service in your area, there is only one company to supply it. That company has a monopoly on local electricity service in your area. You *could* use natural gas, wood, or coal for heating, or diesel oil or gasoline for energy. For most purposes, however, these substitutes are not convenient enough to serve as suitable alternatives. The provision of electrical service is a **natural monopoly**. It is much more efficient to have everyone plugged into one system

than into several systems. Similarly, it is much more efficient to have a single supplier of each of natural gas and water. Thus their supply is also a natural monopoly. As a sole supplier in a given area, a monopolist has considerable control over price. In other words, it is a "price-maker."

Legal monopolies exist when government makes it illegal for more than one company to supply a good or a service. Many municipal transit systems have a legal monopoly on public transit in their area. Inventors of a new product can apply for and receive a patent, which gives them the exclusive right to produce and sell the product for 17 years. The copyright on this book is another example of a legal monopoly.

A group of producers may agree to limit competition by fixing prices, limiting output, or dividing the market geographically among them. In this way, they may be able to raise prices and profits. These kinds of arrangements are usually hard to maintain for any long period of time. First, they are usually illegal. Second, high profits are likely to attract other firms into the industry. These monopolies are called **combines** or **cartels**.

What we see as a monopoly depends on how wide we perceive the market to be. Thus, for example, we could consider that in a small town with only one general store, the store holds a monopoly. If, however, there is a city nearby with many general stores, it makes sense to include the city in our definition of the market. In this case, the small-town general store doesn't have a monopoly: it has to compete for customers with the city stores.

Monopolies in Canada

Since there is only one supplier for local telephone service, electricity, and natural gas supply in an area, monopolies have a great deal of power to fix prices or output in their own interest. For example, most of us consider local electrical service to be an essential, for which there is no real substitute. Demand for the service is inelastic. Given this inelasticity, coupled with the fact that electricity supply companies do not face competition from other companies, they are free within limits to set their own prices. For these reasons, many monopolies are regulated by governments and/or in some cases are owned by governments. Governments monitor the quality of their services, and control the prices of the goods and services they produce in order to protect the consumer. However, where price and service are unregulated by government, the pure monopoly has substantial control over the prices it charges.

Activity 1: Tacit bargaining

Situation 1   You have lost your friend in a large department store without any previous agreement about where you would meet if you became separated. What you will probably do is think of some meeting place that is as obvious to your friend as it is to you. It has to be some place that springs immediately to mind as the most obvious spot for both of you. Where would you meet?

Situation 2   Your class agrees to meet in Ottawa on Saturday but you forget to agree on the place and the time. Where and when do you meet?

Situation 3   You and another member of the class have taken up parachute jumping. Both of you have a copy of the sketch-map shown in figure 7.2 of the small town, Turkey Trot, over which you have jumped. You have not agreed on a place to meet after the jump. Where might you meet?

1. After answering the questions above, compare the responses of all the members of the class.

2. Why could many members of the class arrive at the same conclusion without communicating with each other?

3. What was the reasoning behind the majority selection in each of the situations?

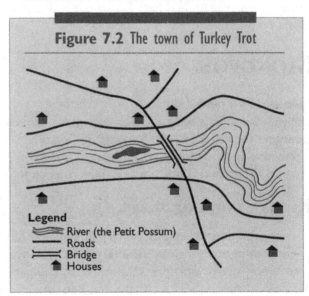

Figure 7.2 The town of Turkey Trot

Legend
≈≈≈ River (the Petit Possum)
── Roads
══ Bridge
🏠 Houses

In each of the above situations there is some spot that is fairly obvious to many as being the logical meeting place. That is why many of you were able to select the same spot from among a number of alternatives, without verbal or written communication with each other.

Activity 2: Gas station game

The situation

Two gas stations, Anita's and Lee's, are located in the tiny village of Big Bad Bear on a remote section of the Trans-Canada Highway. Both stations look the same to prospective customers. The two stations compete with each other with the knowledge that customers will drive to the cheaper gas pump. There are only two choices available to each gas station owner: hold prices or cut prices. To raise prices would be to risk bankruptcy. In this game, the gas stations cannot be driven out of business. The object of the game is for each gas station owner to maximize profits.

Figure 7.3 Scores

Situation	Anita	Lee
Anita holds/Lee holds	+5	+5
Anita holds/Lee cuts	−10	+10
Anita cuts/Lee holds	+10	−10
Anita cuts/Lee cuts	−5	−5

Scoring the game

Profits and losses in the game are determined according to the score chart in figure 7.3.

If Lee holds her price and Anita also holds, then both gain five points. If, however, Lee cuts her price while Anita holds, then Lee gains ten points and Anita loses ten. Scores for Anita and Lee are entered on a chart on the chalkboard by the scorer. See figure 7.4.

Materials

1. Two large cards on which is written HOLD.
2. Two large cards on which is written CUT.

Instructions

1. Two students are selected from the class to play the roles of Anita and Lee, the two owner-managers.
2. Anita and Lee sit at the front of the room so that they cannot see one another but can see the chalkboard.

3. Anita and Lee have two cards: on one is written HOLD and on the other, CUT.

Figure 7.4

Score chart

Round	1	2	3	4	5	6	7	8	9	10	11
Anita											
Lee											

4. Without communicating with each other, Anita and Lee decide whether to hold gas prices or to cut them.
5. At a signal from the game director, each one reveals her decision by raising either the HOLD card or the CUT card.
6. The scorer awards profits or losses to Anita or Lee according to the scoring table.
7. The scores for Anita and Lee are completed on the score chart at the completion of each move.
8. The game is played until a clear pattern of responses emerges.

Questions

1. What is the logical resolution to the gas station game? Explain how you arrived at that conclusion.

2. What was the maximum profit that Anita or Lee could reasonably expect to obtain?

3. What was Anita's total profit or loss? What was Lee's total profit or loss?

4. Ask Anita and Lee the following questions:
a) How did you feel toward the other gas station owner-manager?
b) What was your plan to maximize your profit?
c) Did you attempt to communicate with the other owner-manager? If so, how?

---

d) What did you think was the other player's strategy?

5. How close is this game to reality? How does it reflect the way in which two gas station owners are likely to react to each other's attempts to attract more customers?

6. In what situations are there only two or just a few suppliers of a good or a service?

OLIGOPOLY

If you were to ask a friend what kind of car she drives, chances are the friend would reply with the name of an automobile produced by one of a few manufacturers, e.g., General Motors, Ford, Chrysler, Toyota, Nissan, Honda, or Volkswagen. Most Canadians drive an automobile produced by one of these seven firms. Similarly, when we fill up at a gas station, it is likely that the gas we buy has been refined by one of a small group of huge oil companies, e.g., Shell, Imperial Oil, or Petro-Canada. In Canada, there are a number of other industries in which a few large companies each hold large portions of the market for a particular product. Companies that produce breakfast cereals, steel, chemicals, and cement are examples. These firms are called oligopolies.

Oligopoly is a kind of market in which a few firms supply most of the goods and services. Examples include the steel and automobile markets.

If we were to examine a given industry, we might find that the products of oligopolies are so similar as to be virtually identical. This kind of market is called a **homogeneous oligopoly** because the goods produced are of the same kind. There is little, if any, difference between a litre of gasoline bought from a Shell station and a litre from an Esso station. Steel of a particular kind and quality produced by one steel company is almost indistinguishable from that of another steel company. On the other hand, oligopolies might strive to make their products distinctive or, in other words, to differentiate between their products and those of their competitors. Not surprisingly, this is called a **differentiated oligopoly**. Examples of differentiated products include such items as automobiles, tires, and breakfast cereals.

Why are there markets dominated by oligopolies? The main reason is that certain products require large-scale operations for their manufacture. Take the example of the automobile industry. To build an assembly plant for automobiles requires a huge capital investment. Because of this, the entry of new automobile firms into the car market is extremely limited and the number of firms necessary to supply the market is small.

In oligopolistic markets, firms use various forms of non-price competition. The most obvious one of these is advertising.

Each oligopoly firm is well aware of the actions of the other firms in the same industry. Because there are only a few big firms in the industry, each firm closely watches the actions of other firms. If one firm makes a deep cut in its prices, other firms, afraid of losing their market share, are likely to make a similar move. Similarly, oligopolies tend to raise prices when they think other firms will follow. If there is a great deal of cooperation among the few firms, then prices are likely to be high, tending to compare with what you would expect prices to be in a monopolistic situation. In Canada, there is legislation designed to guard against what is known as "price-fixing." If cooperation is low and competition high among oligopoly firms, prices will be low, more like those in a purely competitive market. On the spectrum of markets shown in figures 7.1 and 7.5, oligopoly is between the opposite poles of pure competition and pure monopoly.

MONOPOLISTIC COMPETITION

After visiting a number of restaurants, it is evident that, just as restaurant prices vary, so does restaurant food, decor, atmosphere, and service. The hamburgers at Harry's Haven are not exactly the same as the hamburgers at

Figure 7.5 A spectrum of markets

Kind of market	Pure competition	Monopolistic competition	Oligopoly (Homogeneous)	Oligopoly (Differentiated)	Pure Monopoly
Number of producers and type of product	• many sellers • identical product	• many sellers • some product distinction	• few sellers • some product distinction	• few sellers • much product distinction	• one seller • no product substitutes
Conditions of entry into the industry	• easy to enter the industry	• easy to enter the industry	• difficult to enter the industry	• difficult to enter the industry	• very difficult or impossible to enter the industry
Influence over price	• no control over price	• some control over price	• limited by interdependence of firms • some control over price	• limited by interdependence of firms — a "price searcher"	• considerable control over price — a "price maker"
Existence of non-price competition	• none	• some—especially advertising	• considerable use made of advertising	• considerable non-price competition—such as advertising	• advertising of firm's "image"
Examples	• stock market • certain agricultural markets	• retail trade • clothing • many service industries	• steel • aluminum • pulp • cement	• automobiles • tires • breakfast cereals • soap	• electrical energy • water • gas • urban transit systems

Dave's Dive. We may favour Harry's food over Dave's, but Dave's atmosphere over Harry's. The fast-food market is an example of monopolistic competition.

Monopolistic competition is a market situation in which there are many sellers providing a similar but not identical good or service. Examples include the markets for fast food and haircuts.

The sit-down restaurant business is a good example of monopolistic competition. First, there are many suppliers or restaurateurs. The products they sell are similar but not identical, thus giving the individual suppliers some measure of control over price. Entry into the business is relatively easy. Imagine the difference in cost between opening a car assembly plant and a restaurant! Price and output in the industry tend to resemble price and output under conditions of perfect competition. By now, you will have discovered why economists say that the restaurant business and others like it are monopolistically competitive. Each restaurant competes with all the others in an area, but each restaurant has a monopoly over the food it serves and the way it is served. No other restaurant serves exactly the same food in the same way as another close by. Monopolistic competition is frequently found in service industries such as hair cutting, auto repair, retail trade, and restaurants, to name a few.

CONCENTRATION IN CANADIAN INDUSTRY

The extent to which an industry is controlled by a few firms can be measured by a concentration ratio. The concentration ratio measures the proportion of an industry's sales made by its four largest and eight largest firms. Figure 7.6 shows that in 1988 the four largest tobacco firms sold almost 99 percent of the sales of domestic tobacco products in the Canadian market. The eight largest tobacco firms sold 100 percent of the sales of domestic tobacco products.

As you can see, petroleum and coal products, rubber industries, and transport are dominated by a few firms. Yet, there are also a number of industries that are not dominated by a few firms, such as construction, clothing, and furniture industries. Finally, figure 7.6 shows the relative importance in domestic sales of producers located in Canada. The degree of concentration in *total sales in Canada* is much smaller in those industries such as transportation and textiles where many of the products come from other countries.

Restricting competition

Competition among companies can be diminished through unfair (predatory) competition; by establishing a cartel; by interlocking directorates; by mergers; and by establishing a holding company.

1. Through unfair competition.   A company that is better able to compete in a market compared to other firms will grow in size at the expense of its competitors. In some cases, firms engage in cut-throat pricing to drive out their competitors. With cut-throat (or predatory) pricing, goods are priced well below the cost of production. This practice drives smaller companies out of the market. Once the small competitors have been forced out of business, the cut-throat competitor can raise prices and increase its share of the

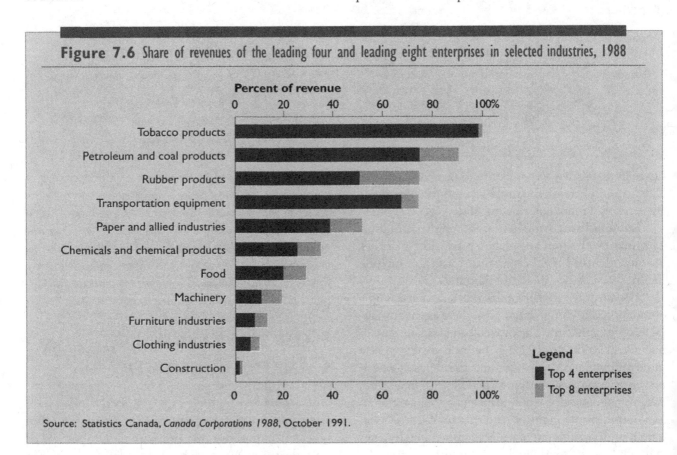

Figure 7.6 Share of revenues of the leading four and leading eight enterprises in selected industries, 1988

Source: Statistics Canada, *Canada Corporations 1988*, October 1991.

market. The classic Canadian case of cut-throat competition was the Eddy Match Company. Between 1928 and 1949, the company succeeded in driving seven competitors out of the wooden match industry using cut-throat competition. In 1951, Eddy was convicted of predatory pricing practices.

2. By establishing a cartel. A **cartel** is an organization of independent producers that enter into an agreement to fix output or prices. Probably the best known and, for a time, one of the most successful of recent attempts to restrain competition and raise prices has been the Organization of Petroleum Exporting Countries (OPEC). OPEC was able to increase the price of oil from $3 a barrel in 1973 to $34 a barrel in 1982. Since the early 1980s, however, the cartel has had less success as other sources of oil outside OPEC such as the North Sea, the Alaska North slope, and the Alberta tar sands have been developed. Other sources of power such as natural gas and nuclear energy are being more widely used and more efficient engines are conserving gasoline. When producers such as OPEC members work together and agree to fix prices, limit output, or divide up markets, the producers are said to be forming a cartel. In Canada, cartels are illegal because they work to restrict competition, to raise prices, and to reduce sales to their own advantage, but to the disadvantage of the Canadian consumer.

3. Through interlocking directorates. When a person is on the board of directors of a number of competing companies, output and pricing policies can be coordinated in a way to lessen competition.

4. Through mergers. Competition can also be restricted by the formation of a merger. A **merger** is the combining of the assets of two companies into a single company. Mergers are usually the result of one company taking over another company.

If A Company merges or joins with a competitor, B Company, then a new company is formed, AB Company, and competition between the two is eliminated. The Toronto-Dominion Bank, for example, was formed in 1957 by the merger of the Bank of Toronto (founded in 1855) and the Dominion Bank, established in 1869.

5. By establishing a holding company. A **holding company** is set up to hold (or own) a significant proportion of the shares of other companies (e.g., 51 percent) and thus to control the activities of these companies. A holding company is another way of eliminating competition between A Company and its competitor, B Company.

If C Company buys 51 percent of the common shares of A Company and 51 percent of the common shares of B Company, then C Company has control of both companies and could act to diminish competition between them. Since C Company holds controlling interest in A Company and B Company, it is called a holding company. When companies of the same type combine by merging or by setting up a holding company, such arrangements are called **horizontal combinations**. See figure 7.7.

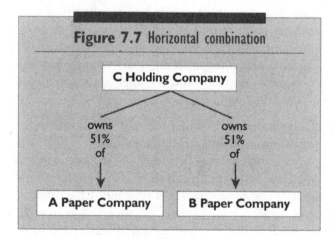

Figure 7.7 Horizontal combination

C Holding Company

owns 51% of → A Paper Company

owns 51% of → B Paper Company

Other combinations

Vertical combination (integration) In addition to combinations that may restrict competition, such as mergers or holding companies, there are other forms of combination, such as vertical combination and conglomerates, that are less likely to reduce competition substantially. Vertical combination is also called "vertical integration." See figure 7.8 on page 148.

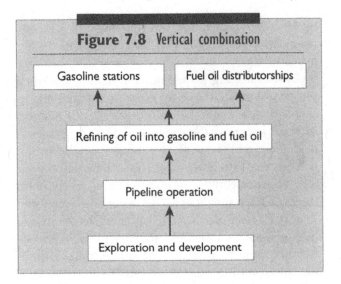

Figure 7.8 Vertical combination

Vertical combination is the control by a company of the various stages of production. Thus a company may control the exploration for and production of the necessary raw materials, the factories necessary to transform the raw materials into finished products, and the retail outlets to sell the goods to the consumer. An example of an integrated firm is Imperial Oil Limited. This company is engaged in the exploration, production, development, refining, and marketing of crude oil and natural gas.

Conglomerates   Another common form of combination in industry is the conglomerate.

A **conglomerate** is formed when companies in unrelated industries combine. A conglomerate could include companies in such diverse industries as insurance, commercial fishing, oil exploration, aircraft production, hotels, and mining. There is a definite advantage to diversification. If, for example, there is a serious decline in mining, this may be offset by a steady growth in insurance. Conglomerates are organized on the principle that it is a good idea to spread business risks over several unrelated industries.

Canadian Pacific Limited is an example of a conglomerate. It is involved in rail, ship and truck transportation; energy; forest products; real estate and hotel operations; telecommunications; industrial products; engineering and construction services; and waste management.

ADVANTAGES OF LARGE-SCALE OPERATIONS

In a number of industries there are two main advantages to large-scale operations. The first relates to the firm's ability to engage in research, and the second to the advantages of large-scale production. A large company with large sales of its products has the incentives and the resources that enable it to research and develop new products and new ways of production. The expenditures on research enable the company to develop profitable new products. Society also benefits as these products become available.

This does not mean that only large corporations can develop new products. Joseph-Armand Bombardier developed the snowmobile in his garage. Steve Jobs and Steve Wozniak began production of the Apple computer in Jobs's garage. However, because of its size, a large firm can produce large quantities of a particular product. The company can make use of specialized machinery and workers in production and, therefore, the cost of producing each individual product declines.

GOVERNMENT REGULATION

As suggested previously, monopolies and oligopolies may sometimes raise prices or restrict output in order to increase profits. Consumers are hurt by these activities in two ways: they are able to buy less and obliged to pay more for the product. Governments, therefore, have moved to protect the interests of consumers in three main ways: by government ownership of the businesses that provide the goods and services; by laws that are intended to ensure that competition between companies is maintained; and by government regulation of the prices charged and services provided.

Government ownership

Governments, today, supply many of the essential services — such as water, electricity, public transit, and sewage treatment — that are natural monopolies. In many cases, governments bought out the private companies that originally supplied these services. The service is still provided by a monopolist but governments do not have the same incentive to take advantage of their power to raise prices unduly. Usually the prices charged are set to cover costs. Whatever profits are made are, for the most part, used for the benefit of the public.

Laws to promote competition

The federal government also promotes competition in Canadian industry. Agreements to fix prices or limit output in order to raise prices or create a monopoly are illegal. Those breaking the law are liable to a fine and imprisonment. It is also illegal for manufacturers to force retailers to sell their goods at "suggested" or "fair" retail prices. Manufacturers also cannot refuse to supply retailers who sell their product at a price that is lower than the "suggested retail price."

Regulation of prices and services

Few if any Canadian households have a choice in deciding what local telephone, natural gas, or electric company they will use. Similarly, we have little choice if we wish to travel between two towns by air, or transport our goods by rail. In order to gain the advantages of having only one company provide the services, and at the same time protect the consumer, government regulates the industry. Thus, provincial governments regulate the rates

SUMMARY

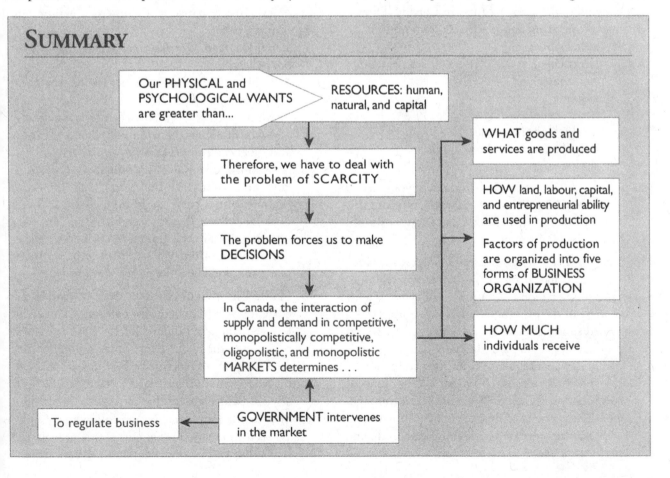

charged for water, electricity, and natural gas. The federal government has jurisdiction over broadcasting, and over air and rail transportation as well.

REVIEW

Explain each concept or term in your own words with an example: monopoly, monopolistic competition, oligopoly, homogeneous oligopoly, heterogeneous oligopoly, pure competition, cartel, OPEC, holding company, vertical combination, horizontal combination.

APPLICATIONS

1. List some brands and manufacturers of the following goods and services found in Canada. Draw a market spectrum and place each item on it.

    automobiles
    electricity
    toothpaste
    gasoline
    hamburgers
    local telephone service
    long distance telephone service
    shoe retailing

2. Are the number of taxicab licences in your city or town restricted? What would be the effect of this restriction? Do you think these licences should be restricted? Explain.

3. Stelco Incorporated is the second-largest steel producer in Canada, producing approximately one-third of the nation's output. The following is a list of some of the main units, and wholly or partially-owned subsidiaries of Stelco. Their activities and products appear in parentheses. Arrange the list of companies in a sequence from the production of raw materials to finished product. What kind of combination is Stelco? What are the advantages and disadvantages of this form of combination?

    Stelco Incorporated (main business: producing steel sheets, plates, rods, and bars)

    Frost Wire Products Ltd. (produces chainlink fence, posts, and barbed wire)

    Stelco Wire Ltd. (processes rod and wire coils and wire products)

    Alta Steel Ltd. (produces steel bars from steel billets)

    Stelco-McMaster Ltd. (produces steel bars from steel billets)

    Jannock Steel Fabricating Company (steel roofing and cladding, metal shelving and store racks, etc.)

    Stelco Fasteners Ltd. (screws, bolts, nuts, rivets, and other fastener products)

    Stelpipe (pipes and tubular products)

    Pikeville Coal Company (Kentucky; coal)

    Kanawha Coal Company (West Virginia; coal)

    Eveleth Expansion Company (Minnesota; iron ore pellets)

    Tilden Iron Ore Company (Michigan; iron ore pellets)

    Hibbing Taconite Company (Minnesota; iron ore pellets)

    Mathies Coal Company (Pennsylvania; coal)

    Wabush Mines (Newfoundland and Labrador and Québec; iron ore pellets)

    Wabush Lake Railway Company (Newfoundland and Labrador; transports iron ore from Wabush Mines part-way to the pellets plant and dock facilities at Pointe Noire)

    Arnaud Railway Company (Québec; transports iron ore from Wabush Mines to the pellets plant and dock facilities at Pointe Noire)

4. Hairstylists in your city have decided that, at the current price they charge for haircuts, they can no longer make a reasonable living. One hairstylist proposes to the Hairdressers' Association that they raise the price of haircuts by $2.00. Before reaching a decision, the hairstylists come to you for your advice. Before giving the hairstylists the benefit of your wisdom, consider the following:

    a) Is the demand for haircuts elastic or inelastic?

    b) What will be the effect of a price increase?

c) Will the Hairdressers' Association be able to ensure that all hairstylists raise the price of haircuts by the same amount?

d) Will the Hairdressers' Association be able to control the entry of new hairstylists into hairdressing in the long run?

Why are the above considerations helpful to you in reaching a decision? What will you advise the hairstylists to do? Why?

5. Parking a car is usually a fairly simple task. At a large concert or sporting event, however, it can be difficult, expensive, and frustrating. The following extract, from an article by Henry G. Manne, describes how the parking situation at one football stadium changed when competition broke down. Henry Manne is a professor at the University of Miami Law School. As you read the extract, consider why competition existed, why it broke down, and what the results of reduced competition were.

The Parable of the Parking Lots

By Henry G. Manne

Producers have a natural interest to narrow the market and raise the price.

Adam Smith, *Wealth of Nations*

Once upon a time in a city not far away, thousands of people would crowd into the local football stadium on a Saturday afternoon. The problem of parking was initially solved by a number of big commercial parking lots whose owners formed the Association of Professional Parking Lot Employees (APPLE). But, as time passed and crowds grew, every plumber, lawyer, and schoolteacher who owned a house in the neighbourhood went into the parking business on Saturday afternoon, and cars appeared in every driveway and on most lawns. Members of APPLE viewed the entry of these "amateurs" into their business with no great enthusiasm, especially since some were charging a lower fee . . .

At a meeting of all members of APPLE, emotions and applause ran high as one speaker after another pointed out . . . that parking should be viewed, not as a business, but as a profession governed by professional standards. In particular, cut-throat price competition with amateurs should be regarded as unethical. The one concrete proposal, quickly adopted, was that APPLE members should contribute $1 per parking spot "to improve their public image, and put their case before the proper authorities."

No accounting was ever made of this money, but it must have been spent wisely, since within a few months the city council passed an ordinance to regulate industry price and to require that anyone parking cars must be licensed. However, it turned out to be difficult for an independent house owner to get a license; it required passing a special driving test to be "professionally administered" by APPLE, a $27 000 investment in parking facilities, and $500 000 in liability insurance. Since every commercial lot found its costs consequently increasing by 20 percent, the city council approved a 20 percent increase in parking fees.

On the next football afternoon, a funny thing happened on the way to the stadium. Since police were out in large numbers to enforce the ordinance, driveways and lawns were empty and long lines of cars were backed up waiting to get into each commercial lot. The snarl was even worse after the game. Some people simply gave up waiting for their cars and had to return to retrieve them next day. (There was even a rumour that one car was never found.) In response, APPLE decided to go ahead with a "statistical-logistic study of the whole socioeconomic situation" by two computer science professors at the local university. Their report cited the archaic methods of the industry and pointed out that what each firm needed was fewer quill pens and more time on a computer.

As the parking lots began to computerize their operations it became quite clear that in the face of these rising costs, a further increase in parking fees was required. The increase was quickly approved by city councillors relieved that, in the modernization of the industry, they had finally found a solution. But, unfortunately, it was no solution after all. The problem, it turned out, was not so much deciding which car should be moved where, as actually moving it — and that continued to be done by attendants who had become surly and uncooperative because of the pressure they were facing.

Relief, however, did appear in two forms. First, many people got fed up with the hassle and started watching the game on TV. Second, small boys who lived in the houses closest to the stadium went into the car wash business on Saturday afternoon. They charged $5, but it was worth the price, since they guaranteed a top-quality job. (In fact, they guaranteed that they would spend at least 2 hours on it.) And they always had as many cars as they could handle, even on rainy days — in fact, especially on rainy days.

Source: *Economics*, Blomqvist et al., 3rd Canadian ed. (Toronto: McGraw-Hill Ryerson, 1990). Originally published as "The Parable of the Parking Lots," *Public Interest* no. 23 (Spring 1971), pages 10-15. Abbreviated with the author's permission.

Questions

a) How did competition work initially to solve the problem of the increased demand for parking space on a Saturday afternoon?

b) How did APPLE solve the parking lot problem? What kind of organization is APPLE? What organizations is it similar to? What negative results followed the APPLE solution?

c) What characteristics of perfect competition are illustrated in the APPLE story?

d) What lesson does Henry Manne suggest can be learned from this parable?

6. As you read the following newspaper article, consider whether the demand for gasoline is elastic or inelastic, what determines the price of gasoline, and why the price of gasoline moves so crazily.

Why gasoline prices move so crazily

By Mathew Ingram
Financial Times of Canada, October 2, 1993

It's a typical week for motorists . . . in most major cities across the country: On Monday, a downtown Petrocan station is charging 53.9 cents a litre for regular unleaded gasoline. The Shell station across the street is offering the same for 52.9, and an Esso a few blocks away is also at 52.9.

The following morning, the Shell has dropped to 49.9 cents a litre, but by that same afternoon, it's back at 53.9. On Wednesday, Shell and Petrocan are both at 49.9, but the Esso station is holding fast at 52.9. On Thursday, Petrocan tries moving up to 51.9, but the Shell stays at 49.9; the Esso is steadfast at 52.9.

By this time a price drop has moved throughout the city: Stations . . . have dropped to 48 or 49 cents. But by Friday, time-honoured tradition kicks in. Stations across [the city] boost their prices to cash in on drivers fleeing the city. Our downtown Petrocan starts Friday with unleaded regular at 53.9, a penny more than the Esso, which has held steady at 52.9. In the morning, the Shell across the street is still at 48.9 — but as the day wears on, it too moves up to 53.5, a rise of almost 10 percent.

A single, typical week. Prices gyrating up and down, even though demand for gasoline — except for Friday — remains relatively consistent. Likewise, the price of crude oil, the raw material from which gasoline is made, fluctuated only a fraction of a cent or so that week — and most major oil companies buy on long-term contracts anyway, either from their own refining divisions or elsewhere. The same goes for refining costs, marketing expenses, payroll and so on: the frantic dance of city gasoline prices can't be explained by variations in any of those routine costs of bringing gasoline to market.

Nevertheless, from day to day and week to week — even from hour to hour — in any given city (although some are more volatile than others) the price of a litre of gasoline can move up and down by as much as 10 to 15 percent. Over the course of the year, an alert motorist — assuming he or she fills up several times a month with 40 litres or so — could save close to $100 by shopping around for the lowest pump prices.

How then to explain these ever-shifting prices? Profiteering oil companies? Greedy station owners? Market forces? Truth to tell, it's none of the above — or rather, a combination of all three. Station owners and oil companies insist price gyrations are evidence of roaring competition throughout the industry. Many motorists no doubt suspect a conspiracy to gouge them at the pump. To date, however, no such thing has ever been proven.

The fact is, gas pricing is the result of a curious combination of both competition and . . . let's call it consultation. Most "branded" station owners get their pricing orders every day from the companies that supply them. Gas stations in the same neighbourhood watch each other closely. They shift their prices, not in response to fluctuating crude prices, shifts in traffic patterns or changes in their operating costs — in the end, they shift them in response to what the station owner across the street is charging. It's an elaborate game of blindman's buff between station owners and managers, between the oil companies who supply them, and between

majors and the independents.

In the above example, the Shell and Esso stations are company-owned and the manager is simply a salaried employee who sets the price wherever head office tells him or her to. The Shell station is strictly self-serve, which means its costs are low relative to its Esso competitor — who is half self-serve and half full service. The Petrocan in our example has the highest costs: it's full-serve, with two service bays for lube jobs and tune-ups.

The Petrocan manager is a so-called "branded independent," who pays monthly rent to the company and buys all his gas from them (about two-thirds of each major oil company's stations fall into this category). The price he pays the company for gasoline is recalculated whenever he tells Petrocan head office that his nearby competitors have moved up or down in price. But he is free to then charge what he feels is necessary — above or below his cost — to get business, thereby increasing or sacrificing his profit.

Recently, one Petrocan owner . . . described how he set his prices on a particular day, when the pump price was 52.9 cents a litre. He explained that the chain's head office had told him he would have to pay them 46.73 cents a litre, including provincial taxes, for his gas. The GST added 3.46 cents to that price, plus a 1.4 cents per litre "participation fee" to Petrocan for processing charges — leaving 2.5 cents a litre to cover operating costs and profit. That's low.

As for the "consultation" part — sometimes it gets personal. Our Petrocan owner says he has known the manager of the neighbouring Shell station for 15 years. When the Shell suddenly dropped its price from 53.9 to 50.9, "I called him and said: 'Terry [not his real name] — what in heck do you think you're doing?'" By that afternoon, after a survey of the area showed everyone else had stayed up, the Shell got his orders from head office: get back up there.

How friendly. Some would call it friendly price-fixing.

But price-fixing in the legal sense involves a considerable degree of collusion — when it comes to gasoline retailing, it's more like a herd mentality. Most stations in a given area will usually point to one as the leader, either in trying to keep prices high, in putting them back up (known as attempting "a restore"), or in dropping them (known as "crashing the market").

"It's always the Petrocan who puts prices up on Friday, and keeps them up longest," says one independent station owner in a large urban centre. "It's usually the Esso owner who tries to stay up," says another.

"I phone in when I see that one of the stations near me has gone up or down a cent or more," says one station manager. And the station across the street? "He looks at me and the station up the block to see if we've moved." All it takes is one station to start it — if another few follow, a wave can be created. If only one moves, the instigator may well give up. Is that collusion? Maybe. Everybody wants to get stations up to a half-decent profit level and keep them there — but some independent usually drags them back down.

Questions

a) Is the demand for gasoline elastic or inelastic i) for individual dealers? ii) in general, over a long period of time? over a short period of time?

b) On a day-to-day basis, what factors determine gasoline prices?

c) In the long run, what determines gasoline prices?

d) How are the gasoline markets described here similar to and different from purely competitive markets?

e) Why do gasoline prices move so crazily?

f) What kind of market is described in the article? Explain why.

g) Survey gasoline prices on a daily basis for a couple of weeks at a number of gas stations in your area. Do gas prices tend to move crazily? Do you notice any patterns in the price changes?

7. **A mystery story**

Mr. Hemlock Shears of Baker Street is trying to find out which one of five suspects is the monopolist. In front of him are the statements of each of the five suspects. Which one is the monopolist? What are the other four?

SUSPECT A: "Look here, I'm not the monopolist. I have lots of competition; if I were to try to raise my prices I'd lose business to Mr. Big Ltd. since he and I produce almost identical products. No, I wait for him to raise prices and follow right along."

SUSPECT B: "I can't afford to advertise. Besides, what good would it do me? My product is the same as that of everyone else."

SUSPECT C: "I have lots of problems. New stores like mine are opening up all the time. I have to spend time and money to convince people that my store is different."

SUSPECT D: "My product is unique. This market is very hard, if not impossible, to break into."

SUSPECT E: "If you were in my business, you would know that I'm not the monopolist. I have lots of competition from big firms that produce goods that are similar to, but in many ways significantly different from, my product. To emphasize the qualities of my products, I spend a lot of money on advertising."

Adapted from *Master Curriculum Guide in Economics, High School Economics Courses*, Joint Council on Economic Education.

CASE STUDY
Will coffee prices perk up?

The association of major coffee-producing countries representing 28 countries growing 85 percent of the world's beans agreed in September 1993 to cut exports starting in October 1993 to help raise prices. The Association of Coffee Producing Nations (A.C.P.N.) is attempting to reverse a four-year collapse in coffee prices in which the price of beans fell from $2.64 to $1.15 a kilo. See figure 7.9. The price collapse caused severe hardship in coffee-producing countries. In Brazil alone some 2 million coffee workers (20 percent of the total) lost their jobs. For many small coffee growers, such as those in Costa Rica, it means bankruptcy and loss of their farms. Total production in Brazil — the largest producer with a quarter of the world's total output — declined by a quarter between 1989 and 1993. Columbia's output decreased by a similar fraction over the same period. Production by African countries as a whole has diminished by 17 percent over six years. Production in Asia and Central America has, however, remained steady.

The objective of the Association of Coffee Producing Nations is to stabilize coffee bean prices between $1.56 and $1.76 a kilo.

Questions

1. Draw a graph to show the supply and demand for coffee in 1989. Label the supply curve SS$_{1989}$.

2. On the graph, show the supply curve in 1993 before the establishment of the A.C.P.N.

3. Assuming that the Association manages to withhold 20 percent of the coffee crop, show the new supply curve. Label it SS$_{ACPN}$.

4. Is the demand for coffee elastic or inelastic? Explain.

5. In what way are the actions of the A.C.P.N. influenced by the elasticity of demand?

6. What kind of an organization is the A.C.P.N.? What organization is similar to it in form?

7. Two heavy frosts, one in late June 1994, and the other in early July 1994, were estimated by Brazil to have cut its 1995-96 coffee crop by 11 million 132-pound bags to 15.7 million bags. Would the frosts help or hinder the aims of the A.C.P.N.? Explain. Use a graph to show the effect of the frosts.

8. What do you think are the A.C.P.N.'s chances of success between 1995 and, say, 1999?

9. Do some library research to bring the coffee story up to date.

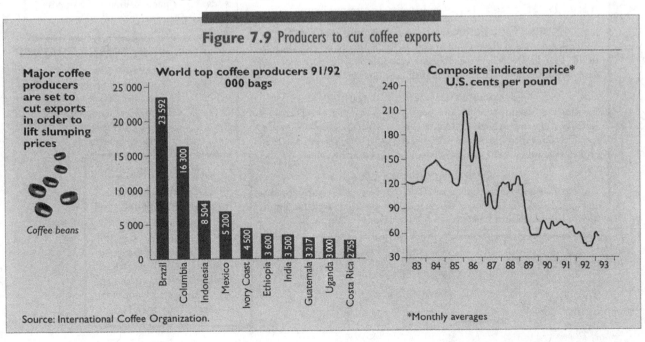

Figure 7.9 Producers to cut coffee exports

Major coffee producers are set to cut exports in order to lift slumping prices

Coffee beans

World top coffee producers 91/92 000 bags

Brazil 23 592
Columbia 16 300
Indonesia 8 504
Mexico 5 200
Ivory Coast 4 500
Ethiopia 3 600
India 3 500
Guatemala 3 217
Uganda 3 000
Costa Rica 2 755

Composite indicator price* U.S. cents per pound

83 84 85 86 87 88 89 90 91 92 93

Source: International Coffee Organization.

*Monthly averages

CHAPTER 8

Distribution

Nanny, live in or out. Driver, some general housekeeping. $1200 net/mo. Immediate.

Construction labourer
Salary: $10.13 per hour
Requirements: Previous experience as a residential construction labourer. Valid Class V driver's licence. Own vehicle an asset.

Electricians needed for installation of Marine Electrical systems. $13-14 per hour plus benefits.

Experienced cosmetic salesperson
Salary: $9 to $10 per hour, plus commission.
Requirements: Experience is mandatory. Good personal sales skills and good phone manners.

Family Program Coordinator
The family program at Community Services is looking for a half-time coordinator to research, develop and implement a viable sliding-scale-fee counselling service. Salary range $22-$24 per hour.

Fitness Centre Instructor
Weight training instructor required. MUST HAVE either degree/diploma in Kinesiology/Physical Ed. OR Basic Fitness Leader-Strength Training certificate. 16/hr wk incl. weekends. $12/hr.

Growing CA firm req's a 3rd yr CGA w/min 3 yrs public practice exp. Salary to $30,000.

Locksmith
Exp'd locksmith req'd for mobile service. Regina. $30K+ per year.

Painter/Sprayer – $20/hr
Central Refinishing is seeking 2 exp'd spray painters for our Calgary area refinishing division.

Qualified Aluminum Welder Fitters
Petroleum tanker experience an asset. Wages $20.50/hour for qualified people plus 100% medical and dental.

Research Officer

$907 - $1,091 per week; Ottawa

If you are highly motivated, explore this 10-month contract opportunity with the **Ministry of Culture, Tourism and Recreation** to conduct economic research studies to analyse and interpret recreation and economic statistical data.

FAMILY PHYSICIAN

This part-time position involves working with a multidisciplinary team to provide excellent primary care to a highly diverse population. Salary range is $80,295 - $117,760 and excellent benefits. Location: Montréal.

NURSE EPIDEMIOLOGIST — $56,800 - $67,100
Your professional skills are in demand at the Ministry of Health, public health branch, for delivery of the provincewide vaccine-preventable diseases and tuberculosis control programs. Location: Halifax.

COUNSELLOR — $34,530 ANNUAL
Exciting opportunity to work on a counselling team providing family and individual therapy to adolescents and their families. Location: Winnipeg. Qualifications: BSW preferred with 3 years' experience serving adolescents and their families. Valid driver's license and road-worthy vehicle required.

MEDICAL SECRETARY
The Pacific Region of the Canadian HIV Trials Network is currently accepting applications for a Medical Secretary. This position, available immediately, carries a salary of $24,000 per annum. Location: Richmond, B.C.

SOFTWARE TRAINER
We have a temporary position available in our District Education Office (30 hours per week). The current wage rate is $17.64 per hour plus 8% in lieu of benefits.

AIR TRAFFIC CONTROLLERS
TRAINEES NEEDED
$28,700-$81,561
Men and women are still needed to fill the many Air Traffic Control positions available. Applications are accepted on a continuous basis. Location: Sydney, N.S.

Question

What influences the wages and salaries of various occupations?

COMPANY NEWS & REPORTS

Hessco Enterprises Inc., Montreal, has boosted earnings and revenues thanks to higher computer sales.

New technology, lower prices and better price performance continue to expand the computer market it serves, Hessco president Lisa Hess said in announcing the results.

What the figures show for Hessco and other reporting companies:

HESSCO ENTERPRISES INC. 2nd quarter

2nd qtr July 30	1995	1994
Revenues	$87,963,000	$64,530,000
Net income	774,000	580,000
Avg shares	11,010,715	10,928,456
Shr income	0.07	0.05

CONSOLIDATED PACIFIC 3rd quarter

3rd qtr July 31	1995	1994
Revenues	$62,073	$75,994
Net income	167,350	(15,666)
Shr income	0.01	nil

METALLONICS LTD. 1st quarter

1st qtr Aug. 31	1995	1994
Revenues	$2,660,000	$3,311,000
Net income	45,000	55,000
Shr income	0.02	0.02

MARK INC. 2rd quarter

3rd		
Reve		
Net		
Shr		

LET

1st		
Reve		
Net		
Shr		

CO

3rd		
Shr		

Question

What factors influence income from interest, rent, and profit?

Activity 1: Who receives how much?

Study figure 8.1 and answer the following questions.

1. The attractiveness of a particular job does not depend solely on pay. What other factors are there?

2. Give reasons why:
    a) nurses earn more than receptionists.
    b) doctors earn more than teachers.

3. What general factors seem to determine the differences in wages and salaries in the comparisons you made in question 2?

4. Check the want ads in your newspaper for the pay scale of jobs in your area.

5. What occupation do you intend to enter? Briefly describe the job. What are the qualifications, pay, and working conditions of the job?

INCOME DISTRIBUTION

In Chapter 2, we saw that each society has to answer the three major questions: what, how, and for whom. In this chapter, our main focus is on the "for whom" question. Here we are concerned with how the incomes of the various factors of production are determined, in other words, with the **distribution** of national income.

Would you like more income? Few people would answer that question with a "no." Why do we want more income? The answer is obvious. With more income we have more money to buy goods and services available in the market; that is, we have more purchasing power.

In our economic system, income is distributed among the different factors of production: land, labour, capital, and entrepreneurial ability. An individual's income depends on what the individual owns of these factors.

Most income earners own at least one factor of production — their own labour. If I offer the services of my labour on the market and I am hired, I will receive a return in the form of wages.

Wages are a regular payment to employees for their labour services.

Similarly, if I have land, capital, or entrepreneurial ability to offer on the market, I will receive a return for the services of these productive factors. The amount of income I receive, whether in the form of rent, wages, interest, or profit, is determined by what I am able and willing to supply, as well as by the prices the different factors command on the market.

The prices of the different productive factors help determine how they are used. Business people examine the prices of the factors to find a combination that will produce a given output as cheaply as possible. The owners of the factors of production also examine prices so that they will receive the best return. Prices serve to allocate the productive factors among the different industries.

But how are the prices of these productive factors determined? In Chapter 6, we examined how supply and demand forces interact in the competitive market to affect the pricing of a single commodity. Here, too, we assume a competitive job market. That is, we assume that workers are free to move from job to job, that there are many employers (buyers or workers' services) and many workers (sellers), that no one has the power to influence wages, and, finally, that all workers are equally productive. In this chapter, we will see the same forces come into play to determine the pricing of the productive factors.

Wages and salaries

Why does a National Hockey League player earn $250 000 or more a year to play hockey, a highly desirable occupation (in the 1993-94 season, 69 players

Figure 8.1 Employment requirements and pay of selected jobs

Group	Qualifications	Pay	Job description*	Working conditions
self-employed physicians and surgeons	minimum of seven years' university training after high school	$113 000 per year (average)	examines patients, diagnoses illness, and prescribes treatment for various disorders and illnesses	varied
trucker	driver's licence; grade 8 minimum; on-the-job training	$17.59 an hour; $34 300 a year plus fringe benefits of about $400 a month	operates trucks to transport goods and materials	lifting 25 kg; good vision
secretary	grade 12 education; ability to input 40 words per minute	$27 465 plus substantial fringe benefits	composes and inputs correspondence and reports; answers telephone(s) and schedules appointments	little physical activity
computer operator	high school graduation; community college; on-the-job training	$29 213; fringe benefits $205 a month single and $267 married	operates and controls computer to process business, scientific, and other information	little physical activity
high school teacher	university; specialized training	$40 000 plus substantial fringe benefits	prepares courses and lessons for presentation to class; administers tests and corrects papers; engages in after-school activities	little physical activity
carpenter	minimum grade 10 education; four-year apprenticeship program	$22.19 an hour; $46 313 a year; fringe benefits $205 a month single and $267 married	assembles wood products to construct buildings, frames, and other structures made of wood; uses power and hand tools	lifting 25 kg; kneeling; some outdoor work
electrician	grade 12 education; four-year apprenticeship program		lays out, installs, assembles, and maintains electric wiring in homes, offices, and factories	lifting 25 kg; some risk
plumber	grade 10; 4–5 year apprenticeship program		repairs and installs pipes and fixtures used in water distribution and waste disposal	lifting 50 kg; kneeling; some risk
registered nurse	2-year college diploma after high school graduation, or university degree in nursing	$17.38 an hour; $33 891 a year plus substantial fringe benefits	provides nursing care to patients in hospitals, in their homes, and in doctors' offices	stooping; lifting 25 kg
garbage collector	grade 8 minimum; physical strength	$16.88 an hour; $35 230 a year plus substantial fringe benefits	empties garbage cans and bags into back of garbage truck	lifting 50 kg; unpleasant work
municipal transit drivers	grade 12; class B driver's licence	$32 000 a year plus fringe benefits of about $4900	operates bus, subway train, or street car to transport passengers	some risk
fourth class constable	grade 12 education; 15-week course	$36 960 a year; fringe benefits of about $6283 a year	enforces municipal laws and regulations and provincial and federal laws; arrests lawbreakers	risk; good vision required; height and weight "in proportion"

* Job descriptions and working conditions are adapted from *Jobs for your future. Bridging the Gap* (Toronto).

earned $1.3 million or more), while a plumber may earn about $46 000 to do a less enjoyable job? Why should a hockey player earn approximately five times the pay of a plumber? Let's explore this question by first investigating the market for plumbers.

Plumbers

Figure 8.2 represents the market for plumbers in a Canadian city. Here we assume that the market for plumbers' services is competitive. The graph tells us that the supply, 400 plumbers, equals the demand for plumbers in this city when the wage rate is $20 an hour. We can also see that a rate higher than $20 an hour, for example $25 an hour, would make plumbing more attractive so that more plumbers would want to enter the market. More plumbers would move into the area, former plumbers doing other things would be tempted to return to this occupation, and more apprentices would think of plumbing as a good trade to be in. Not only would the supply of plumbers increase with the higher rate, but demand would decrease because fewer people would be prepared to pay this higher rate for plumbing services. A surplus of plumbers would result in a tighter market, with all plumbers having to compete for work. The wage rate would start to fall.

Similarly, if the rate were less than $20 an hour, for example $15 an hour, fewer plumbers would be willing to work in the city. Plumbers would leave the occupation or move elsewhere. However, demand would increase because more people would be willing to pay this lower rate for plumbing services. The result would be a shortage of plumbers. Since supply would not meet demand, plumbers would see that they could charge more for their services and the rate would start to rise.

To sum up, we can see from the graph that supply and demand are in equilibrium when the wage per hour is at $20 an hour. With a wage at $25 an hour, 300 workers are demanded but 500 are supplied — there is a surplus. The wage will decline to $20 an hour. With the wage at $15 an hour, 450 workers will be demanded but only 350 supplied. Thus there is a

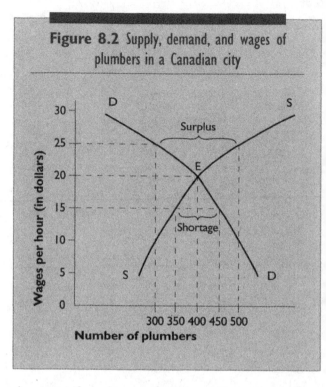

Figure 8.2 Supply, demand, and wages of plumbers in a Canadian city

shortage of workers and competition among those seeking their services will push the wage up to the equilibrium wage of $20 an hour.

Shifts in the demand for labour

As we saw in our examination of markets in Chapter 6, a demand curve shows the relationship between price and quantity. We saw, too, that when there is a change in the quantity demanded for reasons other than a variation in price, the demand curve shifts to the right with an increase in demand, and to the left with a decrease in demand. The same holds true for the demand for labour.

Suppose that, instead of growing, the population of a city is declining, incomes are diminishing, and fewer houses are needed. In this situation, the demand for plumbers will decrease. See figure 8.3. The demand curve for plumbers will shift from DD to D_1D_1. Wages will decrease from OP to OP_1, and the number of plumbers demanded will decline from OQ to OQ_1.

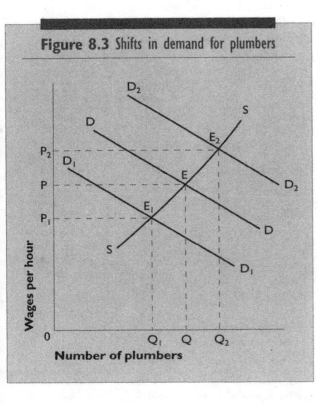

Figure 8.3 Shifts in demand for plumbers

Suppose that the population in a city is growing, incomes are generally rising, and more houses are needed. Builders see opportunities for profit and there is a building boom. In this situation, the services of plumbers are required to install plumbing in the new houses that are being built. The demand curve for plumbers will shift to the right in figure 8.3 from DD to D_2D_2, indicating an increase in the demand for plumbers. Wages will increase from OP to OP_2, and the number of plumbers employed will increase from OQ to OQ_2.

If the demand for plumbers decreases, for example, due to a decrease in the population of a city, the demand curve DD will shift down and to the left. The new equilibrium is at E_1 and the new wage is lower (at OP_1 compared to OP) and the quantity supplied is at OQ_1. If the demand for plumbers increases, for example, due to an increase in income, the demand curve will shift from D_1D_1 to D_2D_2, and the equilibrium to E_2.

Shifts in the supply of labour

There will be a decrease in the supply of plumbers if, for example, there is a significant increase in wages in similar occupations, such as carpentry and bricklaying, or if there is an increase in the pay of plumbers elsewhere. Those who want to train in one of the trades will be attracted to carpentry and bricklaying, and away from plumbing. As shown in figure 8.4 on page 162, the supply curve for plumbers will shift from SS to S_1S_1. With DD as the demand curve, the new equilibrium will shift from E to E_1. The number of plumbers will shift from OQ to OQ_1, and wages will increase from OP to OP_1.

There will be an increase in the supply of plumbers if the wages of plumbers decrease elsewhere, if there is a reduction in the number of years of apprenticeship to become a plumber, or if there is a decrease in the wages of similar occupations. The supply curve for plumbers will shift from SS to S_2S_2. The new equilibrium will be at E_2. Wages will decline from OP to OP_2 and the number of plumbers will increase from OQ to OQ_2.

Hockey players, plumbers, and others

Let's return to our question of why National Hockey League players are paid exceptionally well compared with plumbers.

As you would expect in a country in which hockey is a national sport, there is no shortage of hockey players in Canada. There is, however, a shortage of *exceptionally talented* hockey players. When it comes to hockey, Canadians have very high standards. It is only the truly outstanding hockey players who make it to the NHL. Hockey in Canada is a competitive, big business, spectator sport. The mass TV fans want a good show, and demand is high for players of the calibre of Pavel Buré and Patrick Roy. We could conclude that plumbers can make a good living because there is a demand for their services, but NHL hockey players can do much better because the demand from millions of fans is high for the limited supply of exceptional talent. Television raises the economic value of sports stars.

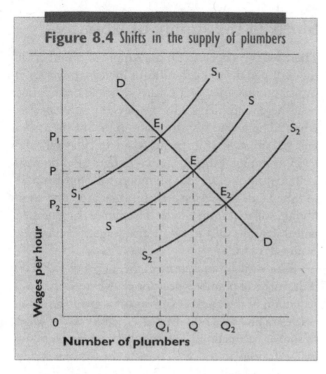

Figure 8.4 Shifts in the supply of plumbers

Wages per hour

Number of plumbers

Table 8.1 The minimum wage in Canada, 1994

	Age 18 and over hourly rate	Employees under 18
Federal	$4.00	no special rate established
Alberta	$5.00	$4.50
British Columbia	$6.00	$5.50
Manitoba	$5.00	no special rate
New Brunswick	$5.00	no special rate
Newfoundland	$4.75	minimum wage does not apply to employees under 16
Nova Scotia	$5.15	$4.55
Ontario Employee serving liquor on licensed premises	$6.70 $5.80	$6.25
Prince Edward Island	$4.75	no special rate
Quebec Employees who usually receive gratuities	$5.85 $5.13	no special rate
Saskatchewan	$5.35	no special rate
Northwest Territories	$6.50	$6.00
Yukon Territory	$6.24	no special rate

Source: *Canadian Labour Law Reports*, CCH Canadian Ltd., 1994.

Other factors affecting wages and salaries

So far we have considered how the forces of supply and demand interact in competitive labour markets to establish the price (wages and salaries) of labour. However, few labour markets are perfectly competitive. Some of the other influences we will examine include the influence of governments, labour unions, professional associations, the importance of large employers, mobility of labour, barriers to admission in certain trades or professions, and discrimination.

Government regulations

Government regulations influence the labour market. Both the federal and provincial governments have fixed minimum wage rates. See table 8.1. Employers cannot legally pay below the **minimum wage**. Governments also influence fringe benefits of workers, for example, in declaring certain days in the year as being holidays or in requiring employers to give employees a number of weeks holiday per year.

Labour unions

Wages and salaries are also affected by the activities of special interest groups, such as labour unions and professional associations. These collective organizations use their power to maintain or increase the salaries of their members, and to improve the working conditions. We will consider their effects in the next chapter.

Large employers

Unorganized workers in towns with a single large employer or a few large employers may be at a disadvantage. The large employer(s) may have considerable power to keep wages lower than if the market were competitive.

Commenting on the statistics in table 8.2 in the *Financial Post* for April 29, 1993, William Watson, professor of economics at McGill University in Montreal, wrote the following. Read his comments, then decide whether you agree with him.

... At the very bottom of Statistics Canada's salary list, below livestock farm workers, bartenders and service station attendants, came child-care workers, who in 1990 earned $13 518 on average (although for how many hours worked during the year was not stated).

A great fuss was made about this in the press. For some reason, livestock farm workers were singled out for attention. How unfair, it was widely proclaimed, for child-care workers to make less than livestock farm workers — although presumably it's more fun working with children than with livestock.

The local Montreal media interviewed a number of parents who agreed most emphatically that, yes, the people who took care of their children did excellent work and certainly should be paid more. As a new parent, I've already figured out that if a TV reporter asks me about the person who takes care of my child, and there's any chance that person owns a TV, I should be generous in my

Table 8.2 Who earns what

Ten highest paying jobs*	Average salary	% in job Men	% in job Women
Judges and magistrates	$102 646	78%	22%
Physicians and surgeons	102 370	77	23
Dentists	95 776	89	11
Lawyers and notaries	76 966	75	25
Senior managers	67 997	81	19
Other managers	64 893	75	25
Airline pilots, navigators and flight engineers	64 316	95	5
Osteopaths and chiropractors	64 299	82	18
Engineering and natural science managers	63 566	88	12
University teachers	62 064	78	22
Ten lowest paying jobs*			
Livestock farm workers	$16 600	64%	36%
Sewing machine and textile workers	16 540	9	91
Other workers in farming, horticulture and animal husbandry	16 227	55	45
Crop farm workers	16 191	51	49
Bartenders	16 067	46	54
Cleaners	15 718	13	87
Service station attendants	15 586	80	20
Housekeepers and servants	14 479	8	92
Food and beverage servers	14 100	22	78
Child-care workers	13 518	3	97

* full-year, full-time jobs
Source: Statistics Canada, 1991 census. Excerpted from *Toronto Star*, May 2, 1993.

Analyse the comic strip

Adam®   by Brian Basset

ANY LUCK GETTING SITTING FOR SATURDAY NIGHT?

ZERO.

PLOP

TRICIA CAN'T 'CAUSE SHE'S GETTING MARRIED, MEAGAN'S HAVING KNEE SURGERY FRIDAY, AND BRITT, BRITT'S PLAYING IN SOME FAR-AWAY JAZZ FESTIVAL WITH HER SCHOOL BAND.

WE GOTTA START PAYING MORE.

praise. But never mind that. If these parents really don't think the people caring for their children make enough money, why don't they pay them more? The answer, of course, is that they'd much prefer that you and I pay them more — out of our taxes.

If more people took economics, more people would understand that the market doesn't reward the intrinsic worth of what you do. It rewards your economic value. If you want to make money, don't choose an occupation lots of other people can do. A couple I know recently advertised for child-care services in a small local weekly newspaper. They got 65 replies in 24 hours. Yes, many child-care workers are wonderful with children. But as a profession they are, not quite literally, a dime a dozen.

If they want to make more money, they'll have to restrict their own supply — either by forming a union monopoly or, like us professors, by raising the credentials required to do the job.

Questions

1. What relationships are shown between pay, training, and percentage of men and women in an occupation in table 8.2?

2. Do you agree with Professor Watson's comments on the pay of child-care workers? Explain your answer.

Mobility of workers

The mobility of the labour force also influences wages. If there are high wages in one part of the country, then workers from other parts of the country will tend to move there, producing a "levelling out" of wage differences. How far the levelling out will go depends on the mobility of labour: the ability and willingness of workers to move from one area to another.

Other factors

Other factors may also result in wage differences. Barriers to entry into a trade or profession in the form of

specialized training will tend to result in higher wages. Discrimination against women and minorities in the past has meant that they have received lower pay for equal work compared to men and the majority. It has also meant that many well-paid trades and professions such as plumbing and law were largely closed to women. The possibility of promotion, too, was often limited for women and minorities. Frequently they encountered a glass ceiling — an invisible but real limit beyond which they could not go.

Interest income

If you have ever borrowed from a financial institution, you know that the price of borrowing is the interest you pay on the money borrowed.

Interest is the price paid to a lender for the use of a sum of money over a period of time.

Conversely, if you deposit your money in a savings account in a bank, you have, in effect, lent the bank your money and you are paid interest for its use. Interest is the price of borrowing money and, like anything else on the market, interest rates fluctuate because they are subject to the forces of supply and demand. But why do we borrow money and why do we lend it?

If you decide that you would like to buy an expensive item like a car, chances are that you will not have enough money on hand to pay for it all at once. However, you may be able to pay for it over the next couple of years. You are faced with a dilemma, similar to that of Elena in Chapter 1. Should you save up for the car and buy it later or go into debt to have it now? If you are like many Canadians, you may decide that it is worthwhile to buy the car now with borrowed funds even though in the long run you pay more than if you had waited and saved the whole amount. You are willing, then, to pay for the use of money so that you can have the use of the car immediately.

Many durable consumer goods such as cars, boats, and houses are purchased with borrowed money. Consumers are willing to pay a rate of interest in exchange for having goods or services immediately.

The same thinking is used by business people who might want to obtain money to purchase capital goods. Business people anticipate that the cost of borrowing will be recovered in the future interest earnings that will be made due to the increased capital investment in the business.

Governments may borrow for reasons similar to those of individuals. Governments may borrow to finance large-scale building projects such as roads, bridges, and dams.

Investment in machines and factories is not the only kind there is. Right now you are investing in yourself — acquiring human capital — through the acquisition of skills, training, and education. In many ways, your acquisition of human capital is similar to the investment in a factory: you reduce current consumption in the hope of a higher income in the future. You give up the income you would have if you were not studying. Students accept low wage rates to receive training that will give them a higher income in the future. Differences in wages very often reflect differences in the investment in human capital. Economists have found that investment in high school education has a high rate of return, similar to that of investment in other capital goods.

The amount of borrowing varies with the price of borrowing, that is, with the level of interest rates. High interest rates discourage businesses from borrowing because borrowing cuts into profit. High interest rates also discourage consumers from borrowing because borrowing cuts into their spending power. Low interest rates encourage borrowing by business and consumers.

Savings

Savings are that part of income that is not spent.

If no saving were done, there would be no money to borrow. The money loaned to borrowers comes mainly from three sources: individuals, business firms, and the banking system. In the case of individuals, money saved is the amount consumers do not spend now. They may be saving to spend at a later date or they may see nothing they immediately want to buy.

Businesses save to replace equipment that is wearing out, to build a reserve against future losses, or to finance future large-scale projects. These savings are deposited in banks and are a major source of loanable funds, as we shall see in Chapter 12.

Rental income

In everyday usage, rent is what you would pay for the use of someone else's property, such as a house or a car. To an economist, **rent** is payment for the use of a resource: land. In the economic sense, it means that if a merchant pays money for the use of a store, she is paying interest because the store is a capital good. Included in the payment, however, is the rent for the land the store stands on.

One thing that we have learned about land is that it is relatively fixed. This becomes apparent when we consider the value of land in the town or city. In every urban centre, there is one area where the crowds are thickest. This is the area of prime commercial land where stores, banks, and other commercial enterprises have the best market. Rents in the commercial hearts of cities are high because there is a demand for prime locations. Land used for stores and offices away from the crowds is less valuable.

Location is not the only factor affecting rents. If a farmer wants to rent agricultural land, the farmer would probably think first about the fertility of the soil. Just as there is prime commercial land, there is prime agricultural, industrial, and residential land, and rents reflect the high demand for the best land in each case.

Income from profits

The word profit, like the word rent, is used by economists in a way that differs from the common usage.

In economics, **profit** is what is left over after all the costs have been met from the income of a business.

Costs include all payments for goods and services used in production. Rent, wages, and interest payments are, of course, part of costs. For a clearer understanding of what an economist means by profit, let's take the example of Martha's Mini Mart.

Martha's Mini Mart makes a profit

Suppose that Martha is the owner of a small corner grocery. She owns the building that has a rental value of $5000 a year. She has supplied the $50 000 capital for the stock and fixtures and she is the only clerk in her grocery. Ten percent represents a fair return on capital invested in the grocery business. Martha knows that if she works in another grocery, she could receive $6000 a year. After paying all her expenses for this year, Martha has $20 000 for herself. Is this profit? To an economist the answer is no because Martha has not included the costs of all the services she used in her business. She has not included the service of her own labour ($6000), interest ($3000) on her capital investment of $50 000, or the rental value of her grocery store ($5000). From an economist's point of view, Martha's profit would be $20 000 minus the total cost of the services of labour, capital, and land that she herself supplied to her own business. These services are valued at $14 000, so Martha's economic profit is $6000.

Though Martha made a profit this year, it is clear that there is nothing automatic about it as there usually is when you work for a salary. As a worker, when you've completed the allotted task or time, you receive an income that was set at the time you were hired. With Martha and other people in business, there is risk involved. Another year, Martha might take a loss. A large supermarket could open just across the street or Maria could open her Mini Mart right next door to Martha's. The city council could ban parking near Martha's store. The population in Martha's area could start to decline or people could suffer widespread unemployment. All of these factors could act to reduce or eliminate Martha's profits.

Why is there profit?

Profit is the reward or return to the entrepreneur for undertaking the risk of establishing and operating a business. Each investment decision made by entrepreneurs has an element of risk. Business people cannot know in advance how consumers will react to their products or how future government legislation will affect them. Profit is the reward for the entrepreneur's efficient combination of the factors of production and the successful anticipation of the wants of consumers.

Profits may also result when businesses act to restrain competition and raise prices. There is legislation that prohibits such practices and government will intervene to prosecute those who breach the law.

Profit is the prime mover in our economy. Its primary function is to motivate people to assume the risk of establishing and operating a business. Without the attraction of profit, people would choose to put their savings where they are safe rather than investing in risky ventures.

When business is most responsive to the wishes of the consumer, profits tend to be high. Profits encourage entrepreneurs to innovate — to bring in new methods of production and new products. Innovation stimulates employment, investment, and output, and is one of the principal causes of economic growth. As costs are diminished by new production methods and revenues are increased from the sale of new products, profits rise.

CIRCULAR FLOW

There is a flow of expenditures from households to businesses going through the product market, and a parallel flow of consumer goods and services going through the final goods market to households. See figure 8.5 on page 167.

There is also a flow of productive resources — land, labour, capital, and entrepreneurial skill — from households to businesses. The prices and quantities of these resources are determined in factor markets. To pay for the productive resources, there is a flow of money from businesses through the factor markets to households. This flow of money represents the income of households — the owners of the four factors of production — and is made up of wages, rent, interest, and profits.

WHO RECEIVES HOW MUCH?

The Gross Domestic Product (GDP)

To answer the question who receives how much, we need to know how much was produced. Just as you or I like to know how much we earned last year and how much we earned last month and whether our earnings are increasing or decreasing, so governments, economists, politicians, and many others like to know how much the country earned last year and last month and whether the country's earnings are increasing or not. One of the measures that is most commonly used for the total amount of goods and services produced in a particular period of time is called the Gross Domestic Product (GDP). This is one of the most widely quoted statistics.

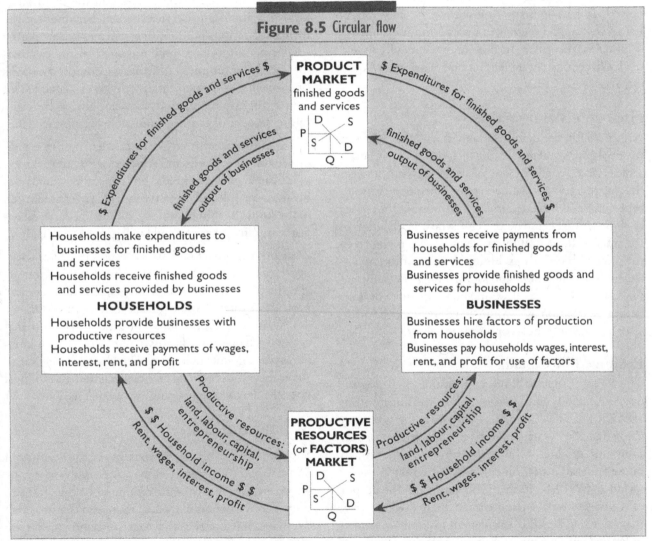

Figure 8.5 Circular flow

To the circular flow we last saw on page 131, we add the productive resources (or factors) market and the money flow from businesses to households. Households sell their productive services (of labour, land, capital, and entrepreneurial skill) through the productive resources market to households. In return, households receive income in the form of rent, wages, interest, and profit.

Gross Domestic Product measures the total value at market prices of all final goods and services produced in Canada over a period of time (usually a year). But why do we emphasize the value at *market prices?* why *final* goods and services? and why *produced in Canada?*

Value at market prices

Our economy produces a huge array of goods and services — airline flights, dental care, and apples are only three among many thousands. The only way in which we can add them is to find a common standard — their market price. In this way we can add apples, teeth extractions, airline flights, and most other things our economy produces.

Final goods and services

Notice that in the definition only the market prices of the final goods and services are included. By final goods and services are meant only those goods and services that are not going to be sold again. The price of bread, for example, is included in the GDP, but not the price of flour and wheat. The price of wheat is included in the price of flour, and the price of flour is included in the price of bread. By excluding the cost of intermediate goods (such as flour and wheat), we avoid counting the same thing twice. If we included the price of flour in our calculation we would have included it twice, once as flour and the second time as wheat.

Produced in Canada

The Gross *Domestic* Product measures the *domestic* output of goods and services, that is, the output from *within* Canada — no matter who owns the product, Canadian, American, Japanese or whoever. The Gross Domestic Product (GDP) differs from another much quoted measure used in the past — Gross *National* Product (GNP) — in that GNP calculates the output of *Canadian-owned* resources no matter where they may be, while the GDP calculates the output domiciled or located within Canada. Because outsiders own more of Canadian industry than Canadians own of industries outside Canada, since 1926 (when Statistics Canada began making the calculations), GDP has always been 3 to 5 percent higher than GNP.

Our circular flow diagram has two halves: a flow of income and a flow of expenditures. Two ways of calculating the total value of output are shown in figure 8.6. We can measure the upper money flow in the diagram (the expenditures on goods and services) or we can measure the lower money flow (the incomes generated in production). Expenditures by households on goods and services become income for the owners of various productive resources. In calculating total expenditures and total incomes, we are calculating the same amount — the market value of a nation's final output — in two different ways. In practice, of course, the two calculations may not give us the same figure because of errors or omissions we might make.

1. Expenditure approach   In calculating the expenditures on final goods and services, we include the expenditures of households on consumer goods, of business people on investment, of government on many kinds of things, and the difference between exports and imports. The total will give us the GDP.

2. Income approach   This is a second way of calculating the size of the income flow to households. Here we add the total amount paid in wages, rent, interest, and profit. The total amount will also give us the GDP.

What is the proportionate distribution of GDP that goes to each one of the factors of production? GDP overstates the amounts that are received by the four factors. Allowances must be made for **depreciation** and **indirect taxes**. In the following discussion, we will see why.

Wheatland I

Suppose we are the sole inhabitants of the country of Wheatland. We produce only one crop — wheat — which we eat raw, without cooking or baking. Wheat, then, is our only final product. Suppose that this year we plant 500 bushels of wheat seed and we harvest 500 bushels of wheat. What is our GDP? Well, since wheat is the only final product, it is 500 bushels. However, if we wish to eat next year, we should set aside

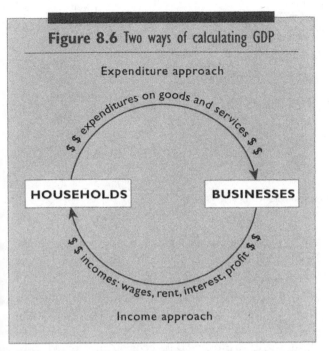

Figure 8.6 Two ways of calculating GDP

Expenditure approach

$ $ expenditures on goods and services $ $

HOUSEHOLDS   **BUSINESSES**

$ $ incomes: wages, rent, interest, profit $ $

Income approach

We can calculate GDP either by adding together all the expenditures on goods and services (the top loop), or by adding all incomes — wages, rent, interest, and profit (the bottom loop).

50 bushels of wheat and consume no more than 450 bushels of wheat. The amount of fifty bushels represents what is used up in the process of production, for example, as seed. This is what we have to replace, if we are to continue production. Therefore, 450 bushels is a better measure of our output than 500 bushels.

How does Wheatland relate to Canada? In the process of production, machinery and buildings slowly wear out or depreciate. In Wheatland, fifty bushels of wheat seed were used up in the production. To arrive at

a reasonable estimate of how GDP is distributed among the productive factors, we must deduct an amount equal to the cost of the capital equipment (buildings and machinery) used up in production or, in other words, allow for **capital depreciation**.

Wheatland II

Let's suppose that Wheatland grows and prospers. With this prosperity, Wheatland starts to use money. Wheat is bought by consumers for $1 a bushel. As conditions improve, Wheatland acquires a government and, as you would expect, taxes. Suppose that Wheatland's government levies on the farmers a tax of $.10 per bushel of wheat produced. Wheat farmers decide to add $.10 to the cost of the wheat they sell to the wholesaler, and the wholesalers decide to pass the $.10 tax on, so now the consumers will pay $1.10 a bushel.

Taxes, like the wheat tax, that are shifted from one person to another are called **indirect taxes**. The imposition of the tax did not increase the output of goods and services but it did increase GDP by 10 percent. Therefore, to arrive at a realistic figure for the income of the factors of production in Wheatland, we would deduct this sales tax.

After making some adjustments for statistical discrepancy, the deduction of depreciation and indirect taxes from GDP leaves us with domestic income. ("Statistical discrepancy" refers to the errors and omissions that occur when calculating the GDP.) See figure 8.7.

The returns to the four productive factors constitute domestic income. Unfortunately, Statistics Canada does not collect data in a way that would show

Figure 8.7 GDP and domestic income (in millions of dollars), 1992

GDP		Domestic income		Indirect taxes		Depreciation		Statistical discrepancy
688 541	=	518 408	+	84 800	+	82 373	+	2960

Source: Statistics Canada, *Canadian Economic Observer, Historical Statistical Supplement,* 1992-93.

Figure 8.8 Net domestic income at factor cost (millions of dollars and percentages, and simplified),* 1992

Net domestic income at factor cost		Wages and salaries		Corporate profits		Interest and investment income		Unincorporated business income
$518 408	=	392 353	+	31 928	+	56 491	+	37 736
Percentages								
100	=	75	+	6	+	11	+	7

* Numbers may not add due to rounding

Source: Statistics Canada, *Canadian Economic Observer, Historical Statistical Supplement*, 1992-93.

precisely the share of the national income that goes to each of the factors. An approximate estimate of these shares is shown in figure 8.8.

The wages and salaries share of domestic income at about 70 to 75 percent has been a relatively stable proportion of domestic income over many years. In addition, perhaps half of the income of *unincorporated* business may include wages and salaries. As we saw in the case of Martha's Mini Mart, much of the income of her business was payment for her own labour. Roughly between 74 and 80 percent of the national income goes to the productive factor of labour (which includes, of course, the return on human capital that goes to skilled workers). The remaining 20 to 26 percent represents payments of rent, interest, and profit.

INCOME INEQUALITY

In the 1993-94 season, the annual salary paid to the goalie, Patrick Roy, under his contract with the Montréal Canadiens was $3 500 000. In addition to his salary from the Canadiens, Roy was earning more money from other activities connected to his celebrity status with the Canadiens. Roy was not alone; many other sports personalities had salaries over a million dollars a year — at least 69 of them in hockey alone.

In 1992, in Canada, the average annual income of a family was $53 676. This is one of the highest average family incomes in the world. It is obvious that

there are substantial differences in incomes in Canada. How much income inequality is there? As you can see from tables 8.3 and 8.4 (on pages 171 and 172), 2.4 percent of families and 25.7 percent of unattached individuals (persons living alone) had incomes less than $10 000 a year in 1992, while over 40 percent of families and just over 10 percent of unattached individuals had incomes over $50 000 a year.

The Lorenz curve

Another way of indicating the distribution of Canadian incomes is shown in figure 8.10. You can see that the lowest 20 percent of the population gets 6.3 percent of total income, while the highest 20 percent gets almost 40 percent.

This inequality in income can be illustrated with a Lorenz curve. The income distribution (column X) can be rearranged into the cumulative income distribution (column Y). For example, in the first row the cumulative population is 20 + 20 percent, or 40 percent, and the share of total income is 6.3 + 12.2, or 18.5 percent. See figure 8.10 on page 171.

To get an idea of what the Lorenz curve shows, consider what the curve would look like if there were complete equality of income, i.e., when any 20 percentage of Canadian families received 20 percent of total income. The "lowest" 20 percent of the population would receive 20 percent (R on figure 8.9) instead of receiving only 6.3 percent (point A on figure 8.9) of

Figure 8.9 Income distribution of Canadian families

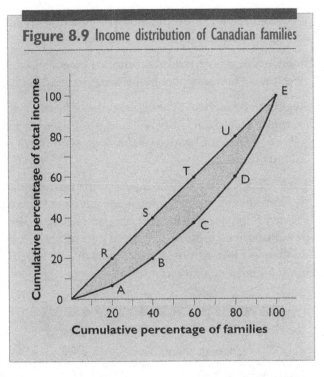

total income. Similarly, with complete equality, the "lowest" 40 percent would be at 5 instead of at B. Complete equality is shown by the diagonal line ORSTUE which is at an angle of 45 degrees. The degree of inequality is shown by the amount of "bow" in the Lorenz curve, OABCDE, or by the amount in the "slice" between the curve and the diagonal line.

Table 8.3 Percentage distribution of families by income groups, 1992

Income group ($)	Percent
under $10 000	2.4
10 000–14 999	3.8
15 000–19 999	5.9
20 000–24 999	7.5
25 000–29 999	6.7
30 000–34 999	6.6
35 000–39 999	7.1
40 000–44 999	6.3
45 000–49 999	6.6
50 000–54 999	6.6
55 000–59 999	5.9
60 000–64 999	5.5
65 000–69 999	4.6
70 000–74 999	4.0
75 000–79 999	3.2
80 000–89 999	5.5
90 000–99 999	3.8
100 000 and over	7.9
Average income	53 676
Median income	47 719

Source: Statistics Canada, *Income Distribution by Size in Canada*, 1992.

Figure 8.10 Percentage distribution of total income of Canadian families

Income distribution (X)			Cumulative income distribution (Y)			
Population		Share of total income	Population		Share of total income	Point on figure
Lowest 20 percent	gets	6.3 percent	First 20 percent	gets	6.3	A
Second 20 percent	gets	12.2 percent	First 40 percent	gets	6.3 + 12.2 = 18.5	B
Third 20 percent	gets	17.8 percent	First 60 percent	gets	18.5 + 17.8 = 36.3	C
Fourth 20 percent	gets	24.0 percent	First 80 percent	gets	36.3 + 24.0 = 60.3	D
Highest 20 percent	gets	39.7 percent	Total	gets	60.3 + 39.7 = 100.0	E

Source: Statistics Canada, *Family Incomes*, 1992.

Causes of income inequality

In our examination of the factors of production, we saw that the returns to the factors were largely determined by the forces of supply and demand. These market forces are impersonal, uninfluenced by any notion of what is "just" or "fair." In Canada, there is considerable variation in personal incomes. Some of the factors contributing to income inequality are summarized below.

Natural ability   We are born with different mental, physical, and artistic abilities. The professional athlete is a good example of an individual who is highly rewarded for physical ability. Natural ability puts some people in a preferred position to draw very large incomes.

Education, training, and opportunity   The opportunity to acquire training and education for a particular occupation is available to all. Opportunities to invest in human capital are not as readily available to the poor as to the affluent.

Property ownership   Property is anything owned — land, buildings, machinery, funds, shares, etc. Income from property takes the form of rent, interest, and/or profit. A study of Canadian families and unattached individuals revealed that the poorest 20 percent of Canadians had debts equal to or greater than their assets. The richest 10 percent of the population had assets greater than the total assets of the other 90 percent of the population. It stands to reason that, because ownership of property is unequal, then the potential to make income from property would be unequal.

Ability to influence wages and salaries   As we have seen in our examination of different markets, there are a number of ways in which businesses can work together to restrict competition and force up prices and, therefore, profits. Similarly, labour unions and professional associations can act to restrict admission to trades or professions, thereby protecting members and influencing income. As we shall see in the next chapter, workers have been able to increase their bargaining power and their salaries by forming unions.

Discrimination   Discrimination against women and minorities may result in lower incomes.

Poor health or physical disability   Some people are unable to work due to poor health or physical disabilities.

Region of residence   Certain regions of Canada, for example, Ontario and British Columbia, have tended to have higher employment and incomes compared to Atlantic Canada.

Luck   Luck seems to play a part in income inequality. Some people might suffer as a result of sickness or accident. Someone else might happen to have a piece of land on which oil is discovered and someone else might win a lottery. Often, luck seems to mean "being in the right place at the right time."

Table 8.4 Percentage distribution of unattached individuals by income groups, 1992

Income group Current dollars ($)	Percent
2 000–4 999	12.4
5 000–7 499	6.4
7 500–9 999	6.9
10 000–12 499	8.2
12 500–14 999	6.8
15 000–17 499	5.7
17 500–19 999	4.7
20 000–22 499	5.1
22 500–24 999	4.4
25 000–29 999	8.3
30 000–34 999	7.1
35 000–39 999	5.8
40 000–44 999	4.5
45 000–49 999	3.4
50 000 and over	10.2

Source: Statistics Canada, *Income Distribution by Size in Canada*, 1992.

Weeks worked   Workers who are employed fifty-two weeks of the year receive an annual salary. For those employed in the forestry, farming, or fishing industries, work may be seasonal and incomes limited to certain periods of the year.

Age   On the average, individuals' incomes rise steadily until they reach the age of forty-five. This rise is due to the increase in workers' skills and experience. After their mid-forties, workers have probably peaked in terms of skills and experience. Older workers may decide to retire early or take a less demanding job.

Government anti-poverty programs

When we think of government anti-poverty programs, those that often come to mind are the old age security pension, unemployment insurance, and welfare. However, these programs only deal with the symptoms of poverty, not the causes. They aim to make poverty more bearable by providing an income. They do not hold out much hope that poverty will be cured, or that the poor will be able to provide themselves with an adequate income. However, these programs may be the only income for the aged, the chronically sick, and the unemployed worker.

A more promising approach is to attack the causes of poverty itself. Such programs include those to reduce the rate of unemployment, and to encourage the development of education and skills.

Programs to reduce the causes of poverty

Governments undertake a number of programs that are intended to reduce the extent of poverty by attacking it at its root.

Governments encourage the **investment in human capital**. Local and provincial governments pay the full cost of instruction in primary and secondary schools. Since education is free, more students finish high school. Provincial governments also pay much of the instructional costs of community colleges and universities, as well as providing loans and grants for post-secondary students.

Government programs to keep the economy operating at a high level also help reduce poverty by providing employment. Government safety programs help protect workers from injuries at the workplace. Provincial health insurance programs are available at little or no cost to the user.

Government and distribution

In addition to programs that are intended to reduce poverty, there are programs that give relief from the symptoms of poverty. These kinds of programs are of two types: social insurance programs in which the whole population is included — rich and poor alike — and those programs specifically targeted for the poor alone.

1. Social insurance programs

To help reduce some of the inequalities of income in our market system, to diminish poverty in the country, and to protect Canadians from the costs associated with sickness, old age, and unemployment, Canadian governments have developed a number of social security programs.

Health insurance

In Canada, we have a health insurance program that provides much of the health care (except for dental care) needed by citizens at little or no cost to the patient. The services are paid for by federal and provincial governments from general taxation.

Unemployment insurance

Introduced in 1940 and greatly expanded in 1971 to cover most of the workforce, unemployment insurance aims to diminish the financial hardship caused by unemployment. The federal government paid unemployment benefits to a maximum of $429 per week in 1994. The amount paid varies with the individual's salary before being unemployed. Benefits may be claimed after an individual has worked a minimum of 12 weeks. Benefits, on average, may be paid to claimants up to a maximum of 32 weeks. Contributions to the scheme are made by the employee and the employer.

Canada and Quebec Pension Plans (C.P.P. and Q.P.P.)

The Canada and Quebec Pension Plans are funded by compulsory employer and employee contributions, varying with amount earned. Benefits from the plan (to a maximum of $694 per month in 1994) are payable when the individual reaches age sixty-five. Like the old age security pension, pensions from C.P.P. and Q.P.P. increase as the cost of living increases.

2. Programs specifically for the poor

The above programs are available to all people. While they may help some poor people, they are not aimed specifically at those with lower incomes. The following programs are.

Old age security pension (OAS)

Upon reaching age sixty-five and having been a resident in Canada for at least ten years, Canadians are eligible for the old age security pension. In 1994, the basic pension was $385.81 per month. This sum increases automatically as the cost of living rises. For those with higher income (above about $53 000 net income in 1994) the federal government claws back an increasing proportion of the pension. The plan is entirely paid for by federal tax revenues.

Guaranteed income supplement

The federal government started the guaranteed income supplement for pensioners on a limited income apart from the old age security pension. Maximum amounts payable in 1994 were $458.50 for a single person and $597.30 for a couple who are both receiving the old age security pension.

Child tax benefit

After half a century, the universal baby bonus or family allowance came to an end as of January 1, 1994, to be replaced by an income tested program — a system whereby more assistance is given to the working poor and families with modest incomes.

Figure 8.11 Incidence of low income among families and unattached individuals by selected characteristics, 1992

	Families	Unattached individuals
All families and unattached individuals	12.1	30.1
By education of head		
0–8 years	17.3	47.3
Some secondary education	17.4	35.3
Graduated from high school	12.2	25.5
Some post-secondary	12.1	39.9
Post-secondary certificate or diploma	9.3	22.2
University degree	5.1	16.0
By number of children under 16 years		
None	8.1	30.1
One child	16.6	. . .
Two children	15.1	. . .
Three or more children	22.3	. . .
By province of residence		
Atlantic Provinces	17.3	43.2
Newfoundland	22.6	43.6
Prince Edward Island	11.3	38.3
Nova Scotia	16.9	45.3
New Brunswick	14.8	40.9
Québec	12.7	37.3
Ontario	9.9	23.0
Prairie Provinces	14.0	32.6
Manitoba	12.8	37.4
Saskatchewan	16.1	34.8
Alberta	13.7	29.9
British Columbia	11.2	25.7
By age of head		
Under 65 years	13.1	30.6
24 years and under	38.6	50.8
25–34 years	17.3	20.4
35–44 years	11.4	23.5
45–54 years	8.3	31.5
55–64 years	11.5	38.6
55–59 years	10.3	38.9
60–64 years	12.8	38.4
65 years and over	6.3	28.8
65–69 years	7.0	25.5
70 years and over	5.9	29.9
By sex and age of head		
Male	8.3	26.7
Under 65 years	8.8	27.8
65 years and over	5.2	19.9
Female	38.7	33.2
Under 65 years	42.9	34.1
65 years and over	14.1	31.9

Source: Statistics Canada, *Income Distribution by Size in Canada*, 1992.

Mothers or single fathers with custody of children receive the allowance for children under 18 years of age. The bonus, though part of a parent's income, is tax free. Families on welfare receive the annual $1020 (in 1993) benefit per child on a monthly basis. The working poor will receive an earned income supplement of up to $500 a year. As family income increases, the family allowance decreases — disappearing completely for a family earning $75 000 a year.

Low income is more likely to exist in families where the head of the family has little education and is very young, where there are many children in the family, where the family is located in Atlantic Canada, and where the head of the family is female.

Canada Assistance Plan

For those not adequately covered by any of the above programs, there is the comprehensive public assistance measure called the Canada Assistance Plan. Those covered under the plan include people who are blind or disabled, unmarried mothers, needy mothers and dependent children, and needy people in special homes for the aged. Half of the costs of the plan are met by the federal government, while the other half comes from provincial sources.

ISSUE
Who is poor?

A bitter debate continues in Canada over the definition of poverty. The debate centres around three different definitions:

1. The minimum level of income that is required to adequately feed, clothe, and shelter a Canadian family. This definition of poverty is suggested by economics Professor Christopher Sarlo of Nipissing University, North Bay, Ontario. Professor Sarlo sets his poverty line at $15 067 (in 1992) for a family of four in a mid-sized Canadian city. Of this, $12 000 is dedicated to food and shelter, leaving $3 000 for everything else. According to this definition, "less than 2 percent of Canada's population lives in poverty." For Professor Sarlo, the "estimates of the extent of poverty in Canada are grossly exaggerated. Poverty as it has traditionally been understood has been virtually eliminated in Canada." Professor Sarlo has been accused of "drawing [his poverty line] one calorie above starvation."

2. A standard that defines what a Canadian needs to live in dignity among other Canadians. This standard was suggested by a House of Commons sub-committee (composed only of Conservatives) headed by Conservative MP Barbara Greene. The committee recommended that a menu of "basic needs" be created which would include food, shelter, clothing, reading material, furniture, school supplies, child care for one-parent families, some ability to give to others, and some entertainment which would include cable TV. This stable standard would remain unchanged from year to year with only the prices of the essentials changing. Greene's committee therefore takes into consideration Canada's high standard of living. Differences in the cost of living in various parts of Canada would be taken into account. Thus the poverty line in Montreal would be between $18 000 and $22 000, and in Toronto between $21 000 and $25 000. Some estimate that using the definition of the Greene committee would cut the number of the poor between 40 and 60 percent.

3. Statistics Canada's Low Income Cut-Off (L.I.C.O.) is a *relative* measure closely tied to the average income and consumption patterns of Canadians. L.I.C.O. was developed by Statistics Canada in 1961 when researchers estimated that the average family spent 50 percent of its income on the essentials: food, clothing, and shelter. Adding 20 percent to this amount, they decided that any family whose income was so low that it would need to spend 70 percent or more on the three essentials (food, clothing, and shelter) would be classified as low income.

Since 1961, the incomes of Canadians in terms of what they can buy have risen steadily and the amount spent on essentials has continued to decline: to 42 percent in 1969; 38.5 percent in 1978; 36.2 percent in 1986; 34.7 percent in 1992. To each of these figures Statistics Canada added 20 percent — just as it did in 1961 to reach the Low Income Cut-Off.

Statistic Canada's L.I.C.O. is widely used by many as the poverty line — although Statistics Canada actually objects to this usage.

Questions

1. In reviewing the three measures of poverty, what effect would each one have on the percentage and number of Canadians defined as poor?

2. In your opinion, which one is the best measure of poverty? Explain why.

The poor

The question of how income should be distributed becomes particularly tough to answer when there is poverty in a country. Statistics Canada defines low income as the situation of a family spending 54.7 percent or more of its income on food, clothing, and shelter. This 54.7 percent "cut-off" or poverty line is related both to family size and area of residence. For example, in 1977 a person living alone in a rural area with an annual income of less than $3231 was considered to have low income, as was a big city dweller with an income of less than $4446. A rural family of four with an income of less than $7110, and an urban family of four with an income of less than $9778, were also considered to be below the low income line.

Using the Statistics Canada definition, about 12 percent of families and 30 percent of unattached individuals were below the low income line in 1992. That amounted to almost $4\frac{1}{2}$ million Canadians (about 16 percent of the total population). Of these, approximately $1\frac{1}{4}$ million were children under the age of eighteen and 625 000 were sixty-five years of age and older (about 1 in 5). In family types, female single-parent families had one of the highest rates of low income in 1992 — at 57.2 percent. This proportion had not changed much since 1982.

Low income trends in the 1980s and early 1990s

In general, the proportion of poor Canadians increased during the economic slowdown of the early 1980s up until 1984, then declined to 1989, but increased again during the economic slowdown of the early 1990s. The proportion of poor Canadians was 16.8 percent (about 1 in 6) in 1992. This represented an increase from the 14 percent of 1989, but a decrease from 18.7 percent — the high for the 1980s. The low income rate for children less than 18 was 18.9 percent in 1992. This percentage was an increase from the 14.9 percent in 1989 but it was less than the 1980s' high of 20.6 percent in 1984.

Table 8.5 Regional and provincial family income, 1992		
Province and region	Average annual income	Percent of national averages
Canada	53 676	100
Atlantic Canada	45 456	85
Newfoundland and Labrador	42 114	78
Prince Edward Island	44 358	83
Nova Scotia	46 872	87
New Brunswick	46 532	87
Québec	48 592	91
Ontario	58 813	110
Prairie provinces	52 287	97
Manitoba	50 262	94
Saskatchewan	48 179	90
Alberta	54 683	102
British Columbia	56 390	105

Source: Statistics Canada, *Income Distribution by Size in Canada*, 1992.

Average family incomes vary considerably in Canada among regions and, even more widely, among provinces — with a low of $42 114 in Newfoundland and Labrador to a high of $58 813 in Ontario in 1992.

Causes of regional income inequality

While family incomes (adjusted for inflation) varied little between 1980 and 1987, there were significant variations in income among the various regions of Canada. Average annual incomes in Atlantic Canada in 1992 were lower than those in any other region in Canada, as they had been for many years. The Atlantic provinces also had all the lowest provincial incomes in Canada, with Newfoundland and Labrador having the lowest income of all. The highest provincial incomes in 1992 were to be found in Ontario and British Columbia. See table 8.5.

A number of factors have tended to bring about the income inequality among regions and provinces. In Atlantic Canada, a smaller proportion of the total population has been of working age (fourteen to sixty-four) than in British Columbia or Ontario. This can result from workers leaving the region to live in areas where the employment prospects are better. Of those of working age, the participation rate (number of persons in the work force or looking for work) was relatively low. The low participation rate is probably due, in large measure, to the limited number of employment opportunities.

The rate of unemployment in the Atlantic provinces and Québec has tended to be significantly higher than the national average. The depletion of fish stocks, especially the northern cod, and the consequent prohibition of fishing off much of the coast of Atlantic Canada have brought widespread unemployment to many fishing communities — especially in Newfoundland and Labrador. The prospects for the replenishment of the fish stocks and the development of alternative employment look equally bleak. These regions have a smaller-than-average percentage of the labour force that has had post-secondary education. These four factors — age composition, participation rate, unemployment rate, and level of educational attainment — account for some regional inequalities.

Natural advantages, such as fertile lands and rich mineral and energy resources of the Prairies and British Columbia, have helped raise incomes per person in these areas. The advantage of large populations centred in and around metropolitan areas continue to attract investment and industry because of the advantages of large markets.

In order to spur economic growth in the poorer areas of the country, the federal government has subsidized the rates of freight travelling from Eastern Canada to Central and Western Canada. Similarly, western grain producers have been assisted by lower freight rates of grain travelling to the West Coast. The federal government provides grants and loans to certain designated areas. These areas have been selected because of their high unemployment, low income levels, and slow rate of economic growth. As well, provincial governments have programs designed to promote the economic health of low income areas of their provinces.

REVIEW

Explain each term or concept in your own words with an example: distribution, wages, interest, rent, profit, gross domestic product, minimum wage, depreciation, indirect taxes, national income, the circular flow, income inequality, the poor, human capital.

APPLICATIONS

1. Why are (a) consumers and (b) business people willing to pay interest on borrowed money?
2. What factors determine the rent of land?
3. In what way does the common meaning of "profit" differ from the economist's use of the word?
4. Why is profit essential to the functioning of a mixed market economy?
5. a) Complete table 8.6 on page 179.
   b) Using the information in table 8.6, draw a Lorenz curve. *(For part c), see page 180.)*

Analyse the cartoon

SUMMARY

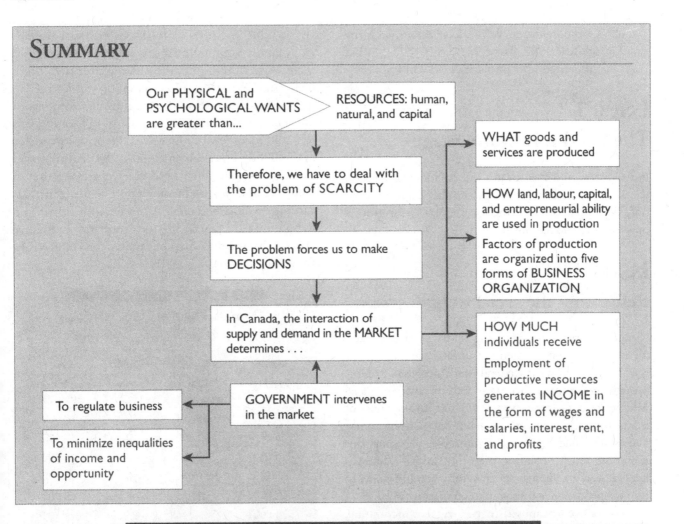

Our PHYSICAL and PSYCHOLOGICAL WANTS are greater than...

RESOURCES: human, natural, and capital

Therefore, we have to deal with the problem of SCARCITY

The problem forces us to make DECISIONS

In Canada, the interaction of supply and demand in the MARKET determines . . .

GOVERNMENT intervenes in the market

To regulate business

To minimize inequalities of income and opportunity

WHAT goods and services are produced

HOW land, labour, capital, and entrepreneurial ability are used in production

Factors of production are organized into five forms of BUSINESS ORGANIZATION

HOW MUCH individuals receive

Employment of productive resources generates INCOME in the form of wages and salaries, interest, rent, and profits

Table 8.6 Percentage distribution of total income of Canadian families, 1985

Income distribution (X)			Cumulative income distribution (Y)		
Population		Share of total income	Population		Share of total income
Lowest 20 percent	gets	6.3 percent	First 20 percent	gets	
Second 20 percent	gets	12.3 percent	First 40 percent	gets	
Third 20 percent	gets	17.9 percent	First 60 percent	gets	
Fourth 20 percent	gets	24.1 percent	First 80 percent	gets	
Highest 20 percent	- gets	39.4 percent	Total	gets	

Source: Statistics Canada, *Family Incomes*, 1985.

c) Compare the curve you have drawn with the one for 1992 (figure 8.9, page 171). What differences and similarities do you notice?

ISSUE 1
The legal minimum wage

Individually, and then in groups, decide whether you think the legal minimum wage should be abolished or not. Be prepared to outline for the class your group's opinion and the reasons for it.

ISSUE 2
Reforming the social welfare system

Mounting criticism and rising levels of welfare payments and unemployment insurance payouts, combined with growing federal and provincial debts brought governments to examine the Canadian social welfare system — the social safety net. In the views of many, the social safety net of unemployment insurance and welfare had become a comfortable hammock for many on which to snooze their time away. What was needed was to change the net into a trampoline to bounce people back into gainful employment.

It has been proposed that a negative income tax (NIT) be established to reform our present social welfare system. One way of implementing this scheme would be to use the present federal income tax system to channel funds to those below the poverty line. At present, income tax is paid only by individuals above a certain income level. Advocates of the NIT propose that the tax system be modified so that Canadians with incomes below the poverty line would receive payments from the government through the income tax system. The advantage of the NIT is that it provides families with a minimum income without destroying the incentive to work. See table 8.7 for an illustration of how NIT would work.

In table 8.7, $10 000 is the poverty line for a family. A family with no income would receive a negative income tax of $10 000, thus raising it to the poverty line. A family with earnings of $5000 would receive a negative income tax of $7 500, thus increasing its total income to $12 500. Similarly, a family with $10 000 income would receive a negative income tax of $5000 for a total income of $15 000. Families with earnings of $20 000 would receive no negative income tax and pay no income tax. Their incomes and earnings would be equal. A family with earnings of $25 000 would pay $2500 in income tax and receive no negative income tax. The family's total after-tax income would equal $22 500.

Table 8.7 Negative income tax plan
Col 4 = Col 1 + Col 2 + Col 3

Col 1	Col 2	Col 3	Col 4
Private earnings	Negative income tax	Income tax	Total income after tax
0	+ 10 000	0	10 000
5 000	+ 7 500	0	12 500
10 000	+ 5 000	0	15 000
15 000	+ 2 500	0	17 500
20 000	0	0	20 000
25 000	0	– 2 500	22 500

Notice that, with the negative income tax, the family has an incentive to go on earning more. As family earnings increase, the family's after-tax total income increases.

Note, too, that our example is merely an illustration. Clearly we can change the poverty line as necessary and we can adjust up or down the incentives to work. (In our example, total income increased by 50 percent of earned income.)

Supporters of the NIT plan suggest that it would replace all welfare programs including programs of subsidized housing.

The NIT in Canada

In the 1970s, Canada undertook a multi-million dollar, multi-year experimental test in which 1300 Canadian families were given a guaranteed income (or a negative income tax) for a number of years. The results showed that fears that the negative income tax would result in a widespread withdrawal from the workforce were unfounded.

Under a three-year experimental program in New Brunswick launched in the early 1990s, more than 1300 single parents get a special income supplement from the federal government, which boosts their earnings from minimum wage jobs and other low-paying work that would normally be less attractive than welfare. The payments from the federal government are 50 percent of the difference between their wages and a target income of $30 000. This experiment is similar to the negative income tax plan outlined in table 8.7, with the main exception that the target income is higher — $30 000 rather than $20 000.

Premier Clyde Wells of Newfoundland also concluded that the system of welfare and unemployment insurance in his province needed a radical overhaul. Here's how his proposal would work:

1. Every adult in Newfoundland and Labrador would be guaranteed a basic income of $3000 annually and every child $1500, totalling $9000 for a family of four.

2. Any income received from any low-paying job would be supplemented by a bonus of 20 percent, up to a maximum of $10 500. Thus there would be an incentive to work as many weeks as possible.

3. The guaranteed basic income would be gradually reduced when a family's income reaches $15 000 and eliminated entirely when family income reaches $42 500.

Thus, Premier Wells' proposal of a guaranteed annual income — or a negative income tax — bore many features similar to our simple negative income tax proposal.

Advantages of the NIT

1. It can replace much of the present welfare schemes that destroy the incentives that people have to get off relief.

2. It would guarantee a minimum income for all.

3. It would treat all families with the same income the same way.

4. It is less humiliating to the poor. Taxpayers and negative taxpayers are treated alike under the same system.

5. Those who worked would receive a higher income than those who did not.

Disadvantages of the NIT

1. The program is obviously very expensive. In our example, those with incomes above poverty level would receive a negative income tax.

2. It is questionable whether the program will provide more incentives to work than present welfare programs.

3. Present programs may be better designed to meet the individual needs of people.

4. Perhaps the NIT and present welfare programs could be joined in some way.

Questions

1. Should we replace our present welfare scheme with the NIT or with one of the provincial guaranteed annual income proposals?

2. Give reasons for your point of view.

CHAPTER 9

Labour Unions

(1)

(2)

(1) This photograph, taken in 1867, shows women sorting chunks of ore with their bare hands at the Huntington Copper Mine in Bolton, Québec. Labour unions have strived to improve the working conditions of labourers.

(2) Governments and labour unions have co-operated to draft legislation designed to protect the health and safety of workers. It is mandatory, for example, to wear ear protectors and other safety gear in certain occupations. This tree service worker is well protected against the hazards of her job.

(3) During the Winnipeg General Strike of 1919, workers held a massive demonstration outside the Winnipeg Board of Trade building on June 4. A Royal Commission concluded that the strike was caused by the high cost of living, poor working conditions, and low wages paid to workers.

(4) Miracle Mart employees went on strike on November 18, 1993 to protest the use of more part-time workers and the roll-back of wages to the "industry standard." A government mediator was eventually called in to resolve the strike, which ended on February 20, 1994.

(6)

(5)

(5) On October 31, 1994, Governor General Ramon Hnatyshyn presented the Governor General's Persons Award to Shirley Carr, former president of the Canadian Labour Congress and the first woman in the world to head a national labour body. With four other women, Carr received the award in commemoration of the Persons Case, a 1929 decision by the British Privy Council that declared Canadian women to be persons and thus eligible for appointment to the Senate.

(6) On May 15, 1993, Canadian Labour Congress president Bob White spoke to more than 25 000 demonstrators from more than 100 unions on Parliament Hill in Ottawa. The union members were protesting the federal government's level of commitment to social programs.

Questions

1. Identify some of the activities in which labour organizations have been involved.

2. Suggest reasons for this involvement.

183

Activity 1: What do you think?

In matters of opinion, it is unlikely that a stand on any issue is either "totally wrong" or "totally right." The following opinion poll relates to labour unions and strikes. In your notebook, copy the answers that most accurately reflect your opinion.

An opinion poll

1. Generally speaking, do you think that labour unions have been good or bad for Canada?
   a) Good
   b) Bad
   c) Partly good and partly bad

2. As you know, the Canadian economy has been adversely affected by major strikes. In your opinion, is this due primarily to the attitude of management or to the attitude of labour?
   a) Management
   b) Labour
   c) Both equally
   d) Don't know

3. Do you think that workers should or should not have the right to strike?
   a) Should
   b) Should not
   c) Undecided

4. What about strikes in occupations where the public is seriously inconvenienced, such as strikes by employees of the postal service, airlines, hospitals, telephone service, or boards of education? Do you think they should, or should not, be permitted to strike?
   a) Should
   b) Should not
   c) Undecided

5. The following are examples of the things that unions try to gain for their members. Choose the one that you think is most important at the present time.
   a) Job security
   b) Better working conditions
   c) Higher wages
   d) Better pension plans
   e) Profit sharing
   f) Shorter working hours
   g) Other
   h) Can't say

6. Some people say that there are too many troublemakers and agitators among union leaders. Others say that this statement is only anti-union propaganda. What are your views on this?
   a) Too many troublemakers among union leaders
   b) Just anti-union propaganda
   c) Another opinion
   d) No opinion

What does the class think?

Take a poll of members of the class to find out what they think about labour unions and strikes. Calculate the percentage that supported each opinion. Keep a survey of the responses. We will return to it later in this chapter.

LABOUR UNIONS IN CANADA

A **labour union** is a recognized (i.e., certified) organization of workers that negotiates matters of wages, working conditions, and other benefits with employers.

The growth of labour unions in Canada

So far in our examination of the markets for labour, we have tended to ignore one important fact: not all labour markets are competitive. Some, in fact, are strongly influenced by the existence of labour unions, even though only about 37 percent of the non-agricultural labour force in Canada belongs to unions. Union membership in the United States is less common than in Canada. Only about 16 percent of U.S. workers are unionized. In other industrialized countries — e.g., Britain, with 43 percent and Sweden, with 90 percent — union membership is more prevalent.

Craft and industrial unions

The first labour unions to develop in Canada were unions of workers in a particular skill or craft, such as printers, shoemakers, masons, bakers, and tailors. Unions of skilled or craft workers — called **craft unions** — began in the 1820s and 1830s in the Maritimes, Québec, and Ontario.

These unions include workers of one trade only, no matter where they are employed. For example, printers from different companies in the same city and in different provinces will be members of the International Printing and Graphic Workers Union.

Industrial unions represent workers in a particular firm or industry, regardless of their trade or level of skill. Developing later than craft unions, industrial unions include skilled and unskilled workers within the same industry. For example, the Canadian Auto Workers includes all kinds of workers employed in the automobile industry, from unskilled floor sweepers to highly skilled machinists.

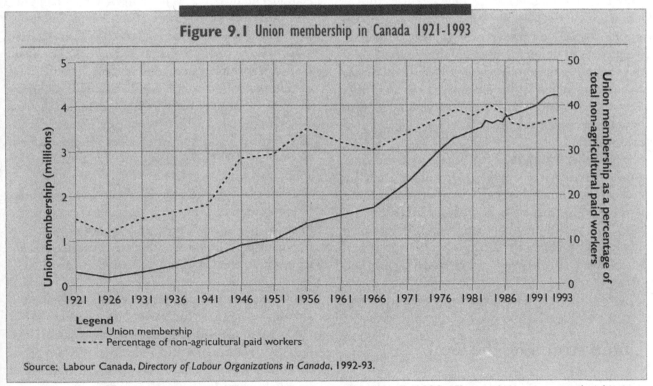

Figure 9.1 Union membership in Canada 1921-1993

Source: Labour Canada, *Directory of Labour Organizations in Canada*, 1992-93.

Since 1926, union membership has grown continuously. During World War II (1939-45), growth in union membership in numbers and as a percentage of the non-agricultural labour force was very rapid. Growth in the 1960s and 1970s was accelerated with the unionization of many civil servants. As a percentage of non-agricultural workers, however, union membership peaked in 1984 at 38.8 percent. The actual numbers of union members have continued to grow in the 1990s, though at a slower rate.

Union membership

In the nineteenth century, union membership grew slowly. It had reached only 166 000 by 1914. During World War I, with the rapid development of industry in Canada, union membership grew significantly. Then, in 1919, The Winnipeg General Strike occurred — this was the most dramatic event in Canadian labour history. The strike failed and many of its leaders were jailed. Membership in unions declined during the Depression of the 1930s. But during World War II, union membership increased markedly, as shown in figure 9.1, as workers gained official right to organize.

Since 1945, union membership has continued to grow so that, by the early 1990s, more than 4 million workers were union members. One recent feature of union growth has been the expansion of membership among clerical and professional groups. Yet despite the growth in union membership during the 1980s, the percentage of non-agricultural paid workers who are union members declined between 1983 and 1989. Between 1989 and 1992, union membership grew in both numbers and as a percentage of non-agricultural paid workers.

Since the 1960s, there has been a relatively rapid growth in national unions (i.e., independent Canadian unions) and a much slower growth in international unions (i.e., those that are associated with American unions). The growth of unions representing government employees has also been particularly rapid since 1965, when federal civil servants were given the right to collective bargaining and the right to strike. The two largest unions in Canada now represent public employees (see figure 9.2).

Union structure: the local

For ordinary union members, the local is the most important part of a union. A person joins the union through the local in his or her plant or town. Union dues are paid to the local. The union member can vote for the officers of the local, including, among others, the president, vice-president, treasurer, and secretary.

Local officers are usually workers like the union member. These local officers are the people who conduct negotiations between workers and employers. The local, however, is one small part of the union organization.

A portion of the union dues paid are retained by the local. The remainder goes to the parent union. Each local sends delegates to conventions where terms of the union's constitution, dues to be paid, division of dues between the local and parent union, and union policy are decided. Elections for the principal offices are also held at the conventions.

National and international unions

National unions, such as the Canadian Union of Public Employees or the National Automobile, Aerospace, and Agricultural Implement Workers of Canada, have locals only in Canada. **International unions**, such as the United Steelworkers or the International Brotherhood of Electrical Workers, have locals in Canada, but most of their locals and membership are in the United States. In the late 1970s, approximately half of the total Canadian unionists were members of international unions. By 1992, this proportion had declined to about one-third.

The two largest unions in Canada represent public employees. In Figure 9.2, the abbreviations in the final column refer to the central labour organization to which each union is affiliated. Most unions are members of the Canadian Labour Congress (CLC). International unions are affiliated with the U.S. central labour organization, called the American Federation of Labour-Congress of Industrial Organizations (AFL-CIO). Most international unions are also affiliated with the CLC. The Social Affairs Federation is a member of the Congress of National Trade Unions and the School Boards Teachers' Federation is independent.

Central labour organizations

Perhaps the labour organization best known to the general public is the Canadian Labour Congress

Figure 9.2 The Top Ten: Membership and related central labour organization, 1992-93

Membership 1992–93 (000s)		Membership of central labour organization
1. Canadian Union of Public Employees	406.6	CLC
2. National Union of Public and General Employees	307.5	CLC
3. United Food and Commercial Workers International Union	180.0	AFL-CIO/CLC
4. Public Service Alliance of Canada	165.0	CLC
5. United Steelworkers of America	160.0	AFL-CIO/CLC
6. National Automobile, Aerospace, and Agricultural Implement Workers of Canada	153.0	CLC
7. Social Affairs Federation Inc.	94.6	CNTU
8. International Brotherhood of Teamsters	91.0	AFL-CIO
9. School Boards Teachers' Federation	75.0	INDEPENDENT
10. Service Employees International Union	75.0	AFL-CIO/CLC

Source: Labour Canada, *Directory of Labour Organizations in Canada*, 1992-93.

Central labour organizations do not play any direct role in negotiations of union contracts. Instead, their function is to act as the principal speaker for labour. When an organization representing a substantial part of the labour force speaks, governments are likely to listen. Provincial labour federations encourage provincial legislatures to pass legislation favourable to labour. Similarly, national labour federations encourage the federal government to pass legislation favourable to labour. Central labour organizations have campaigned for such social programs as health insurance, unemployment insurance, and old age pensions.

COLLECTIVE BARGAINING

When a star hockey player wants to discuss the terms of his contract with his team's management, he is likely to get a friendly hearing. Few individuals have the talent of a Wayne Gretzky, for example, to be in such a good bargaining position. Consider the situation of an assembly line worker in an auto plant. She cannot be sure of a friendly hearing or any hearing at all with management. Auto plants employ hundreds or thousands of workers. Management doesn't have time to talk extensively with individual workers. Management might also think that dissatisfied assembly line workers can easily be replaced.

One way that assembly line workers ensure they receive a fair hearing from management is by forming a labour union and bargaining collectively.

Collective bargaining is the negotiation between representatives of workers and employer(s) with the purpose of establishing terms and conditions of employment that are acceptable to both sides.

A union can be recognized as the bargaining agent either voluntarily by the firm, or by a federal or provincial certification board as a result of balloting that affirms the majority of workers' support.

Labour legislation has come to be regarded as a matter of civil rights. Section 92 of the Constitution Act, 1867, gives the provinces the right to legislate on questions of property and civil rights. Federal labour

(CLC), representing over 2.3 million Canadian union members in 1993. Other central labour organizations include the Québec-based Confederation of National Trade Unions, the Centrale des Syndicats Democratiques (CSD), and the Confederation of Canadian Unions (CCU). Central labour organizations are "unions of unions." Their membership is made up of unions. The CLC, for example, is composed of and financed by national and international unions, as well as by locals.

legislation applies only to such industries as navigation, shipping, interprovincial railways, and radio broadcasting. In other cases, provincial labour legislation applies. Once a union is certified as the collective bargaining agent, other unions are not allowed to deal directly with management.

The purpose of collective bargaining is to reach agreement on such issues as wages, pensions, workload, and holidays.

Union and management set a day for the opening of negotiations for a new contract. The union is represented by its top local and national officials, and advised by its own team of lawyers and research economists. Management is represented by the president or vice-president of human resources and other leading corporate officials, and advised by its accountants and lawyers. Points of agreement are set out in a contract. This contract is known as a **collective agreement**. Also included are the procedures to be followed in the event of a dispute over the terms of the contract.

Arbitration

If, during the term of the contract, there are disputes about interpretation or allegations of a violation of the contract, and union and management cannot agree on a resolution, then the contract must be submitted to arbitration.

Arbitration is an arrangement in a dispute in which both labour and management agree to accept the decision(s) of a third party, or arbitrator.

The arbitrator's decision is final and binding on both parties. Strikes (workers collectively refusing to work) or lockouts (management locking the workers out of the company to prevent them from working) during the life of the contract are illegal.

Conciliation/Mediation

If, when a contract expires, the two sides are unable to reach an agreement on a new contract, the dispute is usually submitted to conciliation.

Conciliation is a situation in a dispute in which both labour and management agree to submit their proposals to a third party, a mediator or conciliator.

The conciliator, or the conciliation board, attempts to bring the two sides to an agreement. Unlike arbitrators, conciliators do not have the power to bind the two parties.

Strike/Lockout

A **strike** is the withholding of labour services by a labour union. If the conciliation process does not resolve the differences, the union may then call a strike and management may lock out its workers (this action is called a **lockout**). With many thousands of collective agreements currently in force in Canada, it is clear that these tactics are used only rarely and as a last resort. Strikes, especially prolonged ones, adversely affect not only workers and companies, but the economy as a whole. However, the right to strike is very important from the union's point of view; withdrawal of labour services is the workers' ultimate weapon. To take away the right to strike would be to diminish workers' ability to bargain with management on close-to-equal terms.

Increase your word power

Sweated labour   Labour employed for long hours at low wages and often under unsafe or unsanitary conditions. The places in which this occurs are called sweat-shops.

Wildcat strike   A spontaneous strike action that is not authorized by the union and that violates the collective agreement. A wildcat strike may be called if workers feel that the employers are trying to violate a previously-concluded agreement.

Blacklist   A list of "undesirable" workers drawn up by some employers and circulated among them. One reason for workers being labelled "undesirable" may be that they were members of, or wished to organize, a union.

Scab   Someone who continues to work when other employees are on strike or who takes a job with an employer whose workers are on strike. A strikebreaker.

Yellow-dog contract   In the past some employers required new workers to sign a document by which they agreed never to join a union. Workers agreeing to this kind of contract were called yellow dogs.

Feather-bedding   Labour unions can sometimes convince employers to agree not to lay off workers, even though their jobs may no longer need to be performed. In this case, the worker may just as well take along a feather bed and take a snooze at work. There's nothing for the worker to do anyway.

Sweetheart agreement or contract   An agreement or contract made through the collusion of dishonest management and union officials on terms favourable to the employer. Such an

agreement would be reached without the workers' approval.

Stoolie   A person employed to act as an informer on union members and on union activities.

Question

Which side, labour or management, is likely to have coined each term?

As indicated in figure 9.3, the actual amount of time lost through strikes is relatively small. The number of labour days lost owing to strikes and lockouts between 1960 and 1993 exceeded one million only in 1975 and 1976. The graph also shows that the percentage of estimated working time lost to strikes exceeded only one half of 1 percent during 1975 and 1976. The average amount of time lost is approximately one-third of 1 percent. In well over 95 percent of the contract negotiations, workers and management are able to resolve their differences without resorting to strikes or lockouts.

Figure 9.3 Time lost from Canadian work stoppages through strikes and lockouts, 1960-1993

Legend
—— Millions of labour days lost   - - - - -   Percentage of estimated working time

Source: Labour Canada, *Strikes and Lockouts in Canada*, 1978, 1983, 1985, 1994.

The percentage of time lost to strikes and lockouts between 1960 and 1993 only exceeded one-half of 1 percent in two years — 1975 and 1976. The average amount of time lost tends to vary between 0.2 and 0.3 percent.

THE CONTRACT

Often union and management reach agreement only after very tough bargaining. Generally, the agreement or **contract** covers four major areas: union security, wages and benefits, seniority, and grievance procedures.

Union security

In the early years of its formation, the union local is at pains to ensure that management recognizes it. Is the firm to be a **closed shop**, where workers must become members of the union within a specified period? Or is it to be an **open shop**, where management can hire workers who are not obliged to become union members? Is there to be an automatic deduction or check-off of union dues from workers' wages? The union is in a much stronger position if it has a closed shop with automatic check-off, rather than an open shop with no check-off.

Once a union has been recognized, all employees must pay dues, although they do not have to become union members.

Wages and benefits

Fringe benefits are payments and services other than wages or salary that are provided by an employer.

Wages and hours of work usually form the central part of any union-management contract. Today, more and more fringe benefits, such as medical, dental, pension, and life insurance plans, are paid partly or wholly by the company. Holidays with pay are also included.

Contracts often include **cost of living allowances** (called COLAs) that keep wages increasing on a par with general price increases.

Seniority

Most union contracts contain seniority clauses specifying the order in which workers should be laid off when times are tough, and rehired when times are good. The most usual principle followed in tough times is "last in, first out" and in good times, "last out, first in."

Grievance procedures

No contract can cover all the situations that may arise over the life of an agreement. In most contracts, a procedure is established for settling any disputes or grievances that may arise either in the interpretation of the contract or in unanticipated situations.

The final contract is typically a compromise reflecting the relative strengths of the union and management and the skill of the negotiators.

UNIONS AND WAGES

As we saw in Chapter 8, a wage is a price determined by the interaction of supply and demand. Unions act in the market with the aim of improving the conditions of workers. How, then, can a union act to increase the wages of its members? The following are just three ways that unions can use their power to gain wage increases.

Restrict the supply of labour

A union can require long apprenticeships or high union initiation fees; refuse to admit new members or to allow non-union members to do the job; or support immigration barriers or maximum hours legislation. Some craft unions have been able to get large firms in important industries, such as construction, to employ only union workers in such skilled trades as plumbing and carpentry. The effect of any such restriction is shown in figure 9.4. SS represents the supply available in the absence of a union. OQ workers are employed at a wage of OW. With the existence of a union that is able to restrict the labour supply, the supply curve shifts to the left and becomes more inelastic. By restricting the supply, the wage rate increases from OW to OW_1, and the quantity of labour employed declines from OQ to OQ_1.

Increase the demand for labour

A union can act to increase the demand for labour (that is, to shift the demand curve to the right) in a

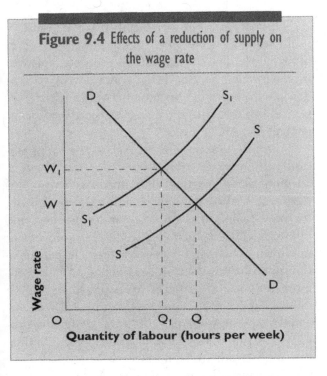

Figure 9.4 Effects of a reduction of supply on the wage rate

power of the employer(s) to some extent, and raise wages. How far wages rise will depend on the relative bargaining strengths of the unions and employer(s).

THE FUTURE OF THE UNIONS

What is the future of the unions in Canada? In the 1980s and 1990s, the labour movement was under great pressure in Canada and internationally. During the 1980s, British trade union membership suffered a 10 percent drop — to about 42 percent of the work force. In 1981, U.S. president Ronald Reagan fired all striking air traffic controllers. By the mid-1990s, union membership in the U.S. had dropped to less than 16 percent of the work force. In Canada, union membership has declined as well — but only slightly, from a high of 38.8 percent in the early 1980s to about 37.5 percent in 1994. Nevertheless, the unions in Canada have been under stress as the federal government, and some provincial governments as well, have succeeded in freezing or rolling back wages of public sector unions — over the powerful opposition of organized labour. In addition, unions strongly opposed the agreements to eliminate trade restrictions between Canada, the U.S., and Mexico — but the agreements came into force despite this opposition.

Rapid changes in technology, for example, the increasing use of computers and robotics, followed the increased international competition as trade barriers fell and the recession of the early 1990s took hold. In this new environment which is redefining the nature of work and the workplace, where do unions fit — if at all?

Leo Gerard, former Canadian director and now international treasurer of the United Steelworkers of America, believes that the 1990s will "chart the future of the labour movement." But there *will* be a future, he believes. People have been predicting the death of the labour movement since the first union certification, but "where is there a democracy without a labour movement?... Countries without labour movements are not democracies."

Unions without a full set of "tools" in their tool box — and not just the adversarial approach to collective

number of ways. It can help employers modernize plants and improve worker productivity. It can encourage fellow unionists, the public, and government to buy union-made products. It can work to keep out or cut down on competitive products coming into Canada by applying pressure on the federal government. The effect of these measures is to increase the demand for labour since, as we have seen, the demand for labour is derived from the demand for the products it makes. The effect of the increased demand is to raise the wage rate and/or the amount of employment.

Balance of power of monopolies or oligopolies

Suppose there is a town where there is only one major employer or just a few major employers and no union. In this situation, the employer(s) may have considerable power to influence the wages set, and wages are likely to be low. If a union is established that includes most of the workers, it will be able to balance the bargaining — may be seriously limiting their options, Gerard asserts. Implicit in this view is the idea that the interests and fates of workers and employers are closely linked and certainly not mutually exclusive. The goal of organized labour, then, must be to seek out a new way of doing things.

In 1990, Leo Gerard played a major part in developing a power-sharing arrangement at the financially troubled Algoma Steel Corporation in Sault Ste. Marie. This deal saw workers ultimately control 60 percent of the company and gain unprecedented influence in management decision-making at all levels. In 1993 Algoma announced its first profit in five years.

But even in a partnership with employers, workers must still be able to use the "tool" of the strike. "Even with a partnership, if they walk all over you, you have to be able to bring out that tool," claims Gerard.

Gerard argues further that the North American labour movement has to regroup after the heavy blows of the job-reducing free trade agreement.

Meanwhile, the Steelworkers are moving beyond their traditional domain and are organizing workers in the private service sector. There's a movement to organize taxi drivers (in four Canadian cities), security guards, and flight reservation agents.

"But we can't get caught up on new workers only. We have to concern ourselves with the jumps in technology and determine what their outcome is. The speed of change is so overwhelming that last year's state-of-the-art equipment is now out of date. Consequently, says Gerard, the union has begun its own steel-industry training courses, because in the past, employers trained their workers for a specific job. As a result, "when the recession came, those workers were caught with insufficient skills."

In the U.S., unions are "starting to come together to brainstorm and develop new strategies," says Gerard. "But that isn't happening in Canada, where it's still every union for itself."

Sam Gindin, research director of the Canadian Auto Workers Union, agrees that unions should work together, but disagrees with much that Leo Gerard has to say.

He does agree, however, that there is a "new reality" in the world of work. "We also know the pressures of history are leading to chaos, and the squeeze on labour is greater than ever. But does that mean we have to lie down in the face of it? No, it means workers need [protective] institutions more than ever, more than in the last half century."

Gindin's union — the CAW — has a significantly different direction from other unions which are emphasizing partnership with management. Instead, the CAW is looking back into labour history for ways to increase militancy, independence, and influence. The union wants to develop "movement unionism" in which the union increases its participation in coalitions with other groups that have common interests. This means focussing its efforts on joining other groups, such as unemployed workers, women, and immigrants, to fight for more jobs, protection of unemployment insurance, and elimination of discrimination and racism.

Since breaking its ties with the American United Autoworkers in 1985, the CAW has changed considerably. In the past, 75 percent of its membership came from the auto industry and members were located mainly in southern Ontario and Quebec. Ten years later, only 35 percent of the membership was from the auto industry, while the others came from such diverse sectors of the economy as airlines, fishing, mining, and electronics. This change in the union's membership suggests that the CAW is moving towards the concept of "one big union" where its diversity and size would give it a lot of strength and influence.

Source: Adapted from Tony van Alphen, "The evolution of a union," *Toronto Star*, September 16, 1994 and Lynda Hurst, "State of the unions," *Toronto Star*, July 9, 1994.

Question

With which of these two views of the future development of labour unions — Leo Gerard's or Sam Gindin's — do you agree? Explain. If you have an alternative view, outline it.

SUMMARY

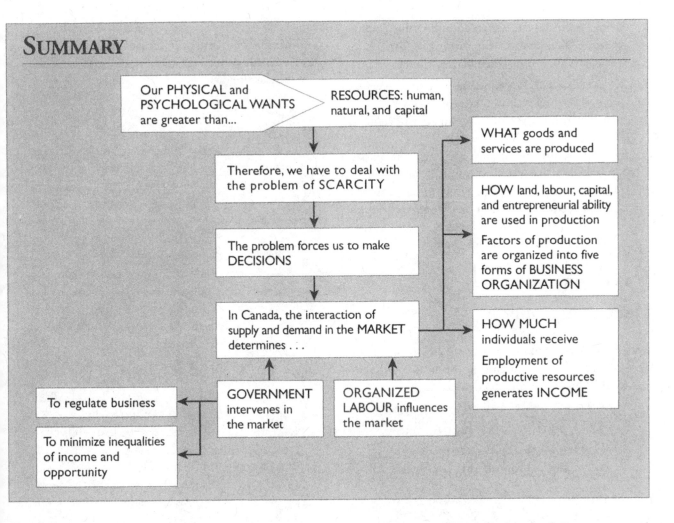

Our PHYSICAL and PSYCHOLOGICAL WANTS are greater than...

RESOURCES: human, natural, and capital

Therefore, we have to deal with the problem of SCARCITY

The problem forces us to make DECISIONS

In Canada, the interaction of supply and demand in the MARKET determines . . .

WHAT goods and services are produced

HOW land, labour, capital, and entrepreneurial ability are used in production

Factors of production are organized into five forms of BUSINESS ORGANIZATION

HOW MUCH individuals receive

Employment of productive resources generates INCOME

GOVERNMENT intervenes in the market

ORGANIZED LABOUR influences the market

To regulate business

To minimize inequalities of income and opportunity

REVIEW

Explain each concept in your own words with an example: labour union, collective bargaining, contract.

Briefly explain the meaning of: international union, craft union, industrial union, national union, lockout, strike, conciliation, arbitration, closed shop, union shop, open shop, fringe benefits, cost of living allowances.

APPLICATIONS

1. Which of the following are craft unions and which are industrial unions? Which are international unions?

   a) The United Brotherhood of Carpenters and Joiners of America
   b) The United Steel Workers of America
   c) International Brotherhood of Electrical Workers
   d) International Chemical Workers' Union
   e) Canadian Chemical and Textile Workers' Union
   f) Canadian Transport and General Workers' Union

2. Which of the following provides the union with the greatest amount of security: closed shop, open shop, or union shop? Explain your choice.

3. Why would the earliest trade unions in Canada be more likely to develop among skilled craft-workers than among unskilled workers?

4. What effect will the following have on the wages and employment of each group?
    a) A law granting public employees the right to strike.
    b) A law requiring all auto mechanics to pass a written examination in English.
    c) An increase in the price of oil on coal miners.
    d) An agreement requiring firefighters to be present on every passenger train, even though there may be nothing for them to do.

CASE STUDY
Organizing a union

As you read the following case study, consider the stages involved in organizing a union and why the fast-food industry is difficult to organize.

Teen achieves rare labour feat
Hamburger helper organizes young co-workers into union

By Virginia Galt
Labour Reporter

Eighteen-year-old high-school student David Coburn has just had the extracurricular "learning experience" of his life — organizing his young co-workers into a union at a fast-food restaurant. He only wished it could count toward his credits at school.

Sitting at his home computer, surrounded by school textbooks and a massive comic-book collection, Mr. Coburn recalled the roller coaster of events in the past four weeks — his discovery that he was being paid less than the legal minimum wage; his telephone call to the union; his

firing and subsequent reinstatement; and, finally, the employer's decision not to challenge the certification of the Hotel Employees and Restaurant Employees Union at the fast-food franchise where Mr. Coburn works part-time as a hamburger flipper.

His feat was all the more remarkable because the Canadian fast-food industry is notoriously difficult to organize. A handful of the 172 franchises across the country are unionized, but the overall rate of unionization in the industry, which relies on a young, part-time work force, is low.

"Everything happened really fast, but it seemed like it was longer because there was so much pressure," Mr. Coburn said in the interview. It was also nerve-wracking for his co-workers, some of whom went against their parents' wishes when they supported the union.

Yesterday's scheduled Ontario Labour Relations Board hearing into allegations of unfair labour practices and the union's application for certification were cancelled after the union and the employer reached a pre-hearing settlement on Oct. 6.

Mr. Coburn skipped classes to attend the closed meeting on Oct. 6. Now, he just wants to buckle down to his studies so he can go to university, while continuing to work part-time so he can save for tuition fees. Whatever course he decides on — he is leaning toward business administration or marketing — he already has some prodigious researching and organizational skills.

Barely four weeks ago, suspecting he was being paid less than the legal minimum wage, Mr. Coburn went to the offices of the Ontario Ministry of Labour to do some homework. On learning that the general minimum wage is $6.35 an hour, while he was earning $6 an hour, Mr. Coburn decided he needed a union.

"I looked it up in the Yellow Pages — simple enough," he said when asked how he knew whom to call. "Unions. Hotel and Restaurant Employees. I thought that should be the one."

On Sept. 17, within days of his initial telephone call to Paul Clifford, an organizer with Local 75 of the Hotel and Restaurant Employees Union, Mr. Coburn had signed up a majority of his co-workers — all in their teens and early 20s.

That same day, the franchisee, who owns and runs the restaurant with her husband, was invited to attend a meeting with the employees on the company's premises. Mr. Coburn said he held the meeting on company property "as a courtesy — we could have done it behind their backs."

Mr. Coburn was fired at the end of his shift on Sept. 17 by the franchisee's husband, who cited problems with punctuality, cleanliness of uniform, and job performance. The franchisee subsequently reduced the firing to a suspension, which has since been expunged from Mr. Coburn's employment record as part of last week's settlement at the labour board, Mr. Clifford said.

The employer has also undertaken to audit its pay sheets for the past two years and ensure that its employees have received all wages, overtime pay, and holiday pay that they are entitled to under the Employment Standards Act. Any shortfall will be made up, Mr. Clifford said, adding that Mr. Coburn has already received a cheque to cover back wages.

The victory was quick, but not easy, for Mr. Coburn and his co-workers. Some feared reprisals if they associated with Mr. Coburn. "Everyone is, like, scared," Mr. Coburn said in an interview early in the process.

Nonetheless, on Sept. 21, Mr. Coburn and several of his off-duty co-workers congregated after school at another restaurant across the street. Some were still dressed in school uniforms, carrying such books as *The Fundamentals of Physics.* Mr. Coburn carried *A Guide to the Labour Relations Act.*

Sharing a single hamburger and fries among eight people, their moods switching from nervousness to the bravado of youth, they related some disturbing things that had happened since they had signed union cards.

Some said their parents had been contacted by the employer, with the message that they would be fired unless they wrote letters saying they wanted nothing more to do with the union. A few reported that they were being paid less than the minimum wage, which is $5.90 an hour for students under 18 and $6.35 for workers 18 and older.

Later, in response to the union's allegations of unfair labour practices, the owners denied that they had put pressure on the parents of employees or threatened the young part-time workers. They issued a blanket denial that they had violated any provisions of the Ontario Labour Relations Act, but did agree to review complaints about pay under the Employment Standards Act.

At the meeting with his co-workers, Mr. Clifford gave the young employees a primer on their rights under the recently updated Labour Relations Act, which now allows for expedited hearings if there are complaints that workers have been fired or disciplined during a union's bid for certification.

Mr. Clifford said the workers had the right to join and be represented by the union and that the law would protect those rights. He said he understood the pressure they were under, but urged them to hold their ground. Mr. Clifford then crossed the street to the franchise, where he sought a meeting with the owner.

The owner asked Mr. Clifford to leave. He also declined to talk to the *Globe* reporter, saying:

"I have nothing to say to you. I'd appreciate it if you would leave my premises right now."

Meantime, the owners had called the main franchisor for advice. The franchisor is available to play an advisory role in addition to ensuring that the restaurants' products and menus are the same in all its franchise operations across Canada.

The manager of human resources for the franchisor made it clear in an interview that the owners operate as "a separate employer." Although the owner had referred all questions to the manager, he said, "I have no comment on anything that is before the Labour Relations Board."

In the absence of comments from the employer, Mr. Clifford said, "There was no admission of wrong-doing and we are not interested in getting one." The goal now, he said, is to establish a professional working relationship with the owners and to negotiate a first collective agreement for the 16 workers in the bargaining unit.

David Wright, the lawyer who represented the union, said the speedy resolution of the dispute shows that the New Democratic Party government's new labour laws are working in the interests of both workers and employers. In the past, he said, "it wasn't uncommon for these things to drag on for a year or more and poison the relationship between the parties."

Mr. Clifford said it is not uncommon that young part-time workers who do not know their rights are taken advantage of.

"David [Coburn] is bright and he does have guts," he said. "A lot of people talk about doing what he did, but few actually go ahead and do it."

Source: *The Globe and Mail*, October 13, 1993.

Questions

1. What are the various stages in organizing workers into a union outlined here?

2. Why do you think that the fast-food industry is "notoriously difficult to organize"?

ISSUE
Strike alternatives

Besides strikes, workers have used the following methods to pressure management into concluding an agreement:

- A **boycott**, organized by a union, is a collective refusal by supporters of the union to buy or use goods or services supplied by a firm or an industry in which a labour dispute is taking place. As one example, members of the United Farm Workers of California and their supporters have picketed supermarkets in Canada in an attempt to convince Canadian consumers not to buy California grapes or lettuce.

- Air traffic controllers and letter carriers have used **rotating strikes** in order to try to bring about a more favourable settlement in a labour dispute. Instead of all air traffic controllers or letter carriers across the country going on strike at the same time, the controllers in one location go out on strike for one day, to be followed by the controllers in another location going out on another day, and so on. Thus, workers are able to put a lot of pressure on management to reach an agreement without closing down the entire industry and bringing about possible return-to-work legislation and large wage losses to their members.

- **Work-to-rule** is a practice whereby workers obey to the letter all the laws and rules that relate to their work — thus bringing about a slowdown. Work-to-rule also involves a refusal to do certain tasks not included in the job description.

Compulsory arbitration

One frequently suggested alternative to the strike is compulsory arbitration. It has been proposed that when both negotiations and attempts at conciliation between union and management have failed, both sides should be required to submit their dispute to arbitration. The decision of the independent arbitrator would be final and legally binding on both labour and management. Workers would be prohibited by law from going out on strike; management would not be permitted to lock out the workers. Some people recommend compulsory arbitration in all deadlocked labour disputes. Others would require it only in essential industries.

Industrial democracy

Why don't we follow the practice of some European countries and institute a form of industrial democracy? In this system, union members would be on the Board of Directors and there would be a considerable degree of joint decision-making by management and unions. Thus, the Board of Directors would ensure that the company would function not only in the interests of the shareholders, but also in the interests of the workers. In this way, conflicts between the company and the union would be minimized.

Final offer selection

If labour and management cannot reach agreement over the contract, then a person acceptable to both sides is selected to resolve the dispute. Labour and management each submit their final and best offer to the selected person who decides which of the two offers is more fair and reasonable. The selected offer is binding on both labour and management. Supporters of final offer selection argue that it forces both sides to moderate their demands and be more reasonable in their bargaining. However, some critics question the ability of a selected person to make a fair judgment as to which offer is the more reasonable.

Questions

1. Does any one of the six options above provide a good alternative to the strike? Explain.

2. In groups, discuss which of the following should be allowed to go on strike: ambulance drivers, airline pilots, doctors, hospital workers, nurses, grocery clerks, local transit workers, postal workers, steelworkers, garbage collectors, coal miners, hydro employees, plumbers, elementary school teachers, lawyers.

3. If you think that some of these occupations should not have the right to strike, then what do you propose in its place?

4. Be prepared to defend your group's position.

Activity 2: What do you think now?

You have now given considerable thought to strikes and strike alternatives. At the beginning of this chapter, you completed a survey of opinion on unions and strikes. Turn back to the opinion poll and, without reviewing your earlier responses, complete the survey again.

What does the class think now?

Poll the class again. Calculate the percentage of the class that supports each option.

1. Compare the two polls taken here with the ones taken earlier.

2. What may account for the changes, or lack of changes, in the surveys?

CHAPTER 10

Consumption and Savings

(1)

(6)

(5)

Questions

1. What influences the way we spend our money?

2. What has the greatest influence on the way we spend money?

CONSUMPTION

Consumption is that part of an individual's income that is spent on goods and services rather than saved.

We are all consumers. We have seen how our economic system operates to meet the demands of consumers, how the purpose of the production process is to produce consumer goods and services, and how the market allocates these goods and services among consumers.

In examining a modified command economy in Chapter 2, we learned that in some countries such as the former Soviet Union, the influence of the consumer is not as important as in a modified market economy like our own. In our economy, consumer purchases indicate to producers what to produce and what not to produce. Producers unable to produce the kind of goods and services in demand are likely to suffer losses, even bankruptcy. Producers supplying goods and services in high demand are likely to make profits. Thus, through the individual decisions of millions of consumers acting through the market system, producers are led to produce what consumers want, when and where they want it.

Clearly not every consumer wish is satisfied. As we saw in Chapter 6, a wish has to be backed up by the ability and willingness to pay for a product before it becomes part of the demand for a product and therefore before it can have an influence on production. I may wish to own the latest Jaguar, but if I cannot pay for it, my wish is of no consequence. Similarly, if I only have five dollars to spend, I can influence production but only to the extent of five dollars' worth. In the market system, individuals who are poor have much less influence on what is produced than those who are wealthy. The poor have fewer dollar votes to influence production, compared to the rich.

Since we are all consumers, we all have some influence. At any point in time, when we buy one thing rather than another, we are voting for the production of one thing rather than the production of another. The collective influence of consumers — called demand — is of paramount importance in influencing what producers will produce.

Factors influencing consumer choice

There is a limit to everyone's income and, therefore, we all try to get the most from our limited resources. Consider, for example, the young person buying a car. She will look at many cars, examine tires and engines, sit behind the wheel, go for test drives, and ask the advice of other people. She is trying to get the best value by purchasing the car that best meets both needs and budget.

Another person might spend the same amount of money on a motorbike, another on a trip, and yet another on a VCR. The differences in expenditures are the result of the different tastes and needs of individuals. All consumer spending is like this. The different preferences of all consumers collectively determine what is purchased.

If you look around your classroom, however, you will probably notice that the clothing that some students are wearing is similar. Fashion strongly influences what we wear. Fashions in clothing, music, entertainment, furniture, and other such items change frequently, and fashion in general affects our purchasing decisions.

Many cultures celebrate the harvest in ways that have been the same for decades. These are customs. Just as fashion affects colours and small styling details, custom determines general characteristics of our clothing and housing. Custom differs from fashion in that it is less subject to change.

Advertising is another powerful influence that affects our choices. The media continually bombard us with the brand names of different automobiles, soft drinks, and detergents. No matter how much we may hate an advertisement, we might end up buying the product it promotes because the brand name is familiar. What advertisers seek is exposure of the product name.

Generally, advertising has an unsettling influence. Many advertisements create new wants. We are led to be unhappy with our present lot and to discover wants that we didn't know we had.

The ultimate determinant of the consumption behaviour of an individual or family is amount of income. Whatever the influences of fashion, custom, or advertising, income imposes restraints.

Size of income influences not only how much but also what the individual or family will buy. A poor family tends to be restricted to essentials — food, clothing, and housing. A more affluent family has a greater choice in what to buy.

Consumer protection

Today consumers are surrounded by the competing claims producers make for a vast number of complex goods and services. Consumers have become increasingly aware that they need help in evaluating the merits claimed for these products. In the days of the pioneer, life was simpler. Choice was largely restricted to what was in the village general store. Products, too, were simpler. Choosing between two brooms is easier than choosing between two vacuum cleaners and their many attachments. If you shop in a large department store in the city, you will note that there are literally hundreds of thousands of possible choices for the consumer. As well, there are many different department stores in the larger Canadian cities.

Besides needing guidance to judge the merits of products, consumers need protection. Unless you happen to be a medical researcher, it is impossible to judge the accuracy of claims made by drug companies for the products they sell. Canadian governments have acted to protect the consumer. For example, the federal government enforces the standards of weights and measures so that when you visit the gas pump or the corner store, you can be reasonably sure you will get a fair measure. Similarly, restaurants are inspected by government to protect the consumer.

Business itself has moved to protect consumers from "shady" operators. Thus, all Canadian cities have Better Business Bureau offices, financed by businesses in the community. The bureau dispenses free advice to consumers related to businesses in their area.

Consumers, too, have established their own organizations for mutual protection. The Canadian Association of Consumers provides consumers with information on many products.

Consumer credit

Consumer credit is the ability to acquire goods and services now in exchange for payments in the future.

We are all familiar with the advertisements that tell us how we can have what we want now even if we can't pay immediately. Payment can be put off until later.

Buying on credit has advantages. We can buy durable goods, homes, cars, and washing machines, and have the use of them immediately instead of waiting to save the total amount needed. Most Canadians obtain credit to buy their homes. Credit can also help us to meet financial emergencies. As well, credit permits us to take advantage of sales when we don't have cash available.

Buying on credit has disadvantages as well. Usually there is a cost attached to buying on credit. Not only do we have to pay back the amount of money borrowed, but we must also pay a rate of interest. Because credit makes purchasing easy, many people are tempted into credit buying and later find they have acquired substantial debts. They may find it increasingly difficult to pay off their debts and may ultimately lose the goods purchased on credit. Banks and other credit-granting facilities may be unwilling to loan money.

The interest you pay is the cost of borrowing. The lower the interest rate you are able to find, the lower your monthly payments will be. If you are a member of a credit union, you may be able to get a lower rate of interest than from a chartered bank. Rates on loans from finance companies can be quite high. Before borrowing, you should comparison shop for interest rates. You should also figure out how borrowing will affect your budget.

Other sources of credit

Credit is so widely used in our society that many of us have used credit without knowing it. For example, when we pay many of our bills for household utilities at the end of the month, we have been given credit for the service. In the case of your electricity bill, you do not pay for the month's electricity until after you have used it. It is the same with natural gas and water bills. On the other hand, in many parts of Canada, people provide the phone company with credit because they are billed ahead of time for regular service. For long distance charges, though, we pay after we have made the calls. This is another case in which we are provided with credit.

Credit cards

One way to obtain immediate credit is by the use of a credit card. Credit cards such as American Express, Visa, MasterCard, and others can be used for a variety of purchases: clothing, meals in restaurants, hotel rooms, airline tickets. Credit card holders are billed monthly for their expenditures. If payment is received within a specified time limit, there are no interest charges with some credit cards. Beyond that time limit, interest charges are high — about 18.5 percent annually, for example, in 1995.

Will that be cash, credit, or debit?

Most of us are familiar with credit cards and most Canadian adults own one or more of them. At first, credit cards were used by people when they didn't have cash. Now, though, they are used as an alternative to cheques and cash. People use them even when they have cash in their wallets.

What's next? The debit card. Like the credit card, you don't need to carry cash or a chequebook with you, but you do have the freedom to make the payment immediately using your debit or direct payment card. In using the debit card, there are three steps:

1. Make sure that the store carries the symbol of the debit card. Then present your card for payment.

2. The cashier passes your card through the store's electronic scanner and enters the total amount of your purchase.

3. You confirm that the total is correct and then enter your personal identification number (PIN) using the keypad you'll be given by the cashier.

That's it — your purchase is completed. The amount of your purchase has been transferred automatically from your bank account to your retailer's account.

There's a processing charge (currently 25 cents a transaction), but it's less expensive than using a cheque. It takes less time than writing a cheque and getting it authorized. Using a debit card is secure — the cashier doesn't know your PIN number or the balance in your account. You don't have to carry large amounts of cash with you. You can use the debit card to buy food and liquor — which in some provinces is not permitted with a credit card. The debit card has another advantage over the credit card: it's harder to spend money you don't have.

But credit cards have many advantages over debit cards. They are convenient to use — most businesses accept them. They allow the postponement of payments to a later date and permit people to "spread" payments over time. For some purchases — such as car rentals and purchases by phone — the credit card is essential.

Question

Do you think the debit card will replace the credit card? Why or why not?

Charge accounts

For many goods such as gas, clothing, hardware, sports equipment, and stationery, the retail outlet may agree to bill us later, usually at the end of the month. Charge accounts are useful for the purchase of smaller items that are stocked in stores. The stores usually allow thirty days without charging interest.

Conditional sales contracts

Large items, like cars, serve as their own guarantee to the seller that the loan will be repaid. In the case of a conditional sales contract for a car, the car itself becomes the pledge. If the buyer fails to keep up the installment payments, the seller may repossess the car.

Spending patterns of Canadians

The spending patterns of typical Canadian consumers are shown in table 10.1. As you can see, expenditures of families with less than $15 000 are mainly limited to food and housing. Expenditures on clothing, on the other hand, are very limited. Despite their restricting expenditures to the essentials, families with incomes less than $15 000 consume on average $12 426. This probably means that many families with incomes under $15 000 spend more than their income. How do they manage to spend more than their income? The answer

is that they go into debt or they draw on their past savings. Those who are retired are particularly likely to draw on their savings.

As incomes rise, expenditures also rise. But, as shown in table 10.1, while the proportion of expenditures on food, housing, and clothing declines, the total of other expenditures increases considerably. Thus, for example, families with incomes of $85 000 and over spend less than four times the amount of families under $15 000 on food and less than three times the amount on shelter.

For discussion

Advertising

As a class, debate whether advertising should be banned or restricted. Consider the arguments outlined here and add others of your own.

"Be it resolved that some advertising be banned or restricted."

For the motion

1. The objective of advertising is not to inform but to persuade. Advertisers often make extravagant and misleading claims that confuse the consumer. Advertising adds weight to our newspapers and annoyance to our television viewing.

Table 10.1 Family expenditures by family income in 17 Canadian cities, 1990

	Families of two or more persons										
	Family income										
	Under $15 000	$15 000– 19 999	$20 000– 24 999	$25 000– 29 999	$30 000– 34 999	$35 000– 39 999	$40 000– 49 999	$50 000– 59 999	$60 000– 69 999	$70 000– 84 999	$85 000 and over
Food	2540	3629	4103	4659	4920	5338	5873	6617	7874	8288	9680
Shelter	4676	5366	5840	6589	6428	7280	7681	8785	10 606	11 315	13 022
Clothing	688	1161	1359	1606	1760	1844	2359	2955	3523	4002	5522
Total current consumption (including transportation, recreation, education and food, clothing, and shelter); excludes taxes	12 426	17 393	20 113	23 851	25 486	28 564	32 243	37 801	43 324	47 130	59 139

Source: Statistics Canada, *Family Expenditures in Canada*, 1990.

2. Expenditures on advertising are unproductive. Resources are diverted from useful purposes. Advertising leads to the overproduction of private luxury goods such as electric toothbrushes and the underproduction of important goods such as libraries, schools, and recreational facilities. The advertising of some products such as alcohol and tobacco can lead to disastrous effects on people's health.

3. Advertising leads to the visual pollution of our cities and towns with its ugly neon signs and billboards.

4. Since advertising revenue is necessary to the financial health of television, radio, and newspapers, large advertisers could have the power to influence the media unduly.

5. Advertising decreases competition. The huge expenditures necessary to advertise give the large companies a competitive advantage, thereby decreasing competition.

Against the motion

1. Advertising provides consumers with information that helps them to make intelligent choices. In a dynamic economy with new products constantly being developed and old products constantly being improved, it is essential that the consumer receives up-to-date information.

2. Advertising is essential to communications media that are dependent on advertising for operating revenue.

3. Since successful advertising increases demand for a particular good, a firm can expand its production of that good and thus take advantage of mass production techniques. In this way, consumers pay a lower price for an article as a result of advertising.

4. Advertising promotes competition. Since consumers are given information about a wide variety of similar products, competition is increased.

5. Advertising promotes full employment by encouraging high levels of spending. While it is not necessary to advertise food to a hungry person in an affluent country like Canada, advertising encourages people to buy a second car, television set, or clock radio. To help ensure employment in such industries, it is essential to stimulate demand by advertising.

BUILDING YOUR SKILLS

Budgeting

Anne Worker is 20 years old. She is single, with no dependents and has a job at $27 000 a year at the Electric Current Company. After graduating from high school, she obtained a diploma in computer programming at a local community college. For a year now, she has had her own apartment, but she has begun to find that, although she has a good income, somehow all her money just disappears. She decides to establish a budget — a financial plan to prevent her money from running out before the end of the month.

Step 1 Income

An appropriate place for Anne to start is with her income. See the budget chart in figure 10.2 on page 206.

Take-home pay

At Electric Current she is paid $2250 monthly. Attached to her cheque is a statement of earnings and deductions. Her monthly statement is reproduced in figure 10.1.

Anne's gross pay for the month is $2250. Electric Current is required by law to deduct income tax, Canada or Quebec pension plan contributions, and unemployment insurance. After deductions, her monthly take-home or net pay is $1543.22.

Other income

Anne does not have a part-time job but she does have savings. She keeps a balance above $4000 in her chequing account. Since the account pays ½ percent on the minimum amount, she earns $20 in interest. She also has a two-year $3000 Canada Savings Bond that, at 5 percent, gives her an income of $150 a year. Her total other income is therefore $20 + $150, which equals $170 or $14.17 a month. Her total monthly income is, therefore, her net pay ($1543.22) plus her other income ($14.17) or $1557.39.

Step 2 Rent and utilities

Anne has a one-bedroom apartment for which she pays $600 a month in rent, $21 for telephone, and $12 for cable television. Anne also pays, on average, $25 a month for electricity, and $30 a month for heat. Her total monthly household expenses amount to $688.00.

Figure 10.1

Electric Current Company
STATEMENT OF MONTHLY EARNINGS AND DEDUCTIONS

Name	Regular earnings	Deductions				Net pay
		Federal and provincial income tax	Canada or Quebec pension plan	Unemployment insurance	Total deductions	
Anne Worker	$2250.00	$536.56	$51.14	$69.08	$656.78	$1543.22

Figure 10.2 Where it came from and where it went

Budget: Anne's monthly income and expenses

Step 1 Income

1 Take home pay	$1543.22	
2 Other income, e.g., part-time job, interest income	$ 14.17	
Total income per month		$1557.39

Expenses

Step 2 Rent and utilities

3 Rent	$ 600.00	
4 Electricity	$ 25.00	
5 Heat	$ 30.00	
6 Cable TV	$ 12.00	
7 Telephone	$ 21.00	
Total household expenses		$ 688.00

Step 3 Transportation

8 Public transportation		$55.00

Step 4 Living expenses

9 Groceries	$ 300.00	
10 Clothes	$ 100.00	
11 Newspapers, magazines, books, etc.	$ 30.00	
12 Entertainment	$ 60.00	
13 Spending money	$ 100.00	
Total living expenses		$ 590.00

Step 5 Regular monthly payments

14 Savings	$ 100.00	
15 Furniture	$ 100.00	
16 Other	$ 24.39	
Total regular monthly payments		$ 224.39

Step 6 Total Expenses per month

		$1557.39

Step 7 Balance

Total income minus total expenses		0

Step 3 Transportation

Anne doesn't own a car so she relies on public transport. The monthly cost is $55.

Step 4 Living expenses

Included here are the regular expenditures on groceries, clothing, newspapers, and entertainment, which total $590.00.

Step 5 Regular monthly payments

Included here are the $100 a month that Anne saves, and her payments of $124.39 on her furniture and a small loan she has from a bank. Notice that Anne counts her savings as if they were regular payments she has to make. This ensures that she will save.

Step 6 Total expenses per month

Anne's total monthly expenses amount to $1557.39.

Step 7 Balance

Anne's income equals her expenses. Her balance is 0.

Comments

Anne is managing to set aside $100 in savings and make $124.39 in payments. Since she can also look forward to a rising income, she is in a fairly healthy situation. What she might consider, though, is repaying her loan.

Practise your skill

What job do you propose to take when you graduate? What is currently being paid for the job? Go through the various steps in our budget exercise to draw up a possible monthly budget. Consult your local newspaper, friends, and relatives to help you get realistic figures for your expenses.

Personal finances

"Where did my money go?" ask people as they examine an empty wallet or purse, or their bank passbook with its low balance. There are a number of reasons for the seemingly mysterious disappearance of our money. Often we make purchases on the spur of the moment with little reflection. Many stores and supermarkets have merchandise arranged to tempt us into impulse buying. Very often we fail to distinguish between real needs and psychological wants. In Chapter 1, we saw how wants are capable of infinite expansion.

There are other reasons our money seems to dwindle away. We may buy the first item we come across instead of comparing prices of similar goods. As well, buying on credit can be expensive because the cost of credit can add significantly to the cost of a good or service. Advertising plays a part because, when we are bombarded day after day with advertising messages, our resistance weakens. There seem to be many traps for the unwary consumer.

Granted there are many temptations. Often, though, we live beyond our means because we have an imprecise idea of our actual disposable income and our expenses.

One way to answer the question of where your money goes is to develop a budget. A budget will help you to understand what your income and expenses are, and how you can plan to use your income wisely.

A **budget** is a financial plan that shows the expected income and expenditures, and indicates the anticipated surplus or deficit.

SAVINGS

Savings are that part of current income that is not spent.

Often we find that we have to make a conscious effort to save. It is helpful to set a savings goal and trim expenditures accordingly. This is where budgeting comes to the rescue again.

Once you have some savings, what can you do with this money? As any financial advisor will tell you, you have worked hard for your money; now it's time to make your money work for you.

There are a number of places where we can put our savings. At first glance, the possibilities may seem a little bewildering. We have come across some already. In our examination of business organizations, we learned of some of the features of stocks, preferred shares, and bonds. However, there are many other places to invest our savings: bank deposits, guaranteed investment certificates, mutual funds, and so on.

The possibilities can be simplified if we keep in mind that there are really only two broad categories of places into which we can put our savings — **loans** or **equities**.

When you loan money to a bank or another institution, you earn a rate of interest until the amount of your loan is returned to you. In this case, you are acting as the bank usually acts. You loan out your money — usually to the government, to a bank, trust company, or credit union — and the borrower pays you an interest rate plus the amount of the loan sometime in the future.

If we used our savings to buy ownership or part-ownership in something, we have equity in it. Kinds of equity include ownership or part-ownership of land, buildings, or stocks. As an equity holder you stand to gain as its value increases, and to lose if its value decreases. Your hope is that the land, building or stock will increase in value before you sell it.

Risky business
By Robert E. Pierce
Special to *The Globe and Mail*

Finding a method to measure how much risk you are willing to take when investing or discovering what type of investor you are is important prior to moving ahead with registered retirement savings plan or other investment decisions.

If you're not sure just how much risk you feel comfortable undertaking, then this quiz is for you. Simply answer the following questions as honestly as possible, choosing the answers that most closely match your attitudes toward investing. The evaluation at the end of the quiz will help you identify what type of investor you are.

1. An investment loses 15 percent of its value in a market correction a month after you buy it. Assuming none of the fundamentals have changed, you:
a) Sit tight and wait for it to journey back up.
b) Sell it and rid yourself of further sleepless nights if it continues to decline.
c) Buy more — if it looked good at the original price, it looks even better now!

2. A month after you purchase it, the value of your investment suddenly skyrockets by 40 percent. Assuming you can't find any further information, what do you do?
a) Sell it.
b) Hold it on the expectation of further gain.
c) Buy more — it will probably go higher.

3. Which would make you the happiest?
a) You win $100 000 in a publisher's contest.
b) You inherit $100 000 from a rich relative.
c) You win $100 000 by risking $10 000 at the race track.
d) Any of the above — you're happy with the $100 000, no matter how it ended up in your wallet.

4. You inherit your uncle's $100 000 house, free of any mortgage. Although the house is in a fashionable neighbourhood and can be expected to appreciate at a rate faster than inflation, it has deteriorated badly. It would net $1000 monthly if rented as is, or $1500 per month if renovated. The renovations could be financed by a mortgage on the property. You would:
a) Sell the house.
b) Rent it as is.

c) Make the necessary renovations, and then rent it.

5. You work for a small but thriving privately held electronics company. The company is raising money by selling stock to its employees. Management plans to take the company public, but not for four or more years. If you buy stock, you will not be allowed to sell until shares are traded publicly. In the meantime, the stock will pay no dividends. But when the company goes public, the shares could trade for 10 to 20 times what you paid. How much of an investment would you make?
a) None at all.
b) One month's salary.
c) Three months' salary.
d) Six months' salary.

6. Your long-time neighbour is an experienced petroleum geologist, and is assembling a group of investors (of which he is one) to finance an exploratory oil well. The well could pay back 50 to 100 times its investment. But if it is dry, the entire investment is worthless. Your friend estimates the chance of success at only 20 percent. What would you invest?
a) Nothing at all.
b) One month's salary.
c) Three months' salary.
d) Six months' salary.

7. You learn that several commercial building developers are seriously looking at undeveloped land in a certain location. You are offered an option to buy a choice parcel of land. The cost is about two months' salary and you calculate the gain to be 10 months' salary. You:
a) Purchase the option.
b) Let it slide — it's not for you.

8. You are on a TV game show and can choose one of the following. Which would you take?
a) $1000 in cash.
b) A 50-percent chance at $4000.
c) A 20-percent chance at $10 000.
d) A 5-percent chance at $100 000.

9. Suppose that you expect that within the next six months or a year, inflation will return. Hard assets such as precious metals, collectibles and real estate are expected to keep pace with inflation. Your assets are now all in long-term bonds. What would you do?

a) Hold the bonds.

b) Sell the bonds and put half the proceeds into money funds and the other half into hard assets.

c) Sell the bonds and put the total proceeds into hard assets.

d) Sell the bonds, put the total proceeds into hard assets and borrow additional money to buy more.

10. You've lost $500 at the blackjack table in Atlantic City. How much more are you prepared to lose to win the $500 back?

a) Nothing. You quit now.

b) $100.

c) $250.

d) $500.

e) More than $500.

Risk-tolerance scoring

Total your score using the point system below for each answer that you gave:

1. (a) 3 (b) 2 (c) 4; 2. (a) 1 (b) 3 (c) 4; 3. (a) 2 (b) 1 (c) 4 (d) 1; 4. (a) 1 (b) 2 (c) 3; 5. (a) 1 (b) 2 (c) 4 (d) 6; 6. (a) 1 (b) 3 (c) 6 (d) 9; 7. (a) 3 (b) 1; 8. (a) 1 (b) 3 (c) 5 (d) 9; 9. (a) 1 (b) 2 (c) 3 (d) 4; 10. (a) 1 (b) 2 (c) 4 (d) 6 (e) 8.

32 and over: You're an adventuresome, assertive investor. The choices available to you promise dynamic opportunities. Remember, though, that the search for more return carries an extra measure of risk.

19–31: You are an active investor who's willing to take calculated, prudent risks to achieve greater financial gain. Your investment universe is more diverse.

Below 19: You are a conservative investor who's allergic to risk. Stick with sober, conservative investments until you develop the confidence or desire to take on more risk.

Robert Pierce is vice-president of Equion Securities Canada Ltd.

Source: *The Globe and Mail*, September 29, 1992.

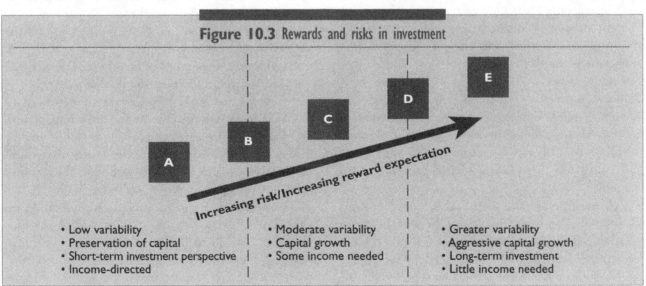

Figure 10.3 Rewards and risks in investment

Increasing risk/Increasing reward expectation

- Low variability
- Preservation of capital
- Short-term investment perspective
- Income-directed

- Moderate variability
- Capital growth
- Some income needed

- Greater variability
- Aggressive capital growth
- Long-term investment
- Little income needed

Which one of the five boxes best reflects your position? Explain why.

Loans

Many different institutions — for example, banks, trust companies, credit unions, governments, and corporations — borrow money from individual Canadians.

1. Banks, trust companies, and credit unions

You can deposit your savings in a bank, trust company, or credit union. Financial institutions have a number of accounts that are designed to meet different needs. As well, rates of interest and services are competitive and are likely to vary from one financial institution to another. It is worthwhile to compare the different accounts available to get the one(s) that best fit(s) your needs.

Personal chequing account

With this account, your name is printed on the cheques. There may be a service charge for each cheque written. Your cheques are returned with a monthly statement, making this account a good one to use for paying your bills. However, there is usually no interest or only a very low interest paid on this account so it is not a good place for your savings.

Chequing/savings account

Cheques may not be returned on this account. There may be a service charge for each cheque written, although some banks offer free chequing if you keep a minimum monthly balance. There is a low rate of interest offered on this account.

Savings account

A more appropriate place to put your savings is a true savings account. While you are usually not permitted to write cheques on this account, you can make cash withdrawals. This type of account offers the highest rate of interest. A passbook is often used for record keeping.

Guaranteed Investment Certificates

Banks and other financial institutions issue savings or Guaranteed Investment Certificates (GICs). You can obtain these certificates for a specified amount (often with a minimum of $1000) and a fixed period of time (usually for a minimum of a year). The advantage of placing your savings in an investment certificate is that you get a higher rate of interest than on a savings account. The disadvantage is that you are "locked into" the program for the fixed period of time and you suffer a penalty if you withdraw your money before the end of the fixed time period.

2. Government

Buy a Canada Savings Bond

Canada Savings Bonds are issued for a specified period of time by the government of Canada and usually pay an interest rate above that offered on a savings account. The one advantage of a Canada Savings Bond over a GIC is that you can cash in your Canada Savings Bond at any time.

Buy federal or provincial government bonds

Federal/provincial government bonds are essentially IOUs issued and backed by these governments. The bond is a promise to pay borrowed money on a particular date and, until that date, to pay interest on the amount owed.

The various ways to save money considered so far have one big advantage over most other kinds of investment: they carry little risk. In other words, your money is safe. It is doubtful that the big financial institutions (and much less likely the federal government) will "go under" tomorrow, taking your life savings with them. As a measure of protection for the depositor, all federally incorporated banks and trust companies are required to be members of the Canada Deposit Insurance Corporation (CDIC).

The CDIC insures deposits to a maximum of $60 000 per person per institution. Deposits made with provincially incorporated companies are also insured by CDIC in every province but Québec. Québec has a similar deposit insurance plan of its own under the administration of the Québec Deposit Insurance Board.

You should be careful, though, to investigate investment options. For instance, if you invest in a five-year investment certificate, you are "locked into" the plan for those five years. The rate of interest that was set when you first invested in the plan might have seemed attractive at the time. If, however, the interest rate rises, the value of your bond will decline. If the interest rate falls, then the value of your bond will increase. An example will show why.

Suppose that I have bought a bond or a GIC for a five-year period for $1000 and that the rate of interest on the bond is 10 percent. Over the next five years I can expect to receive $100 a year (plus, of course, $1000 at the end of the five-year period).

Suppose the rate of interest increases to 15 percent. Now suppose you buy a $1000 bond. Your bond provides you with an income of $150 a year — even though we both paid the same amount for the bond ($1000) and at the end of the fifth year the bonds will be worth the same ($1000). Your bond is worth more than mine because it has a greater rate of return.

If the rate of interest falls to 5 percent, the opposite is true. My bond bought when interest rates were at 10 percent still yields $100 a year. Your bond, though, bought at the new rate of 5 percent, yields only $50. With falling interest rates, the value of bonds will tend to rise; with rising interest rates, the value of bonds will tend to fall.

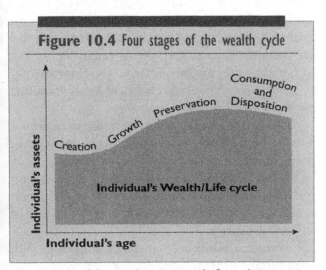

Figure 10.4 Four stages of the wealth cycle

After getting a full-time job, many people focus their energies to create and increase (or grow) their wealth. Later, before retirement, a major concern is to preserve the wealth that has been created. After retirement, the accumulated wealth is slowly disposed of.

3. Life insurance

Many forms of life insurance have a savings as well as an insurance feature. When you buy these kinds of insurance you are saving. We will examine life insurance in more detail later in the chapter.

4. Corporations

As outlined in Chapter 3, you can invest money in a corporation and become a bondholder. The corporate bond is an IOU very much like the federal or provincial bond. It, too, is a promise to repay borrowed money on a particular date and, until then, interest is paid on the amount owed. Corporate bonds are more risky than government bonds and consequently pay a higher rate of interest. Again, however, bonds are liable to suffer from a decline in value if the general rate of interest on corporate bonds rises, and an increase in value if the rate of interest declines.

The value of bonds and preferred shares also depends on the profitability of the corporation. If the corporation suffers heavy losses, it may not be able to pay bond holders and preferred shareholders anything at all. This means there is a greater risk involved with these securities than the other investments we have considered so far.

Equities

Equity investments are investments in those things we can both see and touch. The most common forms of equity investments are in homes and cottages (real estate), and in the common stocks of corporations.

Common stocks

Buying common stocks is a very common form of equity investment. As we have seen, the prices of common stocks tend to vary in accordance with the company's financial performance and future prospects, and with the general state of the economy.

Common stocks are the riskiest form of investment in a corporation because they have last claim on the earnings of the company. They are also likely to have higher rates of return when corporate profits are high than corporate bonds or preferred shares. Common stocks will usually provide better protection against general increases in prices (inflation) than bonds.

Real estate

Many Canadians own their own home. For many people, that is the most expensive item they purchase in their lives. It is therefore appropriate to consider the relative merits of owning versus renting a home.

Many advantages are often cited in favour of home ownership. Pride of possession, feelings of independence, and a general sense of security are associated with ownership of a home. Homeowners may have a greater sense of belonging to their community and have a greater stake in it. Repayments of money borrowed to buy the home (called a **mortgage**) are often fixed for the life of the loan so they are predictable over that period of time.

One of the principal reasons for buying a home is to build up savings. In some kinds of mortgages, part of the monthly payment made by a mortgage-holder goes toward paying off the mortgage. With these kinds of mortgages, as time goes by, the homeowner's equity in the house (the difference between the value of the home and the loans on it) will gradually increase — assuming, of course, that the home does not decline in value.

In Canada, too, homeowners receive favoured tax treatment. Provided that the home is the family's principal residence, profits from its sale (capital gains) are not subject to taxation.

Though there are many advantages to home ownership as a savings investment, there are also advantages to renting. It is sometimes said that it is easy to recognize a homeowner — she's the one coming out of the hardware store. The renter is freed from the day-to-day upkeep of a home. The renter doesn't have to worry about declining home prices or rising interest rates. The renter is mobile, free to move at the end of a lease without having to go through the expensive concern of selling and/or buying a house. The renter is also free to use savings in ways other than making a first or down payment on a home.

Ownership of real estate other than a home is another form of equity investment. The ownership of a cottage, a duplex, or a plot of land may provide an income when rented, and a capital gain (profit) or a capital loss when sold.

Mutual or investment funds

Suppose you have $1000 and you want to invest it in stocks, but you have little knowledge of the stock market. With $1000 you could not spread your investment over a large number of stocks to diminish the risk. You also could not afford a professional manager to look after it. If, however, there were 999 people like you, with similar investment objectives and each with $1000 to invest, you could pool your funds. With a million dollars, you could hire a professional manager and you could spread your risk over many stocks. (You would avoid "putting all your eggs in one basket.") In fact, this is what you are doing when you buy into a mutual fund. The small investor, through the mutual fund, gets the same advantages as the large investor: diversification (the spreading of risk) and professional management. In addition, mutual funds, like stocks, are liquid — they can be sold on any business day.

Essentially there are five different kinds of **mutual (or investment) funds**:

Equity funds are mainly invested in stocks — usually the common stocks of Canada, the United States, Japan, or a number of other countries.

Bond funds invest in government (federal, provincial, or municipal) bonds — as well as those of corporations. Bonds, too, may be from a number of different countries.

Mortgage funds are sometimes lumped in with bond funds and are primarily invested in mortgages.

Money market funds invest in short-term (e.g., three to six months) government treasury bills (bonds).

Balanced funds invest in a mix of equities (or stocks), bonds, and treasury bills. Depending on how the money managers see trends in the economy, they will shift their investments among the three types to maximize their return and minimize the risk.

There were about 800 mutual funds offered to the Canadian public in 1994 — more than twice the number a decade ago — and the numbers are still growing.

The growth of investment in mutual funds in Canada in the 1980s was very rapid. In December 1980, approximately half a million people were fund holders; by mid-1987, the number had mushroomed to 2.2 million, and by 1994 to 7 million. The total amount invested grew even more rapidly from $3.5 billion in 1980, to $24 billion in 1987, and to $130 billion in 1994.

Mutual fund prices are quoted daily (except Monday) in the business section of many newspapers, including *The Globe and Mail*, and in the *Financial Post*. Before investing in a mutual fund, you should obtain a copy of the prospectus of the fund to find out what its objectives are, and to determine what the sales and redemption charges are. (Redemption charges are incurred when the fund is sold.) Find out also how well the fund has performed over a number of years. It is important to know who the fund's investment advisors are, and how well the funds that they have managed have done in the past.

Life insurance

One of the great mysteries of life is the length of it and, fortunately perhaps, it will remain a mystery. We all know that we are going to die but we don't know when. To help deal with that uncertainty, we have life insurance.

Insurance is a contract in which one party (the insurer) agrees to pay another (the insured) a sum of money in the event of a specific loss. Insurance protects against losses due to death, sickness, accident, and fire. In return, the insured makes payments to the insurer.

If you are the principal breadwinner of a family, one way of protecting your family against the financial loss that would occur if you died is through life insurance. Without your income, your family could face serious financial problems. The purchase of insurance on your life is one way of sheltering your family from these problems.

The principle behind life insurance is really quite straightforward. The risk of financial loss due to death can be shared among a large number of people. Each insured individual makes a payment (called a premium) to an insurance company. In the event of the death of the insured, the company makes a payment to an individual (called the beneficiary) chosen by the insured.

While you and I do not know how long we will live, insurance companies have statistics that indicate the probability of death for people of a certain group at a particular age. These statistics, called mortality tables, are used by life insurance companies to predict how many people in a particular group will die in a particular year. The companies assume that what will happen in the near future will be similar to what has happened in the recent past.

Table 10.2 on page 217 is a sample of the tables used by insurance companies. It shows that, of 1000 people aged five, 1.35 of them are expected to die within the next year, and of 1000 people aged eleven, 1.23 are expected to die within the next year, and so on.

Suppose that you set up the Teen Life Insurance Company for young men and women, fifteen to nineteen years of age, and that at each age 100 000 people wanted to buy $1000 each of life insurance. How much would you have to pay out to beneficiaries of the fifteen-year-old group? We can expect that within the next year 1.46 of 1000 fifteen-year-olds will die. Of every 100 000 in this age group in Canada, 146 fifteen-year-olds are expected to die (100 × 1.46). Therefore, your company will have to pay out 146 × $1000 = $146 000. In order to cover the amounts paid out in insurance for the fifteen-year-olds, you would have to receive $146 000 at the beginning of the year from those insured with your company. For each insured, that would be $1.46. In the same way, for the sixteen-year-old group, you would want to pay out $154 000, and so on, for the other ages.

BUILDING YOUR SKILLS

Reading a mutual funds performance survey

The *Financial Post, The Globe and Mail* and many other daily newspapers publish summaries of the performance of Canadian mutual funds. These are useful for comparing the performance of one mutual fund with another, of one kind of mutual fund with another (e g., Japanese equities with Canadian equities), and of comparing mutual funds with other forms of personal investment.

Figure 10.5 includes selections from one mutual funds performance survey, and explanations for the terms used. Test your ability to read a mutual funds performance survey by answering the questions that follow the explanations.

The daily (except Monday) mutual funds performance survey is typically much simpler than the table in figure 10.5. It shows only the fund name, the net asset value per share, and the change from the previous day in cents.

Fund name

In this column appears the name of the fund. The London Life Mortgage Fund invests in Canadian

Figure 10.5 Mutual funds monthly performance survey

| Fund name | Fees | Expense ratio | Volatility | Percentage change in value | | | Average annual compound rate of return | | | | NAVPs | Assets (000s) |
				3 mos.	6 mos.	1 yr	2 yr	3 yr	5 yr	10 yr		
Balanced fund Jones Heward Canadian Balanced Fund	F 9% D 5%	or 2%	2	3.58	2.46	16.73	15.40	14.41	10.91	10.24	15.12	$57 078
International fund Royal Trust Japanese Stock Fund	N	3.1%	7	25.33	7.17	48.51	21.23	11.01	0.37	N/A	17.82	$41 012
Canadian equity fund Trimark Canadian Fund	F 9%	1.57%	3	6.49	13.05	33.93	19.13	17.78	12.97	13.75	16.14	$871 636
Bond fund Investors' Bond Fund	R 3%	1.82%	2	1.05	2.47	10.60	11.04	11.83	11.91	11.58	4.83	$1 750 900
Money market fund Scotia Money Market Fund	N	1.00%	1	0.81	1.71	3.83	4.60	5.78	N/A	N/A	10.00	$149 378
Mortgage fund London Life Mortgage Fund	R 5%	2%	1	2.56	4.57	9.37	9.55	11.42	11.10	11.14	103.87	$310 159

Source: *The Globe and Mail*, March 17, 1994.

mortgages. Often the fund name provides a good description of the nature of the fund.

Fees

Many mutual funds have sales (or front-load) charges. Some funds have redemption charges — charges made when the fund is sold. The amounts shown here are maximum charges; that is, the sales charges are open to negotiation and are frequently lower than the percentages shown here.

The letter N indicates that it is a "no-load" fund — that is, the investor pays no money to buy or sell the fund. Many banks and trust companies have no-load funds.

The letter F with a percentage figure after it indicates the maximum charge levied at the time of investment. This fee is called a front-end load and is usually negotiable. Thus, Trimark Canadian has a front-end load of 9 percent.

The letter D indicates that there is a fee charged when the fund is sold but only on the original amount of the investment. Thus, the Jones Heward Fund has a redemption fee of 5 percent.

The letter R indicates there is a charge on the total amount when the fund is sold. These fees, however, decrease as time goes on. Thus, the Investors' Bond Fund has a fee of 3 percent when the fund is sold.

Expense ratio

The expense ratio is the total costs of running the fund as a percentage of the assets. These costs include payments to the investment advisors, and office and investment expenses. The expense ratio per year for the Trimark Canadian Fund is 1.57 percent of the net asset value per share.

Volatility

This is a measure of how the value of the shares has varied over the previous three years compared with other funds. A "1" indicates low volatility — a fund that seldom changes very much, a steady performer. A "10" indicates a fund that varies a great deal. The degree of volatility gives an indication of the amount of risk in a fund. Thus, for example, the Scotia Money Market Fund with a volatility measure of 1 is very much less variable than the Royal Trust Japanese Stock Fund with a measure of 7.

Percentage change in value

The three-month, six-month, and one-year figures show the percentage change in these funds for this period of time. Thus, for example, over the last three months measured by the table, Royal Trust Japanese Stock Fund turned in a dazzling 25.33 percent, while the Investors' Bond Fund had only a 1.05 percent gain. These figures assume that all dividends are invested and all management fees deducted.

Average annual compound rate of return

The two-year to ten-year columns show the average compound rate of return over that time period. Thus, over ten years the London Life Mortgage Fund has a compound rate of return of 11.14 percent. These figures are useful to compare returns of different mutual funds and to compare these returns with other forms of investment.

Net asset value per share (NAVPs)

This is the value of each mutual (or investment) fund share. Since the value of these shares is dependent on the values of shares and other assets of the mutual fund, the net asset value will vary from day to day. Daily prices of mutual fund shares are listed in the financial pages of many daily newspapers. The selling and buying price of the Investors' Bond Fund, for example, was $4.83. The net asset value per share is calculated by taking the total assets of the fund, subtracting the liabilities, and dividing the sum by the total of the shares. Mutual fund investors buy shares at this price (plus any sales charges) and sell at this price (minus any selling or redemption charges).

Assets

Assets show the total market value of a fund's portfolio at the end of the month. Thus, for example, the total value of London Life Mortgage Fund was $310 159 000.

Questions

1. What are the fees charged by (a) Royal Trust Japanese Stock Fund (b) London Life Mortgage Fund?
2. Which fund has the highest expense ratio?
3. Which fund(s) has (have) the lowest volatility?
4. Over the previous year, which fund has had the lowest rate of return?
5. Over the previous five years, which fund has had the best rate of return?
6. Check the recent performance of the six funds in your newspaper.

There are many different plans of life insurance to suit many different situations. We will examine three main types of insurance: term, straight-life (or whole-life), and limited-payment life insurance.

Term insurance

Term insurance was used in the explanation of the Teen Life Insurance Company. There we saw that the company's premiums were set to pay the insurance on those who died in the one-year period. Once the beneficiaries in that year had been paid, and operating costs, commissions, and profits had been covered, nothing was left over.

Term insurance is often referred to as "pure insurance." It only provides protection for a specified period of time. Once that period of time is over, the policy ends and so does the protection. For this reason, it is the cheapest of the three kinds of insurance. With term insurance, it is possible to acquire more protection than with other kinds of insurance for each premium dollar. See table 10.3 on page 217. At age eighteen, the premium for five-year renewable term insurance is less than a quarter of that for whole-life insurance and less than an eighth of that of twenty-pay life insurance. However, if the insured wants to renew the policy at the end of five years, it is renewed at the rate of twenty-three-year-olds. Insured people who want to renew their term insurance face increased rates

with each renewal. Premiums for whole-life and twenty-pay life insurance remain unchanged.

As the name implies, term insurance is for a certain period of time, or to a particular age. Some kinds of term insurance require medical examinations for renewal and, as a result, insurance may be denied or the rates increased. Renewable term insurance, however, means that the insurance policy may be renewed without a medical examination up to a stated age limit. Term insurance is often not available beyond age sixty-five or seventy.

Straight-life or whole-life insurance

As the name of this kind of insurance implies, the insureds continue paying premiums for the whole of their lives. Straight-life premiums have an insurance component (roughly equal to term insurance) and a savings element. From table 10.3 we can see that the annual premiums for $1000 straight-life insurance at age eighteen are higher than those for renewable term insurance between the ages of eighteen and fifty and lower after age sixty. The savings (and interest) accumulated by the straight-life policy before age sixty are used to lower the premiums after age sixty to maintain a level premium.

The straight-life insurance policy has a cash surrender value. This means that, after the policy has been in existence for more than one or two years, the

Table 10.2 Mortality rates

Age	Deaths per 1000
1	1.76
2	1.52
3	1.46
4	1.40
5	1.35
6	1.30
7	1.26
8	1.23
9	1.21
10	1.21
11	1.23
12	1.26
13	1.32
14	1.39
15	1.46
16	1.54
17	1.62
18	1.69
19	1.74
20	1.79
21	1.83
26	1.96
31	2.19
36	2.64
41	3.84
46	5.83
51	9.11
56	14.21
61	22.24
66	34.74
71	54.15
76	79.18
81	119.35
86	172.82
91	245.77
96	400.56
98	668.15

Source: Canadian Life Insurance Association.

Table 10.3 Sample insurance rates

Age	Whole-Life ($)	20-Pay life ($)	Age	5-Year renewable term ($)
16	7.84	12.91	16	-
17	8.11	13.26	17	-
18	8.35	13.57	18	1.65
19	8.55	13.91	19	1.65
20	8.77	14.20	20	1.65
21	9.00	14.53		
25	10.20	16.16	25	1.62
30	12.12	18.57	30	1.66
35	15.06	21.98	35	1.70
40	19.18	26.37	40	2.15
45	24.46	31.83	45	3.10
50	31.04	38.22	50	4.70
55	38.91	45.45	55	6.95
60	48.19	53.45	60	11.00

Source: 1993 Life Insurance Tables, Stone and Cox.

Of the three types of insurance shown in table 10.3, term insurance has the lowest premiums while whole-life has the highest premiums.

sixty-five), or over a fixed number of years — ten, twenty, and thirty. Twenty years is the most usual.

Because of the higher premiums, the savings for this type of insurance build up more rapidly than with a straight-life policy. Yet, the policy has a cash surrender value after a period of time like the straight-life policy. Once the payments for the limited period of time have been made, no additional premiums are required. However, it is only on the death of the insured that the full amount of the policy is paid.

SHAREOWNERSHIP AMONG CANADIANS

The image of Canadians — that we are afraid to consider any investment that has even a slight odour of risk — is not totally in agreement with reality. Although many Canadians continue to concentrate their assets in

policy holder may terminate the policy and withdraw the savings.

Limited-pay life insurance

As the name suggests, this is a life insurance policy with payments made over a limited number of years. Payments may be made until a particular age (often traditional places such as savings accounts and home ownership, shareownership among Canadians shows very considerable growth. According to surveys published by the Toronto Stock Exchange, in 1993 over 4.2 million (21.5 percent) owned common or preferred stock in publicly traded companies compared to 2.9 million (or 16 percent) in 1989. See figure 10.6. Nearly a quarter of all adult Canadians (almost 5 million) own mutual funds invested in common or preferred stock and nearly 30 percent (5.6 million) own mutual funds invested in mortgage funds, bond funds, or money market funds.

REGISTERED RETIREMENT SAVINGS PLANS

A popular way for Canadians to save for retirement is through a Registered Retirement Savings Plan — popularly known by its initials, **RRSP**. As the future of government old-age benefits becomes increasingly doubtful due to rising government debt and an aging

population, Canadians are beginning to recognize that they cannot rely on government pensions to provide them with an income in old age. Many Canadians use RRSPs to save for the future. Up to a certain limit (18 percent of earned income or $14 500 in 1995, and $13 500 in 1996 — whichever of the two is smaller), every dollar contributed is deductible from taxable income. Suppose, for example, that the highest tax rate on the last $1000 of income is taxed at 30 percent; then for every $1000 you put in an RRSP you save $300 in taxes.

The income earned inside the RRSP is protected from taxes as long as it stays in the RRSP. Outside the RRSP, income earned on investments is subject to taxation.

In making contributions to an RRSP, many people wait until the last minute at the end of the year. A more profitable and more painless way of making contributions is to have the Canadian financial institution that holds your RRSP (such as a bank, trust company, or credit union) deduct a fixed amount monthly from your account. See table 10.4.

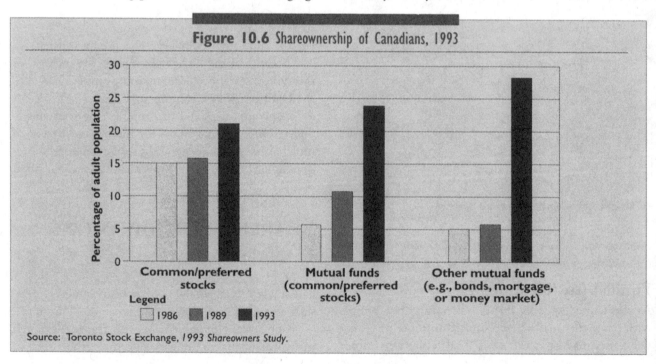

Figure 10.6 Shareownership of Canadians, 1993

Source: Toronto Stock Exchange, *1993 Shareowners Study.*

Within the RRSP, your assets can be held in a number of ways (though a maximum of 20 percent only was permitted outside Canada in 1995): cash, GICs, bonds, stocks, and mutual funds of various sorts are the most popular ways. Here the old adage — "don't put all your eggs in one basket" — is probably a wise idea. In this way you will not have all your funds locked into an underperforming investment.

Most people start to withdraw funds from their RRSPs when they retire and their income (and income tax level) falls. Some Canadians, however, withdraw funds from their RRSPs as a last resort when they have no other income sources. Whatever the reason for the withdrawals, any funds withdrawn will be subject to tax. However, it is likely that the tax rate on withdrawal is lower than at the time of the contribution.

YOU AND YOUR INVESTMENTS

So far we have reviewed a number of possible personal investments but we have yet to consider where you enter the picture. A starting point in any program of personal investment and savings is to consider your objectives. What do you want to achieve? What are your objectives or goals? Is your objective to save for a rainy day? for a round-the-world trip? for a down payment on a home? for a car? to retire by the time you reach age fifty? to have enough money to start your own business? to make a million by age thirty? to get married?

Once you have decided on one or more objectives, then you may have to temper them with some realities about your situation. You will need to consider some, or all, of the following questions.

1. Is your income large enough to support you? There is little point in risking your money in investments if your income is only just enough.

2. How will your income vary in the future? If your job is secure with a well-established company and the possibility of pay increases is good, then you can afford to take more risks than you could otherwise.

Table 10.4 The cost of waiting

Investor A — Age 35	Investor B — Age 35
$5000 per year in *monthly* deposits; 6% compounded annually	$5000 contribution at *year-end*; 6% compounded annually
$408 141 accumulated value at age 65.	**$395 291** accumulated value at age 65.
The Advantage of Monthly Deposits: $12 850	

Source: Royal Trust.

3. How old are you? Your age is an important factor. The younger you are the more you can take risks. As you approach retirement (a long way off!), you will be more likely to look for security.

4. How much time, knowledge, and interest do you have to follow your investments? If you wish to invest in common stocks, you will need to devote time to select and follow your stocks. If you have little time or knowledge available, you should consider other personal investments until you have the time and expertise.

5. What is your tax situation? You should know what your marginal tax rate is. You should also know how the federal and provincial governments treat income from different sources for tax purposes. Governments in the past, for example, have treated income from capital gains and dividends from stocks more favourably than interest from savings accounts, Canada Savings Bonds, or GICs.

6. How much risk keeps you awake at night? When a worried investor complained to J.P. Morgan that his investments prevented him from sleeping at night, the great American financier replied, "Sell down to your sleeping point." In other words, your personality should determine how much risk is appropriate for you.

In establishing your investment plan, be ready to be flexible. Recognize that there is no investment that has the best of both worlds — that is safe while at the same time giving a high return. Generally we are

BUILDING YOUR SKILLS

Applying the "rule of seventy-two"

A useful way of calculating how long it will take to double your money — to make $1 become $2 — at various interest rates is to use the "rule of seventy-two." If you invest your money at 1 percent, it will take seventy-two years for it to double. If you invest at 2 percent, it will take thirty-six years to double, and so on. The rule of seventy-two highlights the need to compare rates when you are considering borrowing as well as lending money.

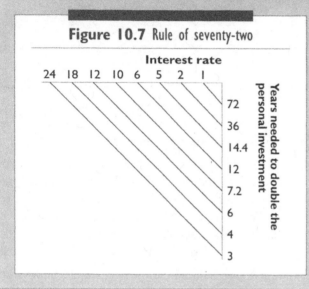

Figure 10.7 Rule of seventy-two

Practise your skill

Assume there are no taxes and no sales charges.

1. You invest $1000 at 6 percent. What is the investment worth at the end of twenty-four years?

2. You invest $1000 at 9 percent. What is the investment worth at the end of twenty-four years?

3. What is the difference in the value of the two investments after twenty-four years?

trading off security for high returns. The higher the returns we seek, generally the greater the risk we run.

REVIEW

Explain each term in your own words and provide an example: consumption, budgeting, savings, insurance, credit.

APPLICATIONS

1. Use a comparison organizer, like the one shown in figure 10.8, to summarize the different kinds of personal investment that have been examined in this chapter.

2. Read the following passage and apply your knowledge of decision-making to help Darjit buy a car. Refer back to Elena's dilemma in Chapter 1 and draw a decision-making grid.

Darjit is pleasantly perplexed. She has just graduated from high school and has accepted a $20 000-a-year job in a large town 30 km away from her parents' home where she lives. Since there is no public transportation between her home and her job, she has decided to buy an automobile. She would like to spend a maximum of $10 000 on the car. But what kind of car should she buy? Examining the want ads in her local newspaper, Darjit narrows it down to three different cars.

Luxury car   She could buy a five-year-old Lincoln Town Car Signature Series with electric moonroof,

SUMMARY

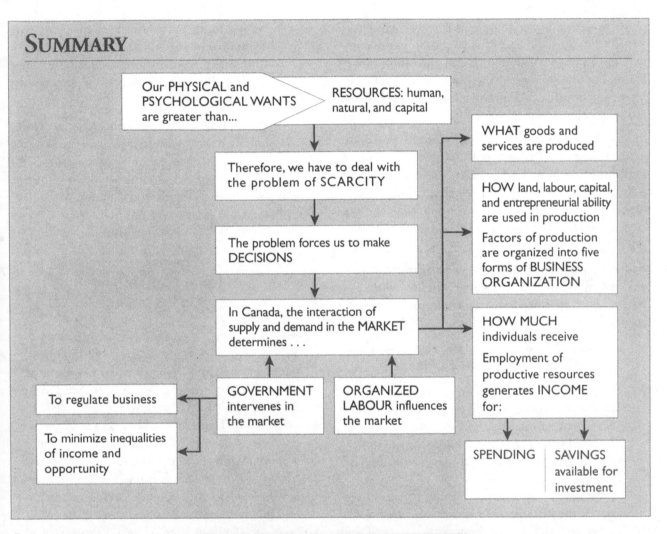

Figure 10.8 Comparison of different investments

Investment	Safety of amount invested	Possibility of increase in value	Income from the investment	Ease of getting cash	Time required to manage the investment
Personal chequing account	High	None	None	Excellent	None
Chequing-savings account					

power steering, power brakes, and power windows, AM/FM stereo radio and cassette player, cruise control, low mileage (76 000 km), and air conditioning. Darjit has always wanted to own a luxury car. She likes a smooth ride. The stereo will keep her company as she drives to and from work.

Sports car   She could buy a three-year-old, two-door white GrandAm Firebird with a V-8 engine, automatic transmission, bucket seats, rally wheels, low mileage (77 000 km), power steering, windows and brakes, radio, tape deck, and air conditioning. She has always wanted a sports car. Her friends would be impressed.

Economy car   She could buy a two-year-old Volkswagen Golf, with two doors, rear window wiper, radio, manual transmission, power steering, sunroof, and very low mileage (42 000 km).

    a)   Before deciding on a particular car, is there anything else Darjit should consider?

3.   Suppose that your wealthy Uncle Ebenezer Scrooge has generously given you $5000 to invest in one mutual fund. Your Uncle Ebenezer has asked you to answer the following questions. Consult four or five other students in your class for their advice.

    a)   What are your most important objectives for the investment? Do you want high rates of growth for your money? the safety of the sales or redemption charges? a low expense ratio? maximum income?

    b)   Examine copies of the *Financial Post* and *The Globe and Mail* and/or your local newspaper for a month. In each you will find one section that contains mutual funds performance surveys. Choose five funds that best meet your objectives.

    c)   Call or write a stockbroker or the mutual funds for a prospectus of your chosen funds. The prospectus usually outlines the objectives

of the fund, its investments, the past performance of the fund, the dividends paid, and other information. Choose the fund that best meets your objectives. Be prepared to explain your choice.

4.   As you read the following extract from an article in *The Economist*, consider whether you agree with Professor Becker that the decision to have children is based on economic laws. Do you think that the laws of supply and demand can be applied to the decision to have children? Explain why you reached your conclusion.

Homo economicus gets his prize

The Nobel prize for economics is worth a juicy $1.2 million — a big enough pot of money to tempt any academic to pursue his or her career in a way that might impress the judges in Sweden. Whether Gary Becker, who has won the [1992] prize, did so is not known, but he would surely approve of the idea. For Mr. Becker, the third winner in a row from the University of Chicago, has been honoured for showing that hard-headed self-interest can explain much human behaviour — ranging from marriage and divorce, to crime and racial discrimination — usually thought of as irrational.

Mr. Becker's first important work was "Human Capital," published in 1964. Education, Mr. Becker argued, is an investment on which people expect to earn rewards later in life. Though this seems obvious enough now, it transformed the way economists thought about labour markets.

In "A Treatise on the Family," published in 1981, Mr. Becker applied the laws of supply and demand to the decision to have children. Contraception, for instance, reduces supply. The cost of having children falls if the child can be put to work at an early age — which is why large families are more common in traditional agricultural societies than in cities. On the other hand, if the mother's time becomes more valuable, the cost of taking time off work to rear a child rises. This, Mr. Becker argues, is why the number of children per family falls as more women get good jobs.

Source: *The Economist*, October 17, 1992.

Becker in demand.

CHAPTER 11

Government Expenditures and Revenues

(1)

(1) Office workers in Calgary, Alberta take a lunch break in Prince's Island Park, located close to the downtown core.

(2) The Parliament Buildings in Ottawa.

(3) Province House in Charlottetown, Prince Edward Island. The first meeting of the Fathers of Confederation was held here in September, 1864. Today it is the seat of the provincial government and a national historic site.

(4) Corporal Corena Letandre, a member of the Canadian Forces' Service Battalion, comforts a hospitalized child in Cambodia.

(5) An aerial view of The Vancouver Trade and Convention Centre, with its unique five-sail roof. This facility is one of several managed by the B.C. Pavilion Corporation, a Crown corporation of the Province of British Columbia. Each year, the Centre hosts approximately 900 events, including conventions, trade shows, consumer shows, meetings, and banquets.

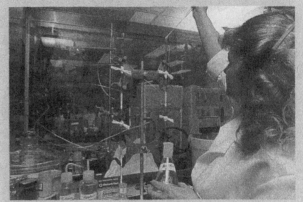

(6)

(6) A National Research Council technical officer prepares a sample of CARP-1, the world's first certified reference material for biological tissue containing the highly toxic substances, dioxins and furans. This reference material is sold to analytical laboratories around the world.

Questions

1. What examples of government expenditure are shown here?

2. List some ways in which you benefit from government spending.

Government business in the bathrooms of the nation

BUZZZZZZZZZZ!! It was the insistent clamour of my radio alarm clock, powered by electricity produced by a provincially-owned Crown corporation and distributed by a municipally-owned utility company. After I had silenced the alarm clock, the modulated tones of the news announcer could be heard . . . brought to us by the Canadian Broadcasting Corporation — a federal Crown corporation.

Bleary-eyed, I took my morning shower with water supplied by another company owned by my local government. That water has been treated with a number of chemicals to protect me from typhoid, tooth decay, dysentery, and sundry other unhealthy horrors.

As I began to shave, the label on my can of shaving cream warns: "Do not puncture or incinerate." Some government agency obviously believes that such warnings are necessary. The same label informs me in both official languages (thanks again to government) that the can contains 454 mL because some other government agency has abolished fluid ounces. The towel I used to dry myself bears a label stating that it was manufactured in South Korea and, of course, the federal government regulates the flow of foreign goods that enter the country.

I glanced out my bathroom window and noticed a neighbour taking her dog for a walk. The local government owns the sidewalk but requires householders to clear snow from it within 24 hours of a snowfall. The dog is on a leash (as required by municipal laws). The neighbour is carrying a small plastic shovel and bag.

Obviously, there's a place for government in the bathrooms of the nation.

Adapted from Richard J. Van Loon and Michael S. Whittington, *The Canadian Political System* (Toronto: McGraw-Hill Ryerson Ltd., 1981).

Activity 1: An opinion poll

What do you think?

Canadians have different opinions about whether government is spending too much, and whether taxes are too high. What do you think?

Question 1: Which of the following statements comes closest to your view?

1. Taxes should be cut, even if it means some reduction in government services such as health, education, and welfare.

2. Things should be left as they are.

3. Government services such as health, education, and welfare should be extended, even if it means some increase in taxes.

4. Don't know.

Question 2: Do you think taxes are too high or about right?

What does the class think?

After you have made a note of your views, find out what the class thinks. Summarize the class response. Keep a record of your responses — we will return to them at the end of this chapter.

Activity 2: Let your fingers do the walking through the blue pages

Are you aware of the extent of government involvement in your community? A quick way to research this is to use the blue pages of your telephone book. Here, under the municipal, provincial, and federal governments, many of the different government departments or ministries are listed.

Instructions

Divide into six groups. Two groups will be responsible for making as complete a list as possible of government activity for any one level of government.

Municipal (or local) government
Examples: local police, garbage collection, fire department

Provincial government
Examples: schools, provincial roads, hospitals

Federal government
Examples: national defence, criminal justice

We could expand our description of the impact of government on our daily lives; but perhaps the brief glimpse on page 226 is enough to show us that government does have a huge effect on our lives.

As we saw in Chapter 2, ours is a mixed market economy: an economy in which governments play a significant role. The defects and weaknesses of the market system provide the major justification for that role.

Governments influence the economy in four major ways: by **spending**; by **taxing**; by **regulating**; and by **directing Crown corporations**. When government increases its spending on schools and hospitals, then more schools and more hospitals are built. Through taxation, government raises the money (or revenue) it needs to function. It takes money from you and me and uses it in a way that is almost certainly different from the ways in which we would use it. Governments may also use taxes to discourage the consumption of certain goods or services. As a result, the prices of these goods or services will increase and less will be consumed. Government regulations also influence the economy through laws. For example, the laws that require all young Canadians to go to school mean that schools must be built and staffed with teachers and provided with teaching resources. Finally, government affects many parts of the economy through its direction of Crown corporations. For example, because the CBC — a Crown corporation

— has a policy of favouring Canadian shows, more Canadian performers and technicians will find work.

We will begin our examination of the role of government in our economy by considering some of the reasons for government involvement. Then we will examine the ways in which government seeks to achieve its goals: through its spending, taxing, and regulating powers.

REASONS FOR GOVERNMENT INVOLVEMENT IN THE ECONOMY

Government expenditures total many billions of dollars and about half of our Gross Domestic Product. Why do Canadian governments engage in such a large number of activities? Couldn't private enterprise provide goods and services presently supplied by governments? How far should government be involved in the economy? These are questions on which Canadians have differed and will continue to differ.

1. Public goods
A **public good** is a good or service with benefits that people cannot be prevented from consuming, no matter who pays for it. It is therefore usually provided by government.

There are certain goods and services that government can provide that private business cannot. National defence is one example.

Goods where the benefits go to the public in general and not to the individual who purchases them are called **public goods**. If public goods, such as defence, are to be produced, then this production can only be done by government. Government can ensure that the general public pays for the production of these goods.

2. Externalities

An **externality** is a good or bad side effect of production or consumption.

A side effect or an externality (as economists call it) is produced when, for example, a factory pollutes the air or water. The external cost is borne by those who breathe the air or who drink or fish in the polluted water. In the case of pollution, we have negative side effects or externalities.

But not all side effects are negative. If owners of a golf club decide not to sell their land to developers, even though the city has grown around them, there is a positive side effect to their actions. People around the club will breathe cleaner air and will enjoy a more beautiful view than if the land were developed.

Because externalities can affect many people, governments may decide to use their powers of spending, taxing, and regulating to encourage positive side effects and to discourage negative ones.

3. Harmful and beneficial goods

Some goods in our society are viewed as being harmful while others are seen as being beneficial. Harmful goods include such products as addictive drugs — cocaine, heroin, cigarettes. Government reaction to such products may include outright prohibition (as in the case of cocaine) to warnings about the dangers of using it (as in the case of cigarettes).

Perhaps the best known example of a desirable good is education. Governments provide free education in elementary and secondary schools and cover much of the cost of post-secondary education.

4. Distribution

As we have seen in Chapter 8, the market distribution of goods and services does not always agree with our views of economic justice. Therefore, government is involved in the distribution of goods and services to the economically disadvantaged.

5. Economic stability

We will examine the role of government in promoting stable prices and full employment in Chapters 13 and 14.

GROWTH IN GOVERNMENT SPENDING

Total expenditures by all levels of government in Canada have increased greatly since 1867. The expenditure of the federal government, for example, was about $14 million in 1867, $306 million in 1926, and estimated to be more than $164 billion in 1994-95.

Why has this dramatic increase in expenditures occurred since 1926? Some of the reasons are obvious. Since 1926, the Canadian population has increased by over two and a half times. With an increase in population, we can expect an increase in government expenditure. The general level of prices increased more than 4.5 times between 1926 and 1994, so that it took more than four dollars and fifty cents in 1994 to buy what one dollar bought in 1926. Also, Canada was involved in two major wars in the twentieth century and we continue to pay pensions to war veterans.

But increases in population and prices and involvement in war are not enough to explain the massive growth in government expenditures, which reached about 48 percent of the Gross Domestic Product in the early 1990s. Since 1926, Canadians have come to expect that government will do much more for them. As a result, Canadian governments have provided greatly expanded pension and welfare benefits. They have made elementary and secondary education free and available to all young Canadians.

Government-subsidized fees and loans help make college and university education widely available. Governments have also provided Canadians with medical and hospital services at no direct cost to the patient. Expenditures on education, health services, and social welfare have continued to increase rapidly over the years.

By the late 1980s and early 1990s, many Canadians had begun to object strongly to higher taxes and they were increasingly concerned about government deficits and the rising levels of debt. As a result, in the 1990s, governments began to cut expenditures and freeze tax levels at the then current rates.

GOVERNMENT EXPENDITURES

What goods and services do we receive for the taxes we pay and what level of government supplies them?

In general, the federal government provides those services such as defence, international trade, and foreign affairs that affect the nation as a whole. The provinces and municipalities handle affairs that affect the individual citizen more directly, by providing such services as police, fire protection, schools, and roads.

Most of the highways and bridges in the province are paid for by the provincial government. Provincial governments also provide and/or control a significant part of the money needed for elementary, secondary, and post-secondary education.

Municipal government expenditures

Municipal governments provide us with local services that generally affect us more closely than those of the federal or provincial governments. Such services include the building and maintenance of local roads, sewers, sidewalks, streetlights, and the services of the local police, garbage collection, and fire departments.

There are some services administered and funded by more than one level of government. Who sits on your local school board is a local matter because we elect local representatives to school boards. The public school system is administered at both the local and provincial levels. Who pays for the public school system is both a local and provincial matter because, usually, local tax money designated for schools is supplemented by provincial grants.

Some services are administered at one level of government but receive financial assistance from another. Medical care in Canada is one example. Health schemes are funded federally and provincially but are administered by the individual provinces.

Provincial government expenditures

During the four years of expenditures summarized in table 11.1 (page 230), provincial government expenditures grew significantly. Expenditures on goods and services (about one-third of the total) paid for provincial public servants and the supplies they needed, and for the maintenance and construction of provincial buildings. **Transfers** are sums of money allocated to individuals and organizations to pay for pensions, welfare subsidies, roads, school boards, capital assistance to businesses, etc.

The provincial debt and deficit

A large and rapidly growing component of provincial expenditures — more than $1/7$ of the total — is composed of interest payments on the provincial debt.

In the early 1990s, many provincial governments became concerned about the rapid growth of the provincial debt and with increasing interest payments on that debt. The governments introduced plans to cut some expenditures and to restrain the growth of others. The effects of some of these measures can be seen in the decline in the provincial deficit between 1992 and 1993. (A **deficit** results when expenditures are greater than revenues.)

Table 11.1 shows that provincial government expenditures grew more rapidly between 1990 and 1991 and between 1991 and 1992 than between 1992 and 1993, when provincial government spending restraints began to take effect. Transfers to persons,

Table 11.1 Provincial government expenditures (in million dollars), 1990-93

	1990	1991	1992	1993
Expenditure ($)	140 792	152 357	162 247	165 719
Goods and services	44 234	46 961	48 846	49 216
Transfers to:				
Persons	27 762	31 119	33 770	34 841
Businesses	6 120	6 457	7 606	6 709
Municipalities	23 934	26 333	27 904	28 166
Hospitals	20 705	22 121	22 561	22 711
Interest on public debt	18 037	19 366	21 560	24 076
Deficit	–3 119	–12 751	–19 345	–16 991

Source: Statistics Canada, *Canadian Economic Observer*, April 1994.

municipalities, and hospitals accounted for about half the expenditures. Interest payments on the provincial debt continued to grow as provincial governments recorded deficits in each of the four years.

Compare the provincial government expenditures in table 11.1 with provincial government revenues for the same four-year period, as shown in table 11.4 on page 233.

Federal government expenditures

For many years after Confederation, the federal government restricted its expenditures to matters of national concern such as defence, trade and commerce, justice, and foreign relations. The federal government also helped finance the construction of transportation facilities, most notably railways. Recently, however, federal government expenditures have extended into areas that were formerly thought to be the concern of provincial or municipal governments.

The growth in federal expenditures was especially rapid in the late 1970s and early 1980s. Federal expenditures more than doubled in seven years — growing from $45 billion in 1978 to nearly $110 billion in 1985.

Since the early 1980s, federal government expenditures have almost tripled, growing from $63 billion in 1981-82 to $160 billion in 1993-94. Total federal budget expenditures increased by more than 60 percent between 1983-84 and 1992-93. Expenditures are

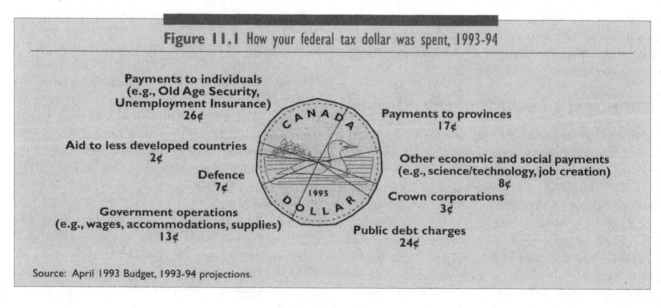

Figure 11.1 How your federal tax dollar was spent, 1993-94

Payments to individuals
(e.g., Old Age Security,
Unemployment Insurance)
26¢

Aid to less developed countries
2¢

Defence
7¢

Government operations
(e.g., wages, accommodations, supplies)
13¢

Payments to provinces
17¢

Other economic and social payments
(e.g., science/technology, job creation)
8¢

Crown corporations
3¢

Public debt charges
24¢

Source: April 1993 Budget, 1993-94 projections.

expected to continue increasing from 1993-94 to 1995-96, despite anticipated reductions in payments for unemployment insurance, transfers to other levels of government, defence, government operations, and payments to Crown corporations.

1. Transfers to persons

Of the eight major components of federal government expenditures, one of the largest is transfers to persons. Included in this category are Old Age Security benefits, guaranteed income supplements, and spouses' allowances. As shown in table 11.2, this category of expenditures is expected to grow from $19.1 billion in 1992-93 to $21.4 billion in 1995-96 as the population ages. Unemployment Insurance payments, on the other hand, are expected to decline, because of decreases in unemployment due to the end of the recession and because of increased eligibility requirements.

2. Transfers to other levels of government

These transfer payments provide financial assistance to the provinces and territories for health care services and post-secondary education. Also included are payments to less wealthy provinces, so that they can provide services comparable to those in more affluent provinces. Finally, these payments include the Canada Assistance Plan, by which the federal government shares the cost of social assistance programs with the provinces.

3. Subsidies and other transfers

Included in this category — and of about equal size in the 1992-93 budget — are grants to business, to Natives and Inuit, to agriculture, and to international assistance programs. Only grants to Natives and Inuit are expected to increase by 1995-96, while the other three subsidies are expected to decline.

Table 11.2 Federal government expenditures (in billion dollars), 1983-84 to 1995-96

	1983-84	1987-88	1990-91	1992-93	1993-94	1994-95	1995-96
1. Transfers to persons	10.4	13.4	16.2	19.1	19.9	20.6	21.4
Unemployment Insurance benefits	9.8	10.4	11.7	19.1	18.4	18.3	17.3
2. Transfers to other levels of government	18.1	20.6	25.1	27.1	27.1	26.3	26.4
3. Subsidies and other transfers	11.6	12.4	13.0	16.2	16.0	17.2	18.0
4. Payments to Crown corporations	4.8	5.0	5.3	5.8	4.9	4.6	4.5
5. Defence	7.7	9.8	11.2	11.2	11.3	10.8	10.5
6. Government operations	13.2	14.4	17.3	20.1	21.5	20.5	19.6
7. Other program expenditures	4.5	3.9	4.1	4.0	2.6	4.3	4.9
8. Public debt charges	18.1	26.7	38.8	39.4	38.5	41.0	42.0
Total budgetary expenditures	98.2	116.6	142.7	162.0	160.2	163.6	164.6

Sources: Government of Canada, *Public Accounts*, 1992-93, and Ministry of Supply and Services, *The Budget Plan*, 1994.

4. Payments to Crown corporations

These payments (such as to the Canadian Broadcasting Corporation, Via Rail, and the Canada Mortgage and Housing Corporation) are expected to decline by about one-fifth between 1993-94 and 1995-96 as subsidies and grants are trimmed.

5. Defence

With the ending of the Cold War, expenditures on defence are budgeted to decline after 1993-94.

6. Government operations

Included in this category are expenditures on government organizations such as the judicial system and government departments. Expenditures are expected to decline after 1993-94, reflecting a four-year wage freeze in public service salaries.

7. Other program expenditures

Other expenditures are relatively small in amount. They include, for example, veterans' allowances and pensions and (until 1992-93) family allowances.

8. Public debt charges

These charges (interest payments) are the final component of federal expenditures. The **federal public debt** (sometimes called the national debt) is the total amount owed by the federal government, to Canadians and foreigners, in the form of government bonds. The debt is a result of federal government budget deficits (when expenditures were greater than revenues) in the past.

The interest payments on the federal debt have mushroomed from about $10.5 billion in 1980-81 to nearly $39.5 billion in 1992-93 as successive federal budgets have increased the total federal debt. Though payments on the debt were expected to fall between 1992-93 and 1993-94, as interest rates fell substantially, the rising amount of debt is expected to push debt charges to $42 billion by 1995-96. By then, public debt charges are expected to be the largest of the eight categories of government expenditures. By 1995-96, more than 25 cents of every dollar paid in federal taxes will go to pay interest on the debt. The growth in the federal debt presents serious problems for Canadian governments. We'll return to this topic later in the chapter.

GOVERNMENT REVENUES

To pay for roads, schools, police protection, hospitals, and other goods and services, governments have to raise money, and that means taxation.

Taxes are obligatory payments made by individuals and corporations to government.

A **direct tax** is one that is levied on a person who cannot pass the tax along to someone else. Provincial sales tax is an example of a direct tax. If I buy a chocolate bar at a corner store, I pay the tax when I make my purchase. I can't pass the tax on to someone else. I'm the final consumer. Similarly, with income tax, the tax is deducted from my earnings and I can't get someone else to pay it. It is a direct tax.

An **indirect tax** is one that can be passed on to other people. For example, those who bring (or import) Japanese cars into Canada for sale to Canadians have to pay the federal import tax. The import tax is an indirect tax that can simply be added to the final cost of the car so that the consumer, not the importer, ultimately pays the tax.

In Canada, personal income taxes are progressive. See table 11.3. With a **progressive tax**, as income increases, the tax rate also increases — in this example, from 10 to 30 percent. With a **proportional tax**, the tax rate remains unchanged as income increases. With a **regressive tax**, the rate diminishes (here from 10 to 6 percent) as income increases.

Municipal government revenues

Local property taxes provide approximately 90 percent of the tax revenue of municipalities. These taxes are levied on the value of property — land and buildings. The property is assessed for tax purposes. For example, my property — my house and the land around it — may be given an assessed value of $10 000. Property tax rates are expressed in terms of mills (or thousandths) per dollar value of the property. For example, if the tax rate is set at 55 mills, then for every thousand dollars of assessment, I pay .055 × $1000 or $55 in property tax. With

Table 11.3 The progressivity of taxes

Income	Progressive		Proportional		Regressive	
	Rate (Percent)	Tax	Rate (Percent)	Tax	Rate (Percent)	Tax
$1000	10	$ 100	10	$100	10	$100
$2000	15	$ 300	10	$200	9	$180
$3000	20	$ 600	10	$300	8	$240
$4000	25	$1000	10	$400	7	$280
$5000	30	$1500	10	$500	6	$300

the assessment of $10 000 on my property, I pay .055 × $10 000 or $550 in local property taxes.

Grants from provincial governments provide local governments with their other major source of revenue. Local government revenues from other sources such as fines, parking meters, and building permits are small by comparison with provincial grants and local property taxes.

Provincial government revenues

Provincial government revenues come from many more sources compared to those of municipal governments. Table 11.4 shows that the bulk of provincial government revenues comes from direct taxes from persons (about one-third), indirect taxes (about one-fourth), and federal government transfers (grants) (about one-fifth).

Federal government revenues

The federal government has a much wider range of taxes than the provincial government. The federal government was given the right, by the Constitution Act of 1867, to raise money, "by any mode or system of taxation."

The federal government has five major sources of revenues: federal income tax, corporate income tax, unemployment insurance contributions, the Goods and Services Tax (GST), and excise taxes. We'll examine each one in turn.

Federal income tax

The federal income tax has been, and continues to be, by far the most important source of federal government revenues, providing almost 50 percent of the total taxes collected.

As everyone who earns an income in Canada knows, April 30 is usually the deadline for filing our federal income tax return. Prior to the end of April, the airwaves and newspapers are filled with articles about income tax and advice about how to fill out the form. Whether we paid too much or too little tax, we must fill out an income tax form.

Table 11.4 Provincial government revenues (in million dollars), 1990-93

	1990	1991	1992	1993
Revenue	137 673	139 606	142 902	148 728
1. Direct taxes from:				
a) Persons	48 595	49 446	48 649	49 388
b) Business enterprises	5 192	4 459	4 467	4 824
2. Indirect taxes	36 844	37 655	39 031	40 116
3. Investments	18 157	18 141	18 711	19 908
4. Federal government transfers	25 778	26 552	28 513	30 733
5. Other	3 107	3 353	3 531	3 769

Activity 3: A fair tax for Nova Queland?

You are a member of a new country, Nova Queland. There are only 100 families in this country and, except for variations in income, the families are alike with only one spouse working and equal numbers of children. The total cost of services that Nova Quelanders want their government to provide is $750 000. The Nova Quelanders decide that an income tax is the best way to raise money. How much income tax should each family pay? The Nova Quelanders have outlined five tax proposals that are shown in figure 11.2. Under each proposal are the percentage and amount the families would pay in taxes.

Instructions

1. In groups of five students, decide which of the proposals your group prefers. Select a leader to represent your group and prepare arguments for your proposals.

2. The leader of each group should present the group's arguments in favour of their chosen proposal.

3. After the arguments have been presented, the citizens of Nova Queland should vote on the proposals.

4. Which income tax proposal is closest to the Canadian income tax system? Explain.

Figure 11.2 Tax proposals

Annual family income	Number of families	Proposal 1 (percent) (total $)	Proposal 2 (percent) (total $)	Proposal 3 (percent) (total $)	Proposal 4 (percent) (total $)	Proposal 5 (percent) (total $)
$ 10 450	10	20 2 090	16 1 672	10 1 045	5 522.50	75 7 837.50
16 500	15	20 3 300	17 2 805	12 1 980	7 1 155	45 7 425
25 500	40	20 5 100	18 4 590	15 3 825	10 2 550	29 7 395
39 000	20	20 7 800	20 7 800	18 7 020	15 5 850	19 7 410
63 000	9	20 12 600	21 13 230	22 13 860	22 13 860	12 7 560
120 000	4	20 24 000	22 26 400	25 30 000	31 37 200	6 7 200 ·
277 500	2	20 55 500	23 63 825	31 86 025	42 116 550	2.5 6 937.50

The amount of federal income tax paid by the individual is arrived at after a number of rather complicated calculations.

First, total income from *all* sources — wages, interest, rent, dividends, profits, and capital gains, and from all places inside and outside Canada are calculated. Some types of income such as dividends may qualify for a partial tax exemption.

Second, *allowable deductions* are subtracted from total income to get the taxable income. Examples of

Table 11.5 Rates of federal income tax, 1993		
	Taxable income	**Tax rate**
line 1	less than $29 590	17%
line 2	$29 590 to $59 180	$5 030 on the first $29 590, plus 26% on taxable income over $29 590
line 3	more than $59 180	$12 724 on the first $59 180, plus 29% of the taxable income over $59 180

Source: Revenue Canada, *1993 Tax Guide.*

allowable expenses include deductions for a dependent spouse or children and expenses connected with employment (e.g., professional association fees or union dues).

Third, taxes payable are calculated from a schedule or table, a small part of which is shown in table 11.5.

If your taxable income in 1993 was $40 000, for example, you can calculate your tax by using line 2 of table 11.5. Your federal income tax would be:

$5 030 plus 26% of $40 000 – $29 590

= $5 030 plus 26% of $10 410

= $5 030 + $2 706.60

= $7 736.60

On a taxable income of $40 000 you would pay $7 736.60 in federal income tax.

Corporate income tax

This significant source of revenue for the federal government generated more than $8 billion in 1992-93. See table 11.6 on page 236. The tax is paid on the profits of the corporation. Revenues from corporate income tax vary directly with the health of the economy and with variations in a corporation's profits. During the prosperous years of the late 1980s, corporate income tax revenue was much higher compared to that in 1992-93.

Unemployment insurance contributions

These contributions are made by most workers in Canada and by their employers. Exceptions to the compulsory scheme include the self-employed, some part-time workers, and workers over the age of sixty-five. With rising employment and increases in contributions, revenue is expected to increase in the mid-1990s.

Goods and Services Tax (GST)

On January 1, 1991, the Goods and Services Tax replaced the Federal Sales Tax (FST). The tax base of the FST was much narrower than that of the GST — services, for example, were excluded. In addition, while Canadian export goods were taxed, import goods were exempt, which put Canadian industry at a competitive disadvantage.

To overcome these problems, the GST was introduced. As the name implies, services (such as haircuts) are taxed, as well as goods, such as automobiles. Goods produced in Canada but which are to be exported are GST-free, while imports are subject to the full GST. In this way, the competitiveness of Canadian business is enhanced.

Since its introduction, the tax has received widespread criticism. Part of the criticism stems from the

Analyse the cartoon

Merle Tingley, Ting Cartoons.

fact that, unlike its predecessor, the FST, the GST is highly visible — we know when we pay it and how much it is. The ruling federal Liberal party has promised to replace the GST. One thing is certain: the government will seek to ensure that the generated revenue is maintained or increased.

As shown in table 11.6, revenues from the GST are expected to grow in the first half of the 1990s, along with the anticipated growth in the economy.

Excise taxes and duties

Excise taxes are imposed on the sale of many luxury or non-essential items, such as tobacco, liquor, and playing cards. Customs duties are collected on goods that are brought into the country. International trade agreements cutting customs duties and huge cuts in federal government excise taxes on tobacco are expected to result in reductions in revenue by the mid-1990s.

Other revenues

Other sources of revenue for the federal government include the returns on other taxes and on government investment.

Questions

1. Refer again to table 11.6. Look at the sources of government revenue on a proportional basis. For example, individual income taxes are expected to generate $64.4 billion in 1995-96, compared to anticipated revenue of $12.2 billion from corporate income taxes. Do you think the proportions of government sources of revenue are fair? Why or why not?

2. Suppose you were the federal finance minister. What adjustments, if any, would you make to the various sources of government revenue? For example, what proportion of revenue would come from the private sector (individuals), and what proportion from business? (Keep in mind that if businesses perceive corporate taxes to be too high, this could discourage investment and lower profits. Lower profits would mean higher prices for goods and services.)

Table 11.6 Federal budgetary revenues (in billion dollars) for selected years, 1983-96

	1983-84	1986-87	1989-90	1992-93	1993-94 E	1994-95 E	1995-96 E
Personal income tax	27.0	37.9	51.9	58.3	52.1	59.5	64.4
Corporate income tax	7.3	9.9	13.0	8.3	8.8	10.3	12.2
Unemployment insurance contributions	7.3	9.6	10.7	17.5	18.0	19.3	20.3
Sales tax	6.6	4.2	17.7				
Goods and Services Tax	—	—	—	14.9	15.6	16.5	17.5
Excise taxes/duties	9.6	9.0	10.3	11.2	10.5	10.1	9.8
Other revenues	5.5	7.4	9.6	11.3	9.7	8.2	7.8
Total budgetary revenues	63.3	78.0	113.2	121.5	114.7	123.9	132.0
Percent of GDP (%)				17.6	16.1	16.8	17.0

E = estimates
Source: *Public Accounts,* 1992-93 and *The Budget,* 1993.

The underground economy

The underground economy is economic activity that is unreported to Revenue Canada. It includes both legal activities and illegal activities (such as the narcotics trade). According to a 1993 report by University of Alberta economist Roger Smith, the size of the underground economy almost doubled between 1976 (10 percent to 12 percent of GDP) and 1990 (15 percent to 20 percent of GDP). A number of factors have contributed to this dramatic increase: higher personal income taxes; growth in the self-employed sector of the economy; and the Goods and Services Tax. Proposed ways to stamp out the hidden economy include lower tax rates on a broader tax base and increased enforcement of the tax laws.

Merle Tingley, Ting Cartoons.

CONTROLLING FEDERAL AND PROVINCIAL DEBTS AND DEFICITS

Facts about the federal debt

How fast was the debt growing in 1993-94?
In one hour, by more than $5 million.
In the time it takes to watch a hockey game, by more than $15 million.
In one day, by more than $123 million.

How much do we owe?
In 1980, the debt totalled about $4 800 per person in Canada.

In 1985, the debt totalled about $10 000 per person in Canada.
In 1990, the debt totalled about $15 700 per person in Canada.
In 1994, the debt totalled about $18 750 per person in Canada.

The average federal, provincial, and territorial debt in 1994 was about $23 000 per person.

What are the interest charges?
In 1969, 12 cents of every dollar of federal revenue went to pay interest on the debt.
In 1981, it was 25 cents.
In 1988, it was 30 cents.
In 1994, it was almost 40 cents.
And the debt continues to grow.

The growth of the federal public debt

The size of the federal public debt increased more than 18 times between 1966 and 1994, from more than $27.4 billion in 1966-67 to more than $546 billion in 1995.

How did the federal debt get to be so high?

Both federal revenues and expenditures increased rapidly after 1966. Expenditures outpaced revenues by an average of about $26 billion a year. The main reason for the increase in expenditures was a significant increase in the costs of new social programs, such as the Canada and Quebec Pension Plans (1965), the Canada Assistance Plan (1966), and Medicare (1966). In addition, the costs of programs such as Family Allowance and federal contributions to post-secondary education increased substantially. Consequently, federal spending tripled, jumping from $10 billion in 1966-67 to $31 billion in 1974-75. In the same period, the federal debt increased from $27 billion to $49 billion. Even though the debt was growing, the economy was growing at a good rate as well. Thus, it was assumed that the federal government would have little difficulty in paying the interest on the debt.

But after 1975, annual deficits increased considerably, averaging about $30 billion during the period 1980-1995, with a peak deficit of $45.6 billion in 1993. The total debt grew from $48.8 billion in 1974-75 to $600 billion in 1995, and debt charges grew from $4 billion to $42.5 billion in the same period. In fact, the fastest-growing component of the federal budget in the 1980s was the interest paid on the national debt. Compared with other leading industrial nations, only Italy had a consistently worse deficit record compared to Canada. See figure 11.3.

Effects of the federal public debt

The payment of interest on the federal debt — like any other debt — involves the transfer of funds from one group of people now to another group of people now; from taxpayers now to government bondholders now. For those people who are both government bondholders and taxpayers, it may mean transferring money from one pocket to another. But the debt may cause a number of problems:

1. Redistribution of income Paying the interest on the debt causes income to be transferred from taxpayers to bondholders. This may bring about an undesirable

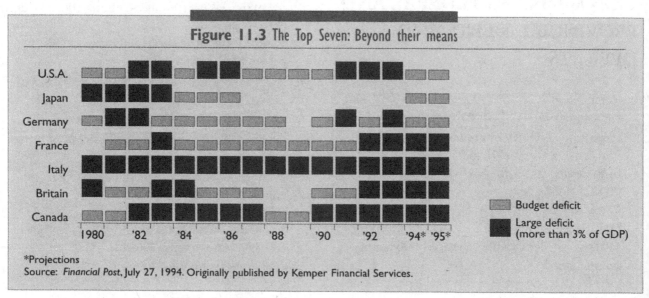

Figure 11.3 The Top Seven: Beyond their means

U.S.A. · Japan · Germany · France · Italy · Britain · Canada

1980 · '82 · '84 · '86 · '88 · '90 · '92 · '94* · '95*

Budget deficit

Large deficit (more than 3% of GDP)

*Projections
Source: *Financial Post*, July 27, 1994. Originally published by Kemper Financial Services.

distribution of income. If the bondholders are mainly wealthy people and taxpayers poor people, the effect of the increasing debt may be to increase the inequalities of income.

2. Debt held by foreigners   Interest on debt held by foreigners —about one-third of the total in 1994 — must be paid by exports. There is therefore less left to pay for imports of goods and services, the Canadian standard of living will decline, and the Canadian dollar may decrease in value.

3. The cost of collecting the tax   One obvious cost of increased taxes is the cost of collecting them. Another less obvious cost is the energy expended by people looking for ways to avoid the taxes needed to pay the interest on the debt. The government needs to support a costly apparatus to monitor these activities. In addition, high taxes may discourage people from seeking higher incomes, thus limiting economic growth.

4. The danger of the debt feeding on itself   A large debt with large interest payments may make it difficult for governments to bring the debt under control. Interest payments on the debt may be met by increasing the debt. Public confidence in the government and the economy may be weakened, leading to a spiral of higher interest payments, increasing deficits, and even weaker confidence in government.

5. "Crowding out" investment   If the debt occurs at a time when there is a need for investment in the economy, the government will discourage investment by absorbing the savings needed to finance production. Interest rates will be higher as borrowers compete for scarce funds and economic growth will be slowed.

6. A burden on future taxpayers   Future taxpayers will be obliged to pay the interest on the debt without benefitting from the expenditure or without having a say in the debt's acceptance. In other words, it is taxation without representation.

   If some of the debt is assumed to build such things as roads and hospitals, then future taxpayers will benefit. If, on the other hand, the debt is the result of

expenditures such as interest on the debt or welfare payments, then future taxpayers will receive no benefit. The only beneficiaries are those who inherit the federal government bonds.

7. Restrictions on government spending and taxing policy   During periods of sluggish economic activity (recessions), an appropriate policy may be to cut taxes and raise government spending. However, when faced with a large debt and deficit, government may not be able to exercise this option. We'll return to this problem in Chapter 13.

Curbing the federal debt and deficit

There are several ways the federal government can try to control the deficit: (1) by cutting federal government expenditures; (2) by increasing revenues; (3) by relying on rising incomes to increase government revenues and lower expenditures; or (4) by combining two or more of the above.

1. Cut federal government expenditures
Attempts by the federal government to cut expenditures have included freezing the pay of federal public servants; reducing unemployment insurance payments; reducing transfer payments to provincial governments; and ending the universality of some social security programs. These attempts have met with widespread opposition from those affected. Moreover, as the population ages, we can expect expenditures on health care and pensions to continue to increase. In addition, as long as we continue to have deficits, we can expect that interest payments on the federal debt will continue to grow.

   It seems likely, then, that only the most determined of federal governments will have the political will to make substantial cuts in government expenditure.

2. Increase revenues
Revenues may be increased by increasing individual taxes or by broadening the tax base, or by some combination of the two. The tax base was extended, for example, when the Federal Sales Tax was replaced with the Goods and Services Tax (GST). However, attempts

by governments to increase taxes have met with wide-spread opposition. Governments have therefore been reluctant to increase them.

3. Rely on economic growth and rising incomes

The unpopularity of raising taxes and of cutting government expenditures has led governments to look to rising incomes resulting from economic growth as a means of reducing the deficit. How would this occur? As incomes rise, government revenues from income tax and corporate taxes from the GST and from excise taxes would also rise. With economic growth, too, unemployment declines and welfare roles diminish; thus, unemployment insurance and welfare payments decline. With rising revenues and decreasing expenditures, the federal deficit would diminish.

However, while it would seem that this approach should work, during the prosperous 1980s the federal government was unable to bring the average annual deficit much below $30 billion a year. Again, it would appear that in prosperous times only the most determined of federal governments will be able to control the growth in the federal debt.

Provincial debts and deficits

Provincial government deficits in total peaked in 1992-93 and then began to decline. By 1992-93, all provinces had deficit-reduction plans in place to try to attain balanced budgets by the late 1990s. For all provinces, deficit reduction was well underway by the mid-1990s, so that some provinces anticipated a budget surplus and, therefore, the beginning of a reduction in the size of the debt. See figure 11.4.

In most cases, the reductions in the provincial deficits were due to increases in taxes, to reductions in expenditures, and to improvements in the economy following the end of the recession of the early 1990s.

GOVERNMENT AND THE CIRCULAR FLOW

To our earlier circular flow diagram (figure 8.5), we add government. See figure 11.5. Governments collect taxes from households (income, excise, and property taxes) and from businesses (corporate income, sales,

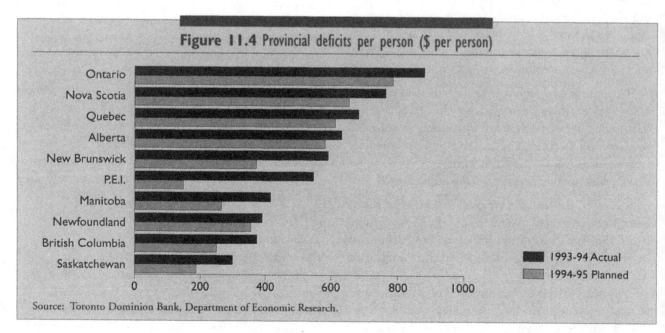

Figure 11.4 Provincial deficits per person ($ per person)

■ 1993-94 Actual
■ 1994-95 Planned

Source: Toronto Dominion Bank, Department of Economic Research.

and property taxes). Governments also make transfer payments to businesses (e.g., subsidies) and to households (e.g., welfare payments). In effect, government is transferring income from businesses and households through taxes, and giving it to other businesses and households through subsidies and other payments.

Governments provide services to households (e.g., education) and to businesses (e.g., roads and police protection). Thus, there is a flow of services from govern-

ment to households and back to government. To provide these services, governments buy productive resources in the resource market, and final goods and services in the product market. Thus, there is a flow of resources from the productive resources market to government and a flow of payments to the resources market from government. Also, there is a flow of finished goods and services from the product market to government and a flow of payments from government to the product market.

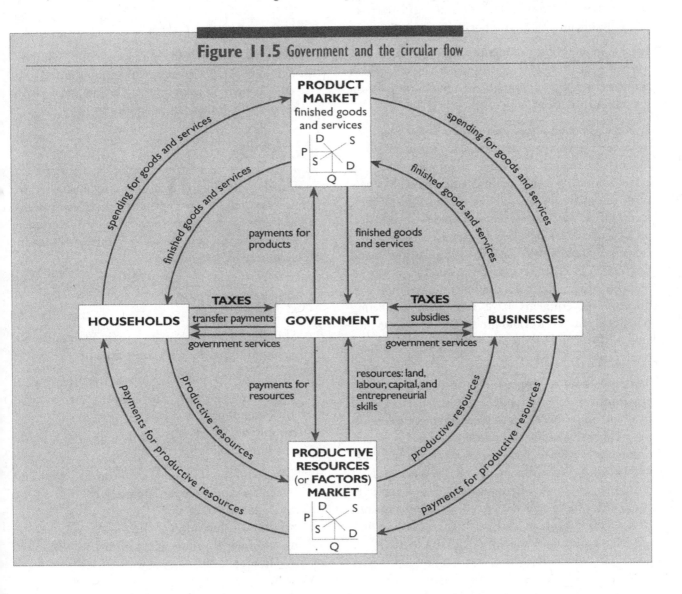

Figure 11.5 Government and the circular flow

GOVERNMENT REGULATION OF BUSINESS

Government spending and taxing greatly influence what is produced and for whom it is produced. But government influence does not stop there. Government rules and regulations also affect Canadian business in three principal ways: laws to prevent the reduction of competition; controls of prices; and regulations of safety, health, and the environment.

1. Laws to prevent the reduction of competition We have already seen that governments act to prevent agreements between companies to limit competition between them. (See Chapter 7.)

2. Regulation of prices and production Again, as we have seen, governments intervene to regulate prices that may be charged by natural monopolies such as local telephone services or natural gas companies. These companies have a monopoly in the provision of their services to us — we cannot shop around for a good deal on local telephone and electricity service.

Governments have also acted to regulate prices and production in other parts of the economy. In various branches of agriculture (for example, egg and milk production), governments have established marketing boards to control prices and production in order to provide stable incomes for producers and stable prices for consumers.

3. Regulations to improve health, safety, and the environment These types of regulations are applied in all industries. Measures to promote improved working conditions and improved health and safety protection in the workplace have been introduced by federal and provincial governments. Similarly, both levels of government — especially since the 1970s — have become much more aggressive in their attempts to control and diminish pollution.

The increasing regulation of business in the 1960s and 1970s brought increasing criticism from those who thought that government intervention had gone too far, and that business should be given greater freedom to act without government controls. Sensitive to those criticisms, governments began to dismantle some of the regulations affecting business. In the 1980s, the federal government began to deregulate transportation, for example. By the 1990s, trucking companies, airlines, and railways had been given increased freedom to establish rates and routes.

Crown corporations

Finally, government also influences the economy through the ownership of Crown corporations. As we saw in Chapter 5, government decides what these businesses will produce, and for whom.

REVIEW

Explain the meaning of each of the following terms: public debt, transfer payments, federal excise tax, indirect tax, direct tax, property tax, income tax, regressive tax, progressive tax, government revenues, government expenditures, deficit.

APPLICATIONS

1. Should pensioners who own their own homes be required to pay school taxes? Explain.

2. Which of the following taxes are progressive? Which are regressive? Explain your answers.
    a) federal income tax
    b) provincial sales tax
    c) municipal property tax

3. Which of the following are indirect taxes and which are direct taxes? Explain why.
    a) federal income tax
    b) import duty on Scotch whisky
    c) municipal property tax on owner-occupied houses

SUMMARY

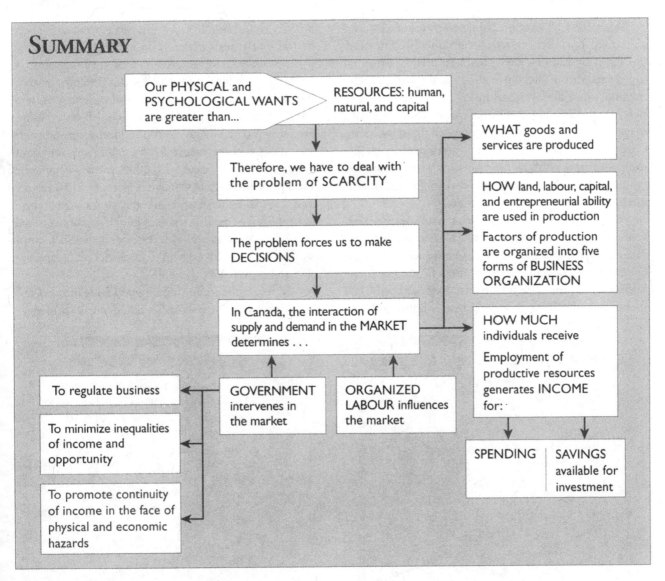

Our PHYSICAL and PSYCHOLOGICAL WANTS are greater than...

RESOURCES: human, natural, and capital

Therefore, we have to deal with the problem of SCARCITY

The problem forces us to make DECISIONS

In Canada, the interaction of supply and demand in the MARKET determines . . .

WHAT goods and services are produced

HOW land, labour, capital, and entrepreneurial ability are used in production

Factors of production are organized into five forms of BUSINESS ORGANIZATION

HOW MUCH individuals receive

Employment of productive resources generates INCOME for:

GOVERNMENT intervenes in the market

ORGANIZED LABOUR influences the market

To regulate business

To minimize inequalities of income and opportunity

To promote continuity of income in the face of physical and economic hazards

SPENDING | SAVINGS available for investment

d) provincial sales tax

4. List some of the taxes a person would pay even if his or her income were too low to pay personal income tax.

5. In groups, decide what either the federal government or your provincial government should do about the deficit. If you propose to decrease it, explain why and how. If you propose to leave it alone, explain why.

ISSUE
Smuggled smokes

Prior to 1991, tobacco smuggling in Canada had never been a serious enough problem to alarm governments and/or the police. However, between 1991 and 1993, the percentage of cigarettes entering Canada illegally soared from less than 18 percent of total sales to an estimated 40 percent (60 percent in Québec). Why?

After 1991, in an effort to increase revenues, Ottawa had raised so-called "sin taxes" substantially. The taxes on cigarettes sold in Canada had increased by $6 a carton. To maximize sales while avoiding this tax, cigarette manufacturers almost quadrupled their export sales to U.S. wholesalers. These wholesalers sold these cigarettes to customers, some of whom smuggled them back into Canada. With the cost of legal cigarettes rising, people took advantage of these lower-priced illegal cigarettes. Consequently, the federal and provincial governments were losing millions of dollars in taxes.

Therefore, to discourage export sales of cigarettes, Ottawa imposed an export tax of $8 a carton. Cigarette manufacturers retaliated by threatening to move their operations out of Canada. (This is a tactic used by many businesses to protest high Canadian taxes.) About 4100 manufacturing jobs and the livelihood of 3900 tobacco

farmers would be affected if this threat were carried out. So the government removed the export tax, temporarily.

As evidence mounted that cigarette smuggling was becoming epidemic, Ottawa tried a different strategy. The federal tax on a carton of cigarettes was cut by $5 while another $8 export tax was levied. Tobacco manufacturers also had to pay a $200-million surtax on profits over the next three years to pay for an anti-smoking campaign aimed at teenagers. Other measures included raising the legal age to purchase cigarettes to 18 from 16 and a $150-million enforcement program to curtail smuggling. Several provinces cut their tobacco taxes (with Ottawa matching this decrease up to $5 a carton) so that the price of a carton of cigarettes fell from about $48 to between $23 and $30.

While smokers and storeowners were pleased, anti-smoking groups were worried that decreased prices

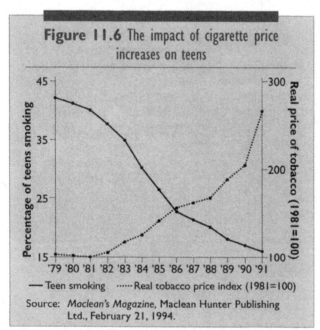

Figure 11.6 The impact of cigarette price increases on teens

— Teen smoking   ······ Real tobacco price index (1981=100)

Source: *Maclean's Magazine*, Maclean Hunter Publishing Ltd., February 21, 1994.

"Real tobacco price index" refers to the price adjusted to eliminate changes in the value of money. As the real price of tobacco products rose between 1979 and 1991, the percentage of teenagers smoking dropped from about 42 percent to about 15 percent. How do you think the 1994 tax reductions have affected teenage cigarette consumption?

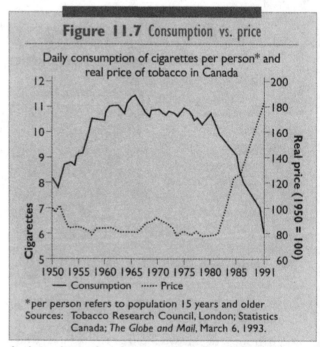

Figure 11.7 Consumption vs. price

Daily consumption of cigarettes per person* and real price of tobacco in Canada

— Consumption   ······ Price

*per person refers to population 15 years and older
Sources: Tobacco Research Council, London; Statistics Canada; *The Globe and Mail*, March 6, 1993.

As the real price (i.e., the price adjusted to eliminate changes in the value of money) of cigarettes fell in the 1950s, cigarette consumption per person increased. As the real price rose rapidly in the 1980s and early 1990s, consumption fell dramatically.

would increase cigarette consumption among teenagers. (See figures 11.6 and 11.7.) These groups proposed various measures aimed at increasing the price of exported cigarettes to match that of domestic cigarettes, thereby discouraging export and the profitability of smuggling — without lowering the price of domestic cigarettes and thereby increasing consumption.

Results of the program

After the adoption of measures to make smuggling less profitable, sales of legal cigarettes soared and smuggling almost ceased. The government began to recoup lost tax revenues and cigarette manufacturers kept making profits (the loss in export sales was compensated by the increase in domestic sales). Now everyone — except the anti-smoking groups — was happy.

Questions

1. Individually, then in groups, consider the situation faced by the Canadian government, and assess the various actions taken by the federal and provincial governments, the tobacco manufacturers, smokers, and anti-smoking groups. Comment on both the short-term and long-term effectiveness of these actions. Which group(s) do you support, and why?

2. Canada faces a similar, but less serious problem with the illegal importation of liquor. Liquor company officials estimate that smuggling costs Canada about $1 billion in lost revenue each year. These officials recommend lowering taxes to counter this illegal action and to raise revenue. Do you agree or disagree? Why?

3. What role, if any, do you think the federal government should play in decreasing cigarette consumption in Canada (especially by teenagers)? In your answer, pay attention to the effect that decreased tobacco consumption would have on health care costs, government revenues, jobs, and the presence of industry in Canada.

Activity 3: Comparing opinion polls

What do you think?

Without looking back at your earlier responses at the beginning of this chapter, answer the following questions. Canadians have different opinions about whether government is spending too much, and whether taxes are too high. What do you think?

Question 1: Which of the following statements comes closest to your view?

1. Taxes should be cut, even if it means some reduction in government services such as health, education, and welfare.

2. Things should be left as they are.

3. Government services such as health, education, and welfare should be extended, even if it means some increase in taxes.

4. Don't know.

Question 2: Do you think taxes are too high or about right?

What does the class think?

After making a note of your responses, see what the class thinks. Compare the class's response with the earlier response.

a) Are there any differences?

b) If there are differences, what reasons can you suggest for the differences?

CHAPTER 12

Money and Banking

(1)

(2)

Questions

1. What is money?

2. What are some of the uses of money?

APPLICATION

Royal Bank
Visa

Reduced-Rate Option Included

New Added-Value Benefit!

PANORAMA
Club

See details inside.

It's the only card you need.

Just think ...

A NEW WAY TO PAY CASH

Canada Trust AccessCard
brings you the
convenience
of Interac®
Direct Payment

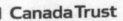

Canada Trust
Thinking like a customer

Una carreira sem fronteira

Une carrière sans frontière

Una carrera sin fronteras

A career without frontier

无边境的事业

Una carriera senza frontiere

Một nghề không ranh giới

Кар'єра без границь

وظيفة بلا حدود لبواسها

Yon karyè ki pa gen fwontyè

Για μια καριέρα χωρίς σύνορα

BANQUE LAURENTIENNE

Questions

1. What are some of the services provided by Canadian banks and trust companies?

2. List the names of some banks, trust companies, caisses populaires, and credit unions in your area.

4)

Activity 1: What is money?

a) **Wampum**   Wampum was made from white and purple Atlantic coast seashells. The shells were threaded onto string, and woven into belts and sashes. Wampum was valued highly by Native people of Eastern Canada, who used them for ornamental and ceremonial purposes. Wampum was used as currency, especially in the seventeenth and eighteenth centuries.

b) **Beaver pelt**   The standard of value of the fur traders in early Canadian history was the prime quality adult beaver pelt. Goods were often quoted in terms of their value in pelts.

c) **Brass and copper tokens**   These tokens were issued, by the Hudson Bay Company, in denominations that amounted to the value of one beaver pelt or a fraction of it. The tokens could be spent just like money at the stores of the Hudson Bay Company.

d) **Playing card money** Canada's first currency was the playing cards of New France that were signed by the governor of the colony. Though the playing cards had no intrinsic value, their inscribed value was supposedly guaranteed by the colonial government of New France. First issued in 1685 to supplement the short supply of currency in the colony, their use as money came to an end in the 1760s.

1. What kinds of things have been used as money in the past?

2. What are the characteristics of money?

3. What are the functions of money?

4. In what ways are some of the things that were used as money in the past, less appropriate than our present form of money? In what ways have they been more appropriate? Why are they not accepted as money today?

MONEY

Money is anything that people are willing to accept as payment for goods or services.

Money is a familiar article. You are probably carrying some in your pocket or purse at this very moment.

Though familiar to us, money is puzzling. The pennies, nickels, dimes, quarters, and loonies that jingle in our pockets are only bits of metal. These bits of metal are not even worth a penny, nickel, dime, quarter, or dollar. As for bills of various dollar amounts, they are only coloured pieces of paper. They can't be eaten or worn; they

Activity 2: The great Canadian auction

Situation

Today your economics teacher walks into class and writes on a piece of paper:

I, _____ , will pay the person who
       name of teacher
has this note the sum of $1 upon its presentation

to me by the start of the next class period.

Signed _____
                    signature of teacher

Procedure

Your teacher auctions the note off to the members of the class.

Questions

To the people who bid for the note but not sufficiently high to get it:

1. Why didn't you bid the price at which the note sold?

To the person who bought the note:

2. Why did you pay so much for it?

To the other members of the class:

3. What factors determine the value of the note?

4. Suppose the owner of the note stopped at a local restaurant and tried to use it to pay for a hamburger. What do you think would be the restaurant manager's reaction?

5. Suppose that the owner of the note became "hard-up" for cash. To whom could she sell the note? From whom would she probably get the highest price? From whom would she get the lowest price?

6. If, instead of selling the note, your teacher had auctioned a personal cheque, would the class pay more or less for it? Explain.

7. Is the note money? Explain.

---

have no value in themselves. Contrary to popular belief, the Canadian government does not keep a stock of gold somewhere in its vaults equal in value to all the dollar bills issued. Yet, with these pieces of paper and bits of metal, we are able to acquire the things we want to buy.

Money has been many things in the past: cows, stones, beads, beaver pelts, and even playing cards. What was it that made these things money? What is it that makes a piece of paper or a bit of metal money today?

If we generally and readily accept sharks' teeth as payment, then sharks' teeth are money. Canadian dollars are generally accepted by Canadians as payment for goods and services. By law, creditors must accept Canadian dollars as payment for debts — that is, Canadian dollars are legal tender. Therefore, Canadian dollars are

money in Canada. Subway tokens, streetcar tickets, Canadian Tire Corporation bills, credit cards, or traveller's cheques are not always, and therefore not generally, accepted as payment. These are not money in Canada.

What does our money supply consist of? Part of the answer is just what you would expect, that is, our currency. Our currency is all the Canadian dollar bills of all denominations and all the coinage in circulation at any one time. The other part of the answer is perhaps more surprising.

Many stores accept cheques in payment for purchases. Occasionally, however, we see signs in restaurants saying: "We have made an agreement with our banker: she will not sell hamburgers and we will not cash cheques." If we are 100 kilometres away from home, we may find it difficult to buy gas or food with a cheque. These, however, are exceptions. Cheques are generally accepted as payment for goods and services. By far, the greatest proportion of payments made by Canadians is accomplished by means of a cheque. A **cheque** is simply an order to pay an individual or a group of individuals a particular amount of money from a chequing account. Since money can be withdrawn from these accounts on demand, they are also known as **demand deposits**. These deposits — not the cheques that authorize the transfer — are considered as money. Money is, then, composed of currency plus chequing accounts or demand deposits.

Read the following newspaper article. As you read, consider the arguments for and against withdrawing the penny from circulation. Do you think the penny should or should not be withdrawn?

A penny saved
. . . soon a penny gone?

By Joseph Hall
Staff reporter

The federal government is considering a move that could eventually leave Canada without a cent.

The Public Works Minister, who holds a key to the crown-owned Royal Canadian Mint, told a government operations committee last week he may consider dropping production of the penny, as a money-saving measure.

The copper coin of a million cookie jars now costs about twice its face value to produce. And the government, which only likes to make money when it makes money, may stop producing the one-cent piece in coming years.

"There are a lot of people who have fortunes in old tin cans, and what have you, of pennies that are not circulating," ministry spokesperson André Tessier said.

"So what he [the minister] was basically explaining was that we are looking at other possibilities,

and one could be eliminating the penny . . . the possibility is there."

The mint is now in the midst of a two-year study of the coin, says spokesperson André Girard.

"It's costing us too much money to produce the pennies," he said.

"The banks are ordering pennies all the time and they keep ordering them every year and the pennies don't circulate; they stay in people's cookie jars. So it's nonsense. Why should we produce coins if they don't circulate?"

In 1992, the mint produced 678 522 000 pennies, down from 696 629 000 the previous year.

But Girard says the mint could find ways to encourage people to put their hoarded pennies back into circulation. And changing the metal or size of the coin could also reduce costs, he says.

Girard says both New Zealand and Australia have already chosen to stop their penny production.

If that happened here, a numismatics [coin] expert says, it would almost surely mean the coin would gradually vanish from circulation, melted down by the mint or left to languish in jars and drawers across the country.

While the penny would remain legal tender, its use would probably cease, says Robert Aaron, a Toronto coin collector, lawyer and Toronto Star columnist.

"It would disappear . . . I can't see it being used," he said.

"The banks will say, 'Why should we ship it out if nobody's using them?'

"In fact they (the banks) may even assist the government in withdrawing them so that whenever they get $1000 in pennies, they'll send them off to Ottawa in exchange for a credit of $1000 and the mint will melt them."

Aaron says that as billions of pennies are removed in this way, people would start to withhold their hoards, leaving few for transactions.

"People would say, 'Hey, they're not making these any more. I'm going to hang on to them and maybe I'll be rich some day.'"

Aaron argues that Canadians should put their two cents' worth in to save the penny, both because of its heritage and to prevent inflationary mark-ups.

"When I go into a drugstore and I buy something that ends in a three (cents) I don't want to pay five (cents). It annoys me. It's as simple as that," he said.

"The question is, if you bought something in the store and the clerk threw down a penny as change or was reaching into the drawer, would you say, 'Oh forget it, I don't want the penny'...or would you say, 'Darn it, that's my money.'

"Sure, you wouldn't stoop down to the ground, because that's work. But if it's sitting there on the counter and you're picking up your quarters and dimes and nickels, would you grab the penny or leave it there?"

Aaron says the federal government, which makes money on coins and bills by contracting-out production to the mint and bill-makers at a cost that's a fraction of the face value Canadians pay for them, could still make a profit on the penny.

"They say they are losing money on it the way they calculate it," he said.

"I say that if they're losing money on it, then we should find somebody else to produce them. If the Canadian mint can't make them profitably, I'll find them half a dozen mints in the world in one morning that will make them cheaper."

Source: *The Toronto Star*, March 28, 1994.

1. What are some arguments in favour of withdrawing the penny from circulation?

2. What are some arguments against withdrawing the penny from circulation?

3. How might the cent be withdrawn from circulation?

4. Do you think the cent should be withdrawn? Why or why not?

Money supply

The **money supply** is equal to the total amount of currency in circulation plus the total amount held in chequing accounts by individuals and businesses. This definition of the money supply is called M1 to distinguish it from the other definitions of the money supply, M2, M2A, M3, etc., which count other kinds of bank accounts as money.

Barter

One way of finding out how much we need or rely on someone or something, is to imagine what it would be like without that person or thing. In the case of money, we can see how useful it is by imagining what it would be like to be without money or, in other words, to use a system of barter. In a system of barter, one good or service must be exchanged directly for another. The farmer who has a sheep to exchange has to find a hungry shoemaker if she needs a pair of shoes, a hungry hairdresser to get a haircut, a hungry tailor if she needs a new outfit, and so on.

Now we are obviously faced with a problem. A great deal of the farmer's time has to be spent in finding not only someone who wants what she has to exchange but also someone who has what the farmer wants. *The wants of the two people must coincide.* Finding someone

Figure 12.1 Canadian money supply (in million dollars), May 1994	
1. Currency outside banks	24 772
2. Chequing accounts (or demand deposits)	30 392
Money supply (M1)	55 164

Source: *Bank of Canada Review*, May 1994.

else whose wants coincide with our own — a double co-incidence of wants — can involve a great waste of time.

But there is another problem — that of **indivisibility**. Suppose our sheep farmer finds a shoemaker who would like mutton for supper. Suppose the shoemaker wants only one leg of lamb — after all, a whole sheep is rather a lot. If the pair of shoes is worth half a sheep, what happens next? Does the farmer exchange one leg of mutton for one shoe? Does the farmer hope to find another hungry shoemaker in the hope that he will provide the farmer with a matching shoe?

The problems of double coincidence and indivisibility make barter a very time-consuming system of exchange. With money, these problems disappear. It is no longer necessary for the sheep farmer to find someone whose wants coincide with her own. All she needs is someone who is willing to buy the sheep from her. With the money from the sale of the sheep, the farmer can buy the shoes she wants from the shoemaker she prefers. With money too, the farmer solves the problem of indivisibility. With money, it doesn't matter how much, or how little, mutton the shoemaker wants. He will always be willing to accept money for the shoes he makes.

Uses of money

Money has three principle uses. It is used as a medium of exchange, as a measure of value, and as a store of value.

As a **medium of exchange**, money frees us from the difficulties of barter. Since money is generally acceptable, we can exchange our goods and services for money and use the money later to buy any goods and services we want. Efficient production requires specialization and, in turn, requires that we satisfy most of our needs by consuming goods produced by others. Specialization requires the use of money.

To serve as a medium of exchange, money must have a number of qualities. It must be *generally acceptable* because, if it were not, it obviously could not serve as money. It must be *portable* (easy to carry around). Otherwise, it would be very inconvenient to use. It must be *divisible* because, otherwise, as we saw with the mutton, it would be impossible to use it for small transactions. It must be *hard to duplicate or counterfeit* by individuals. Otherwise, it would lose its value. Finally, it should be *uniform in value* so that the

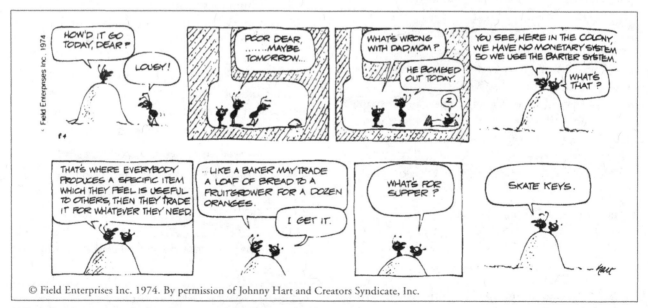

© Field Enterprises Inc. 1974. By permission of Johnny Hart and Creators Syndicate, Inc.

What disadvantages of a barter system does the cartoon illustrate?

Activity 3: The ancient village of Much-Binding-in-the-Marsh

The thatched cottages of Much-Binding-in-the-Marsh surround the village green where, once a week on Saturdays, the villagers gather to exchange their surplus goods or services for things they need. Today is Saturday and, like every good Much-Binding-in-the-Martian, you are going to the green. But what do you need? And what do you have to exchange?

Materials

Need cards: Make up a set of cards (of one colour) to correspond to the list below.

2 chairs	3 hens
1 cartload of wood	3 ducks
1 day's work ploughing	3 geese
1 week's use of a plough	1 pair of boots
1 week's use of 4 oxen	1 cart
1 day's work thatching	1 cord of firewood
1 week's use of an oven	3 water pitchers
1 day's work milling	2 bushels of apples
1 bushel of wheat	1 spade
1 load of hay	1 hoe
48 eggs	1 metal cooking pot
12 loaves of bread	1 axe
1 breeding sow	1 cow
1 litter of piglets	1 dog
1 bowl of salt	1 bag of flour

1 bolt of woollen cloth	1 plough
1 ox	1 scythe
1 calf	1 pot of peas
1 horse	1 ram
1 harness	1 sheep

Surplus cards:

Make up a set of cards (of a second colour) corresponding to the same list.

Playing the game

1. Each student is given one need card and one surplus card.

2. The objective is to obtain through trading a surplus card that matches a need card.

3. If you find that after a period of time you are unable to satisfy your need, you may exchange your need card for one that was not distributed.

Questions

1. What happened in the game?

2. What did you learn from the game?

3. How could the game be changed to better reflect the real situation in an ancient village?

value of each unit should be evident at a glance without the need for weighing it.

As a **measure of value**, money simplifies our exchanges. The value of any item is expressed in dollars and cents in Canada. Because each good has a money price, comparisons between the price of one good and another can easily be made. Through money, we can measure the value of one good against another.

As a **store of value**, money performs a highly useful service. Goods can be sold today and the money stored until needed. With barter, some other good has

to be taken in exchange and kept until needed. Some goods cannot be stored and others may be expensive to keep.

In order to be a satisfactory store of value, the value of money — that is, what you can buy with it — must remain fairly stable. In the early 1980s, however, the value of the Canadian dollar declined sharply, as the prices of most goods and services rose steeply. This is called inflation, which we will examine more fully in Chapter 14. Inflation weakens the usefulness of money as a store of value.

Money is one of the great inventions. It is highly useful in a modern economic system. Without it, the gains that could be realized from specialization would be hard to achieve. Just imagine trying to acquire the goods and services you needed this past week through a barter system! It would probably be impossible or at least tremendously time-consuming. Before very long, we would be reduced to supplying most of our own needs. Our standard of living would decline significantly.

As essential as money is to our economy, it is a mixed blessing. Significant variations in its value can erode or destroy some of its functions and thus cause serious problems. We will explore this later in Chapter 14.

REVIEW

Explain each term in your own words with an example: money, money supply, medium of exchange, measure of value, store of value.

APPLICATIONS

1. What are the disadvantages of a barter system of exchange?

2. In what ways does a money system of exchange overcome the disadvantages of barter?

3. Describe the functions of money.

4. "For the love of money is the root of all evil" (*I Timothy 6:10*). Suppose the Canadian government believed this and decided to eliminate money. How might this action affect your life?

5. *Adanac I.* In the country of Adanac, there is only one form of money — the physical commodity of wheat. What problems might result from this? What would the value of wheat be?

   Adanac II. In Adanac, a change takes place. Pieces of paper, promising to pay so much wheat to the bearer and issued by the Bank of Adanac, replace the physical commodity of wheat as the form of money. The wheat certificates become legal tender. In what ways does Adanac I differ from Adanac II?

   Adanac III. Suppose now that everyone in Adanac uses the wheat certificates for money. One year there is a drought and a plague of grasshoppers so that the wheat crop (but not the certificates) is destroyed. What do you think might happen now?

6. In the following extract, R.A. Radford describes the development of the system of exchange in the prisoner-of-war camps in which he was detained in World War II.

The economic organization of a prisoner-of-war camp

Our supplies consisted of rations provided by the detaining power and (principally) the contents of Red Cross food parcels — tinned milk, jam, butter, biscuits, bully [beef], chocolate, sugar, etc., and cigarettes. So far the supplies to each person were equal and regular. Private parcels of clothing, toilet requisites, and cigarettes were also received, and here equality ceased owing to the different numbers despatched and the vagaries [unpredictability] of the post [the mail]. All these articles were the subject of trade and exchange.

We reached a transit camp in Italy about a fortnight after capture and received one quarter of a Red Cross food parcel each a week later. At once exchanges, already established, multiplied in volume. Starting with simple direct barter, such as a non-smoker giving a smoker friend his cigarette issue in exchange for a chocolate ration, more complex exchanges soon became an accepted custom. Within a week or two, as the volume of trade grew, rough scales of exchange values came into existence. It was realized that a tin of jam was worth half a pound [227 g] of margarine plus something else; that a cigarette issue was worth several chocolate issues; and a tin of diced carrots was worth practically nothing.

In this camp we did not visit other bungalows very much and prices varied from place to place. By the end of a month, when we reached our permanent camp, there was a lively trade in all commodities and their relative values were well known, and expressed not in terms of one another — one didn't quote bully [beef] in terms of sugar — but in terms of cigarettes. The cigarette became the standard of value. In the permanent camp people started by wandering through the bungalows calling their offers — "cheese for seven" (cigarettes) — and the hours after parcel issue were bedlam. The inconveniences of this system soon led to its replacement by an Exchange and Mart board in every bungalow, where under the headings "name," "room number," "wanted" and "offered," sales and wants were advertised. When a deal went through, it was crossed off the board. The public and semipermanent records of transactions led to cigarette prices being well known and thus tending to equality throughout the camp, although there were always opportunities for an astute trader to make a profit from arbitrage [price differences]. With this development everyone, including non-smokers, was willing to sell for cigarettes, using them to buy at another time and place. Cigarettes became the normal currency, though, of course, barter was never extinguished.

The permanent camps in Germany saw the highest level of commercial organization. In addition to the Exchange and Mart notice boards, a shop was organized as a public utility, controlled by representatives of the Senior British Officer, on a nonprofit basis. People left their surplus clothing, toilet requisites [needs], and food there until they were sold at a fixed price in cigarettes.

Only sales in cigarettes were accepted — there was no barter — and there was no haggling. For food at least there were standard prices: clothing is less homogeneous [uniform in value] and the price was decided around a norm by the seller and the shop manager in agreement; shirts would average say 80, ranging from 60 to 120 according to quality and age. Of food, the shop carried small stocks for convenience; the capital was provided by a loan from the bulk store of Red Cross cigarettes and repaid by a small commission taken on the first transactions. Thus the cigarette attained its fullest currency status.

Although cigarettes as currency exhibited certain peculiarities, they performed all the functions of a metallic currency as a medium of exchange, as a measure of value, and as a store of value, and shared most of its characteristics. They were homogeneous, reasonably durable, and of convenient size for the smallest or, in packets, for the largest transactions. Incidentally, they could be clipped by rolling them between the fingers so that tobacco fell out. [Clipping refers to the practice of trimming the edges of coins that are made of a valuable metal.]

Cigarettes were also subject to the working of Gresham's Law. Certain brands were more popular than others as smokes, but for currency purposes a cigarette was a cigarette. Consequently buyers used the poorer qualities. The more popular brands, cigarettes such as Churchman's No. 1, were rarely used for trading. At one time cigarettes hand-rolled from pipe tobacco began to circulate. Pipe tobacco was issued in lieu [place] of cigarettes by the Red Cross at a rate of twenty-five cigarettes to the ounce [28 g] and this rate was standard in exchanges, but an ounce would produce thirty home-made cigarettes. Naturally, people with machine-made cigarettes broke them down and re-rolled the tobacco, and the real cigarette virtually disappeared from the market. Hand-rolled cigarettes were not homogeneous and prices could no longer be quoted in them with safety: each cigarette was examined before it was accepted and thin ones were rejected, or extra demanded as a make-weight. For a time we suffered all the inconveniences of a debased currency.

Source: R.A. Radford, "The Economic Organization of a POW Camp," *Economica*, vol. XII, no. 48 (November 1945). London School of Economics and Political Science.

a) Why were cigarettes accepted as money? Why not canned carrots? or tinned beef?

b) What functions of money did cigarettes perform? Give an example of each one.

c) What characteristics of money did cigarettes have?

d) What disadvantages did cigarettes have as a currency? Explain.

e) The article gives an example of Gresham's Law, but it does not explain this law precisely. In your own words, what do you think Gresham's Law states?

BANKING

Chartered banks

You are probably familiar with a branch of one of the national banks in Canada. These branches are usually located on street corners or in local shopping centres. You might have an account in one. Each of the federally **chartered banks** has received a charter from the government, and most Canadians do their banking with a local branch of the Bank of Montreal, Bank of Commerce, Bank of Nova Scotia, Royal Bank, Toronto-Dominion Bank, or National Bank. Five of these banks have about 85 percent of the total number of branches of all the federally chartered

banks in Canada, and 90 percent of the total assets. Four of them have over 1000 branches (as shown in Figure 12.2) and three have assets over $100 billion.

Schedule 1 banks and schedule 2 banks

The Canadian banking system is divided into two types of banks known as **schedule 1 banks** and **schedule 2 banks**. Both types of banks are chartered under the Bank Act and both are subject to review and control by Parliament — but there are significant differences between them.

Schedule 1 banks   The six major schedule 1 banks are listed in figure 12.2. No individual may own more than 10 percent of the shares. No group of foreign (except U.S.) investors can own more than 25 percent of the shares. These banks have immense financial power. Their reserves and demand deposits make up more than 95 percent of our definition of the money supply M1.

Schedule 2 banks   There are 59 schedule 2 banks — most of which are subsidiaries of foreign banks. Their total assets are only a fraction of the big six schedule 1 banks. Consequently, schedule 2 banks have much less impact on the Canadian economy. In our discussion of Canadian banks our major focus will be on the big six.

Many Canadian banks do a great deal of business in foreign countries. The Bank of Nova Scotia international banking division, for example, operates branches, representative offices, and subsidiaries in forty-three countries outside Canada. Just like many other businesses, chartered banks are privately owned and are in business to make a profit.

Branch and unit banking

As can be seen from figure 12.2, Canada has a system with few banks, each with a large number of branches. This is called a **branch banking system**. The emphasis has been on consolidation and safety. Managers are moved frequently to preserve their objectivity. Contrasting with our system is the **unit banking system** of

Figure 12.2 The six largest Canadian schedule 1 chartered banks and their branches and assets

Name of bank	Number of branches	Assets (billions $)
Bank of Montreal	1168	109
National Bank	650	40
Bank of Nova Scotia	1376	88
Canadian Imperial Bank of Commerce	1600	137
Royal Bank of Canada	1731	138
Toronto-Dominion Bank	900+	83

Source: *Corpus Almanac and Canadian Sourcebook*, 1994.

the United States, where there are some 15 000 separate banks. The amalgamation of banks and the creation of a branch banking system have been strongly discouraged in the U.S. The power of large banks with many branches is feared — the emphasis in the U.S. is on the need for banks to serve their local community.

One of the advantages of the branch banking system is that relatively few bank failures have occurred. Since the 1920s, only two banks have failed in Canada — the Canadian Commercial Bank and the Northland Bank (both in 1985) — and these were small banks. In the United States, many banks collapsed, and bank failures have continued to be fairly common there since that time.

Major services that banks provide may be familiar to you. Banks hold deposits for individuals, companies, and governments. They will transfer money from one customer's account to another customer's account in the same bank, or in another bank. They make loans to individuals, companies, and governments, and accept loans from them.

The Bank of Canada

Another component of the Canadian banking system is the central bank — the Bank of Canada. Founded in 1935, the Bank of Canada is now a Crown corporation.

Look at a two-dollar bill. If you examine it closely, you will see that it is a note of the Bank of Canada and it is signed by the bank's governor and deputy governor. One of the bank's functions is to supply the economy with the needed paper money, Bank of Canada notes.

Many of us find it convenient to have an account with a chartered bank. In our accounts, we hold our personal financial reserves that we use to pay our bills. In the same way, the chartered banks have accounts with the Bank of Canada and they use these accounts to pay what they owe to other banks. The Bank of Canada acts as the bankers' bank.

The federal government also uses the services of the Bank of Canada to help manage its financial affairs — the collection of revenues and payment of its bills. The Bank of Canada also handles the sale and redemption of government bonds.

The tasks mentioned so far are routine by nature if you compare them with the Bank of Canada's prime function — the regulation of the money supply. Regulation of the money supply requires the bank to act in accordance with the needs of the economy as a whole. Whatever action the Bank of Canada takes to regulate the money supply affects the lives of all Canadians.

Other financial institutions

Other institutions that perform banking functions are trust companies, mortgage companies, and credit unions.

Trust companies

Trust companies may be established under provincial or federal law. In addition to providing trustee services (such as the management of property and investments), these companies perform services like those of the chartered banks. They are in competition with the banks. They accept deposits, make loans, have chequing facilities for their customers, which include corporations as well as businesses, and issue Guaranteed

Investment Certificates. With long hours, convenient locations, and competitive interest rates, deposits in trust companies have grown about 300 percent in the past 10 years.

Mortgage companies

Like trusts, mortgage companies may be registered with either the federal or provincial governments. Mortgage companies may accept deposits for short or long terms. As the name of the company suggests, most of these funds are invested in mortgages.

Credit unions and caisses populaires

These are consumer-owned financial institutions. They provide many of the same services as banks and trust companies. At the beginning of 1993, there were over 2600 caisses populaires and credit unions in Canada, with a combined membership of over 9.5 million and assets totalling almost $86 billion. In our discussion of banking in Canada, we will concentrate on the Bank of Canada and the chartered banks because of their particularly important role in our economy.

Creation of money in the banking system

Banks accept deposits from their customers in savings or chequing accounts. These deposits represent claims that the customers have against their banks. At this moment, Canadians have on deposit billions of dollars in banks across Canada. Does this mean that the banks' vaults are filled with billions of bank notes to cover all the deposits? The answer is no. It is not necessary because deposits are transferable from one person to another by means of cheques.

Suppose you decide to use a cheque to pay for a $700 stereo system. The owner of the store where you make your purchase deposits the cheque in the store's business account. All that has occurred in this transaction is a change in two figures in two bank accounts — minus $700 in your account and plus $700 in the storeowner's account. In this transaction, no actual cash changed hands, yet the transferral of money was accomplished.

A typical day at the bank

Suppose I go to My Bank and deposit $1000 in my chequing account. Similar transactions happen all the time. What happens to the balance sheet at My Bank?

In the first transaction (figure 12.3), My Bank's assets (money in bank) increased by $1000 and its liabilities (claims against bank) increased by $1000. I have deposited my $1000 with the bank and can, if I wish, withdraw $1000. The total amount of money (the money supply) remains unchanged. Before depositing my $1000, I had $1000 in cash; after depositing it, I have $1000 in a chequing account. Since cash and chequing accounts are both money, then the amount of money available to the public has remained unchanged. Remember that cash held by banks is not included in the calculations of the money supply. Shortly after my deposit of $1000, a second transaction occurs. Ms. Ima Debtor enters the bank and requests a loan of $900. After checking her references and the bank's financial condition, the bank's loan officer grants her request and Ima Debtor's chequing account is credited. This transaction would appear on My Bank's balance sheet, as shown in figure 12.4.

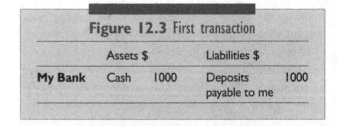

Figure 12.3 First transaction

My Bank	Assets $		Liabilities $	
	Cash	1000	Deposits payable to me	1000

Figure 12.4 Second transaction

My Bank	Assets $		Liabilities $	
	Loan to Ima Debtor	900	Deposits payable to Ima Debtor	900

As a result of this transaction, the bank increased both its assets and its liabilities by $900. Since chequing accounts are money, then the bank increased the money supply by $900. But where did the $900 come from? Answer: My Bank simply created money out of thin air! (In case you are thinking that the action of My Bank was illegal, be assured that the situation just described takes place many thousands of times a day in banks in Canada.) Far from the transaction being illegal, it is expected by the government. In the process of making loans, banks create money in the form of new chequing accounts.

The balance sheet for My Bank after the two transactions would read as shown in figure 12.5.

As you can see, the total demand deposits have increased from $1000 to $1900. The total money supply has also increased from $1000 to $1900. Currency held by a bank is not considered money; therefore, the money supply is $1900, not $2900.

If banks can create money out of thin air, they can cause it to disappear as well. When Ms. Ima Debtor repays her $900 loan, My Bank's balance sheet will show minus $900 on the assets side and minus $900 on the liabilities side. The money supply will be diminished by $900. It will have just vanished.

As has been shown, My Bank created $900 of new money from the deposit of $1000. Other banks, too, can create money by making loans. What, then, can prevent the supply of money from being increased indefinitely by the banking system? The answer is the **cash-reserve requirement**. Some cash will always be drawn out of the banks by depositors. Thus, banks will always need to keep a cash reserve. The cash reserve need only be a fraction of the banks' total deposits — hence the term **fractional reserves**. In the example, the fractional reserve was 10 percent. My Bank kept 10 percent of my demand deposit of $1000 as a reserve. The remaining $900 was excess reserve that the bank could loan out to anyone. Conveniently, Ms. Debtor just happened to need a loan of $900.

Let's return to Ms. Debtor. She now goes to the nearest store and buys a stereo system costing exactly

$900 and pays for it with a cheque from My Bank. The store owner, I.D. Posit, places the $900 in his account in Your Bank. This third transaction diminishes the deposits at My Bank by $900, reduces the reserves it is required to hold by $90, but leaves the increased assets in the form of a loan of $900 unchanged. At the same time, Your Bank has increased its deposits by $900 and increased its reserves by a similar amount by the transfer of the excess reserves from My Bank. With deposits of $900, Your Bank has required reserves of 10 percent of $900 or $90 and excess reserves of $900 minus $90 or $810. See figure 12.6.

In the fourth transaction, Mr. John Dough obtains a loan of $810 from Your Bank that is credited to his account. Further loans could be granted in diminishing accounts by banks. Over the course of the four transactions, the amount of money (cash + demand deposits) has increased from my initial $1000 to $2710 ($1000 + $900 + $810). (See figure 12.7 on page 260.) It could go on increasing up to a maximum amount of $10 000!

Notice the statement that a maximum of $10 000 can be created from an initial deposit of $1000. It may

Figure 12.5 First and second transactions

	Assets $		Liabilities $	
My Bank	Cash	1000	Deposits payable to me	1000
	Loan to Ima Debtor	900	Deposits payable to Ima Debtor	900
		1900		1900

Figure 12.6 Third transaction

	Assets $		Liabilities $	
My Bank	Reserves	−$900	Deposits	−$900
Your Bank	Reserves	+$900	Deposits	+$900
	required reserves	$ 90		
	excess reserves	$810		

Figure 12.7 Chartered banks' balance sheet changes

Transaction	Bank	Assets $		Liabilities $		Money Supply $
1	**My Bank**	Cash	+1000	Deposits	+1000	unchanged
		required reserves	100			
		excess reserves	900			
2	**My Bank**	Loans	+900	Deposits	+900	+900
3	**My Bank**	Reserves	-900	Deposits	-900	
	Your Bank	Reserves	+900	Deposits	+900	unchanged
		required reserves	90			
		excess reserves	810			
4	**Your Bank**	Loans	+810	Deposits	+810	+810

very well be less than that amount. Individuals and firms may be unwilling to borrow the maximum amount from the banks. Banks may be unwilling to lend it to them. Borrowers may wish to have some of their receipts in the form of cash rather than simply adding to the size of their bank balances. These three factors would diminish the total volume of money that could be created by the banking system from any initial deposit. Nevertheless, chartered banks are able to increase and decrease the supply of money as the demand from business people, consumers, and governments varies. A flexible money supply has considerable advantages and disadvantages.

REGULATION OF THE MONEY SUPPLY

Banks can vary the money supply considerably by expanding or contracting the loans they grant. Banks have an interest in expanding loans. Just like other businesses in Canada, their aim is to make a profit and the more money they can loan safely, the larger that profit is likely to be. The Bank of Canada's major function is to control the money supply in accordance with the best interests of Canada. In carrying out its mandate, the bank works closely with the Minister of Finance.

How does the bank regulate the money supply?

Open market operations

Open market operations are the buying and selling of federal government bonds by the Bank of Canada to control the money supply.

Expansion of the money supply

Let's suppose that the Bank of Canada buys a Canada Savings Bond worth $1000 from you. You will probably deposit the $1000 in your account with one of the chartered banks. See figure 12.8. The chartered bank will present the $1000 cheque to the Bank of Canada, which will credit the account that the chartered bank has with the central bank. Chartered banks' deposits with the Bank of Canada constitute the major part of their cash reserves.

After your deposit, bank deposits increase by $1000. But the process does not end here. Let's assume again that the cash reserve ratio is 10 percent. This means the chartered bank is only required to hold $100 in reserves against your demand deposit and it can loan the excess reserves of $900. Sound familiar? As we have seen, with a 10 percent cash reserve ratio, the entire banking system could create additional money so that the maximum amount could equal $9000. The purchase of a $1000 federal bond by the Bank of Canada could increase the total money supply by a maximum

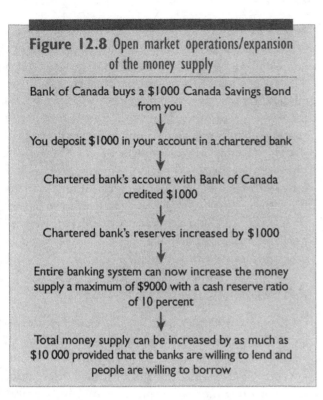

Figure 12.8 Open market operations/expansion of the money supply

Bank of Canada buys a $1000 Canada Savings Bond from you

↓

You deposit $1000 in your account in a chartered bank

↓

Chartered bank's account with Bank of Canada credited $1000

↓

Chartered bank's reserves increased by $1000

↓

Entire banking system can now increase the money supply a maximum of $9000 with a cash reserve ratio of 10 percent

↓

Total money supply can be increased by as much as $10 000 provided that the banks are willing to lend and people are willing to borrow

of $10 000: $1000 would come from the repayment of the bond, but a maximum of $9000 could come from the creation of demand deposits. In this open market operation, the money supply has been expanded.

When the Bank of Canada wishes to increase the chartered bank reserves and thus make possible an increase in the money supply, it buys government bonds.

Contraction of the money supply

The contraction of the money supply through open-market operations works by reversing the above process. When the Bank of Canada sells a $1000 bond to you, then your account with the chartered bank is reduced by $1000 and the account of the chartered bank with the Bank of Canada is similarly reduced. The bank's cash reserves have contracted by $900 since $100 in reserves was held against the $1000 deposit. If the bank's loans are at a maximum, it will have to reduce its loans by $900. Thus, the process of contracting the money supply can go throughout the entire system

to reduce the money supply by a maximum of $10 000 (see figure 12.9 on page 262).

When the Bank of Canada wishes to decrease the chartered bank reserves and thus make possible a decrease in the money supply, it sells government bonds.

Through the process of buying and selling government bonds, i.e., open market operations, the Bank of Canada can vary the money supply. By buying government bonds, the Bank of Canada can expand the money supply; by selling government bonds, the Bank can contract the money supply.

There is, however, one large difference between the expansion and contraction of the money supply. The expansion of the money supply depends on whether the banks are able and willing to loan their excess reserves. People may not be willing to borrow the excess reserves. On the other hand, when the Bank of Canada sells government bonds, the full extent of the contraction of the money supply must take place, unless the banks are holding excess reserves.

Open market operations influence the rate of interest. An increase in the money supply will tend to bring interest rates down. Since banks have more money to lend, competition between banks for loans will lower interest rates. Similarly, a decrease in the supply of money will tend to bring interest rates up. Since banks have less money available to loan and there is less competition among banks to make loans, interest rates tend to rise.

The rate of interest that the banks charge on their least risky loans is called their **prime rate**. The prime rate usually varies with the bank rate set by the Bank of Canada.

Changes in the bank rate

One weekly event that is carefully analysed by economists, bankers, and investors is the Tuesday announcement of the Bank of Canada rate.

The **bank rate** is the interest rate charged by the Bank of Canada on loans it makes to the chartered banks.

Variations in the rate act as signals to the chartered banks to change their own lending rates in the same

Figure 12.9 Open market operations/contraction of the money supply

Bank of Canada sells a $1000 Canada Savings Bond to you

↓

Your account in your chartered bank is reduced by $1000

↓

Your chartered bank's account with the Bank of Canada is debited $1000

↓

Your chartered bank's reserves are reduced by $900

↓

If entire banking system is fully loaned up, then bank deposits will be reduced by a maximum of $9000 (with cash reserve of 10 percent)

↓

Total money supply may decrease by a maximum of $10 000

direction as those of the bank rate. If the central bank raises the bank rate, then the chartered banks will tend to raise their rates; if the central bank lowers the bank rate, then the chartered banks tend to lower theirs. Increases in interest rates tend to discourage businesses and consumers from borrowing money. Decreases in interest rates tend to encourage borrowing. Variations in the bank rate are used to encourage or discourage borrowing from the chartered banks. In this way, the Bank of Canada can influence the supply of money.

Chartered banks tend to follow the bank rate signals of the Bank of Canada because they know that the bank can force them to follow its lead by means of market operations.

Moral suasion

The governor of the Bank of Canada can try to persuade the chartered banks to vary their lending policies in the best interests of the country. In heeding the governor's request, the banks forego profit for the sake of the national interest; thus the term **moral suasion**.

Moral suasion can be very selective in its action. The government can call on the chartered banks to cut lending to a particular sector of the economy and increase it to another. With the limited number of chartered banks in Canada, moral suasion is an effective way of achieving the Bank of Canada's objectives. However, the chartered banks are in competition not only with each other but also with other financial institutions (trust companies, credit unions, caisses populaires, etc.), and agreement to support the governor of the Bank of Canada's policies could result in others profiting at their expense.

An assessment

Of the tools available to the Bank of Canada for regulating the money supply, open market operations and changes in the bank rates have become the most important. Changes in the Bank of Canada rate influence the prime and other interest rates. In this way, the Bank of Canada influences the money supply. Open market operations have the advantage of flexibility; government bonds can be bought or sold in large or small amounts as the situation requires. Open market operations are rapid in their effect. The size of the amount of government bonds held in relationship to the cash reserves of the chartered banks is such that the Bank of Canada could, in theory at least, reduce their cash reserves to zero.

What differences do variations in the money supply make? In the next two chapters we will examine the influences that the money supply and other factors have on unemployment and inflation.

REVIEW

Explain each term in your own words with an example: chartered bank, open market operations, changes in the bank rate, prime rate, moral suasion.

SUMMARY

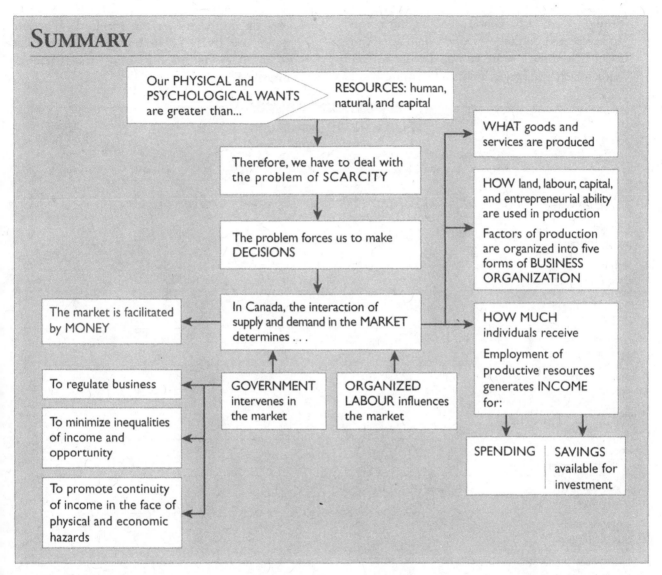

Our PHYSICAL and PSYCHOLOGICAL WANTS are greater than...

RESOURCES: human, natural, and capital

Therefore, we have to deal with the problem of SCARCITY

The problem forces us to make DECISIONS

In Canada, the interaction of supply and demand in the MARKET determines . . .

The market is facilitated by MONEY

WHAT goods and services are produced

HOW land, labour, capital, and entrepreneurial ability are used in production

Factors of production are organized into five forms of BUSINESS ORGANIZATION

HOW MUCH individuals receive

Employment of productive resources generates INCOME for:

GOVERNMENT intervenes in the market

ORGANIZED LABOUR influences the market

To regulate business

To minimize inequalities of income and opportunity

To promote continuity of income in the face of physical and economic hazards

SPENDING | SAVINGS available for investment

APPLICATIONS

1. Explain how money is created in our banking system.

2. What are the major functions of the Bank of Canada?

3. Explain the various ways in which the Bank of Canada can:

a) expand the money supply;
b) contract the money supply.

Which way of varying the money supply is most important? Explain.

4. If banks hold only a fraction of their deposits in the form of cash, is it safe to deposit your cash there? Explain.

5. If I lend you $30 so that you can buy a T-shirt, this transaction does not create money. Suppose,

though, I am rich, famous, and highly trusted and respected, so that everyone would accept my I.O.U. Suppose I write you an I.O.U. for $30 with which you buy a T-shirt. The store owner uses the I.O.U. to pay an employee. The employee uses the I.O.U. to buy some groceries and so on. Does that mean that my loan has created money? Explain.

Figure 12.10 Banking chart

	Chartered bank 1	Chartered bank 2	Trust co. 1	Trust co. 2	Credit union 1	Credit union 2
features of savings accounts						
features of chequing-savings accounts						
features of chequing accounts						
range of rates on personal loans						
range of rates on first mortgages						
range of rates on second mortgages						
penalty for N.S.F. cheques						
cost of certifying cheques						
commission on traveller's cheques						
safety deposit box fee per year						
twenty-four hour cash dispenser fee						
cost of other services provided (itemize)						
business hours						
number of branches in your area						
safety of deposits						

6. Suppose the total deposits of the public in the banking system equal $1 billion and the required cash reserve ratio is set at 10 percent. In what ways could the central bank bring about
   a) an increase in the deposits in the amount of $100 million?
   b) a decrease in the deposits of $100 million?

7. Where would you bank?
   To investigate this question, divide into six groups. Two groups will be responsible for investigating the services of each of the following:

- two different chartered banks
- two different trust companies
- two different credit unions

To facilitate the collection and comparison of information, use a chart like the one in figure 12.10.

   a) Which banking facility would you choose? Why?
   b) Where would you obtain the best return on your money?

CHAPTER 13

Unemployment

Questions

(1) Economists often classify people such as these as being frictionally unemployed. Why might they be unemployed?

(2) There are virtually no people in this occupation today. What happened to eliminate their jobs? This kind of joblessness is called structural unemployment. In what occupations are similar developments taking place today?

(3) When are these workers most likely to experience unemployment? This is called seasonal unemployment.

(4) Many workers were unemployed in the 1930s. What was the period called when this kind of unemployment became widespread? Economists call this kind of unemployment "cyclical unemployment."

What do you think?

Make a note of your response to each of the following questions.

1. What do you think is the most important problem facing this country today?

2. Do the federal government's policies for tackling the country's economic situation give you a feeling that the government is or is not handling the situation properly?

What does the class think?

Summarize the opinions of the members of your class. Make a note of these opinions for future reference. We will return to these questions at the end of the next chapter.

WHAT IS UNEMPLOYMENT?

One of the biggest problems affecting Canada is unemployment. The economic cost of unemployment is the output that would have existed if the workers were employed. In Canada today, this would total many billions of dollars. But, in addition to these costs, and probably much more important, are the social and psychological costs to the unemployed and their families. These costs are especially heavy when unemployment drags on for a prolonged period of time. It is therefore important to examine the extent and causes of unemployment in Canada and some of the suggested remedies. But, first, we'll examine what is meant by unemployment.

Unemployment rate

Usually, when we refer to unemployment we are speaking of the unemployment of labour rather than the other productive factors. In Canada, the official unemployment figures are calculated monthly by Statistics Canada by means of the Labour Force Survey, that is, by the simple means of asking questions. Roughly 56 000 households across Canada are asked a series of questions regarding employment status.

The **unemployed** are those over age fifteen who are temporarily laid off, and those who are without work and who are actively seeking employment.

The **unemployment rate** is the percentage of members of the total labour force who are unemployed.

Rates of unemployment grew significantly in the early 1980s, declined in the late 1980s, and then began to grow again in the early 1990s with the onset of the recession. Unemployment rates tend to be much higher in some provinces (e.g., Newfoundland) than in others (e.g., Saskatchewan).

Not included in the official statistics are the **discouraged workers**. These are people who would like to work but who have stopped looking for employment because they believe there are no jobs for them. When they stop looking, they are no longer counted in calculations of the unemployed.

What, then, is **full employment**? Zero percent unemployment? The answer is no. Some economists have suggested that an unemployment rate of between 6 and 7 percent constitutes full employment. Even in a healthy economy, some people will be looking for a better job, some people will be temporarily out of work because of a seasonal change, and others will be unemployed because of changes in consumer taste or technology.

Who are the unemployed?

The burden of unemployment does not fall equally on all sections of Canadian society.

Regional rates

In the 1980s and early 1990s, unemployment rates in Atlantic Canada, British Columbia, and Quebec were higher than those in the Prairie provinces and in Ontario, remaining above 10 percent for most of the time. See table 13.1. The unemployment rate in Newfoundland and Labrador remained particularly high — even exceeding 20 percent in four years.

Young adults

The unemployment rates for young adults between the ages of fifteen and twenty-four have been typically at least twice the rate of those twenty-five years of age and older. See table 13.2 on page 270. Teenage unemployment rates are especially high in Atlantic Canada. In Newfoundland and Labrador, teenage unemployment reached 40 percent in 1982! Rates between 30 and 40 percent continued well into the mid-1990s in Newfoundland. Men fifteen to twenty-four years of age have higher rates of unemployment (exceeding 20 percent at times during recessions) than women aged fifteen to twenty-four.

Women

Historically, unemployment rates for women have been higher than those for men. However, unemployment rates for females came closer to the male unemployment rate in the 1980s and were lower during the recession of the 1990s. See table 13.2.

Types of unemployment

Economists generally categorize unemployment into four types: seasonal, frictional, structural, and cyclical. We will examine each of the four types in turn. However, since cyclical or inadequate-demand unemployment is generally regarded as our most serious problem, we will devote much of the chapter to examining it.

Seasonal unemployment

Seasonal unemployment is the loss of jobs due to changes in the climate and other seasonal conditions.

The cycle of the seasons causes variations in the unemployment rate. Fishing, lumbering, farming,

Table 13.1 Average annual provincial unemployment rates (in percentages), 1970-1995

	1970	1975	1980	1981	1982	1983	1984	1985	1986	1987	1988	1989	1990	1991	1992	1993	1994	1995 (Jan.)
Nfld.	7.3	14.0	13.3	13.9	16.7	18.7	20.2	20.8	19.2	17.9	16.4	15.8	17.1	18.4	20.2	20.2	20.4	19.4
P.E.I.	N/A	8.0	10.6	11.2	12.9	12.2	12.8	13.3	13.4	13.2	13.0	14.1	14.9	16.8	17.7	17.7	17.1	15.3
N.S.	5.3	7.7	9.7	10.1	13.1	13.2	13.0	13.6	13.1	12.3	10.2	9.9	10.5	12.0	13.1	14.6	13.3	12.8
N.B.	6.3	9.8	11.0	11.5	14.1	14.8	14.8	15.1	14.3	13.1	12.0	12.5	12.1	12.7	12.8	12.6	12.4	13.1
Que.	7.0	8.1	9.8	10.3	13.8	13.9	12.8	11.8	11.0	10.3	9.4	9.3	10.1	11.9	12.8	13.1	12.2	12.0
Ont.	4.4	6.3	6.8	6.6	9.7	10.3	9.0	8.0	7.0	6.1	5.0	5.1	6.3	9.6	10.8	10.6	9.6	8.6
Man.	5.3	4.5	5.5	5.9	8.5	9.4	8.4	8.2	7.7	7.4	7.8	7.5	7.2	8.8	9.6	9.2	9.2	7.7
Sask.	4.2	2.9	4.4	4.6	6.1	7.3	8.0	8.1	7.7	7.4	7.5	7.4	7.0	7.4	8.2	8.0	7.0	5.9
Alta.	5.1	4.1	3.7	3.8	7.7	10.6	11.1	10.0	9.8	9.6	8.0	7.2	7.0	8.2	9.5	9.6	8.6	7.7
B.C.	7.7	8.5	6.8	6.7	12.1	13.8	14.7	14.1	12.5	11.9	10.3	9.1	8.3	9.9	10.4	9.7	9.4	8.8
Canada	5.7	6.9	7.5	7.5	11.0	11.8	11.2	10.5	9.5	8.8	7.8	7.5	8.1	10.3	11.3	11.2	10.4	9.7

Source: Statistics Canada, *Canadian Economic Observer*, 1992-1993, and February 1995.

Table 13.2 Annual average unemployment rates by age and sex, 1970-1995

	1970	1975	1980	1981	1982	1983	1984	1985	1986	1987	1988	1989	1990	1991	1992	1993	1994	1995 (Jan.)
Total both sexes	5.7	6.9	7.5	7.5	11.0	11.8	11.2	10.5	9.5	8.8	7.8	7.5	8.1	10.3	11.3	11.2	10.4	9.7
Total men	5.6	6.2	6.9	7.0	11.0	12.0	11.2	10.3	9.3	8.5	7.4	7.3	8.1	10.8	12.0	11.7	10.8	9.9
Total women	5.8	8.1	8.4	8.3	10.9	11.6	11.3	10.7	9.8	9.3	8.3	7.9	8.1	9.7	10.4	10.6	9.9	9.4
Both sexes, 15-24 years	10.0	12.0	13.2	13.2	18.7	19.8	17.8	16.4	15.1	13.7	12.0	11.3	12.8	16.2	17.8	17.7	16.5	14.8
Men, 15-24 years	11.2	12.5	13.7	14.1	21.1	22.3	19.3	18.1	16.4	14.8	12.9	12.4	14.0	18.8	20.2	20.2	18.5	16.0
Women, 15-24 years	8.6	11.4	12.6	12.3	16.1	17.0	16.1	14.5	13.6	12.4	11.0	10.1	11.4	13.4	15.2	15.0	14.3	13.4
Both sexes, 25 years and over	4.2	5.0	5.4	5.6	8.4	9.4	9.3	8.7	8.0	7.5	6.7	6.6	7.0	9.0	9.9	9.9	9.2	8.7
Men, 25 years and over	4.1	4.3	4.8	4.8	8.2	9.2	9.0	8.3	7.6	7.0	6.0	6.1	6.8	9.1	10.4	10.1	9.4	8.8
Women, 25 years and over	4.4	6.5	6.5	6.7	8.8	9.6	9.7	9.4	8.6	8.3	7.5	7.3	7.3	8.8	9.3	9.6	8.9	8.5

Source: Statistics Canada, *Canadian Economic Observer*, 1992-1993, and February 1995.

construction, and tourism industries are all affected by the change of seasons and, thus, there is seasonal unemployment. Governments have acted to diminish this type of unemployment with winter works projects. Seasonal unemployment is becoming less important in Canada. A smaller percentage of the labour force is engaged in primary industries. More Canadians enjoy winter sports and thus tourism is becoming more and more a year-round industry.

Frictional unemployment

Frictional unemployment is temporary unemployment due to the time required to change jobs.

Since workers in Canada are free to change jobs and employers are free to fire workers, there will always

be some people "between jobs." Because the flow of workers from one job to another is not perfectly smooth, there is friction in the flow. Economists use the term frictional unemployment to describe this situation. Students leaving school and seeking employment are included in this category of unemployment.

In our economic system, frictional unemployment is inevitable. It is also partly desirable because workers move from low-paying, less productive jobs to higher-paying, more productive jobs. Thus, there is a clear benefit in this mobility to the individual worker and to the economy as a whole.

Governments have attempted to diminish the amount of frictional unemployment by establishing employment offices (under the Ministry of Human

The scoop on future jobs

The best research available says that the **top ten** fastest-growing areas of employment will be those listed below.

- Medical labs
- Hospitals
- Personal and household services
- Auto manufacturing and parts
- Aircraft manufacturing and parts
- Business services
- Professional business services
- Chemical industries
- Food processing
- Education

Source: Government of Canada, *Your Life... Your Decision... Your Future....*

Resources Development Canada) across the country so that workers can find jobs more quickly. Privately-owned employment agencies also help to reduce the amount of frictional unemployment.

Governments have attempted to reduce the amount of frictional unemployment among teenagers looking for their first job by improving guidance and job counselling services. Governments have also provided financial help to employers who hire young workers.

Structural unemployment

Structural unemployment is the loss of jobs due to long-term changes in consumer demand, the decline in natural resources, the development of new technologies, and shifts in trade between nations.

Today we see few blacksmiths at work shoeing horses. At one time, many people worked as blacksmiths but, gradually, they lost employment because of changes in demand. In this case, the change in demand was brought about by the introduction of the new technology of car building. As the demand for cars increased, the horse was gradually replaced by the car as a means of transportation. The blacksmith was

replaced by the auto mechanic. As another example, continuing changes in computer and communications technology have radically altered the jobs of many white-collar workers and, in some cases, have led to their replacement as businesses strive to cut costs. In addition to the changes that technology brings, changes in consumer taste can cause structural unemployment.

The rapid decline in the East Coast cod stocks, due in part to overfishing, led the federal government to impose a ban on much of the cod fishery. Thus, many of those involved in fishing were thrown out of work and faced the bleak prospect of finding new employment in some other occupation.

The opening of the Canadian market to free trade with the United States and Mexico and freer trade with many other countries means that some Canadian industries will be lost forever, while other industries will expand. Workers in the vanished industries face long-term unemployment or the need to retrain and/or relocate.

Structurally unemployed workers often have to be retrained so that they can acquire new skills for jobs that are in demand. An office worker, accustomed to a manual filing system, can learn to program the filing system by computer. For older workers in an economically depressed region who have limited general education and who are structurally unemployed, the prospects are particularly grim. It is hard to know what jobs will be available and where. Also, it is not easy to acquire the necessary skills. At best, the workers will face the likelihood of having to move elsewhere. With continuing developments in technology and the constant changes in taste, it may well be that all of us will have to retrain continuously throughout our working lives to stay abreast of changes in technology and consumer tastes.

Governments have helped to retrain structurally unemployed workers by providing training in skills that are in demand. In some cases, unemployed workers are given an income while they acquire needed skills. They may also be given financial assistance to relocate to an area where those skills are required.

However, despite the efforts of government to reduce unemployment levels, many economists believe that unemployment will remain high (18 percent or more) throughout the 1990s.

Cyclical or inadequate-demand employment

If we were to examine the history of the Canadian economy, we would see that economic activity does not proceed at an even pace. Instead, there are times of recovery (an expansion of economic activity) followed by recession (a contraction of economic activity), followed by periods of recovery, and so on. Economic activity has tended to follow a cyclical pattern of highs and lows. This is what is known as the **business cycle**.

Cyclical unemployment results from inadequate demand during the declining economic activity of the business cycle.

Business cycles differ considerably in length and severity. Each period of recovery is different from any other. Each recession is different from any other.

"We're so proud to see our family climbing the ladder of success . . . your father an unemployed bricklayer and you an unemployed architect."

Len Norris from the *Vancouver Sun*.

What categories of unemployment are shown in this cartoon? Explain your answer.

However, each cycle goes through four phases: trough, recovery, peak, and recession. See figure 13.1.

1. Trough

In the low point or trough phase of the business cycle, people who are employed are cautious about spending their money. Many people are unemployed. Sales are low. Business executives are unwilling to make investments. Banks are unwilling to lend money. Bankruptcies are common. Economic activity is at a low level. Pessimism about the present and the future is widespread.

2. Recovery

The trough cannot last forever. People who have deferred expenditures on clothes, home repairs, and the like cannot put them off forever. The stocks of goods of businesses run out and they start to order more. Government spending on public works and relief projects increases demand for goods and services. Business machinery starts to wear out and has to be replaced. Some business people foresee the end of the recession, and take advantage of low prices, low interest rates, and ample supplies of labour to make a profit. Gradually, the economy recovers and pessimism declines. As more people get jobs, they spend more money. Consumers borrow money to finance some of their purchases.

3. Peak

A high level of employment is reached. Costs of production rise as workers are able to ask for and get higher wages. Prices start to rise.

The final phase of the peak of the business cycle may be characterized by an upsurge in speculation. As people see the prices of real estate and stocks rising, they anticipate further increases and they buy. As more people buy, prices increase.

4. Recession

But the good times don't last forever. The seeds of recession are to be found in the period of prosperity. Businesses often overestimate the size of the consumer

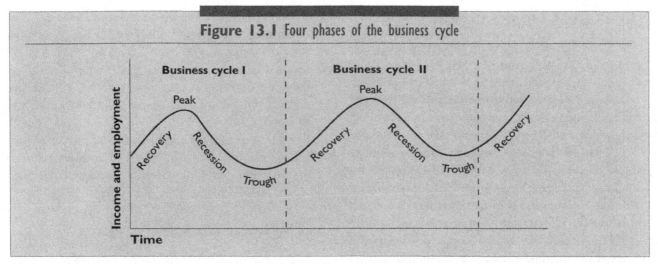

Figure 13.1 Four phases of the business cycle

market and are forced to cut back production and employment of workers. Demand for goods declines which, in turn, brings about declines in output and employment. Prices of many goods start to fall. Banks may raise interest rates and call in their loans. The Bank of Canada may restrict the money supply and raise the rate of interest. Investment falls. If a recession is very prolonged and very deep, it is called a depression.

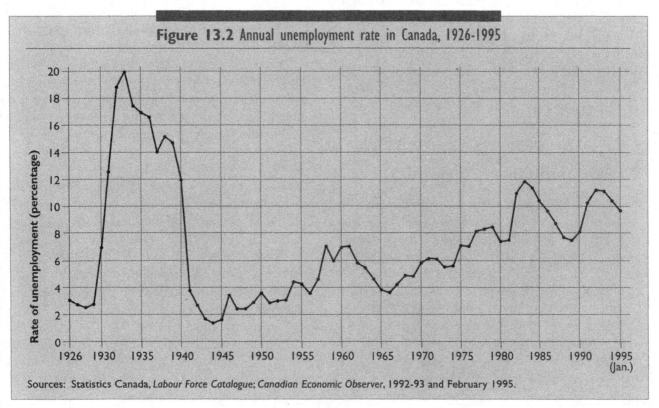

Figure 13.2 Annual unemployment rate in Canada, 1926-1995

Sources: Statistics Canada, *Labour Force Catalogue*; *Canadian Economic Observer*, 1992-93 and February 1995.

The Great Depression

The Great Depression of the 1930s still influences our lives today. Unemployment in the 1930s was very high — exceeding 20 percent in 1933 — and very prolonged, lasting until after the outbreak of World War II in 1939. Incomes, output, and prices fell markedly. Bankruptcies were widespread. Misery was the lot of many Canadians.

A **depression** is a prolonged period of greatly reduced economic activity, with little investment, high unemployment, declining prices, and many business failures. A depression is more severe than a recession, and lasts for a longer period of time.

The Great Depression was worldwide in scope. Large-scale unemployment was common in most countries.

Unemployment since 1945

Unemployment since the 1930s has been low compared to that during the Great Depression. But our economy has continued to experience business cycles with their related periods of high unemployment. Our rates of unemployment in the recessions of the early 1980s and of the early '90s were the highest we have experienced since the 1930s. Since the 1950s, average rates of unemployment have tended to increase during each ten-year period. See figure 13.2 on page 273.

Macro- and micro-economics

The emphasis in this chapter and the two that follow is on the whole economy. What is the rate of unemployment in the economy as a whole? What is the production of the economy as a whole? What is the general level of prices? What changes are taking place in the general rate of unemployment? Because we are concerned with questions about the economy in general, these questions are called "macro-economic" questions. "Makros" means "large" in Greek.

Macro-economics is the study of the economy as a whole, such as the overall level of consumption, investment, government spending, prices, and employment.

So far, we have examined such questions as: What determines the wages of plumbers? What determines the price of potatoes? What factors contribute to the increased demand for a particular good or service? We have been putting the economy under a microscope to find out how particular parts function and why they work that way.

Micro-economics is the study of the economic actions of individuals and groups of individuals, such as consumers, households, and businesses. "Micros" means "small" in Greek.

The leaky bucket economy

Have you ever tried to fill a leaky bucket with water? As you pour water into the bucket, it will continue to fill only if the flow of water into the bucket is greater than the flow of water out of the bucket. As soon as you stop filling the bucket, the water level starts to fall. It is at this point that you discover (if you haven't been soaked already!) that you have a problem.

Every economic system resembles this leaky bucket. This model will help you understand the functioning of the economy. No model is a perfect representation of something else, but the leaky bucket analogy will help you visualize what happens in our economy.

A simple bucket

We'll start our examination of the economy by describing our bucket. The bucket is unusual. See figure 13.3. The right side of the bucket has measuring marks on it like a ruler. These graduations measure the level of total output or GDP. The fuller the bucket, the greater the total output. When the flow of money fills the bucket to the brim, we have the maximum output possible in the economy.

A pipe, attached to the bottom of the bucket, leads to the top of the bucket. Money can be pumped from the bottom of the bucket, around the outside of the bucket, and into the top. This pipe represents consumer spending or consumption (C).

A simple economy I

Our bucket represents a simple economy — one with no saving, no investment, no trade, and no government. Let's also assume that total output is at maximum, and that there is thus full employment and maximum income. This is shown by the full bucket in figure 13.3. Let's suppose that all households in our economy decide to spend their entire income of $100 million. In our bucket economy, this is represented by $100 million being pumped out of the bottom of the bucket through the pipe on the side and into the top. The level in the bucket remains unchanged. The $100 million spent by households is received by businesses. Businesses, in turn, spend the entire sum on the productive resources of households. Thus, householders receive $100 million in income.

As long as householders continue to spend their entire income of $100 million, we will have the maximum GDP and maximum output and income, and full employment will be maintained. The level of money in the bucket will remain full to the brim. Money will continue to flow smoothly through the bucket and pipe.

A simple economy II, with savings

It is unusual that no one would save any of their income. So now let's assume that we have the same simple economy but that householders decide to spend $90 million of their income and save $10 million. See figure 13.4. What happens now? Consumer spending declines to $90 million. Businesses receive only $90 million. They are forced to cut production. This is shown by a decline in the money level in the bucket economy. Employment declines and incomes diminish. Households receive only $90 million in income. If households continue saving, then output, incomes, and employment will continue to decline. Savings act as a drain, or a leakage, on the economy.

A simple economy III, with savings and investment

Now let's add business investment to our simple economy. As before, let's assume that households spend $90 million and save $10 million. Let's also assume

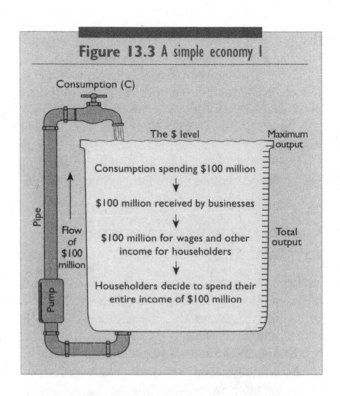

Figure 13.3 A simple economy I

Consumption (C)

The $ level — Maximum output

Consumption spending $100 million
↓
$100 million received by businesses
↓
$100 million for wages and other income for householders
↓
Householders decide to spend their entire income of $100 million

Pipe

Flow of $100 million

Pump

Total output

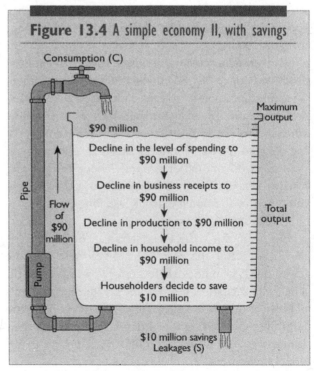

Figure 13.4 A simple economy II, with savings

Consumption (C)

$90 million — Maximum output

Decline in the level of spending to $90 million
↓
Decline in business receipts to $90 million
↓
Decline in production to $90 million
↓
Decline in household income to $90 million
↓
Householders decide to save $10 million

Pipe

Flow of $90 million

Pump

Total output

$10 million savings Leakages (S)

that business invests $10 million, and that output is less than at the maximum level. See figure 13.5.

Now what happens? Business investment spending on machines and factories raises the output of goods and services in the economy by $10 million. It also increases incomes by $10 million. Total income now equals $100 million. Since the savings leakage ($10 million) is balanced by the investment injection ($10 million), the simple economy is in equilibrium.

Causes of changes in savings and investment

Variations in the level of economic activity in our simple economy are brought about by changes in the level of savings and investment. What causes changes in savings and investment?

Savings decisions by householders are mainly influenced by their level of income. The larger our income, the more we can save. Since savings are what is left over after spending, all those factors that influence spending (such as custom, fashion, and advertising) influence savings.

Investment decisions are made mainly by business executives. They buy additional plants and equipment on their expectations of future profit. These expectations are influenced by their general view of the future, whether they see reasons for optimism (for example, rising demand for their products, favourable government policies) or pessimism (for example, labour unrest, rising foreign competition). The time frame that they have in mind may be five or ten years or even longer.

Future profit is also influenced by the cost of borrowing money — the interest rate. The higher the rate, the greater the cost of an investment and the fewer the possibilities there are of making a profit. The lower the rate of interest, the greater the prospects of profit. Business executives' investment decisions are not only influenced by cost but are also based on their anticipations of what they might earn on any additional investment.

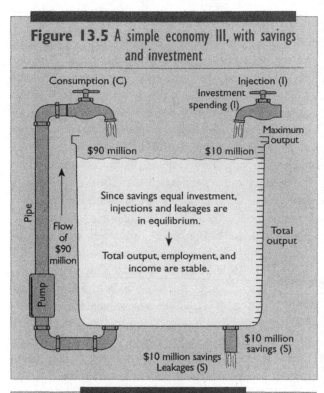

Figure 13.5 A simple economy III, with savings and investment

Consumption (C)

Injection (I)
Investment spending (I)

Maximum output

$90 million $10 million

Pipe

Flow of $90 million

Since savings equal investment, injections and leakages are in equilibrium.
↓
Total output, employment, and income are stable.

Total output

Pump

$10 million savings (S)

$10 million savings Leakages (S)

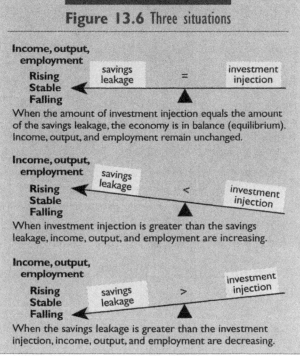

Figure 13.6 Three situations

Income, output, employment

Rising
Stable
Falling   ← savings leakage   =   investment injection

When the amount of investment injection equals the amount of the savings leakage, the economy is in balance (equilibrium). Income, output, and employment remain unchanged.

Income, output, employment

Rising
Stable
Falling   ← savings leakage   <   investment injection

When investment injection is greater than the savings leakage, income, output, and employment are increasing.

Income, output, employment

Rising
Stable
Falling   ← savings leakage   >   investment injection

When the savings leakage is greater than the investment injection, income, output, and employment are decreasing.

We can see, then, that investment and savings decisions are made largely by two different groups acting from different motives. Because of this separation of decision making between savings and investment, we cannot be sure that savings will equal investment at a point when we have full employment. Thus, in the absence of any other influences, we cannot be sure that our economy would automatically provide us with high and stable levels of employment, total production, and income.

In our simple economy, there are three possible situations. (See figure 13.6.)

1. When savings equal investment (S = I), the economy is in equilibrium. Income, output, and employment are stable.

2. When savings are less than investment (S < I), the economy expands. Income, output, and employment increase.

3. When savings are greater than investment (S > I), the economy declines. Income, output, and employment decrease.

REVIEW

Explain each concept in your own words, with an example: unemployment rate, frictional unemployment, seasonal unemployment, structural unemployment, cyclical unemployment, investment injection, savings leakage, business cycle, micro-economics, macro-economics.

APPLICATIONS

1. You are the world-famous economics detective Mr. Homlock Shears in a mystery entitled "The Case of the Frictionally Unemployed Workers." Here we have the statements of five suspects. Who is the frictionally unemployed worker? And what are the others? Of course, just like all good detectives, you will be able to explain how you know which one is the suspect and what the others are.

SUSPECT A: "I am a ski instructor. I'm still looking for work, even though it is July, but I can't find anything."
SUSPECT B: "I have just graduated from high school and I'm looking for my first job."
SUSPECT C: "I worked for a company that made vacuum tubes; now I'm unemployed because the tubes have been replaced by transistors."
SUSPECT D: "I looked for work for six months but all they want are people who have experience and I have none. I think it's a waste of time for me to look for a job."
SUSPECT E: "I was laid off when the recession hit our business."

2. Which of the following are examples of (a) micro-economics, or (b) macro-economics? In each case, explain why.
    a) the supply of potatoes
    b) the price of hamburgers
    c) the unemployment rate in Canada
    d) the business cycle
    e) the supply of pizzas in your school cafeteria.

3. Use the leaky bucket model to explain what happens to the level of employment and output, in an economy.

4. In a simple economy, without government and foreign trade, where savings equal investment, there is less than full employment and less than maximum output. What will happen if the rate of investment increases? Use the leaky bucket model to explain what happens.

5. Why is it unlikely that savings will equal investment at the level of full employment and maximum output?

A simple economy IV, with government injections

We have seen, in Chapter 11, that government (federal, provincial, and local) plays a significant role in the functioning of the economy through its expenditures and taxation. In figure 13.7, the injection of **government spending (G)** is added to our simple economy. As government spends money, it raises the levels of employment, output, and income in the same way as investment. Government spending (G) is an injection — similar to investment. **Taxation (T)**, on the other hand, functions as a leakage (just like savings), diminishing the level of employment, output, and income.

Government expenditures and taxation need not be equal. Governments may choose to collect more taxes than they spend; in this case, they will have a budget surplus. They may decide to spend more than they receive in taxes, thus having a budget deficit. Governments can, therefore, use their taxing and spending powers to raise, lower, or maintain the level of employment, income, and output.

A simple economy V, with foreign trade

Now we add the last pieces to our leaky bucket economy by examining the effects of foreign trade.

If you examine the labels of the goods you use, you will discover that many of them are produced in other countries: shoes from Italy, cars from Japan and Germany, sweaters from Britain. These shoes, cars, and sweaters are imported. Similarly, we sell many goods to other countries. Goods such as wheat, wood pulp, and newsprint are Canadian exports. As you can guess from the volume of goods and services we buy from other countries and the amount we sell to them, foreign trade has an important impact on our level of employment, income, and output.

Exports (X)   As foreign consumers, business people, and governments buy Canadian goods and services,

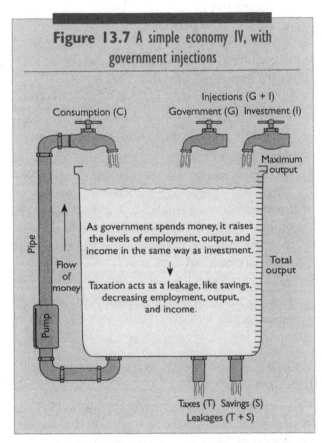

Figure 13.7 A simple economy IV, with government injections

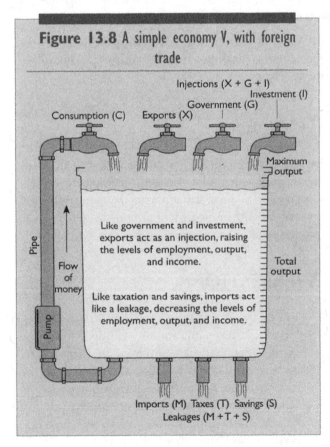

Figure 13.8 A simple economy V, with foreign trade

Canadians are provided with income and employment. In our leaky bucket economy, exports appear as an injection. See point X in figure 13.8.

Imports (M)   On the other hand, what we spend on imports acts as a leakage. Your purchase of a Japanese stereo serves to increase Japanese employment, income, and output rather than those of Canada. A business's purchase of capital equipment from the United States or the federal government's purchase of goods from Britain serves to increase the employment, output, and income of those countries. Thus, our expenditure on imports acts as a leakage. See point M in figure 13.8.

Changes in imports and exports   The level of Canadian imports is mainly dependent on the level of Canadian income. As our income rises, we tend to spend more on imports; as it falls, we tend to spend less. Unlike imports, our exports tend to follow variations in the domestic incomes of other countries. As their income rises, they buy more Canadian products; as it falls, they buy less. Our exports account for more than one-quarter of our income. Thus, exports have an important impact on our employment rate. Like investment spending, other countries' expenditures on our exports are not directly dependent on the level of our domestic income.

Summary

One of the major problems that Canadians face is unemployment. Of the four types of unemployment, cyclical unemployment is most severe. In our examination of the causes of fluctuations in the economy, we saw that these fluctuations take place when leakages (imports, taxes, and savings) differ in amount from injections (exports, government spending, and investment). When leakages exceed injections, the economy declines, unemployment increases, and income and output diminish. When leakages are less than injections, the economy increases, unemployment decreases, and income and output increase. See figure 13.9.

The inequalities between injections and leakages are likely to continue because those factors that determine

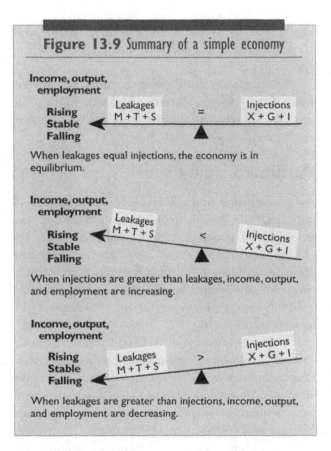

Figure 13.9 Summary of a simple economy

Income, output, employment

Rising
Stable ◀
Falling

Leakages M + T + S   =   Injections X + G + I

When leakages equal injections, the economy is in equilibrium.

Income, output, employment

Rising
Stable ◀
Falling

Leakages M + T + S   <   Injections X + G + I

When injections are greater than leakages, income, output, and employment are increasing.

Income, output, employment

Rising
Stable ◀
Falling

Leakages M + T + S   >   Injections X + G + I

When leakages are greater than injections, income, output, and employment are decreasing.

the amount of injections are different from those controlling the leakages. Therefore, we can expect that the employment rate will vary and we have no assurance that it will settle automatically at full employment.

FISCAL POLICY AND EMPLOYMENT

Government spending and taxing decisions have an effect on the level of employment, income, and output. These spending and taxing decisions are called **fiscal policy**. Changes in spending and taxing take place through automatic stabilizers or through government discretion.

Automatic stabilizers refer to changes in taxation and expenditures that occur automatically with changes in the levels of employment, income, and output. These changes have the effect of stabilizing the economy.

Discretionary fiscal policy occurs when government acts to change its taxation and expenditure policies deliberately to influence the levels of income, output, and employment.

Automatic stabilizers

When total injections (X + G + I) are less than total leakages (M + T + S), then output declines and unemployment increases. As unemployment increases, the number of people collecting unemployment insurance increases. Government expenditures on unemployment compensation increase automatically; government spending injection into the economy increases automatically.

In the same way, as the level of unemployment decreases, government expenditures on unemployment insurance decrease. Government expenditures on unemployment insurance **increase** as income, output, and employment are declining, and **decrease** as income, output, and employment are increasing. In this way, unemployment insurance payments act automatically to help stabilize the economy. Thus, stabilizers are built into the economy.

The Canadian income tax structure also acts as an automatic stabilizer. Because our income tax is progressive, as personal income declines in a recession, smaller proportions are taken in taxes. The tax leakage declines. In a recovery, as the output increases, incomes rise. With the rise in incomes, the amount collected in income tax increases and the tax leakage in our economy also increases. Income tax thus acts automatically to help stabilize the economy.

Automatic stabilizers are always at work in the economy. As output declines, stabilizers such as income tax and unemployment compensation act to slow down the decline in income, output, and employment. Similarly, stabilizers are also at work as the economy expands. No specific action is necessary on the part of the government. Once the stabilizers have been put in place, they work automatically.

Discretionary fiscal policy and unemployment

We are now in a position to examine how governments can act to increase the level of employment and, with it, income and output. Let's suppose that employment is declining, that is, we have an increasing rate of unemployment. This means that the total injections into the economy are less than the total leakages. To slow, stop, or reverse the increases in unemployment, government can act in a number of ways. Government can increase injections, decrease leakages, or do both.

Government action to cut leakages

1. Tax leakage

The leakage most easily influenced by government is taxation. A cut in personal income tax leaves consumers with more disposable income. Consequently, we can expect consumer spending to increase. Similarly, a cut in business taxes leaves businesses with more funds for investment and/or distribution to shareholders; thus, consumer and/or investment spending will increase.

2. Import leakage

Government can also move to diminish imports. The imposition of taxes and other restrictions on imports increases the price of imports and encourages Canadian consumers to consider buying a similar product made in Canada.

Government action to increase spending

1. Government spending injection

The injection most easily influenced by government is its own spending. Governments can increase their own spending on goods and services, and increase the amount of transfer payments they make. Clearly, governments have a wide range of options.

2. Export injection

Governments can also encourage exports in a variety of ways. For example, subsidies and low interest loans to exporters are likely to encourage exports.

By stimulating spending in the economy and diminishing leakages in these various ways, government can deal with the problem of cyclical or inadequate-demand unemployment.

The multiplier effect

Suppose that, as a result of a federal government public works program, my income increases by $100. Suppose, too, that everyone saves one-fifth of any increase in income and spends the remaining four-fifths (and we assume that government doesn't take a tax "bite" and there is no trade with other countries). This $100 increase in my income sets off a chain reaction. Of my $100 increase, I save one-fifth or $20 and spend the

remaining $80. Let's say I buy something from you and give you my $80. You, in turn, save one-fifth of this, or $16, and spend $64. You buy something from Lori and give her your $64. Lori saves $12.80 and spends $51.20. This process goes on until the total income generated is $500. See figure 13.10. In this case, since we all save one-fifth of the additional income, the multiplier is 5.

We can see from figure 13.10 that the initial government expenditure of $100 in four rounds of expenditures generates $295.20 in income. The total amount by which incomes are multiplied depends on the tendency to save. The greater the proportion that individuals save, the smaller the multiplier effect. The smaller the proportion of savings, the greater the effect. You can easily check this assertion by using a different proportion saved. For example, suppose that instead of individuals saving one-fifth of additional income, they saved one-half. In this case, the multiplier would be 2. The multiplier effect would operate as shown in figure 13.11.

When we compare the two figures, we see that total additional income generated with one-fifth saving is $500, while total income generated with one-half saving

Figure 13.10 The multiplier effect I

Expenditure	Total income generated	
Government spends $100	$100	Initial government expenditure
I spend $80	$180	Additional spending brought about by the initial government expenditure = $400
You spend $64	$244	
Lori spends $51.20	$295.20	
*	*	
*	*	
*	*	
Total increase in output from initial government expenditure	$500	

Figure 13.11 The multiplier effect II

Expenditure	Total income generated	
Government spends $100	$100	Initial government expenditure
I spend $50	$150	Additional expenditure brought about by the initial expenditure = $100
You spend $25	$175	
Lori spends $12.50	$187.50	
*	*	
*	*	
*	*	
Total increase in output from initial government expenditure	$200	

is $200. With the greater tendency to save, the multiplier effect is less, so the total income generated is less.

The effect of the multiplier is to magnify the impact of a change in expenditures or a change in the tax level. An initial tax cut or expenditure increase of $1 million, for example, will generate incomes in excess of the initial amount. Similarly, a tax increase or an expenditure cut of $1 million will also be magnified by the multiplier — thus reducing total incomes by some multiple of the initial amount. The effect of the multiplier is, then, to magnify the impact of fiscal policy.

Limitations of fiscal policy to combat unemployment

From our examination of fiscal policy and the multiplier effect, it would appear that government has a lot of power to resolve the problems of inadequate-demand unemployment. While things might look relatively simple on paper, they are much more complicated in reality. One problem is evident from the start. Government has a number of choices. Should taxes be cut? Should government expenditures be increased? Can the deficit and the debt be safely increased? Should exports be stimulated? Should imports be cut? Should some combination of tax cuts, expenditure increases, and trade measures be undertaken? Once a general decision has been made about taxes, expenditures, and trade policy, government has to work out the specifics. Just what expenditures are to be increased and by how much? What taxes are to be cut and by how much? By how much can government safely increase the deficit and the debt? What imports are to be restricted, and how? What exports are to be stimulated, and how?

Timing of fiscal policy

Decisions about the appropriate fiscal policy are complicated by the fact that government cannot be certain which way the economy is headed. Is the economy headed towards increasing unemployment? If so, then an expansionary or stimulative fiscal policy may be appropriate. On the other hand, the economy may be headed in the direction of full employment. An expansionary fiscal policy could bring about another problem — inflation. (We will examine inflation in the next chapter.)

The problem of knowing what will be happening in the economy at some point in the future is heightened by three problems of timing. There is a period of time, or **recognition lag**, between the onset of a recession and the recognition of the nature of the problem. It is only at this point that government can start to do something about the problem.

Once the problem has been recognized by government and private economists, there is a further delay, or **decision lag**. In a democracy, it usually takes a significant amount of time for us to reach a decision about what should be done about a problem.

Finally, there is an **implementation lag**, or a period of delay until fiscal policy changes start to take effect. A decision to increase expenditures on public works, for instance, takes a long time to plan and to start.

National and regional effects

The federal government must gauge the effects of policies on different parts of the country. If unemployment is high in Atlantic Canada and low in the rest of the country, should government do nothing on the grounds that in most of the country unemployment is low? Or should it cut taxes to help stimulate employment in Atlantic Canada while running the possible risk of inflation elsewhere? In the case of high unemployment in one region only, it may be better to develop specific public works programs, designed to put people to work in the high unemployment areas, rather than a program of general tax cuts.

MONETARY POLICY

Monetary policy is a government policy to bring about changes in the money supply.

So far, we have examined how government fiscal policy can be used to influence the level of employment. We have seen that increased government expenditures

Analyse the cartoon

Reprinted by permission of Newspaper Enterprise Association.

and/or reduced taxes can increase spending flows and reduce leakages to raise the level of income, output, and employment in the economy. Government (or more specifically the Bank of Canada) can also influence the size of the spending flows by varying the money supply. In Chapter 12, we outlined three main methods the Bank of Canada uses to vary the money supply: open-market operations, moral suasion, and adjusting the bank rate.

Easy money policy

In times of recession when there is widespread unemployment, a policy that stimulates the economy may be appropriate. The Bank of Canada can act to increase the money supply to make it easier for banks to lend money, and for consumers, businesses, and provincial and local governments to borrow more money. This kind of action by the central bank is called an **expansionary** or **easy money policy**.

Let's look at how an easy money policy works. See figure 13.12. By buying government bonds, or lowering the bank rate, the Bank of Canada acts to increase the excess reserves of the chartered banks. The chartered

banks have more money to loan and, to encourage borrowing, they are likely to lower their interest rates.

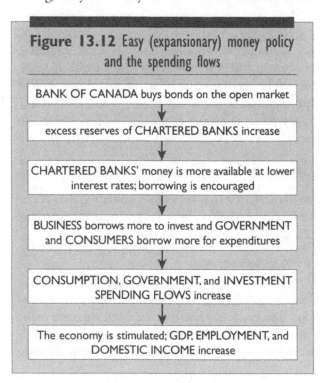

Figure 13.12 Easy (expansionary) money policy and the spending flows

BANK OF CANADA buys bonds on the open market

↓

excess reserves of CHARTERED BANKS increase

↓

CHARTERED BANKS' money is more available at lower interest rates; borrowing is encouraged

↓

BUSINESS borrows more to invest and GOVERNMENT and CONSUMERS borrow more for expenditures

↓

CONSUMPTION, GOVERNMENT, and INVESTMENT SPENDING FLOWS increase

↓

The economy is stimulated; GDP, EMPLOYMENT, and DOMESTIC INCOME increase

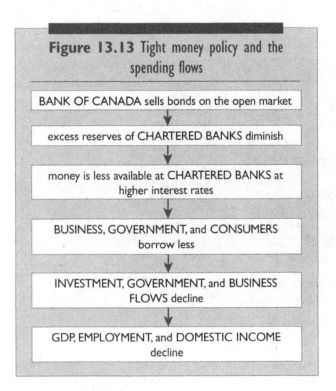

Figure 13.13 Tight money policy and the spending flows

BANK OF CANADA sells bonds on the open market

↓

excess reserves of CHARTERED BANKS diminish

↓

money is less available at CHARTERED BANKS at higher interest rates

↓

BUSINESS, GOVERNMENT, and CONSUMERS borrow less

↓

INVESTMENT, GOVERNMENT, and BUSINESS FLOWS decline

↓

GDP, EMPLOYMENT, and DOMESTIC INCOME decline

Similarly, with money being cheaper and easier to borrow, consumers, business people, and governments will be encouraged to borrow. Thus, consumer spending, investment, and government injections are likely to increase. The economy will be stimulated. Employment output and income are likely to rise. Compare the easy money policy shown in figure 13.12 on page 283 to the tight money policy in figure 13.13.

Limitations of monetary policy

Just as there are a number of limitations to fiscal policy as a means of combatting unemployment so, too, there are a number of limitations to monetary policy.

1. Excess reserves

There is a problem with an expansionary or easy money monetary policy that can be summed up in the expression, "You can lead a horse to water but you can't make it drink." Though an expansionary monetary policy can ensure that the chartered banks have excess reserves,

it cannot guarantee that banks will increase their loans or that the public will borrow money. The effectiveness of a monetary policy ultimately depends on how the banks and the public respond.

2. Timing problem

When we investigated weaknesses of fiscal policy, we saw that one big problem was identifying which way the economy was heading. This recognition time lag applies to monetary policy as well. However, monetary policies can be implemented fairly quickly.

REVIEW

Explain each concept in your own words with an example: automatic stabilizer, discretionary fiscal policy, monetary policy, the multiplier effect, decision lag, recognition lag, implementation lag, easy money policy.

APPLICATIONS

1. Suppose that in a situation where there is widespread cyclical unemployment, government has the choice of doing one of the following. Explain what effects each action would have on the economy.
   a) cut income taxes by $2 billion
   b) raise income taxes by $2 billion
   c) raise expenditures on public works by $3 billion
   d) cut imports by $1 billion
   e) institute an easy money policy

2. Which of the following are automatic stabilizers? Explain why.
   a) personal income tax
   b) corporate income tax
   c) unemployment insurance payments
   d) welfare payments
   e) federal public works program
   f) local property tax

SUMMARY

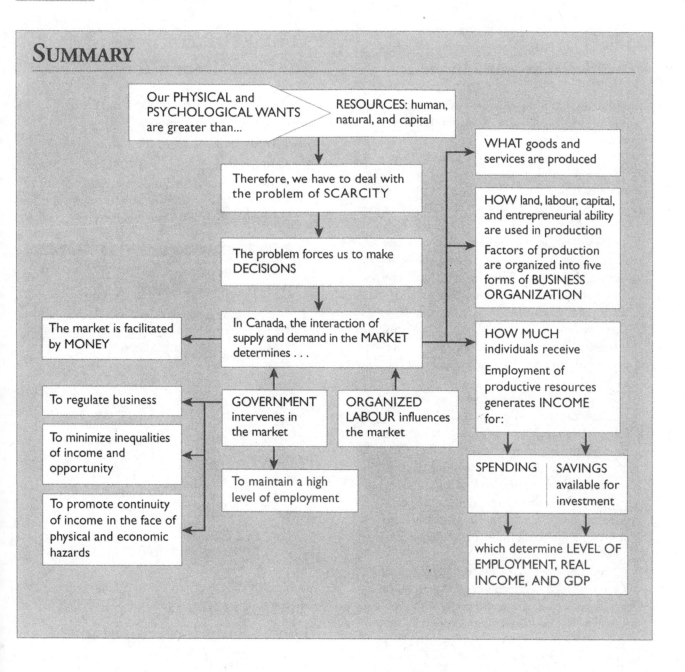

Our PHYSICAL and PSYCHOLOGICAL WANTS are greater than...

RESOURCES: human, natural, and capital

Therefore, we have to deal with the problem of SCARCITY

The problem forces us to make DECISIONS

WHAT goods and services are produced

HOW land, labour, capital, and entrepreneurial ability are used in production

Factors of production are organized into five forms of BUSINESS ORGANIZATION

The market is facilitated by MONEY

In Canada, the interaction of supply and demand in the MARKET determines . . .

HOW MUCH individuals receive

Employment of productive resources generates INCOME for:

To regulate business

GOVERNMENT intervenes in the market

ORGANIZED LABOUR influences the market

To minimize inequalities of income and opportunity

To maintain a high level of employment

SPENDING | SAVINGS available for investment

To promote continuity of income in the face of physical and economic hazards

which determine LEVEL OF EMPLOYMENT, REAL INCOME, AND GDP

3. Suppose Canadians face a situation of rising unemployment, declining output, and declining incomes.

    a) What monetary and fiscal policies would be appropriate to deal with the situation?

    b) Explain how the appropriate policies would influence the economy.

    c) What policies would affect the economy most quickly?

ISSUE
Would you accept a buyout?

Individually, and then in groups, decide what you would do in the following situation. Outline the reasons for your decision.

You are a middle manager with a secure job at a manufacturing company.

Your firm, like most others, is feeling the pinch of recession. It has announced a round of layoffs which will be mitigated [offset] by a voluntary retirement package. For every person who takes the buyout, the number to be laid off is reduced by one.

You've worked there for 25 years and you're three years shy of retirement. Your children are on their own and you own your home. Your pension is adequate, but you've always wanted to travel and you're working now to give yourself that long anticipated luxury.

At a meeting of senior managers the day of the buyout deadline, you are given a list of people to be laid off. Among them is a member of your staff who is the sort of employee the company badly needs to keep: young, hard working, enterprising and loyal. You know she has a young family, is a single parent and has a large mortgage. Because she lacks seniority, her severance would not be very much and it would be difficult for her to find a job quickly.

You can save her job by accepting the buyout.

You would be entitled to a good severance package, though by leaving earlier than planned your retirement dreams would not be realized.

What would you do?
a) Take the buyout.
b) Do nothing, it's not your problem.
c) Plead with your superiors that she's a special case.
d) Take some other action.

Source: *Toronto Star*, December 5, 1993.

TIME STUDY
The Great Depression

Use the information given in tables 13.3 and 13.4 to answer the following questions.

1. Identify four phases of the business cycle.

2. Suppose that at the end of 1931, Prime Minister Bennett asked you for suggestions to improve the economic situation. What would you have suggested? Explain your reasons.

Table 13.3 Canadian employment (in thousands), 1926-1935

Year	Total civilian labour force	People with jobs	Number of unemployed
1926	3658	3550	108
1927	3757	3690	67
1928	3861	3796	65
1929	3964	3848	116
1930	4060	3689	371
1931	4151	3670	481
1932	4211	3470	741
1933	4275	3449	826
1934	4338	3707	631
1935	4466	3895	571

Source: M.C. Urquhart and K.A.H. Buckley, *Historical Statistics of Canada* (Toronto: Macmillan, 1965).

TIME STUDY
The Canadian economy in World War II

1. Using the information in tables 13.4 and 13.5, explain what happened to employment, income, and output in the Canadian economy during World War II (1939-1945).

Table 13.4 Aggregate demand, GNP, and national income (in millions of dollars at market prices), 1926-1945

Year	Consumption expenditures	Investment	Government expenditures	Exports	Imports	Error of estimate	GNP	National income
1926	3 542	837	488	1 650	1 522	157	5 152	4 129
1927	3 893	1 083	531	1 618	1 629	53	5 549	4 356
1928	4 314	1 166	560	1 773	1 808	41	6 046	4 737
1929	4 621	1 213	640	1 632	1 945	27	6 134	4 708
1930	4 367	1 003	721	1 286	1 625	24	5 728	4 399
1931	3 773	517	688	967	1 142	114	4 699	3 382
1932	3 194	219	584	804	901	73	3 827	2 641
1933	2 984	143	462	826	828	77	3 510	2 368
1934	3 182	330	503	1 018	948	101	3 984	2 783
1935	3 338	408	542	1 143	1 017	99	4 315	3 099
1936	3 549	386	544	1 428	1 183	71	4 653	3 367
1937	3 884	633	619	1 591	1 409	70	5 257	3 887
1938	3 897	592	666	1 356	1 257	33	5 278	4 001
1939	3 984	874	683	1 451	1 328	28	5 636	4 236
1940	4 488	1 058	1 116	1 808	1 629	98	6 743	5 063
1941	5 103	1 173	1 635	2 467	1 976	74	8 328	6 305
1942	5 500	1 199	3 674	2 361	2 307	100	10 327	8 098
1943	5 808	707	4 177	3 444	2 917	131	11 088	8 802
1944	6 274	755	4 978	3 561	3 569	149	11 850	9 583
1945	6 969	720	3 656	3 597	2 910	197	11 835	9 665

Source: M.C. Urquhart and K.A.H. Buckley, *Historical Statistics of Canada* (Toronto: MacMillan, 1965).

Table 13.5 Employment in Canada, 1939-1945

Year	Total people with jobs (in thousands)	People without jobs and seeking work (in thousands)	Total labour force (in thousands)	Percentage unemployed
1939	4120	529	4649	11.4
1940	4184	423	4607	9.2
1941	4271	195	4466	4.3
1942	4434	135	4569	2.8
1943	4491	76	4567	1.7
1944	4485	63	4548	1.4
1945	4447	73	4520	1.6

Source: M.C. Urquhart and K.A.H. Buckley, *Historical Statistics of Canada* (Toronto: MacMillan, 1965).

CHAPTER 14

Inflation

(1934)

25.95

Special! Elswick
BICYCLES

HOME LOVERS CLUB
TERMS—$3 now and $3
a month. No extras.

English-made, with coaster brake, chromium-plated parts. In maroon or blue. Dropside mudguards, coil spring saddle. Roller chain. A strong, sturdy bicycle with pump, tool bag and bell. Sizes 20/18, 22/20, 24/22.

Sporting Goods—Fourth Floor

(1934)

CORNERS SCHOOL DISTRICT No. 2579 REQUIRES teacher with first-class certificate to commence at once. Four pupils in school. Grades 8 and 9. Want French 1 or Latin 1. Also oversee literature composition and geography in Grade 11. Board 1 mile. Salary $950 per year. Apply W. F. Anderson, Secretary, Wardlow, Alberta.

TEACHER WANTED FOR CHERRY VALLEY School District No. 3087. Salary $1,000 per year. Apply to J.P. Rorabeck, Secretary-Treasurer, Box 10, Oyen, Alberta.

(1

HOUSES AND FLATS TO LET

Heated upper flat of four rooms and bath, newly decorated. Rental $25.00 per month.

House of six rooms and bath, breakfast-nook, open fireplace, oak floors, hot-water heating, fine view. Rental $35.00 per month.

New five-room bungalow. Tupper Street, hardwood floors, furnace heated, open fireplace. Rental $30.00 per month.

(193

(1934)

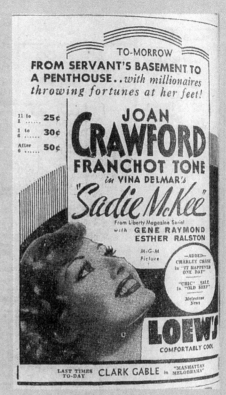

(1934)

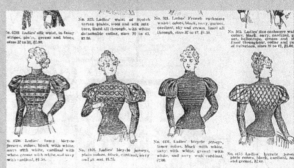

(1898)

Questions

1. Use a recent newspaper to compare some prices today with those in the past.

2. What prices have probably risen the most?

289

Figure 14.1 The effects of inflation

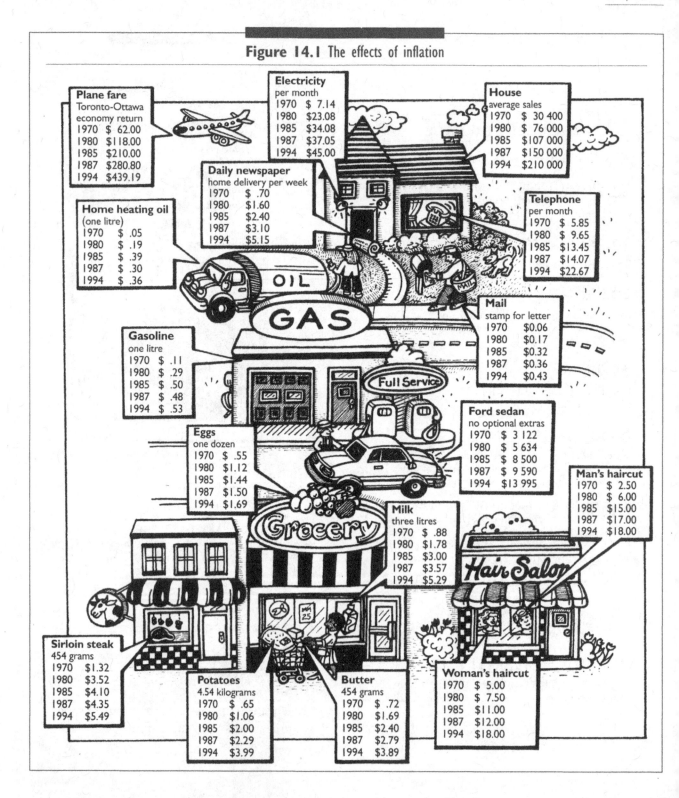

Plane fare
Toronto-Ottawa
economy return
1970	$ 62.00
1980	$118.00
1985	$210.00
1987	$280.80
1994	$439.19

Electricity
per month
1970	$ 7.14
1980	$23.08
1985	$34.08
1987	$37.05
1994	$45.00

House
average sales
1970	$ 30 400
1980	$ 76 000
1985	$107 000
1987	$150 000
1994	$210 000

Daily newspaper
home delivery per week
1970	$ .70
1980	$1.60
1985	$2.40
1987	$3.10
1994	$5.15

Telephone
per month
1970	$ 5.85
1980	$ 9.65
1985	$13.45
1987	$14.07
1994	$22.67

Home heating oil
(one litre)
1970	$ .05
1980	$ .19
1985	$ .39
1987	$ .30
1994	$ .36

Mail
stamp for letter
1970	$0.06
1980	$0.17
1985	$0.32
1987	$0.36
1994	$0.43

Gasoline
one litre
1970	$ .11
1980	$ .29
1985	$ .50
1987	$ .48
1994	$ .53

Ford sedan
no optional extras
1970	$ 3 122
1980	$ 5 634
1985	$ 8 500
1987	$ 9 590
1994	$13 995

Eggs
one dozen
1970	$ .55
1980	$1.12
1985	$1.44
1987	$1.50
1994	$1.69

Man's haircut
1970	$ 2.50
1980	$ 6.00
1985	$15.00
1987	$17.00
1994	$18.00

Milk
three litres
1970	$ .88
1980	$1.78
1985	$3.00
1987	$3.57
1994	$5.29

Sirloin steak
454 grams
1970	$1.32
1980	$3.52
1985	$4.10
1987	$4.35
1994	$5.49

Potatoes
4.54 kilograms
1970	$ .65
1980	$1.06
1985	$2.00
1987	$2.29
1994	$3.99

Butter
454 grams
1970	$ .72
1980	$1.69
1985	$2.40
1987	$2.79
1994	$3.89

Woman's haircut
1970	$ 5.00
1980	$ 7.50
1985	$11.00
1987	$12.00
1994	$18.00

WHAT IS INFLATION?

If we look back to the 1970s, we can see that there has been a general increase in prices since then. It is true that the prices of some goods, for example, ballpoint pens and electronic calculators, have decreased, while the prices of some other goods have remained approximately the same. But in general, prices have risen. We find that our dollar buys fewer and fewer goods and services. We have been experiencing inflation.

Inflation is the general increase in the prices of goods and services over a period of time. (See figure 14.1.) In this chapter, we will examine how inflation is measured, how different social groups are affected by it, what causes it, and how we can deal with it.

Questions

1. In general, what happened to prices (a) between 1970 and 1980? (b) between 1980 and 1985? (c) between 1985 and 1987? (d) between 1987 and 1994? (e) between 1994 and today?

2. In general, in what period was the increase most rapid? Which prices increased most rapidly? Which prices increased least rapidly?

3. How are you affected by price increases? How do increases affect other people? Who is most likely hurt by price increases?

HOW TO INCREASE YOUR INCOME WITHOUT DOING MORE WORK

Suppose that during the last three years you have had a weekly income from a part-time job of $30.00. However, you have begun to notice that your income buys less and less. Therefore, you decide to show your expenses to your employer to convince her that, since the prices of the goods and services you purchase have increased, you should get an increase in your pay. You show her a chart like the one in figure 14.2.

YOU: As you can see from the chart, the costs of the goods and services I buy have increased from $20.00 to $25.00, an increase of 25 percent. Therefore, I'd like to request an increase in pay of 25 percent, from $30.00 to $36.50.

EMPLOYER: You may request an increase in pay but you haven't proved to me that a 25 percent increase is fair. The prices of milk and fruit haven't changed very much and they are much more important in your consumption than records or movie tickets.

YOU: (*Disappointed*) I see what you mean. But I'll have to think it over.

You decide to seek the advice of your friendly economist about how you can better present your case. You outline what happened in your interview with your employer.

FRIENDLY ECONOMIST: Your employer's comments are valid. I presume that you buy milk, fruit, and hot dogs every school day (that is, five times a week), a cassette tape once a week, and a ticket to a movie once a week?

YOU: Yes, that's right. But I don't see . . .

FRIENDLY ECONOMIST: In the chart you gave your employer, you didn't take into account the *relative frequency* of each purchase. Since you buy milk, fruit, and hot dogs five times a week, and tapes and movie tickets only once a week, then the food items should count five times more in calculating your expenditures. In other words, each purchase should be *weighted*, as I've shown in this chart. . . .

Figure 14.2 Increase in costs

Purchases	Costs three years ago	Costs today
Two hot dogs	$ 1.60	$ 1.90
Milk	.40	.55
Fruit	.50	.55
Cassette tape	12.00	14.00
Ticket for movie	5.50	8.00
Total	$20.00	$25.00

YOU: I see. So I would need to show my employer a comparison chart that included the frequency of each purchase.

FRIENDLY ECONOMIST: Yes. As you can see, it costs you $37.00 to purchase today what it cost $30.00 to purchase three years ago. Another way of comparing the expenditures is to show today's expenditures as a percentage of those three years ago. Here's how to calculate such a percentage:

$$\frac{\text{Costs today}}{\text{Costs three years ago}} \times 100\% \quad \frac{\$37.00}{\$30.00} \times 100\% = 123\%$$

You could say, then, that your cost of living rose 23 percent.

YOU: Thank you very much.

You present your employer with this new information. Needless to say, she is completely convinced by the brilliance of your new argument. Your pay is increased by 23 percent immediately!

Figure 14.3 Your price index

Purchases	Cost per item three years ago	Weight	Costs three years ago
Two hot dogs	$1.60	5	$ 8.00
Milk	.40	5	2.00
Fruit	.50	5	2.50
Cassette tape	12.00	1	12.00
Ticket for movie	5.50	1	5.50
Total			$30.00

Purchases	Cost per item today	Weight	Costs today
Two hot dogs	$1.90	5	$ 9.50
Milk	.55	5	2.75
Fruit	.55	5	2.75
Cassette tape	14.00	1	14.00
Ticket for movie	8.00	1	8.00
Total			$37.00

THE CONSUMER PRICE INDEX

As you saw when you approached your employer about an increase in pay, some method to measure change in price is useful. We saw in Chapter 5 that the Dow Jones industrial average and the Toronto Stock Exchange 300 composite index were both developed to measure changes in the prices of stocks. Similarly, it is useful to have a measure of how prices, in general, vary over time. To measure changes in the prices of consumer goods and services, Statistics Canada constructs the Consumer Price Index (CPI) in basically the same way as shown in figure 14.3.

The **Consumer Price Index** is a measure of the general changes in market prices of a selected group of goods and services purchased by a typical urban family.

To calculate the index, a survey of the spending habits of Canadians is made. From this survey, a relatively small number of items (less than 400) is chosen to reflect the spending patterns of Canadians living in Canadian cities of over 30 000 people. To determine the CPI each month, the prices of the chosen goods and services ("the shopping basket") are collected by survey takers in urban centres. The items are "weighted" according to the proportion of the household budget spent on them — in the same way you weighted your expenditures. The shopping basket of goods and services is determined through regular family income surveys. The current basket is based on surveys carried out in 1986.

The CPI includes seven components to reflect the spending patterns of Canadians. These major components and their weights are shown in figure 14.4. From the chart, we can see that food, clothing, and shelter account for about two-thirds of total spending. The remaining third is made up of transportation, health and personal care, recreation, reading and education, and tobacco and alcoholic beverages.

Rather than describing the CPI in terms of the cost of the "basket" of goods and services, the CPI is expressed in terms of how much it has changed from a base year. Presently, the base year (in which the CPI

Figure 14.4 Weights of components of the Consumer Price Index

Components	Weights
Food	18.1
Housing	36.3
Clothing	8.7
Transportation	18.3
Health and personal care	4.2
Recreation, reading, and education	8.8
Tobacco products and alcoholic beverages	5.6

Source: Statistics Canada, *The Consumer Price Index*, March 1994.

is 100) is 1986. In 1990, for example, the CPI was estimated at 117.0. In money terms, that means that the amount of goods you could buy for $1 in 1986 would cost you $1.17 in 1990.

The CPI has many uses. One of them you can guess from the construction of your price index. Increasingly, labour-management contracts include cost of living allowances. Some wages are linked to CPI increases. Many pensions are also adjusted upwards as the CPI increases. The CPI is perhaps most used as an approximate measure of the rate of inflation from year to year. In addition to the unemployment rate and GDP, it is one of the most widely quoted measures of how well our economy is performing.

Questions

1. In what years were there rapid increases in prices?

2. In what year was there deflation (i.e., a reduction in the general level of prices)?

3. How do prices in the 1990s compare with those in the 1970s and 1980s?

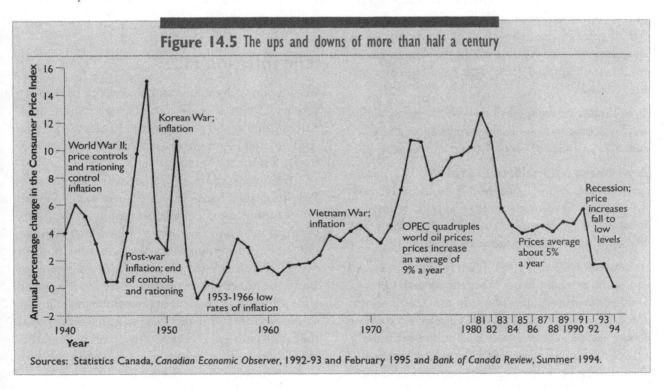

Figure 14.5 The ups and downs of more than half a century

Sources: Statistics Canada, *Canadian Economic Observer*, 1992-93 and February 1995 and *Bank of Canada Review*, Summer 1994.

INFLATION SINCE 1940

Since 1940, there have been significant increases in prices. In every year except 1953, prices have increased. See figure 14.5 on page 293. At the beginning of the Second World War in 1939 and 1940, employment, national income, and output began to rise as government demand for war materials rose sharply. Prices began to increase rapidly. To prevent continued rapid increases in prices, the federal government intervened in 1942 to control rising prices, to ration goods, and to boost taxation. From 1942 until the end of the war in 1945, the general level of prices rose, but at rates lower than those in 1941.

With the end of the war, there was a huge demand for goods and services. After the shortages experienced during the war, Canadians were in a buying mood. Business people invested heavily in anticipation of good profits. Government also pursued an expansionary policy and cut taxes. With the removal of government price controls and rationing, prices rose rapidly. The rate of price increase slowed in 1949 but picked up again in 1951 with the outbreak of the Korean War.

Since the early 1950s, there have been five distinct periods.

1. **In the period from 1953 to 1965**, the rate of inflation was low, with an average increase in the Consumer Price Index of about 1.5 percent per year.

2. **In the second period, from 1966 to 1972**, the annual increase in the Consumer Price Index averaged 4.8 percent. This was the time of heavy U.S. involvement in the Vietnam War which, like the Korean War, had a major impact on Canadian price levels.

3. **Between 1973 and 1982**, prices increased at a rapid rate again, averaging about 9 percent per year. One factor that played a significant role in these increases was the activity of the Organization of Petroleum Exporting Countries, the oil cartel, which led to the quadrupling of world prices for oil in 1973. Other large increases in the price of oil were imposed by the cartel in subsequent years. A decline in the value of the Canadian dollar compared to the currencies of other countries also led to an increase in the cost of imported goods.

4. **From 1983 to 1991**, following the recession of the early 1980s, the rate of increase in prices fell to an average of less than 5 percent per year.

5. **From 1991 onwards**, recession and the determined efforts of the Bank of Canada and other central banks pushed average inflation rates in Canada below 2 percent.

INFLATION: THE WINNERS AND THE LOSERS

The costs of inflation are much less obvious than the costs of unemployment. Unemployment represents a clear loss. What the unemployed do not produce is gone forever. In the case of inflation, though, there are winners and losers. Those who owe money win. Those who are owed money lose.

The inflation race

Keeping up with rapidly rising prices can be seen as a race with inflation. Let's consider the situation of inflation running at 8 percent a year. In order to keep up with inflation, your income would have to be increasing by 8 percent a year.

Let's imagine the entire nation out running in an "8 Percent Inflation Race." In general, what would we see?

Running ahead of inflation would be the hearty — those who find themselves in healthy, expanding industries. This group would include those business people who are able to keep the price of their products above the growth in the general price level. It would also include those workers in powerful bargaining positions who are able to negotiate wage settlements over the 8 percent figure. Finally, this category would include those who had borrowed money when the inflation rate was less than 8 percent.

Running behind inflation and starting to feel winded would be the business people and workers in declining industries. Workers in weak bargaining positions would find it difficult to negotiate wage raises in keeping with the high cost of living.

The people losing ground fast in the Inflation Race would be those on low or fixed incomes. Among this group would be retired people on fixed pensions, those who had invested in long-term bonds when the rate of inflation was below 8 percent; and those who live at or near the poverty line.

Others in the race

Inflation acts to alter the relationship between debtors and creditors. Suppose, for example, that you borrow $100 for one year and that the price level doubles in that year. While you still have to pay back $100 (if we ignore interest charges), the actual purchasing power of money you pay back is only half of what you borrowed. Thus, there has been a transfer of wealth from your creditor (the person from whom you borrowed) to you (the debtor).

Those who put their savings into bonds, savings accounts, and insurance policies would also be hurt by inflation unless the return on the money invested exceeded the rate of inflation. Since stock prices are flexible and determined by supply and demand, these prices could keep pace with inflation.

Hyperinflation: inflation run wild

Extremely high rates of inflation (known as **hyperinflation**), like that experienced in Germany in the early 1920s and Bolivia in the 1980s, have a devastating effect on the economy. In Bolivia in 1984, prices zoomed 2700 percent, compared to 329 percent the year before. The 1000 peso bill, the most commonly used, cost more to print than it purchased. It could be used to buy one bag of tea.

What are the effects of hyperinflation? The value of savings accounts, government and corporate bonds, insurance policies and annuities are wiped out. The real incomes of those on pensions are reduced to zero. The value of money declines rapidly. People resort to barter, preferring to exchange their goods for other goods rather than for money with its declining value. With widespread barter, specialization (one of the advantages of money) is lost. Money promotes specialization. Without continued specialization, income and output diminish rapidly.

Deflation

Deflation is a decrease in the general level of prices over time. In periods of deflation, the purchasing power of money rises.

Deflationary periods, such as the early 1930s, are associated not only with declining prices, but also with declining national income, employment, and output.

As you would expect, the effects of a deflationary period on distribution are the opposite of an inflationary period. Creditors, savers, and those on fixed incomes gain. Debtors will tend to lose since the real value of their debts — the value of their debts in terms of what it will buy — will increase.

WHAT CAUSES INFLATION?

We have all been affected by inflation. For the most part, prices have continued to rise in the 1960s, 1970s, 1980s, and 1990s, and we have seen some of the effects inflation can have. What causes inflation? Economists have identified two major types of inflation, which they call "demand-pull inflation" and "cost-push inflation" (also known as "sellers' inflation").

Full employment and no inflation

Before we start to examine demand-pull inflation, we should notice one change in our measure on the side of the leaky bucket. It measures real output. In other words, it measures output adjusted for changes in the level of prices. When we compare real output at two different times, we are comparing the amount of real goods and services produced. Changes in the output due solely to changes in prices have been eliminated.

Let's start with the economy in an ideal situation. Suppose our injections are equal to our leakages. See figure 14.6. Our bucket is full, and we have maximum real output, maximum real income, and full employment. This is an ideal situation!

Demand-pull inflation

Let's suppose that we have full employment but that total injections exceed total leakages. See figure 14.7. Now we have a situation in which there's an overabundance of money in relation to the goods and services it

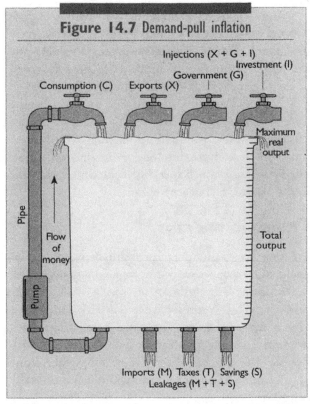

Figure 14.7 Demand-pull inflation

At full employment, injections are greater than leakages; investment, government, and exports are greater than savings, taxes, and imports; the bucket overflows and we have demand-pull inflation.

can buy. Our leaky bucket economy overflows and this overflow represents inflation. In this situation, there can be no further increase in real income or in real output because there is already full employment of the factors of production. We are in the situation where we are producing as much as we can. While it may be possible to increase the production of one good, perhaps cars, it can only be done at the cost of diminishing the output of another good, perhaps trucks. In response to the high demand for goods and services, prices rise and will continue to rise as long as the amount of spending continues to increase. Real output can only increase to the rim of the bucket; money output may go on rising. Total injections or total demand pull(s) up prices. This is called **demand-pull inflation**.

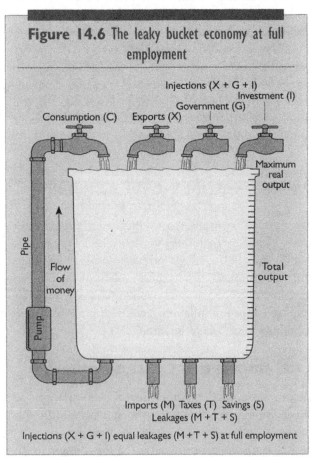

Figure 14.6 The leaky bucket economy at full employment

Injections (X + G + I) equal leakages (M + T + S) at full employment

Demand-pull inflation is caused by excessive total spending or demand compared to the total amount of goods and services that can be produced in the economy. Demand "pulls up" prices. Demand-pull inflation is therefore often described as "too much money chasing too few goods."

Government policies to control demand-pull inflation

A glance at figure 14.7 suggests some of the actions that government can take to control demand-pull inflation. To lower or eliminate the rate of inflation in our leaky bucket economy, government could increase the leakages and/or decrease the injections by fiscal and monetary policies.

1. Contractionary fiscal policy In using its spending and taking powers, government could engage in a contractionary fiscal policy. By cutting its expenditures and/or increasing taxation, government can lower the amount of injections into the economy and increase the leakages, thus lowering the rate of inflation. In this case, government revenues increase and expenditures decrease.

We saw that during periods of inadequate demand unemployment, an appropriate policy for government is to spend more than its revenues, that is, to have a budget deficit. On the other hand, in times of demand-pull inflation, it is an appropriate policy for government to aim for a budget surplus, a situation in which revenues are greater than expenditures. Over the course of the business cycle, the budget would be balanced with deficits during depressions and surpluses during times of prosperity and demand-pull inflation.

2. Contractionary or tight money policy In addition to a contractionary fiscal policy to fight inflation, government can also adopt a contractionary or tight money policy. By acting to diminish the money supply by the sale of bonds, raising the bank rate, or by exercising moral suasion, government makes bank credit less readily available and more expensive. Thus,

a tight money policy serves to diminish the spending flows, thereby diminishing the rate of inflation.

Applying fiscal and monetary policies to demand-pull inflation

Sounds easy, doesn't it? Why, then, do we have inflation? Needless to say, applying appropriate policies is much more difficult in practice than in theory.

1. Unemployment One major difficulty is that contractionary fiscal policies and tight money policies may ease the problem of inflation at the expense of widespread unemployment. To return to our leaky bucket economy, if government cuts the injections and increases the leakages through its monetary and fiscal policy, it may lower the rate of inflation. However, it may also cause the level of GDP and employment to drop significantly, thus bringing the economy into a recession. A vigorous attack on inflation may bring in its wake unemployment, and reduced national income and GDP. Conversely, an easy money policy and an expansionary fiscal policy may ease the problems of inadequate-demand unemployment, but may bring inflation as well.

2. Delays in applying the policy In our examination of government policies to meet the problem of inadequate-demand unemployment, we saw that there were three different kinds of delays or lags that made it difficult to apply the appropriate policy. First, there is a period of time between the onset of unemployment and the recognition of it. This **recognition lag** also occurs in the case of inflation. Second, there is a **decision lag**, a period of time in which decisions are made about what mix of fiscal and monetary policies is most appropriate. Finally, there is the **implementation lag** — the delay up until the fiscal and monetary policies start to take effect.

3. Cost-push inflation Besides the danger of creating unemployment and the delays in applying policy, there is a further problem: cost-push inflation.

Cost-push or sellers' inflation

Clearly, the task of managing the economy to eliminate either inadequate-demand unemployment or demand-pull inflation is tricky. What do you do when you have both rising unemployment and inflation together? This is a situation known as **stagflation**, which made its appearance in the late 1950s in the Canadian economy. Stagflation exists when a high level of unemployment (or *stag*nation) and a high level of in*flation* occur at the same time.

Our demand-pull explanation, taken alone, does not explain the simultaneous existence of high unemployment and inflation. Inflation occurs when we are at, or close to, full employment. How, then, can high unemployment and inflation exist at the same time? Simply stated, the reason is because we have only looked at part of the picture. We have examined only how total demand affects price and the economy. We must also examine how producers (or the supply side of the economy) can affect prices.

Even in a situation where employment is high, powerful unions may be able to use the threat of a strike to gain higher wages. A large corporation with few rivals may be able to raise prices even though demand for its products is slow. At the same time, it may also be able to increase its profit margin. If the corporation is producing goods that are essential in other industries (such as raw materials or essential parts), then the costs to other industries will increase. These industries may also pass along these costs to the consumer in the form of higher prices. The result is cost-push or sellers' inflation. As the general level of prices rises, workers will feel that their wages are not keeping up. There will be wage demands reflecting labour's desire to "catch up" with inflation and keep ahead of expected inflation. In this way, prices may continue to rise.

Cost-push or **sellers' inflation** occurs when wages or other costs rise and these costs are passed along in the form of higher prices. Costs are "pushed up" by rising prices. Cost-push inflation can occur when there is widespread unemployment and sluggish demand.

One cause of cost-push inflation in the 1970s and early 1980s stood out above all others: the Organization of Petroleum Exporting Countries. This organization, composed of petroleum exporting countries, was able to increase the price of oil eight-fold in approximately ten years. Since oil is an essential source of power for industry, fuel for transportation, and heat for homes and businesses, prices rose dramatically.

The leaky bucket economy and cost-push inflation

In our leaky bucket economy, we have a number of holes cut in the side of our bucket. See figure 14.8. Let's suppose that in our economy, output is at AA — at a point less than full employment and maximum output.

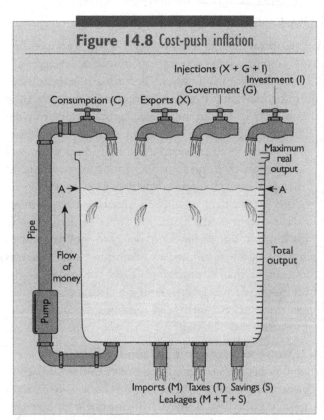

Figure 14.8 Cost-push inflation

If employment rises above AA, more money flows out of holes in the side of the bucket. As employment increases, inflation increases.

Suppose that at this point cost-push inflation appears. It is shown as the leakages through holes in the side of the bucket below AA. At this point, it is clear that employment could decrease (the level in the bucket could decline) while we continue to have inflation. With cost-push inflation, we can have high levels of inflation and unemployment appearing at the same time; in other words, stagflation.

A glance at the leaky bucket economy represented in figure 14.8 shows that, while government can control leakages and injections by various fiscal and monetary measures, it is unable to eliminate both unemployment and inflation. Instead, in applying fiscal and monetary policies, the government has to make choices. By trying to reduce unemployment, government runs the risk of adding to inflation. By trying to combat inflation, it runs the risk of adding to unemployment.

A VIEW OF THE ECONOMY FROM THE PERSPECTIVE OF MONEY

So far we have looked at total spending as the sum of its parts. As we have seen, there are four basic spending groups: consumers (C), businesses (I), government (G), and foreigners (X – M). We have combined these as four great spending flows to get total spending or aggregate demand. We can, however, look at total spending from another perspective, as being a large flow of dollars.

Total spending flow as a mass of moving money

Total spending can be looked at as the total money supply and the speed at which it is flowing. If our total money supply is $10 billion, if each dollar is spent to buy something once a month, then the total size of the spending flow is $10 billion a month or $120 billion a year.

M is used to symbolize the **supply of money** in existence and **V** to denote the **velocity of circulation of money** (the average number of times the money is spent). **Total spending** is therefore **MV**.

If the total money supply is spent just once a year, then total spending is equal to the money supply times the velocity of circulation, or one. If the total money supply is spent at a faster rate, for example, on average three times a year, then the total spending is three times the money supply, since the velocity of circulation is three. The money supply times the velocity of circulation (MV) is C + I + G + (X – M) described in a different way.

As we have seen, total demand or spending is equal to total output or GDP. One way of measuring GDP would be to multiply the total quantity of goods produced (Q) by the average price (P) per unit. Thus, for example, if we produce 1000 goods (Q) a year and the average price (P) is $2 each, then total output is $P \times Q$ or $1000 \times \$2 = \$2000$. The average price (P) multiplied by the number of goods and services produced (Q) is the national output. $P \times Q$ is simply GDP stated in a different way.

Now we can state what economists call the equation of exchange. The total spending flow equals total output, or:

$$MV = PQ$$

which is simply the following equation expressed in a different way:

$$C + I + G + (X - M) = GDP$$

The money supply (M) and total spending (PQ) are linked by the velocity of circulation (V). If the velocity of circulation is fairly stable, then it follows that the money supply is of crucial importance in the economy. In a period of recession, an increase in the money supply will bring about an increase in the quantity of goods produced.

$$M \uparrow \times V = P \times Q \uparrow$$

As M increases, Q increases. If, however, we are in a period of full employment, an increase in the money supply will bring about an increase in the price level; this causes inflation. As M increases, P increases.

$$M \uparrow \times V = P \uparrow \times Q$$

Changes in the money supply have a direct impact on the GDP.

Monetary rule

Though the money supply is the critical element in the economy, some economists, known as Monetarists, do not advocate the use of "tight" and "easy" money to control the economy. They maintain that government actions to vary the money supply have often been wrong or that government influence has tended to make matters worse. One of the difficulties, as we have seen, is the implementation lag. Studies by economist Milton Friedman have shown that it can take between four and thirty months for a monetary policy to have an impact. Thus, selection of the appropriate monetary policy may very well be impossible.

Friedman advocates the legislation of a **monetary rule** by which the money supply would increase by the same rates as the annual increase in potential GDP. Thus, our money supply would be increased by between 3 and 5 percent per year.

$$M \uparrow \times V = P \times Q \uparrow$$

Because the money supply would match the increase in the quantity of goods and services produced, there would be no inflation. If the economy slid into recession, the increase in the money supply would lead to increases in the quantity of goods produced. The economy, the Monetarists argue, would be saved from the disruptive policies of government.

Summary

The debate between the Monetarists and the Keynesians — between those who oppose and those who advocate government intervention in the economy — is likely to go on for some time. This debate involves not only questions of economic theory, but also of policy. There are significant differences as well in the way they see the market system working. They perceive two conflicting roles for government in the economy.

The Keynesians believe that there are inherent weaknesses in our economic system that prevent it from providing full employment without inflation. The role of government is to intervene in the system to see that the goals are achieved.

The Monetarists, on the other hand, see the economic system as being fundamentally sound. It can function best without interference by government. Government intervention, they say, tends to be inefficient and harmful. If freed from government, the economy would tend to provide high levels of output, income, and employment without inflation. The role of government would be to provide an atmosphere conducive to the growth of the private sector. This would include maintaining the appropriate growth in the money supply of 3 to 5 percent.

DIRECT GOVERNMENT WAGE AND PRICE CONTROLS

We have seen some of the problems involved in trying to use fiscal and monetary policy to control inflation and unemployment. Canadian governments have looked for ways to deal with these problems. Some economists, most notably the economist J.K. Galbraith, have recommended the use of wage and price controls.

Wage and price controls (or guidelines) are policies aimed at restraining inflation by holding wage and price increases below a specific level. By imposing wage and price controls, government attempts to enlist business and labour in its fight against inflation.

Wage and price controls since 1945

Wage and price controls have been imposed during wartime to hold in check inflationary pressures caused by excess demand. In World War II, wage and price controls were successful in restraining the rate of inflation. Since World War II, Canadian governments have made two attempts to control wages and prices.

The Prices and Incomes Commission

In 1969 the federal government established the Prices and Incomes Commission. It attempted to obtain support from workers and business for a program of **voluntary controls** on prices and wages. The commission failed to win the support of labour unions. There was no attempt to impose compulsory guidelines. The commission ended in 1972.

The Anti-Inflation Board (AIB)

In 1975, the Liberal government introduced **compulsory wage and price controls** for a three-year period. Price and wage changes were to be monitored by the Anti-Inflation Board, commonly called the AIB. Wage and salary increases were to be limited to increases of 10 percent in the first year, 8 percent in the second, and 6 percent in the third year. Businesses were allowed to increase prices only to the extent of their increases in costs. Profit statements and collective bargaining agreements were examined by the board to ensure compliance with the controls.

At first, the board was successful in its program of restraining wage and price increases. However, when the board approved wage increases above the limits, those who had agreed to increases within the regulations were outraged. As the program continued, and price increases exceeded wage increases, fewer unions were willing to go along with the controls.

Some of the problems of wage and price controls

Wage and price controls have been used on only two occasions since 1945, despite inflation since then. It is obvious, therefore, that controls are not an easy answer to inflation. What are the problems?

Lack of united support

As we have seen, union leaders and business leaders have difficulty supporting controls voluntarily. Union leaders seek higher wages for union members. Business leaders seek higher profits for their shareholders.

Large bureaucracy

To administer wage and price controls requires a large bureaucracy to keep up with the many complex transactions that occur hourly in a modern economy.

Interference with the operation of the market

As we saw in Chapter 5, prices provide information and rewards to producers. When goods are in short supply, prices rise and business is encouraged to increase production. If prices are controlled, they cannot perform this function.

Import prices

One set of prices is largely beyond the reach of the Canadian government (or its agencies, such as the AIB). The government cannot control the prices of goods that Canadians buy from other countries. About one third of our total spending is on goods and services we buy from other countries.

REVIEW

Explain each of the following in your own words with an example: inflation, Consumer Price Index, hyper-inflation, tight money policy, contractionary fiscal policy, deflation, demand-pull inflation, cost-push inflation, stagflation, velocity of circulation, the monetary rule, wage and price controls.

APPLICATIONS

1. What effect is a period of unexpected inflation likely to have on each of the following (see bottom page 302)? Explain your answer.

SUMMARY

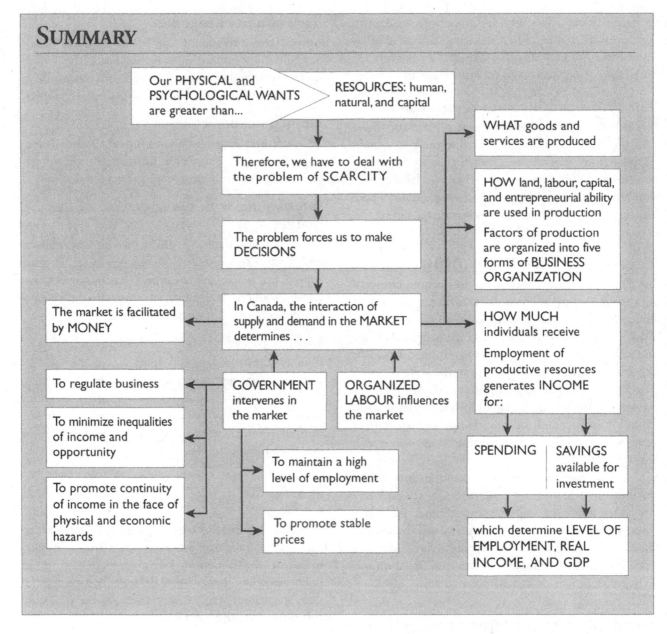

a) creditors

b) debtors

c) pensioners on a fixed income

d) a person whose major asset is a house worth $100 000 and whose major liability is a mortgage of $50 000

e) a person who works in a declining industry and does not belong to a union.

2. Suppose that creditors, pensioners, and unionized workers anticipate that there will be inflation. In each case, explain how they can protect themselves from it to some extent.

3. Indicate whether each federal government action listed below is expansionary or contractionary. Then indicate whether it is an automatic or discretionary stabilizer.
   a) The favourable tax breaks on dividend income are abolished.
   b) As the recession deepens, unemployment insurance expenditures increase.
   c) Federal and provincial taxes on gasoline are increased.
   d) As the economy slows, income tax collections diminish.
   e) As the pace of economic activity quickens, the amount from sales taxes increases.
   f) In the midst of the recession, the federal government cuts income tax.

4. For each fiscal and monetary policy listed below, decide which one would be more effective in combatting a period of widespread unemployment, and which would be more effective in combatting rising inflation. In each case, explain your answer.

   I. Fiscal policy:
   a) Increase sales taxes
   b) Decrease sales taxes
   c) Increase public works
   d) Decrease public works

   II. Monetary policy:
   a) Lower the bank rate
   b) Raise the bank rate
   c) Sell government bonds
   d) Buy government bonds

5. Suppose that during a period of full employment, stable prices, and maximum real output, government changed its fiscal policy from being mildly contractionary to being highly expansionary, and its monetary policy from being fairly tight to being very easy. Explain the effects that the change in policies would have on the following.
   a) injections into the economy
   b) leakages out of the economy
   c) level of real output
   d) level of real national income
   e) price level
   f) employment rate

6. The most famous (or infamous) example of hyperinflation occurred in Germany between 1920 and 1923. In 1921, $1 (U.S.) could be exchanged for 75 German marks. By the beginning of 1922, that dollar was worth 400 marks and, a year later, 7000 marks. During 1923, the inflation rate quickened. By July 1, the dollar was worth 160 000 marks; by August 1, 1 000 000 marks; and by November, 4 000 000 000 marks.

   The first bank note was issued in December 1922. In 1923, it was overprinted "one billion marks." The second bank note, issued in August 1923, was printed on one side only.
   a) The practice of overprinting some bank notes and of printing on only one side of other notes was common in Germany during 1923. Suggest reasons why.
   b) What would each bank note be worth in terms of the U.S. dollar in (i) August 1923, and (ii) November 1923?
   c) What might have been some effects of the change in the value of the German mark?

7. When he left office in 1993, former Prime Minister Brian Mulroney was highly unpopular. Here are some of the key economic statistics for 1983, when he assumed the office of prime minister, and for the end of 1992 — just before he left office in early 1993.

   Governments often take credit for good performance of the Canadian economy, but blame "prevailing general economic trends" for poor performance. Use the data in figure 14.9 on page 304 to assess the performance of Mulroney's Progressive Conservative government. In groups, use the statistics in the chart to answer the following questions.
   a) Where did the Mulroney government succeed?
   b) Where did it fail?

Figure 14.9 Mulroney years in numbers

	1983	1993*
Income of average two-parent family	$45 411	$46 575**
Unemployment rate	11.2%	11.3%
Inflation rate	4.4%	1.5%
Number employed (April '84 and '93)	10 839 000	12 333 000
Federal debt	$244.0 billion	$491.0 billion
Federal deficit	$38.5 billion	$35.5 billion
GDP rate of growth	6.3%	2.9% (projected)
Canadian dollar in U.S. funds	75.7¢	78.0¢

* most figures are for year-end 1992
** figures are from 1991 Survey of Consumer Finance
Sources: Bank of Canada, Statistics Canada.

8. Use table 14.1 as a guide in analysing a recent federal or provincial budget. An example is provided in the table.

CASE STUDY
Prime ministers' report card

In summer, we are familiar with the discomfort index — the combination of temperature and humidity — and in winter, the wind chill factor — the combination of temperature and wind velocity. The U.S. economist, Arthur Okun, devised a similar kind of measure for our economic "climate." He called it the "misery index." This index is a simple addition of two key economic variables: inflation and unemployment rates. See table 14.2. In the table, two figures are missing — the inflation change and the employment change in the final row "Chrétien 1993-."

To calculate the inflation change, we average the inflation rate for each year that Prime Minister Jean Chrétien is in office and we deduct from that the rate in the last year of the previous term. Let's suppose that Mr. Chrétien is in office from 1993 to 1997 and that the following are the inflation rates as measured by the

c) In general, how would you assess the economic performance of the Mulroney government?
d) What additional data would you need in order to assess the Mulroney government?

Table 14.1 Federal or provincial budget analysis

Example: Federal budget

What specific changes were made in taxing or spending policy?	What effect does the government hope the change will have?	What goals or purposes will the change achieve?	How might the change conflict with some other purpose or goal?
1. Increase the number of weeks of employment necessary to qualify for unemployment insurance.	Reduce the expenditures on unemployment insurance.	Reduce the federal government deficit.	*Full employment:* Reduced expenditures by the unemployed, therefore reduced employment *Equity:* Income of unemployed reduced.
2. Continue the freeze on public servants' salaries.			
3. Etc.			

CPI: 1994: 2 percent; 1995: 3 percent; 1996: 4 percent; 1997: 3 percent.

The average of the four numbers is

$$\frac{2 + 3 + 4 + 3}{4} = \frac{12}{4} = 3$$

The average inflation rate would then be 3 percent. (Note that we do not include the year 1993 in these calculations, since Mr. Chrétien did not become prime minister until the fall of that year.)

The CPI inflation rate in the last year of the previous administration (1992-1993) averaged 2 percent. Thus, the inflation change would be represented by a "+1" in the table.

We make a similar calculation for the unemployment rate to measure the change in unemployment during Mr. Chrétien's term in office.

To calculate the misery index, we simply add the inflation change and the unemployment change. For recent statistics on unemployment and inflation, see Bank of Canada's *Bank of Canada Review* or Statistic Canada's *Canadian Economic Observer*, available in most public libraries.

Questions

1. Calculate the inflation change and the unemployment change during Mr. Chrétien's term as prime minister and for any subsequent prime minister(s).

2. Calculate the misery index for each prime minister's period in office.

3. Rank the prime ministers according to the misery index. According to the index, which one was the best prime minister?

4. What other economic criteria might you add to give a better basis for assessing the success of a prime minister?

Table 14.2 Canadian prime ministers' report card, 1949-1993 (and beyond)

Prime minister* and term**	Inflation change (average CPI rate during the prime minister's term minus the rate in the final year of the previous term)	Unemployment change (average unemployment rate during the term minus the rate in the final year of the previous term)	Misery index	Rank
St. Laurent 1949-57	−11.4	1.2		
Diefenbaker 1958-63	−1.7	1.8		
Pearson 1964-68	1.4	−1.3		
Trudeau 1 1969-79	3.1	1.8		
Trudeau 2 1980-82	2.1	1.2		
Mulroney 1983-92	−6.2	−1.5		
Chrétien 1993-				

Source: *Financial Post*, March 5, 1993.

* Note that three prime ministers — Joe Clark, John Turner, and Kim Campbell — are not included in the list because their period in office was very brief.

** Note that the dates are those of the statistics used and not of the period in office.

AN OPINION POLL

What do you think?

Make a note of your response to the following questions without referring to your earlier replies.

1. What do you think is the most important problem facing this country today?

2. Do you think the federal government's policies for tackling the country's economic situation gives you a feeling that they are or are not handling the situation properly?

Table 14.3 Gallup Poll in percentages*

Most important problem	Jan/ 94	Sept/ 93	Nov/ 92	May/ 92	Oct/ 91	Jan/ 91	Feb/ 90	July/ 89	Mar/ 89	June/ 88	Feb/ 88	Feb/ 87	June/ 86	Dec/ 85
Economy/Inflation	17%	37	33	25	30	43	29	20	21	14	19	16	21	21
Unemployment	45%	25	22	34	23	17	18	16	18	27	28	41	44	50
Gov't. debt/deficit	21%	20	3	na	na	na	na	na	na	na	na	na	na	na
National unity	1%	1	11	11	11	8	4	2	2	1	1	1	na	na
GST/Taxes	1%	3	4	5	10	na	na	na	na	na	na	na	na	na
Gov't.	2%	4	8	10	7	8	5	8	5	6	9	10	9	8
U.S. trade relations	1%	1	1	3	3	2	7	5	6	9	9	3	na	na
Environment	—	1	3	3	2	4	14	17	16	9	4	3	na	na
Other	9%	6	12	8	11	17	22	28	29	29	26	21	22	17
DK	4%	2	4	2	2	1	2	4	3	5	5	5	4	5

By region Jan/94

	Atlantic	Quebec	Ontario	Prairies	British Columbia
Economy/Inflation	14	21	17	11	10
Unemployment	51	42	52	38	36
Gov't. debt/deficit	17	23	12	31	33
National unity	—	1	1	1	—
GST/Taxes	—	1	2	1	1
Gov't.	2	1	2	3	—
U.S. trade relations	—	—	1	—	2
Environment	1	1	—	—	1
Other	5	8	11	7	11
DK	10	2	2	8	6

Source: Gallup Canada, January 1994.
na = not available; DK = don't know
* Percentages may not add exactly to 100 due to rounding.

What does the class think?

Summarize the opinions of the other members of your class, and make a note of them. Compare the replies with those the class made earlier. Has the class's opinion changed? What may have caused the change, or the lack of it?

What do Canadians think?

A sample of over 1000 Canadians, aged eighteen years and older, were asked the first of these questions by the Canadian Institute of Public Opinion in January, 1994, and during various years in the past. A sample of the size used in these polls is accurate to within a 3.1 percentage point margin of error, nineteen in twenty times. The results are summarized in table 14.3.

a) How have the Gallup Poll results varied since December 1985?

b) Why might the results have changed?

c) What differences are there between different regions of the country? What might account for the differences?

d) In what ways do the results of the poll of your class differ from the results in the whole country?

CHAPTER 15

Economic Growth and Productivity

(1a)

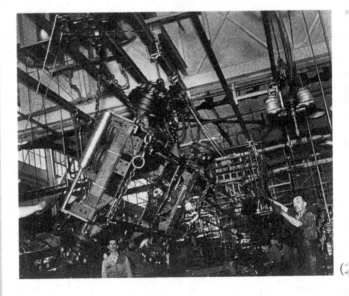

(1b)

(2)

(1a) Logs being loaded through the bow of a ship at Margaretville, Nova Scotia, about 1892.

(1b) This Seaway-size self-unloading vessel is unloading approximately 25 000 tonnes of St. Lawrence-region iron ore at a steel mill in Ontario.

(2a) A General Motors car assembly plant, around the time of the Second World War.

(2b) A modern General Motors car assembly plant.

(3a) Operators at Maritime Telegraph and Telephone Company in the 1930s.

(3b) Operator at MT & T in the 1990s.

(3a)

(3b)

(2b)

Questions

1. What changes have taken place in the shipping industry since the 1890s?

2. What changes have taken place in the manufacture of automobiles since 1945?

3. In what other industries have similar changes taken place? Give some examples.

4. What changes have taken place in the telecommunications industry since the 1930s?

309

Activity 1: Shipwrecked

After days of hurricane-force winds in the South Seas, your ship hits a coral reef and is smashed to pieces. You, the only survivor, wash ashore on a tropical island.

The island proves to be uninhabited. From your travelling experience, you know that in this part of the South Seas the cold, rainy season will soon begin. You know, too, that there is little chance that you will be rescued in the near future. Therefore, you resolve to make your life as pleasant as possible.

You decide to make an inventory of your resources. The maximum amount of time you can work each day is twelve hours; after that it gets dark. The waters around the island are teeming with fish and other edible sealife. On the island there are animals (some dangerous!) and an abundance of berries and tropical fruits. In the twelve hours you have available for work each day, you must provide yourself with everything you need, including enough food and water.

Figure 15.1 lists a number of tools useful for hunting and fishing, and the number of hours it takes to make each one. Construction time for shelter is also provided.

Figure 15.2 gives the number of hours it takes to obtain one day's food supply with these tools.

With no tools, it is necessary for you to work eleven hours to gather one day's supply of food. However, by devoting ten hours to fashioning a rod and hook (figure 15.1), you reduce the time needed to provide yourself with food for one day to eight hours (figure 15.2). Similarly, by providing yourself with a spear, which takes twenty hours to make, you can reduce the time necessary to provide yourself with food for one day to six hours.

How to play the game

Study the sample game chart (figure 15.3). It is divided into nine periods of five days each. In each period you have sixty hours available for work. For an idea of how to play the game, go over the first three periods that have been filled in.

When you first land on the island, you find that it takes you eleven hours a day just to gather enough food to feed yourself. Refer to period one in figure 15.3. Over the first five-day period, you spend fifty-five hours gathering food. With the remaining five hours, you decide to fashion a rod.

Figure 15.1 Construction time for tools and shelter

Item	Hours
Rod and hook	10
Net	25
Raft	50
Spear	20
Bow and arrow	30
Trap	25
Shelter	70

Figure 15.2 Time required to obtain one day's food supply with tools

Tools	Hours
Rod and hook	8
Net	7
Rod, hook, and net	6
Net and raft	4
Spear	6
Bow and arrow	4
Trap	8

In period two, it still takes you fifty-five hours to feed yourself. With the five remaining hours, you finish your crude rod and hook.

In period three, you have moderate success in catching fish with your rod and hook, thereby reducing the time spent on obtaining food. You spend the remaining fifteen hours on constructing a shelter.

Play the game

You might decide to use your time in a way that is different from those described in figure 15.3.

Draw a game chart in your notebook, leaving out the values that are given, and decide on your own goals.

1. Establish your goals

What is most important to you? food? shelter? protection? leisure? clothing? Make a list of your goals in your notebook.

2. Achieve your goals

How will you allocate your scarce time to achieve your goals? Complete your game chart.

3. Compare your decisions with the class

Compare how you filled in your chart with others in your class. Decide who best achieved her/his goals.

a) What were your goals?

b) What were the goals of others in your class?

c) Did your goals differ significantly from theirs? If so, why?

d) How did you allocate your resources?

e) What was the opportunity cost of the first decision you made? the second? the third?

f) Why did you have to make decisions?

Productive resources

On the tropical island you again came face-to-face with that formidable foe — scarcity. You could not spend all day on the beach and at the same time have enough food, shelter, and clothing. You had to choose and to weigh the opportunity cost of each decision you made.

In the simulation, you had a one-person economy, but as in all economies, you had to answer the three major questions: **What is to be produced? How is it to be produced? For whom is it to be produced?** In the one-person economy, the last question was easy — all production was for yourself. In doing step 1 of the game when you established your goals, you answered the question "what to produce." You likely found that the most complex part of the game was the "how" question. You had to allocate your resources in order to maximize the satisfaction that you could derive from them.

Figure 15.3 Sample game chart

Five-day periods	1	2	3	4	5	6	7	8	9
Total work hours available per period	60	60	60	60	60	60	60	60	60
Hours spent collecting, hunting, and fishing	55	55	40						
Remaining hours	5	5	15						
Hours spent on shelter	0	0	15						
Hours spent on protection	0	0	0						
Hours spent on tool making	5	5	0						
Type of tool	rod	hook							
Hours spent on clothing	0	0	0						
Hours spent on leisure	0	0	0						

In making your decisions about what you would produce and how you would produce it, you relied heavily on your knowledge of what natural resources were available. The island and sea were rich in fish, game, and fruit. Another resource you had was a human resource: your own labour. You spent most of your time, at least at first, working for simple survival. But you applied your intelligence. You found that you could reduce your expenditure of time and energy by adding to the process another resource: handmade tools. By using your resources to make tools that produced food more efficiently, you were able to diminish the impact of scarcity. The key to increased efficiency was your decision to spend some of your time making tools. Tools, which are a means to an end in production, are capital resources.

ECONOMIC GROWTH IN CANADA

Compared with the early settlers in Canada, we enjoy more varied clothing, food, and entertainment; better housing; and better and more varied opportunities for travel, recreation, and education. Or, to put it another way, our **standard of living** is higher. We enjoy more goods and services than the early settlers. We also enjoy more goods and services than many people in the world, especially those in Asia, Africa, and South America. What brought us to this very favoured position? Our economic growth.

In the two previous chapters, two goals of the Canadian economy were examined: full employment and price stability. We saw how Canada had been affected by the problems of unemployment and inflation and the various ways of dealing with these two problems. Here, another macro-economic goal identified in Chapter 2 will be examined: economic growth. In examining unemployment and inflation, our view was essentially short-term. With economic growth, we look at the performance of the economy over a period of years.

What is economic growth?

Economic growth is the increase over a period of time — usually a year — in a country's (or a region's) output of goods and services. Economic growth is usually measured by the annual rate of increase in the real Gross Domestic Product (GDP) per person.

GDP measures the output of all final goods produced during a period of time, usually a year. Since GDP is expressed in money terms, it is subject to inflation. Thus, if we are trying to measure how much the economy has grown over a period of time, we have to take into account changes in the general level of prices. Otherwise, we cannot know to what extent there has been a change in the output of goods and services.

Suppose we want to find out by how much the economy grew between 1973 and 1993. From table 15.1 we learn that in 1973 the GDP at market prices or in current dollars was $127 372 million. In current dollars, by 1993, GDP had increased to $710 723 million — an increase of more than five times. However, a dollar in 1973 would buy much more than a dollar in 1993. These two amounts cannot be compared directly. By adjusting the GDP of 1973 and of 1993 with an index of prices so that both amounts are expressed in terms of the same dollar (that of 1986), we can compare them directly. In terms of the 1986 dollar, the 1973 GDP equalled $326 848 million, and the 1993 GDP equalled $573 433 million. In **real terms** — that is, in terms of the total amount of goods and services produced — the GDP for 1993 was about three-quarters more than that of 1973. The comparison in real terms is a more appropriate indication of growth than that in money terms.

We should note that the growth rate is expressed as real GDP growth *per person*. As the population grows, the labour force increases. We can expect that more workers will produce more goods. But it doesn't necessarily follow that more goods will be available for each person. Therefore, economic growth is measured

Table 15.1 GDP and population, 1973-1993

Year	Population (in thousands)	GDP in current dollars (millions)	GDP in 1986 dollars (millions)	GDP per person in 1986 dollars (millions)
1973	22 043	127 372	326 848	14 828
1974	22 364	152 111	341 235	15 258
1975	22 697	171 540	350 113	15 426
1976	22 993	197 924	371 688	16 165
1977	23 273	217 879	385 122	16 548
1978	23 517	241 604	402 737	17 125
1979	23 747.3	276 096	418 328	17 616
1980	24 043	309 891	424 537	17 657
1981	24 342	355 994	440 127	18 081
1982	24 583.1	374 442	425 970	17 327
1983	24 787.2	405 717	439 448	17 729
1984	24 978.2	444 735	467 167	18 703
1985	25 165.4	477 988	489 437	19 449
1986	25 353	505 666	505 666	19 945
1987	25 617.3	551 597	526 730	20 562
1988	25 909.2	605 906	552 958	21 342
1989	26 240.3	650 748	566 486	21 589
1990	26 603	670 952	565 576	21 260
1991	26 442	675 928	556 029	20 600
1992	27 436	688 541	560 048	20 429
1993	27 753	710 723	573 433	20 675

Sources: Statistics Canada, *Canadian Economic Observer, Historical Statistical Supplement* 1990-91, and April 1994, and *Bank of Canada Review,* Spring 1994.

While GDP in current dollars grew more than five times between 1973 and 1993 in current dollars, in constant (1986) dollars it grew by only about three-quarters. Over the same time period, GDP per person grew by about 40 percent.

by **GDP per person.** As we can see from table 15.1, Canada's population grew between 1973 and 1993 from about 22 million to about 27 3/4 million. In considering our economic growth between these dates, we must take into account this increase in population. Thus, GDP per person between the two dates was approximately 40 percent.

Standard of living

GDP per person cannot be taken as a precise measure of the standard of living. It has two major weaknesses. There are things included in the GDP per person that

do not lead to an improvement in the standard of living and there are things excluded that do.

If a crime wave occurs, we will spend more money on police, lawyers, and jails. Our GDP per capita will increase. But we would not say that our standard of living had increased. There are, then, some items included in GDP per person that do not indicate a better standard of living.

Other items are excluded from our calculations of GDP per person that do contribute to our standard of living. These items include leisure, and the "missing" GDP.

Leisure. One of the most striking exclusions from GDP per person — but one that is an indicator of our standard of living — is the amount of leisure time we have available. As the economy grows, we can choose to enjoy more goods and services, more leisure, or more of both. Since 1926, the GDP per person has grown significantly. Since 1926, the average work week in Canada has declined by 35 percent. The choice of taking part of the benefits of growth in greater leisure is not shown in our GDP per person.

Goods and services that are omitted from the GDP because they are not sold.   Examples include the services of the homemaker and the amateur housepainter, carpenter, and gardener. Clearly, all these services are important in our society and they do contribute significantly to our well-being, but they are not included in estimates of GDP per person.

Side effects.   While the production of automobiles and cigarettes is included in our calculation of growth, the side effects of these products are not. The pollution, lung cancer, and heart attacks caused by these goods are not counted in our calculation of growth. Indeed, as pollution and lung cancer bring about more demands on medical services, they have the opposite effect — they act to raise the GDP per person.

Underground economy.   This includes the activities of workers who perform services but who do not report their income. For example, suppose I hire someone to build a garden shed for me and I pay her in cash rather than by credit card or by cheque. If she does not report my payment as income, then she avoids — illegally — paying tax on this part of her income. Unreported incomes do not figure in Statistics Canada's estimates of GDP per person. Estimates of the size of the unreported income range from 6 to 17 percent of GDP; in other words, from about $42 billion to $114 billion.

Kinds of goods produced.   GDP measures only the money value of output; it does not discriminate between those goods that may be harmful, e.g., alcohol, and those that may be beneficial, e.g., milk. Alcohol and milk both selling at $20 are given equal treatment in GDP.

Distribution of income.   GDP per capita tells us nothing about how it is distributed in the population. It contributes less to a society's well-being to have most of the GDP in the hands of a privileged few than to have it distributed equitably in the society.

In spite of its weaknesses, GDP per person does provide us with an important measure of the performance of our economy. Long-term increases in real GDP per person provide us with an important indication of the economic progress of our economy — especially if we temper our use of GDP with a knowledge of its limitations.

Economic growth and the production possibilities curve

Economic growth can be illustrated by a production possibilities curve. See figure 15.4. Let's assume we are producing wheat or tractors and that our present production possibilities curve is at PP.

Economic growth is shown by an outward shift of the entire production possibilities curve from PP to P_1P_1. If population has not increased, more goods are produced per person. If formerly we produced at point A, we can now have the same amount of tractors and more wheat as at point B, the same amount of wheat and more tractors as at C, or more of both products as at D. In sum, we have economic growth.

Economic growth since 1900

Since 1900, real GDP per person has increased more than five-fold. However, this growth has not been at a uniform rate throughout the period. During the Depression of the early 1930s, the output of the economy declined. In the 1950s and 1960s, the economy grew at a rapid rate, averaging between 4 and 5 percent. In the last half of the 1970s, the rate slowed dramatically to a mere 0.5 percent. Following the recession of 1981-1982, the economy again grew vigorously. See table 15.1 on page 313.

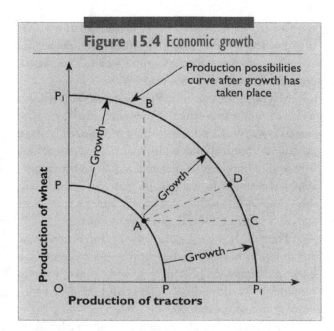

Figure 15.4 Economic growth

Production possibilities curve after growth has taken place

Causes of economic growth

To bring about growth in the economy, we have to raise productivity. **Productivity** is the output per person employed. With increases in productivity, the economy will grow, and the standard of living will increase.

Four major factors bring about increases in productivity:

1. Specialization;
2. Technological progress;
3. Increase in the amount and quality of education;
4. Increase in the amount of capital available.

1. Specialization

In the early days in Canada, pioneers supplied most of their own needs. Early settlers would raise their own sheep, spin their own wool into yarn, and weave it into blankets and clothing. They would grow their own wheat, grind it into flour, and bake the flour into bread. The pioneer was basically self-sufficient.

Today, most Canadians are almost totally dependent on others for their food, clothing, and shelter. We rely on other people to supply our needs. And most of these other people have specialized in the production of a good or a service. With specialization, productivity increases.

A farmer today might concentrate on the production of one crop only instead of a wide range of crops. Certain geographical areas of Canada specialize in the production of particular crops. The Prairies specialize in wheat; the Niagara Peninsula in grapes; the Annapolis Valley in fruit; southern Quebec and eastern Ontario in dairy farming; and Prince Edward Island in potatoes.

Division of labour

In addition to geographical specialization, there is specialization or division of labour within industries. The task of producing a suit of clothing is most likely divided among many people. One person may cut the cloth, another may sew the parts together, another may add the button holes and buttons, and yet another may press it. In the automobile industry, division of labour has developed to a striking degree. One individual may perform the same minute task many times a day, day in, day out. Literally hundreds of people are involved in the production of one automobile. The same technique is used in the production of home appliances, electronic equipment, and even in the construction of ships and homes.

The division of labour has several advantages.

Time-saving

Jobs on an assembly line are quickly and easily learned. Extensive training is not necessary and a new worker can be productive almost immediately. A worker doing a repetitive task becomes very skilled at performing that task, and thus can speed up production. Similarly, since the worker does only one job at a time, there is no need for that worker to leave that task to go to another.

Rising standard of living

Division of labour has increased productivity and has therefore made possible an increase in real incomes. It is clear, however, that there are drawbacks to the division of labour.

Loss of pride in craftsmanship

If work consists solely of tightening a pair of nuts with a wrench for eight hours a day, there is no sense of pride or achievement in the work. The work may just be boring.

Growing dependency

With increasing job specialization, we become more dependent on others. Anything that disrupts others is liable to have an impact on us. Frosts, floods, and work stoppages in other parts of the country are likely to affect us more now than they would have a century ago.

2. Technological progress

We have seen that specialization (and division of labour) can lead to increased productivity. Here, the contribution that technological change can bring to economic growth will be examined.

Technology is the body of knowledge that can be applied to the production of goods and services. Technological progress can take several forms: the development of better ways of organizing production; the discovery of new types of products; and the development of new types of machinery.

i) Better ways of organizing production

Three ways of organizing production have increased and continue to increase productivity: mass production, automation, and work study.

Mass production

The mass production of automobiles began in 1909 when Henry Ford produced 10 000 Model T Fords. Before then, cars had been completely assembled in one place. Ford used the idea of a moving assembly line to which parts were added to the Model-T frame as it moved along the line. Today's assembly lines are much more complex but the basic principle is still the same. Assembly line techniques have been used in many industries — for the production of trucks, snowmobiles, and even bread.

The use of assembly line techniques of production can lead to increases in productivity and thus to economic growth.

Automation

Automation is the automatic and self-regulatory control by machines of the whole, or a part of a process of production. Automation is the logical extension of assembly line production. With automation, the task of the worker is taken over by a machine or robot. The use of robots (mechanical or computerized devices designed to do the work of human beings) increased considerably in the 1980s and 1990s.

Machines are constantly being developed to do the work formerly performed by workers. In fully automated systems, the role performed by humans is that of centralized control and maintenance of the machines involved in the production process. Generally, automation has resulted in marked increases in productivity. This increased productivity has meant a rise in the standard of living for industrialized countries.

There is, however, a cost involved in automation. Automation has led to the elimination of many jobs and marketable skills. Automation has meant unemployment for individual workers and the fear of unemployment for others.

Automation has also meant the end to a lot of undesirable jobs that are dirty, dangerous, back-breaking, or boring. Those employees replaced by robots can be trained for more skilled and interesting work.

The trend to automation is likely to develop more rapidly as computer technology develops. For instance, by using silicon chip computer parts for robots' brains, robots can be made to walk and talk. Some futurists are predicting a "silicon chip revolution" that will change our definition of work and transform our living patterns.

Work study

Through the scientific study of the way in which workers complete certain jobs, improved ways of accomplishing the tasks can be developed.

ii) Development of new machinery

Examples of machines that have increased productivity include the steam and electric engines used to power factories and trains; the telephone, which made communication easier and quicker; nuclear power, which harnessed the power of the atom to produce electricity; and the computer, which can do the work of thousands of clerks and mathematicians. Obviously, this list could be almost endless.

iii) New types of products

Many of the products we use today that add to our standard of living have replaced other goods that were less able to meet our needs. Nylon socks have replaced woollen stockings. Compact discs have replaced long-playing records. Ballpoint pens have replaced fountain pens, and electronic calculators have replaced slide rules. Again, we could go on and list many more items.

3. Increase in the quality of education

The training, skills, and education of workers are directly related to their productivity. Those workers with better education, greater skills, and more experience are able to produce more than other workers.

4. Amount of capital available

The more capital available — machines, railways, factories, and so on — for any given number of workers, the more the output per worker is likely to be. The amount of capital available can be increased by the action of business and government.

The amount of capital that we will have in the future is largely determined by the decisions we make now. Our choices are illustrated in two graphs in figure 15.5. If we choose A, we have high consumption with little capital investment. By the year 2001 the production possibilities curve has only grown slowly, to P_1P_1. If we choose B, we restrain our consumption and devote a lot of our resources to capital investment. The result is that by 2001 the production possibilities curve has expanded to P_2P_2.

CASE STUDY
Robo-shop

Plant 41 is an aircraft engine factory located half an hour's drive from Halifax, Nova Scotia. As you read the following extract, consider how it differs from a conventional machine shop and what are the advantages and disadvantages of this kind of establishment.

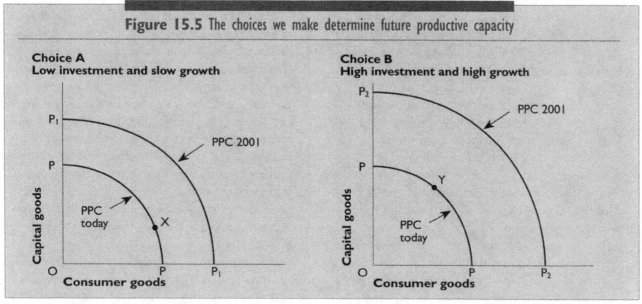

Figure 15.5 The choices we make determine future productive capacity

Choice A
Low investment and slow growth

Choice B
High investment and high growth

Most of production is directed towards the production of consumer goods (point X). There is little investment. Growth is slow.

With most production directed to the production of capital goods, at point Y, investment is high. Growth is rapid. Productive capacity by 2001 is much greater than with choice A.

Though far from any mountain, Plant 41 represents the pinnacle of social and technological organization for United Technologies Corp. of Hartford, Connecticut. UTC is a multinational aerospace, construction and automotive systems giant, the 16th-biggest industrial company in the United States, with $22 billion (U.S.) in revenues in 1992. It employs about 173,000 people worldwide at subsidiaries including Pratt & Whitney, Sikorsky helicopters, Otis elevators and Carrier air conditioning. The UTC colossus has designed Plant 41, which epitomizes flexible manufacturing by blending computer-aided design and manufacturing with an innovative employee structure, as the model for all of its plants worldwide. Just 320 highly skilled men and women working in carefully designed teams run the 25,000-square-metre plant around the clock every day of the year. Plant 41 performs in about four weeks tasks that would take 20 weeks at an older Pratt & Whitney plant. UTC is betting the model facility will help Pratt & Whitney increase productivity, retain its lead in the world market for small aircraft engines, and show the way for other UTC subsidiaries to remain globally competitive. UTC has abandoned traditional assembly-line production in favour of worker teams that assemble products from start to finish. The teams give workers more responsibility, resulting in fewer mistakes and reduced downtime.

"Plant 41 is a very good indication of where manufacturing is going in the future," says Jan Grude, assistant dean of the faculty of management at Dalhousie University. "The speed of change is so rapid now that production of standard items is rare. There is much more customization to meet market niches, there are shorter production runs, plus the absolute need for quality and flexibility."

Grude points out that Plant 41 has effectively combined "socio-tech" theories developed in Norway in 1963 with Japanese concepts of continuous improvement and the creativity of a North American workforce — a combination that's only now working its way into Canada's economy. The men and women who run Plant 41 are highly skilled, socially well-rounded team players who, with little supervision and much help from machines, can outperform the much larger plants that use time clocks and traditional assembly-line methods. There are also far fewer of them than a traditional plant would employ, which is why Plant 41 also exemplifies the term "jobless recovery" from recession — improvements in productivity and quality without increases in employment.

Consultants from Japan have been hired to inculcate in Plant 41 employees the concept of *kaizen*, the Japanese term for continuous improvement. Employees are asked to develop better ways of doing things, from tool-storage boxes to plant layout, and their suggestions are entered into a computer programmed to monitor the time it takes to respond to each idea.

Plant 41's shop floor is divided into two main areas. In the half where robots handle the largest engine parts, like casings, the plant computer supervises most operations with little human intervention. The other half of the plant, where smaller parts are machined, is more balanced between robots and people, yet even there the humans interspersed between the huge machines seem almost incidental. The job for most of these workers is to load engine parts from numbered carts onto computerized grinders, push a button and ensure that the machining process—which ranges from minutes to hours, depending on the part—proceeds smoothly.

Just as important as Plant 41's robots are the facility's team-based system and a flat management structure, in which just eight managers supervise a 320-member workforce. Plant 41's employees are highly skilled, young (the average age is 32), psychologically screened and hired for their ability to work well with other people on teams that are so autonomous that the members have a say in who Pratt & Whitney will hire to work with them.

Pratt & Whitney doesn't say so outright, but it was easier to set up a non-union shop in Halifax than in central Canada. Not surprisingly, the Canadian Auto Workers is not pleased with the plant's non-unionized status and is working to organize Plant 41. The CAW insists that the Halifax plant is so new that worker discontent has not had much time to grow, and says that several of Plant 41's employees have expressed interest in helping a union drive.

Other employees, such as Darell Bunn, 37, plan to work at Plant 41 until retirement. "This is the cleanest plant I've seen and the management system is the easiest to work with," says Bunn. Possibly because Plant 41 represents the cutting edge in robotic technology, the flesh and blood personnel at the facility seem determined to set new, higher standards in labour relations. Says Bunn, "There's a lot of other places where the plant managers wouldn't know your name."

Source: Adapted from an article by Deborah Jones in *Report on Business Magazine*, March 1994.

Questions

1. Why is this plant able to outproduce more conventional plants?

2. What are some of the advantages and disadvantages of this kind of plant to Pratt & Whitney, its customers, and its employees? Explain why in each case.

This Pratt & Whitney worker is a manufacturing specialist whose job is to operate a milling machine. She is standing beside the gearbox housing for an airplane engine.

THE STAPLES THESIS

In your studies of Canadian history, you may have noticed how important certain primary products were at different times. In the sixteenth century, European fishermen were attracted to our waters by the fertile seas off Atlantic Canada. Later, in the seventeenth and eighteenth centuries, many French and British traded goods for fashionable beaver pelts. In the nineteenth century, central and eastern Canadian timber and wheat were important. In the twentieth century, prairie wheat, pulp and paper, minerals, oil, and natural gas became leading Canadian exports.

The development of each of these primary products (or staples) had ripple effects throughout the economy. For example, the development of prairie wheat as a principal Canadian export between 1896 and 1914 is associated with the construction of railways, a boom in grain elevator construction, an increase in the GDP by 150 percent, and a 50 percent increase in the population.

According to the staples thesis, as formulated by economic historian Harold Innis, economic growth in Canada has been connected with the development of staples or primary products. Staples have not only been important as exports, but they have also given rise to developments in many other parts of the economy. Thus, the export of staples has been a major force in the development of Canadian economic growth.

Benefits and costs of growth

The benefits of our economic growth are easy to see, if we examine the period from 1945 to the present. This period has been one of substantial economic growth, the benefits of which have been widely shared by Canadians in higher standards of living. During this time, Canadian governments have introduced social security schemes such as family allowances, unemployment insurance, health insurance, and contributory old age pensions. Canadians were given greater access to secondary and post-secondary education. Economic growth made these things possible. We are now more critical of deprivation, poverty, and pollution than we could have afforded to be in the early 1940s.

There are costs associated with economic growth. In part, growth depends on technological advances; technological change disrupts the lives of individual workers. As a consequence, they may be forced to leave their jobs, to relocate, or to retrain. Also, without proper anti-pollution and conservation measures, increased growth will be accompanied by more pollution, waste, and resource depletion.

Growth has proceeded at an uneven rate across the country. In central Canada and especially in Ontario, the rate of growth has been high. However, even in rapidly growing and relatively affluent British Columbia, certain regions (such as the North) have had lower growth rates and higher unemployment rates compared to the provincial average. In other parts of Canada, and especially in Atlantic Canada, economic growth has lagged behind the Canadian average, with consequent lower incomes and higher rates of unemployment. The wide inequalities that exist have also resulted in strains on our political system.

ECONOMIC DEVELOPMENT IN OTHER COUNTRIES

As mentioned earlier, Canada has one of the highest standards of living in the world. How, though, does it compare with living standards in other countries? The World Bank divides countries in the world into three main categories, according to their Gross National Product (GNP) per person. The **low income economies** are those with a GNP per person less than $635 U.S. in 1991. **Middle income economies** are those with a GNP per person of more than $635 but less than $7911 in 1991. **High income economies** are those with a GNP per person of $7911 or more in 1991. Let's examine each one of the three groupings in turn.

1. Low income economies

Countries in this classification had a combined population of about 3.1 billion people — about 60 percent of the world's population in 1991. Included in this category are the world's two most populous nations: China and India. Low income economies are located mainly in Africa south of the Saharan desert, and in southern Asia. Four nations in the Americas — Haiti, Guayana, Honduras, and Nicaragua — are also in this category.

Low income economies have a number of other characteristics in common. Population growth rates are high — total population is expected to grow by over 2 billion to exceed 5 billion by the year 2025. Growth rates in GNP per person between 1980–1991, in general, were low — many countries had negative rates of growth. The exceptions were China, with nearly 8 percent, and India, with 3.2 percent. Life expectancy at birth was low; again, China was a notable exception at 69 years. Literacy rates were low and the ratio of physicians to population very high, compared to high income economies.

2. Middle income economies

In this category are two different groups. One group, in Eastern Europe, includes many of the members of the former Communist bloc, such as Hungary and Poland. Most of the members of this group are moving towards a mixed market economy and away from a mixed command economy. These countries have relatively low rates of population increase, high literacy rates, and high life expectancies, compared to low income economies.

The second group comprises some developing countries in Latin America and in Africa north of the Sahara. These countries have a significant GNP per person, but have high rates of population growth, high inflation rates, lower literacy rates, and lower life expectancy rates compared to other middle income countries. Included in this group are countries such as Ecuador and Jamaica. Also included are countries such as Brazil, Korea, and Malaysia — each of which is in the process of developing an industrialized economy.

3. High income economies

This group includes the market economies of Canada, the United States, Western Europe, Japan, Hong Kong, Singapore, and Australia. These countries have high GDP per person (over $21 000 in 1991), life expectancy at birth averaging 77 years, and high literacy rates.

REVIEW

Explain each term in your own words with an example: economic growth, productivity, automation, low income economies, middle income economies, high income economies.

APPLICATIONS

1. Suppose that our GDP in money terms has risen by $20 billion this year compared to last year. Has there been growth? What further information do you need before you can determine whether there has been growth?

2. Is this Jo's job the most boring?

The gleaming piles of three-foot strips of tin are always there beside Jo Laing's punchpress. Every fifteen seconds she picks one up; puts it beneath the press; steps on a pedal; watches the press descend and — presto! — there's another bucket bottom.

Then she picks up another strip of tin; puts it beneath the press; steps on a pedal. . . . .

Jo Laing does that maybe 1300 times a day at Vulcan Industrial Packaging, in Rexdale. Somewhere along the line the bottom she made becomes part of a completed pail, but Jo can't see them from where she sits.

What she knows is that she takes a strip of tin; puts it beneath the press; steps on a pedal. . . .

Boring? You bet. Ontario Federation of Labour officials say working a punchpress is about the most numbing, unstimulating, repetitive, just plain boring job you can find.

And like thousands of other assembly line workers, she's stuck in a boring job that offers little reward but the paycheque.

"You need the money and you just continue to work," says Jo, who has done nothing but factory work since leaving school at sixteen.

Source: Joan Barfoot, *Sunday Sun.*

a) What do the terms "division of labour" and "mass production" mean?

b) What are the advantages and the disadvantages of division of labour?

c) Do the advantages outweigh the disadvantages? Explain.

3. Identify some of the possible benefits of a 5 percent increase in real terms in our GDP next year. Identify some of the effects if Canada's GDP declined by 5 percent in real terms next year.

SUMMARY

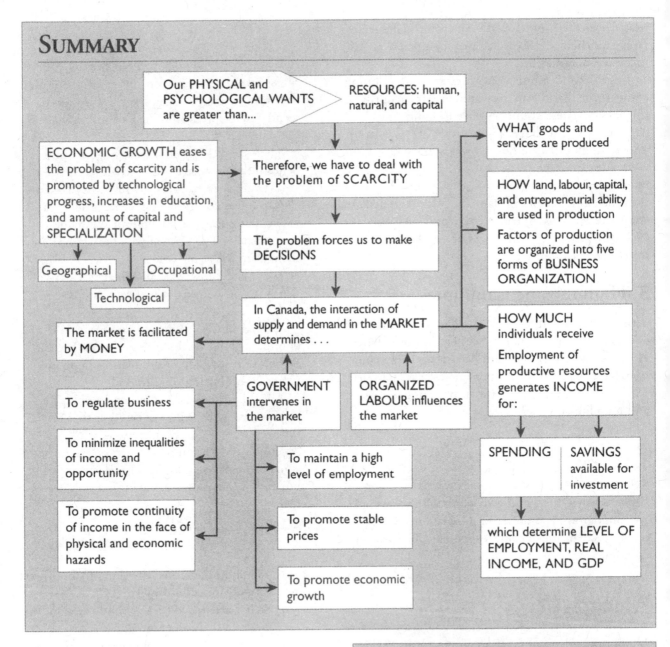

Our PHYSICAL and PSYCHOLOGICAL WANTS are greater than...

RESOURCES: human, natural, and capital

ECONOMIC GROWTH eases the problem of scarcity and is promoted by technological progress, increases in education, and amount of capital and SPECIALIZATION

Geographical

Occupational

Technological

Therefore, we have to deal with the problem of SCARCITY

The problem forces us to make DECISIONS

In Canada, the interaction of supply and demand in the MARKET determines . . .

The market is facilitated by MONEY

GOVERNMENT intervenes in the market

ORGANIZED LABOUR influences the market

To regulate business

To minimize inequalities of income and opportunity

To promote continuity of income in the face of physical and economic hazards

To maintain a high level of employment

To promote stable prices

To promote economic growth

WHAT goods and services are produced

HOW land, labour, capital, and entrepreneurial ability are used in production

Factors of production are organized into five forms of BUSINESS ORGANIZATION

HOW MUCH individuals receive

Employment of productive resources generates INCOME for:

SPENDING | SAVINGS available for investment

which determine LEVEL OF EMPLOYMENT, REAL INCOME, AND GDP

CASE STUDY
Ecuador

As you read the following case study, identify the economic and environmental problems that Ecuador faces.

Ecuador provides an instructive example of the interrelationship of economic, social, resource, and environmental problems in a Latin American country. In Ecuador, despite past attempts at agrarian reform, 1.2 percent of the landholders control 66 percent of the arable land, and 90 percent of farmers own fewer than 10 hectares each, often on steep slopes that scarcely seem arable. Soil erosion is severe, partly as a result of farming on steep slopes. Estimates of average soil loss run as high as two hundred tonnes of soil per hectare per year. The small farmers, whose lots are usually the areas with the steepest slopes, feel the effects of land degradation first.

Farms have a tendency to get smaller with divisions among each succeeding generation, and the population in Ecuador is growing at a rate of over 2.6 percent annually. This growth will be hard to slow in the near future, since, in 1990, 40 percent of the population was under the age of 14, and the entire population is expected to double by the year 2025.

For many small landowners, the crops they can grow do not support their families. As a temporary solution, the men migrate to cities or provide seasonal labor to harvest the crops of large landowners. Thus, over 50 percent of family farm work is done by women.

Migrating to the Amazon

Another common solution is for the whole family to migrate to the Amazon region, where new roads are opening up virgin tropical forests. Estimates based on the extent of roads and studies of the forestry practices lead experts to conclude that at least 100 000 hectares — and perhaps as many as 340 000 hectares — of Ecuador's forests are cut down each year. Thus, Ecuador is losing its forests at the rate of perhaps 2.4 percent per year — the second highest rate in South America.

The migrant colonists clear land wherever roads penetrate the forest, usually in the wake of oil companies exploring new sites to drill. In 1989, 32 oil companies were drilling in an area of 3.5 million hectares, 80 percent of which is in the Amazon region. The Ecuadoran government itself estimated that these companies observed only half of the relevant environmental regulations; oil slicks have oozed out of leaky pipes to float down the rivers.

Gold mining a national park

Oil is not the only business lure in the forests, but it is the one that is officially sanctioned. Ecuador has not entirely escaped from the attentions of drug traffickers, who dominate parts of all its neigboring countries, but cocaine is not a major source of income for the country — yet. The effect of the drug trade is similar to another phenomenon that draws desperate people into the wilderness to seek a fast route out of poverty: gold. In southeastern Ecuador, a gold rush has begun to devour Podocarpus National Park, an area containing cloud forests rich in endangered species. Approximately 500 miners are currently panning for gold there while more than 90 percent of the park has been sold under concessionary rights to national and international mining companies. The mountain streams that flow from the park and provide water for nearby towns are now threatened with mercury contamination owing to on-site gold processing. In northern Ecuador, the ecosystems of Sangay National Park and Cayambe-Coca Reserves face similar destruction due to gold mining activity.

Mining in the Podocarpus Park is not an isolated example of the weak environmental protection offered by Ecuador's park system. The borders of the Cuyabeno Wildlife Reserve in the Amazon, home of the Cofan and Siona Indians, have been changed to accommodate African palm oil plantations and petroleum companies, both of which continue to challenge the borders of this and other parks.

Ecuador's foreign debt is more than $11 billion. Oil used to provide about 50 percent of Ecuador's export earnings, but when the debt crisis hit simultaneously with the drop in oil prices, Ecuador turned to other natural resources. Patterns of agriculture changed over the 12-year period ending in 1986, with the land dedicated to basic foods — corn, rice, beans, and potatoes — dropping by 25.7 percent. The planting of soybeans, African palm for oil, sugar cane, and feed corn expanded by 171 percent in the same period. Ecuador's cattle pastures expanded by 31 percent nationwide between 1977 and 1983, most cleared from forests in the Amazon region. Despite these efforts, however, agricultural exports for Ecuador as a whole, measured in dollars, have not grown appreciably over the past decade.

The soils and the forests are not the only resources that are under pressure to produce exports. The shrimp business grew until exports reached $360 million, enough to pay one third of the service costs of the nation's debt. To make way for the shrimp-growing pools, however, 100 000 hectares of mangroves were cleared.

Urban services

Ecuador is finding it difficult to provide sanitation and services for its residents at a time of austerity imposed by the economic crisis. More than half of all Ecuadorians — 52 percent — live in urban areas. Guayaquil and Quito are both growing at an annual rate of 4.5 percent. The government estimated the housing shortage at 840,000 homes in 1985, and found that 400,000 existing homes lacked the basics of plumbing and water, or were considered uninhabitable. Guayaquil, Ecuador's second-largest city, with a population of 1.2 million, is located on the estuary of two rivers that have been fouled by untreated sewage, garbage, and industrial wastes. Air pollution, like water pollution, is not monitored carefully in Ecuador, although the smog is clearly visible in Guayaquil and Quito.

One indication of the health threat from pollution is the amount of lead allowed in the gasoline used by Ecuador's motor vehicles; the level is more than 20 times that permitted by the U.S. Environmental Protection Agency.

Ecuador is thus facing a conjunction of environmental and economic crises — and yet is better off than many other countries of the region. Ecuador's per capita gross domestic product fell only 1 percent in total from 1981 to 1989. This is much better than in Mexico (-9 percent) or Argentina (-23 percent). Ecuador's inflation rate fell to 59 percent in 1989, far below that of Brazil, Peru, Argentina, or Nicaragua.

Trying to rationalize the use of natural resources under these economic conditions requires a strong political commitment on the part of Latin Americans. In the 1970s, environmental problems were not even discussed. Today there are environmental agencies within the governments, a dozen organizations outside advocating better protection of resources, and hundreds of articles in the press on these issues. Even the constitutions, like those recently written in Brazil and Chile, give citizens the right to a healthy environment.

Signs of hope

Today in Ecuador there are instances of peasant cooperatives reforesting hillsides, ecology being taught in grade schools, and indigenous people's organizations drawing up their own forest management plans. While these initiatives are still on a small scale, they point toward the solutions. As Ecuadoran environmentalists themselves put it:

"The fundamental prerequisite for any action is to recognize the problems ... to identify and analyze their roots, and above all, to understand that these are not simply technical problems — on the contrary, they are strongly woven into our idiosyncrasies, our behavior, and the way that we conceive our rights."

Source: *World Resources 1990-91* (Oxford University Press).

Questions

1. Into which one of the World Bank's categories does Ecuador fit? Explain.

2. What obstacles are there to economic development? Explain why in each case.

3. What environmental problems does the country face?

4. What social problems does the country face?

CASE STUDY
Malaysia

As you read the following case study, consider the progress Malaysia has made in the last twenty years and the factors that have promoted this development.

Over the past few decades Malaysia has made outstanding progress in economic growth and in raising standards of health and education while reducing poverty. Economic growth has averaged 6 to 7 percent annually over the past two decades. Per capita production has far outstripped the developing country average.

The Malaysian government, a constitutional monarchy, has encouraged private industry to provide economic growth while devoting a relatively high share of public resources to human services such as health, education, and reduction of poverty. Of the three Asian rapidly industrializing countries (RICs) — Indonesia, Thailand, and Malaysia — Malaysia has the smallest percentage of population below the poverty line (26 percent). It also has the highest gross national product (GNP) per capita ($2,130) and spends the largest percentage of its GNP on human services. These expenditures are having an effect: life expectancy, for example, has increased from 63 to nearly 71 years since the early 1970s. Virtually all Malaysian children attend primary school and more than half also attend secondary school. These are remarkable achievements for a country formed in the early 1960s amidst a civil war and severe racial tensions.

Once dependent on commodities such as palm oil, rubber, timber, and oil for export earnings, Malaysia's economy now increasingly relies on manufacturing. The electronics industry has led the way; Malaysia is now the world's biggest exporter of semiconductor devices.

The government officially encourages population growth, yet growth rates have been relatively modest and birth rates have been falling. Some 92 percent of the urban population and 68 percent of those in rural areas have access to clean water supplies.

Malaysia is well endowed with natural resources, from tropical forests to offshore oil fields. More than half of Malaysia's merchandise exports are still primary products such as timber and oil. Both the government and citizens' groups are beginning to define sustainable development plans. The government's forest management system on the Malay Peninsula, for instance, is considered one of the few examples of sustainable forestry in the world. Nevertheless, in outlying regions such as Sabah and Sarawak, where local officials control large concessions, forests are being rapidly cut. In addition to damaging natural resources, deforestation threatens the livelihood of native peoples.

Source: *World Resources 1992–93* (Oxford University Press).

Questions

1. What progress has Malaysia made in the last two decades in economic growth, health, and education?

2. What factors have promoted progress in these three areas?

ISSUE 1
Investment in low income economies

A year ago your broker recommended a mutual fund for your retirement savings plan that invests in the economies of Latin American countries. You bought the fund and you're very happy with its performance. In the past year its return has been more than double the market average.

You meet your broker for lunch to celebrate and he's brought along the mutual fund's annual report to show you. You notice the best performing company is one that was recently in the news.

The company owned a factory that burned down, killing dozens of people. There were no fire alarms or fire escapes, the building was poorly ventilated and many of those killed were children. They were legally employed, working 12 hour days, but under conditions that are unacceptable by Canadian standards.

You tell your broker you want to sell, but he says that's a foolish knee-jerk reaction.

"The best way to improve things for kids in those countries is to invest in funds like this," he says.

"Your investment creates jobs, jobs create wealth and gradually conditions improve for everybody. You're helping their economy, them and yourself at the same time. Everyone wins."

What he says seems to make sense, but you're still not sure.

Would you:

a) sell the fund?
b) keep the fund?
c) switch to another non-Latin American fund?
d) choose another option?

Source: *Toronto Star.*

Question

In groups, examine each of the options and the reasons for and against each one. Try to reach a consensus on one option.

ISSUE 2
Subsidizing anti-pollution measures

(Note: This issue is fictional but is based on actual events.)

Seven days a week, 365 days a year, 50 million litres of a black liquid containing at least 40 chemicals flow into the province's major river system from a pulp and paper plant located on the river's bank near the town of Bear's Paw. These 40 pollutants are causing a dilemma for the provincial government. It has to decide whether it will enforce an order passed by the previous administration ordering the company — the Pulp and Paper Company of Canada — to install expensive pollution-control equipment. Company officials say they can't afford the devices. Town officials and residents and union members are afraid that rather than comply with the order, Pulp and Paper will simply close the mill and lay off its 1500 workers.

In his electoral campaign a year ago, the premier promised to get tough with polluters. His minister for the environment tightened the previous administration's pollution laws by providing heavy fines and jail terms for polluters. A recommendation from the environment ministry officials to postpone the enforcement of the order against Pulp and Paper because of the company's financial problems was rejected by the environment minister. An independent audit of the company by a well-respected accounting firm confirmed Pulp and Paper's claim that it had lost $100-million in the last seven years and therefore cannot afford to install the $15-million pollution-control devices. Some members of opposition parties in the provincial legislature are urging the government to be more flexible in its approach. They point out the devastating impact that the enforcement of the order could have on the 5000 inhabitants of Bear's Paw and on the surrounding region, where unemployment at 15 per cent is already very high. They suggest that the provincial government provide subsidies to Pulp and Paper to enable it to install the anti-pollution equipment and to survive financially.

Other members of the legislature supported the environment minister's stand, pointing out that it was necessary to uphold the law and to protect the environment. Moreover, the granting of a subsidy to Pulp and Paper Ltd., would set an expensive precedent. Any other company that was required to install anti-pollution devices would make its way to the provincial premier expecting also to be subsidized.

Question

In this situation, what do you think the provincial government should do?

CHAPTER 16

International Trade

(1)

(1) A Seaway-size self-unloading vessel loading grain in Thunder Bay, Ontario. Canada sells grains such as wheat and canola to many countries around the world.

(2) California growers market about 150 000 cartons of artichokes to Canada each year.

(3) According to the British Tourist Authority, 600 000 Canadian tourists visited Britain in 1994.

(4) This Candu reactor, produced by the Atomic Energy Commission of Canada Limited, was bought by South Korea.

(5) Whistler Resort in British Columbia has the most extensive high-speed lift system in the world and the highest vertical drops in North America. The Whistler Resort Association markets this renowned four-season destination to the North American, European, and Asian market.

(a)

(5b)

(6)

(6) Japan is one of Canada's major suppliers of electronic equipment, for example, portable tape players.

Questions

1. Which of these photos show Canadian exports, that is, goods or services that are produced by Canadians and sold to people in or from other countries?

2. Which of these photos show Canadian imports, that is, goods or services that are produced by people from or in other countries and sold to Canadians?

Activity 1: South Seas simulation

You are an inhabitant of one of the six sun-drenched coral islands in the South Seas. Each island produces two products, fish and coconuts, that are all the inhabitants need for survival. The fish are caught by hand in the sea, and the coconuts are gathered by scaling the trees. Thus, no tools are required.

Each island country can produce as many fish and coconuts as the inhabitants wish with the expenditure of the amounts of labour indicated on the sketch map in figure 16.1. Each individual on each island has no preference for producing fish or coconuts and is just as skilled at producing them as anyone else on his or her island. For a balanced diet, each islander should consume approximately equal quantities of fish and coconuts.

As you can see by the sketch map below, the six islands are divided into three groups. There is communication only between the two islands in each group. There are no costs of transportation of either product between islands in the same group. The inhabitants of the islands are not allowed to migrate from one island to another.

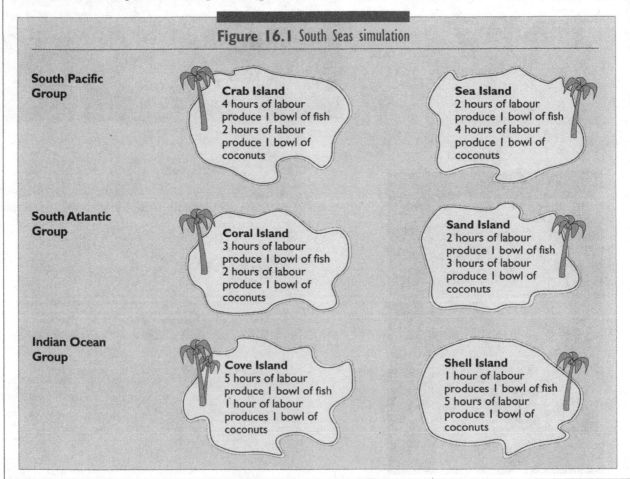

Figure 16.1 South Seas simulation

South Pacific Group

Crab Island
4 hours of labour produce 1 bowl of fish
2 hours of labour produce 1 bowl of coconuts

Sea Island
2 hours of labour produce 1 bowl of fish
4 hours of labour produce 1 bowl of coconuts

South Atlantic Group

Coral Island
3 hours of labour produce 1 bowl of fish
2 hours of labour produce 1 bowl of coconuts

Sand Island
2 hours of labour produce 1 bowl of fish
3 hours of labour produce 1 bowl of coconuts

Indian Ocean Group

Cove Island
5 hours of labour produce 1 bowl of fish
1 hour of labour produces 1 bowl of coconuts

Shell Island
1 hour of labour produces 1 bowl of fish
5 hours of labour produce 1 bowl of coconuts

Instructions

The class divides into six groups, each representing the inhabitants of one island. The groups should arrange themselves in the classroom so that Crab Island is near Sea Island, Coral Island is near Sand Island, and Cove Island is near Shell Island. Refer to figure 16.1 to answer the questions.

Playing the game

The leader of your island has selected your group to advise her/him about the economic life on the island, and presents you with the following questions:

1. What is the total amount of fish that could be caught on our island in thirty hours?

2. What is the total amount of coconuts that could be gathered in thirty hours?

3. What is the opportunity cost (your leader obviously knows some economics!) of one bowl of fish on our island?

4. On our island, what is one bowl of fish worth in terms of coconuts?

5. On the other island in our group, what is one bowl of fish worth in terms of coconuts?

You report your findings to the leader, who replies: "As you know, there have been mutterings of discontent on our island because I was forced to raise taxes to keep myself and my family adequately supplied with fish and coconuts, thus diminishing the food supply available to other people. Is there any way that I can increase the amount of fish and coconuts available to the people on the island (or to raise their standard of living) without increasing the hours of labour or buying any of those new-fangled inventions such as fishing nets? Please present me with a detailed scheme as soon as possible."

Each section should present their scheme to the rest of the class.

Discussion of the game

As you saw in the South Seas simulation, Sea Island had what is known in economics as an "absolute advantage" in the production of fish, compared to Crab Island. This means that Sea Island could produce fish with less expenditure of labour than Crab Island. Similarly, Sand Island had an absolute advantage in the production of fish over Coral Island and Shell Island over Cove Island. Cove Island and Crab Island, on the other hand, were able to produce coconuts with less expenditure of labour than the other island in their group. They had an absolute advantage in the production of coconuts.

Each island stands to gain by specializing in the production of that good by which it has an absolute advantage. Crab, Coral, and Cove Islands gain by specializing in the production of coconuts. Sea, Sand, and Shell Islands gain from specialization in the production of fish.

This simulation may seem a little removed from reality, but a moment's reflection will reveal that it is similar to situations that are common in everyday life.

INTERNATIONAL TRADE

Before arriving at school today, you probably made use of a large number of goods that came from foreign countries. If you had coffee for breakfast, it probably came from Brazil. The cup from which you drank may have been made in England. The sugar you sprinkled on your cereal may have come from Jamaica. The sweater you own may have been knitted in Hong Kong. The Walkman you listened to on the way to school may have been manufactured in Japan. At every turn, you use imports.

Imports are goods and services that are produced in one country, such as Jamaica, but consumed in another, such as Canada. The sugar you sprinkled on your cereal this morning may have been produced in Jamaica but it was consumed by you here in Canada. The sugar is a Canadian import.

In the same way, people in other countries use many Canadian products. The Japanese may eat bread baked from Canadian wheat. The British read magazines printed on Canadian paper. Many countries in the world use Canadian-made farm machinery. The goods we sell to other countries are our exports.

Exports are goods and services that are produced in one country and are then shipped or sold in another. For example, the wood pulp that is produced in Newfoundland and Québec, and is sold in the United States is a Canadian export, while to the Americans it is an import.

Trade between nations of the world is called international trade. In non-communist countries, international trade is carried on mainly by private businesses. If a German firm wishes to import Canadian paper, it contacts a Canadian paper company and makes the necessary arrangements. In communist countries, foreign trade is carried on by some branch of government. Purchases of Canadian wheat by China are made by a department of the Chinese government.

Why do nations trade?

We obtain a great number of goods from other countries. Many of these goods, however, could be produced in Canada. Canadians could produce the cups, sweaters, and stereos we need, instead of importing them from England, Hong Kong, or Japan. Canadian farmers could grow more sugar beets so that we would not have to rely on Jamaicans for our sugar. Why, then, do we import goods from other countries when we could produce them ourselves?

Absolute advantage

Few individuals today produce all the goods and services they themselves need. Individuals tend to specialize in the production of a good or a service. Because of

training or natural ability, I may specialize in word processing and you in tuning automobiles. As a result, I am able to input more pages in one day than you, and you are able to tune more cars than I in the same length of time. Thus, it will be to my advantage to let you tune my car, and to your advantage to let me do your word processing. You and I both gain by specialization.

Canada has an absolute advantage over the United Kingdom in the production of wheat. Manitoba, Alberta, and Saskatchewan have an absolute advantage in the production of wheat over other provinces. You may have an absolute advantage over me in the tuning of cars.

Absolute advantage is the ability of one person, region, or country to produce a good or a service at a cost lower than a competitor's.

Absolute advantage applies to individual countries. Because of the natural advantages of climate and soil, Brazil can produce coffee with less expenditure of resources than Canada. Brazil has an absolute advantage over Canada in coffee production. Canada, on the other hand, has an absolute advantage over Brazil in the production of wheat. Thus, it is to the advantage of both countries to specialize in the production of those goods and services in which they have an absolute advantage, and to exchange these for whatever other goods and services they may need.

Comparative advantage

Comparative advantage is the ability of one person, region, or country to provide a good or a service relatively more cheaply than other goods or services.

Suppose, again, that I specialize in word processing and you in tune-ups, but, in this case, you are not only better at tune-ups, you're a faster word processor. You have an absolute advantage in word processing and tuning cars. Would it be to my benefit to trade with you? Or, more to the point, could it be to your advantage to trade with me?

Suppose that, in a day, I can input 20 pages or tune 2 automobiles. Suppose you can input 25 pages or tune 5 automobiles in a day.

For you — 1 day's work =
5 tune-ups = 25 pages, or
1 tune-up = 5 pages, or
1 page = 1/5 tune-up

For me — 1 day's work =
2 tune-ups = 20 pages, or
1 tune-up = 10 pages, or
1 page = 1/10 tune-up

Could it be to my advantage to buy tune-ups from you for input pages?

As you can see, if I tune a car, it takes me half a day and I have to give up the possibility of inputting ten pages. The opportunity cost of one tune-up to me is ten pages. However, since you can do five tune-ups per day or input twenty-five pages, then the opportunity cost of a tune-up to you is five pages. I have a comparative advantage in word processing, and you have a comparative advantage in tuning cars. I can input more efficiently than I can tune cars, and you can tune cars more efficiently than you can input. Clearly, then, it could be to my advantage to exchange input pages for tune-ups, providing your tune-ups cost less than ten pages. Similarly, for you, it could be advantageous to buy input pages from me with tune-ups, providing that you can sell tune-ups for more than five input pages. Moreover, there is room for bargaining the terms of trade between the limits of one for ten and one for five, the actual terms depending on the relative strength of demand for tune-ups versus input pages.

Thus, despite the fact that you can input more pages and tune cars better than I can, it can be to your advantage to exchange tune-ups for input pages with me. It can also be to my advantage to buy tune-ups from you for my input pages. You have an absolute advantage in both tune-ups and word processing, but a comparative advantage in tune-ups. I have a comparative advantage in word processing. It can be to our advantage to specialize in the production of goods and services in which we have a comparative advantage.

In the same way, countries specialize in those goods and services in which they have a comparative advantage.

It is to their mutual advantage to engage in trade, just as it was in our exchange of tune-ups for word processing. Our example was simplified, concerned only with the exchange of two goods or services between two individuals. We ignored such things as transportation costs, the use of different currencies, and the existence of government restrictions. However, even if we were to complicate our models by adding these factors, it still can be said that nations benefit from international trade.

APPLICATION
A fable of advantage

In a time past, Minnie the lawyer hired a splendid young assistant/word processor named George.

Her friends sniggered, because they knew that Minnie was an excellent word processor in her own right. In fact, they said, the lawyer could input documents faster than this young man, and she could easily do her own word processing and save money. Minnie ignored them, because her motives were very practical.

Of course, Minnie could practise law at the going rate of $200 an hour. Given a forty-hour week, she could spend thirty hours on law to earn a whacking $6000, and then knock off all her word processing in the other ten hours.

Instead, Minnie chose to practise law all forty hours of the week, to take in $8000. She paid George the going rate of $20 an hour, or $800 for his forty-hour week, leaving herself with a decidedly improved net income of $7200.

Regardless of Minnie's superior word processing skills, it paid her to spend her time doing that which maximized her gains — that is, "exporting" legal services, and "importing" word processing services.

Thus, Minnie gave us the Law of Comparative Advantage. In short, always export the goods you have the *relative* advantage in, and import the rest.

(continued on page 336)

Activity 2: South Seas revisited

As a result of terrible volcanic activity, the original six islands in the South Seas have disappeared beneath the deep blue water. In their stead have emerged six new sun-drenched coral islands. The new islands are very much like the old islands in all ways but two. Different amounts of time are available for the production of coconuts and fish, and different expenditures of labour are needed to produce fish and coconuts in all cases. Otherwise there are no changes. See the new sketch map in figure 16.2 for details.

Initially, there is no trade between the two islands in each group. No tools are used to produce coconuts and fish. Island inhabitants need both coconuts and fish for a balanced diet. There are no costs of transportation, and no migration between islands.

Instructions

The class divides into six groups, each group representing the inhabitants of one island. The groups representing the six different islands should arrange themselves in the classroom so that Crab Island is

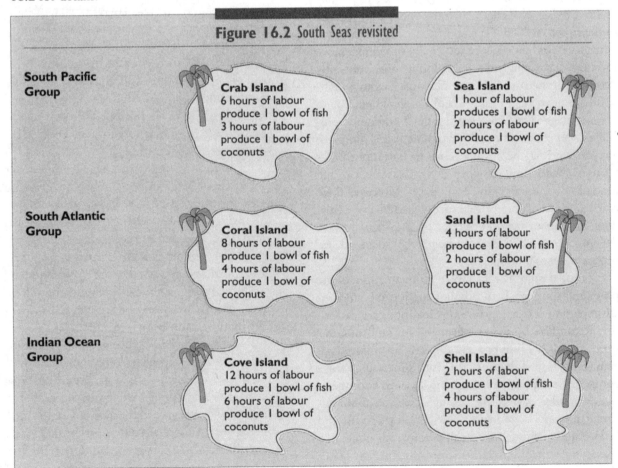

Figure 16.2 South Seas revisited

South Pacific Group

Crab Island
6 hours of labour produce 1 bowl of fish
3 hours of labour produce 1 bowl of coconuts

Sea Island
1 hour of labour produces 1 bowl of fish
2 hours of labour produce 1 bowl of coconuts

South Atlantic Group

Coral Island
8 hours of labour produce 1 bowl of fish
4 hours of labour produce 1 bowl of coconuts

Sand Island
4 hours of labour produce 1 bowl of fish
2 hours of labour produce 1 bowl of coconuts

Indian Ocean Group

Cove Island
12 hours of labour produce 1 bowl of fish
6 hours of labour produce 1 bowl of coconuts

Shell Island
2 hours of labour produce 1 bowl of fish
4 hours of labour produce 1 bowl of coconuts

near Sea Island, Coral Island is near Sand Island, and Cove Island is near Shell Island. Use the sketch map to answer the questions.

Playing the game

The island leader requests your group's advice, stating the problem as follows:

"As you know, there have been loud protests on the island since I was forced to raise taxes to keep myself and my family adequately supplied with fish and coconuts, thus diminishing the food supply available to the other people. How can we increase the amount of food available to the inhabitants of the island without increasing the hours of labour and investing in new-fangled contraptions such as fishing rods? Please present me with a detailed plan as soon as possible."

Draw up a plan and report to the class.

Questions

1. Who would gain by trade between the islands?

2. Suppose that the leader of each island imposed a substantial tax on imported fish or coconuts. What effect would the tax have on the amount of trade between the islands in each group and the standard of living of each island?

3. Generally speaking, in what circumstances is trade most likely to take place?

4. Suppose people were given the freedom to migrate. What incentive is there for them to move? To which islands would they tend to move? Why?

Discussion of the game

In our second South Seas simulation, we might expect that trade between the two islands in each group would not take place. After all, Sea, Sand, and Shell Islands have an absolute advantage in the production of both fish and coconuts. With the equivalent expenditures of labour, they can produce more coconuts and fish than the other islands in the group. But, as you no doubt discovered, trade between the two islands in each group is not only possible, it can also be advantageous to both islands.

Let's examine Sea and Crab Islands. Would it be more advantageous for Sea Island to produce whatever it needed and to ignore Crab Island totally? A comparison of the costs of production of fish and coconuts on both islands is summarized in figure 16.3.

Sea Island has an absolute advantage in the production of both fish and coconuts. It has, however, more advantage in fish (1:6) than it has in coconuts (2:3). Looking just at Sea Island's production, we see that Sea Island produces fish at less cost than coconuts (1 hour for 1 bowl of fish compared to 2 hours for 1 bowl of coconuts). Sea Island has a comparative advantage in fish. Similarly, Crab Island produces coconuts more efficiently than fish (3 hours for 1 bowl of coconuts compared to 6 hours for 1 bowl of fish). Therefore, Crab Island has a comparative advantage in coconuts.

Would trade be advantageous to both Sea and Crab Islands? Let's take the situation of Sea and Crab Islands having to produce 8 bowls of fish and coconuts each, with no trade.

Before trade

Sea Island — 8 hours would be devoted to catching fish for 8 bowls of fish; 16 hours would be devoted to collecting coconuts for 8 bowls of coconuts. **Time required: 24 hours.**

Figure 16.3 Production costs on Sea and Crab Islands

| | Labour cost of production (in hours) | |
	1 bowl of fish	1 bowl of coconuts
Sea Island	1	2
Crab Island	6	3

Crab Island — 48 hours would be devoted to catching fish for 8 bowls of fish; 24 hours would be devoted to collecting coconuts for 8 bowls of coconuts. **Time required: 72 hours.**
Total Production — 16 bowls of fish and 16 bowls of coconuts.

Now let's have Sea Island and Crab Island each specialize in the production of the product in which each has a comparative advantage, using the same amount of time.

With trade
Sea Island — would produce 24 bowls of fish in 24 hours.
Crab Island — would produce 24 bowls of coconuts in 72 hours.
Total Production — 24 bowls of fish and 24 bowls of coconuts.

We can conclude from the example above that both Sea Island and Crab Island could gain from trade since they are able to produce more of each product with specialization than without specialization.

Her friends gathered around Minnie in awe — all except one who stood back, frowning.

But what if George should join a powerful wage-fixing cartel? the skeptic asked.

Or what if hard times came, and Minnie could "export" only twenty hours a week of legal services? Clearly, her wisest course then would be to eliminate the "imports" and do her own word processing.

The lawyer replied, "Whoever heard of such one-sided interventions? And won't there always be full employment? Why let such thoughts muck up a perfectly good theory?"

All exited laughing.

Source: Adapted from *Financial Post*.

Questions

1. Who has an absolute advantage in word processing? in law?

2. Who has a comparative advantage in word processing? in law?

3. In what circumstances, if any, should Minnie do her own word processing? Explain your answer.

4. Give examples of situations where you or people you know make use of the law of comparative advantage.

Barriers to international trade

Even though international trade promotes the efficient allocation of resources, thus raising living standards, governments have sought to restrict the movement of goods and services between nations in a number of ways. These include imposing protective tariffs, embargoes, and quotas.

1. Protective tariffs are taxes imposed on imported goods in order to raise prices and thus restrict the amount sold. A protective tariff may be specific (that is, of a certain amount per unit) or ad valorem (that is, varying directly with the cost of the item).

2. An **embargo** is a ban on, or a prohibition against, the import or export of certain goods. Governments may prohibit trade in certain goods for reasons of health, politics, or national security. In the past, exports of high-technology goods to the former Soviet Union were embargoed for national security reasons. In Canada, for instance, there is an embargo on the importation of hashish. Canada has prohibited the exportation of uranium to various countries at various times.

3. Quotas are a way of protecting home industry from foreign competition. A quota is a restriction on the amount of foreign foods that may be imported. For instance, clothing and textile imports have been subject not only to tariffs, but also to quotas. Thus, only restricted amounts of the foreign goods are allowed into the country.

4. **"Red tape"**: Governments can employ restrictive rules and regulations through the Customs bureaucracy to delay or even prevent the importing of foreign goods.

Arguments against international trade

If we examine absolute and comparative advantage, a strong case can be made for international trade. However, even though arguments in favour of freedom of international trade seem strong, there are many arguments to be made in support of restriction.

Infant industry argument

If certain new industries are given protection from older, well-established companies in other countries, then in time, when they are well-established and operating at low cost, they will be able to compete. At this time, tariffs and other forms of protection may be lowered and perhaps eliminated. While this argument has merit, it is difficult to determine which infant industries will grow to adulthood. Tariffs and other forms of protection are not like old soldiers — they don't just fade away. Once imposed, they are difficult to eliminate since many people have an interest in their continuation.

Vital industries argument

There are certain key industries that need to be protected from foreign competition since these industries are essential to our survival. Oil production is one example. If we become overly reliant on foreign sources for oil, or for any other good or service, then we are vulnerable to pressure from those sources. Two other vital industries are shipbuilding and aircraft production. Without these industries, we would be forced to rely on foreign sources to supply us with the planes and ships we would need to defend ourselves in the event of war or other national emergencies.

Cheap foreign labour argument

This argument finds a great deal of support. Its supporters say that since Canadian workers are more highly paid than workers in Hong Kong, for example, then Canadian industries are unable to compete with those producers. If Canada is flooded with cheap Asian products, then Canadian wages will have to be cut or Canadian firms will go out of business. Supporters of this argument urge the government to protect Canadian industry and its workers from unfair competition due to cheap foreign labour.

This argument ignores the reason for the high wages in the first place. Wages are higher in Canada than in Hong Kong because productivity is higher. Canadian wages may be twice those in Hong Kong, but, generally speaking, if Canadian workers produce twice as much because they are twice as productive, then labour costs per unit are the same in Canada as in Hong Kong. In certain industries we may be unable to compete with foreigners because they have a comparative advantage.

Employment argument

When a country slips into a recession and workers are laid off, calls for protective tariffs are heard more frequently. As we saw with our leaky bucket economy, when employment, income, and GDP are declining, it seems to make sense to cut the leakage. One of the leakages is, of course, imports.

The immediate effect on restricting imports might be to stimulate domestic industries and employment. Over a longer period of time, however, other nations may have to cut their imports to balance their exports. In engaging in international trade, nations become dependent on each other. The imposition of restrictions on imports by country A means, of necessity, a cut in the exports of country B. This results in a decline in country B's ability to pay for its imports. Country B, then, may be obliged to cut its imports from country A. Thus, both countries ultimately lose from A's action. These "beggar-my-neighbour" policies were prevalent in the 1930s. They resulted in a reduction in the flow of trade and the loss of the advantage of international specialization, thus reducing the standard of living for all. This type of policy is likely to produce no winners, only losers.

Some of the arguments for restricted international trade, particularly those in favour of the protection of defence and infant industries, seem legitimate. There are, however, alternatives to setting up protective barriers. In some cases, alternatives — such as government **subsidies** to certain industries — are preferable to tariffs. The cost of the subsidy is a known quantity; the cost of the tariff is hidden.

Tariffs, once imposed, are difficult to eliminate since many people have a vested interest in their continuation. One of the most powerful reasons for not eliminating tariffs is the disruptive effect elimination would have on those industries that have been sheltered. In Canada, as elsewhere, many industries have grown and prospered behind tariff barriers. To remove protection abruptly would bring unemployment and dislocation. If tariffs and other forms of protection are to be removed, it is probably best done slowly and with considerable assistance to cushion the shocks to workers, employers, and local governments.

INTERNATIONAL TRADE AND THE CIRCULAR FLOW

Now we can make the final addition to the circular flow diagram. See figure 16.4.

To figure 11.5 on page 241, we now add international trade — to complete the diagram. Canadian imports of goods and services from other countries are shown by the line and the box linking our product market to other countries. Payments for these imports are shown by the line going from the product market to the other countries' box. Canadian exports are depicted by the arrow from the product market to the other countries' box. Payments for Canadian exports are shown by the arrows from other countries to the product market.

Canadian households buy goods and services from other countries through the product market. As a result, there is a flow of payments from Canadians to foreign countries. From these foreign countries, there is a further flow of goods and services (our imports) to Canada. Also through the final goods market, Canadian businesses provide other countries with a flow of goods and services — our exports. To pay for these exports, there is a flow of payments.

Domestic and international trade

The sale of a Chevrolet in British Columbia by General Motors of Oshawa, Ontario, is a fairly simple transaction. The sale of a Nissan in British Columbia by Nissan of Japan is more complicated. The importer of Nissans has to pay the tariff on the vehicle. The British Columbia purchaser will pay for the Nissan in Canadian dollars. The importer must convert the Canadian dollars into Japanese currency to pay the Nissan manufacturer in Japan. Even though international trade is more complicated than domestic trade, there is no basic difference between trade within a country and trade between nations. Ontario sells automobiles to British Columbia and, in turn, buys lumber from British Columbia. Canada sells wheat to Japan and, in turn, buys automobiles from Japan. Trade between Canadian provinces, and between Canada and its trading partners, is fundamentally the same.

Questions

1. What country is our biggest trading partner? Explain.

2. Which countries sell more to us than they buy from us?

3. List as many reasons as you can why Canada buys and sells so much in the United States.

Canada's trade partners

We use a great number of goods and services produced in other countries. Similarly, people in other countries consume a large number of Canadian-produced goods and services. More than one-quarter of our GDP is sold abroad. The livelihood of many Canadians directly depends on our ability to continue to sell large

Figure 16.4 International trade and the circular flow

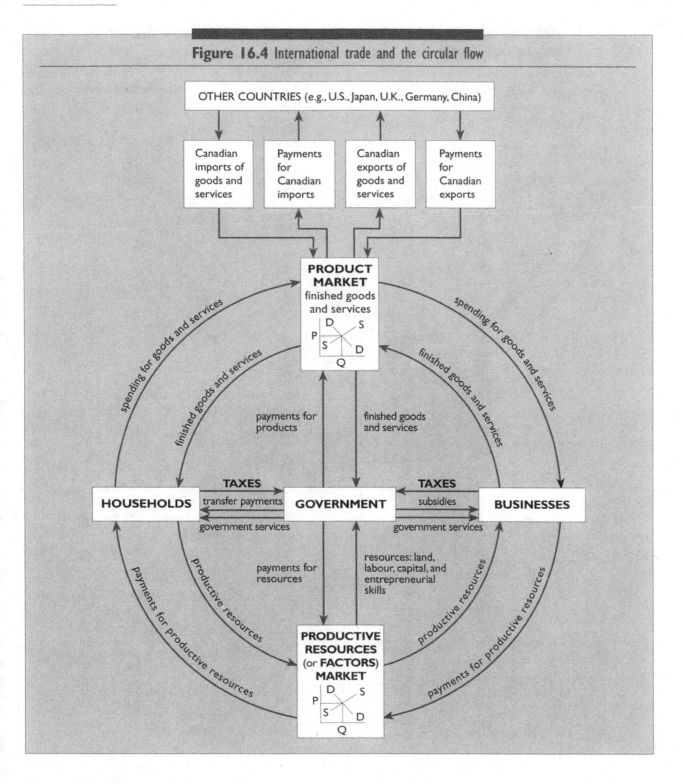

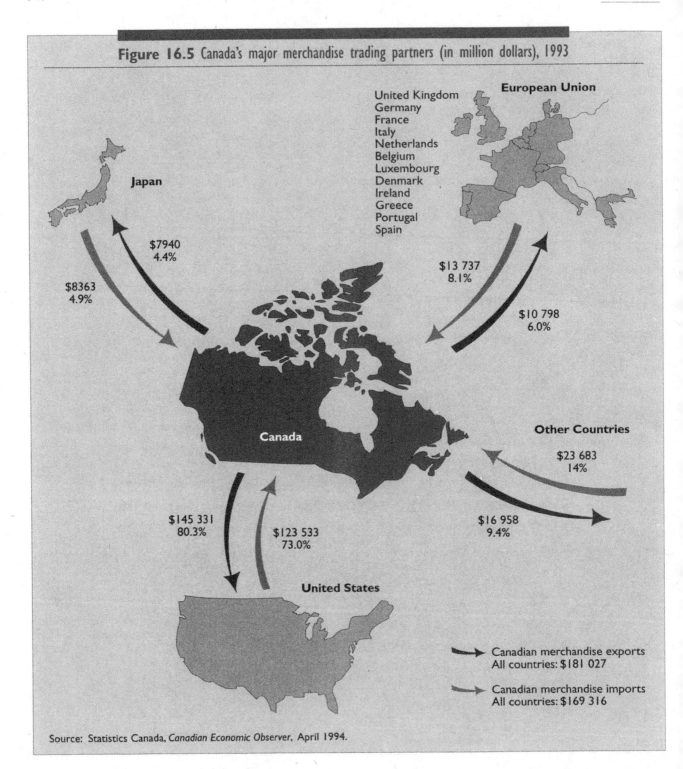

Figure 16.5 Canada's major merchandise trading partners (in million dollars), 1993

Japan

United Kingdom
Germany
France
Italy
Netherlands
Belgium
Luxembourg
Denmark
Ireland
Greece
Portugal
Spain

European Union

$7940
4.4%

$8363
4.9%

$13 737
8.1%

$10 798
6.0%

Canada

Other Countries

$23 683
14%

$145 331
80.3%

$123 533
73.0%

$16 958
9.4%

United States

Canadian merchandise exports
All countries: $181 027

Canadian merchandise imports
All countries: $169 316

Source: Statistics Canada, *Canadian Economic Observer*, April 1994.

amounts of goods and services in other countries. Most Canadians would be seriously affected by a significant decline in Canadian exports. Likewise, the livelihood of people in other countries depends on their ability to sell their products here in Canada.

Canada's major trading partner is the United States. See figure 16.5. In 1993, more than four-fifths of our merchandise exports were sold in the U.S. and almost three-quarters of our merchandise imports came from the U.S. In matters of international trade, then, we are very dependent on the United States.

A recession south of the border is likely to result in a reduced demand for our exports, causing unemployment in those industries exporting to the U.S. American policies that act to diminish the volume of their imports will have similar effects. As for those goods and services that we import from the U.S., inflation in the United States will be transmitted to Canada through higher-priced imports. On the other hand, prosperity in the United States will bring prosperity to the export industries in Canada. As well, lower American tariffs will probably result in increased Canadian exports to the United States.

Our other major markets and suppliers are the United Kingdom, Japan, and countries in the European Union.

Canadian merchandise trade

1. Exports

Canada's major exports of goods for 1993 are shown in figure 16.6 (a). Automobile products (motor vehicles and parts) head the list. By the terms of the Canada-U.S. Automotive Agreement of 1965, tariffs were removed on these goods so that free trade in new automobiles has existed for more than 30 years between the two countries. Thus, there are large amounts of motor vehicles and parts crossing the Canada-U.S. border in both directions. Very substantial amounts of other manufactured goods are sold in other countries: communications equipment, industrial machinery, aircraft and aircraft parts, and consumer goods. Other exports are more closely associated with Canada's "staples," such as fish, wheat, lumber, pulp and paper, metals, and minerals. Canada is also an important exporter of energy (petroleum, natural gas, electricity, and coal), chemicals, and fertilizers.

2. Imports

Figure 16.6 (b) shows Canada's major merchandise imports. A large portion of our imports are fully manufactured or finished products. Just less than one quarter of our imports are of motor vehicles and parts, and just less than one third are of machinery and

Figure 16.6 Canada's merchandise trade (in million dollars), 1993

(a) Exports: Total: $191 036 millions

Agricultural and fish products	Energy products	Forest products	Industrial goods	Machines and equipment	Automobile products	Consumer goods	Other
$15 546	$17 998	$23 590	$31 188	$36 368	$48 016	$4937	$13 393

(b) Imports: Total: $179 316 millions

Agricultural and fish products	Energy products	Forest products	Industrial goods	Machines and equipment	Automobile products	Consumer goods	Other
$10 983	$6932	$1563	$31 092	$53 112	$39 858	$21 197	$14 579

Source: Statistics Canada, *Canada's Balance of International Payments, Fourth Quarter*, 1993.

equipment. Other substantial merchandise imports include industrial goods (iron and steel, chemicals, and plastics), consumer goods, foodstuffs, and energy products (mainly petroleum).

As can be seen by comparing Canadian exports and imports in 1993, Canada exported more agricultural, fish, energy, and automobile products than were imported. Imports of machines and equipment and consumer goods exceeded exports. In 1993, Canadian exports of goods exceeded our imports (as usually happens) by about $11.7 billion.

Visible and invisible trade

Figure 16.6 on page 341 gives us a picture of Canada's merchandise trade. Another term applied to merchandise trade is **visible trade** because merchandise trade involves the import and export of visible, tangible goods. Parts of our international commerce are **invisible trade**, involving the import or export of services, investment income of foreigners, and transfers. These parts of trade cannot be seen or touched and are therefore called invisible imports or exports.

Canadian invisible imports involve payments Canadians make to foreigners. When Canadians travel to a foreign country, they buy many goods and services in the country they are travelling in: plane tickets, hotel accommodation, theatre tickets, meals, post cards, etc. Since these purchases by Canadians involve payments made to foreigners, they count as invisible imports. Canadian travel and tourism account for a large part of Canada's invisible imports. See figure 16.7 (a). Other invisible imports include freight and shipping charges (paid when Canadians use foreign transportation services); business services (payments for insurance, management fees, and payments for research, patents, and royalties); interest and dividend payments (that are incurred when Canadians borrow from foreigners and when foreigners invest in Canada); and transfer payments (that occur when foreigners receive inheritances in Canada).

Similarly, a major part of our invisible exports involve payments received by Canadians from foreigners travelling in Canada. See figure 16.7 (b). Canadian invisible exports also include the payments made by foreigners to Canadians for Canadian freight and shipping services, business services, interest and dividends on Canadian funds loaned and invested in other countries, and the transfer payments that occur when Canadians receive inheritances in other countries.

Figure 16.7 Canada's non-merchandise trade (in millions of dollars), 1993

(a) Invisible imports: $77 466

Travel and tourism	Services			Investment income	Transfers
	Freight and shipping	Business services	Other		
$16 389	$5913	$15 043	$2450	$33 690	$3981

(b) Invisible exports: $40 536

Travel and tourism	Services			Investment income	Transfers
	Freight and shipping	Business services	Other		
$8703	$6137	$10 331	$2070	$9010	$4285

Source: Statistics Canada, *Canada's Balance of International Payments, Fourth Quarter,* 1993.

Typically, Canadian invisible imports exceed invisible exports. As is indicated by comparing figure 16.7 (a) with figure 16.7 (b), the main sources of the disparity are travel — on which we spent almost twice as much as we earned — and investment income, on which we spent more than three times our earnings.

Capital movements

In addition to the movements of goods and services in international markets, there are also transfers of capital between countries. Suppose you buy a U.S. government bond for $1000. You will acquire the $1000 bond and, in exchange, you will pay the $1000. In order to pay what you owe the U.S. broker, there will have to be an exchange from Canadian dollars into U.S. dollars. The $1000, then, is an outflow of Canadian funds. It represents an inflow of $1000 to the United States.

My purchase of U.S. stocks, or of a U.S. corporation, is also an outflow of funds from Canada and an inflow to the U.S. The sale of your bond and my sale of the U.S. stocks would represent an inflow of funds to Canada and an outflow from the U.S. In the same way, a purchase of Canadian bonds or stocks by Americans represent an inflow of funds to Canada and an outflow from the U.S.

Canada's capital imports totalled $51 584 million in 1993 and capital exports equalled $19 384 million, for a balance of $32 200 million. See figure 16.8.

Balance of payments

The **balance of payments** is the summary of all the visible, invisible, and capital transactions that have taken place between one country and the rest of the world over a period of time — usually a year.

Balance of trade

The **balance of trade** is the difference between the value of merchandise (or visible) exports and the value of merchandise (or visible) imports. The balance of trade is favourable if we export more than we import, and unfavourable, if we import more than we export.

In 1993, Canada's merchandise exports exceeded our merchandise imports by over $11 710 million. See figure 16.8. Our balance of trade was therefore favourable.

Balance of trade on current account

The **balance of trade on current account** is the difference between the money value of our visible and invisible exports and the value of our visible and invisible imports. The balance of trade on current account is favourable if our visible and invisible exports exceed our imports. It is unfavourable if our visible and invisible imports exceed our exports.

In 1993, our visible and invisible imports exceeded our visible and invisible exports by more than $25 million. We had an unfavourable balance of trade on current account. See figure 16.9.

Capital account

In 1993, the investments by foreigners in Canada exceeded those by Canadians in other countries by

---

Figure 16.8 Balance of trade (in million dollars), 1993

Merchandise exports	Merchandise imports	**Favourable balance of trade**
$181 026	$169 316	**$11 710**

Source: Statistics Canada, *Canada's Balance of International Payments, Fourth Quarter*, 1993.

Figure 16.9 Balance of trade on current account (in million dollars), 1993

Merchandise exports		Invisible exports			**Unfavourable balance of trade on current account**
$181 026	+	$40 537	=	$221 563	
Merchandise imports		Invisible imports			**$25 219**
$169 316	+	$77 466	=	$246 782	

Source: Statistics Canada, *Canada's Balance of International Payments, Fourth Quarter*, 1993.

Figure 16.10 Balance of payments (in million dollars), 1993

Merchandise exports $181 026	+	Invisible exports $40 537	+	Capital imports $51 584		Errors and omissions −$6981	=	Balance of payments −$598
Merchandise imports $169 316	+	Invisible imports $77 466	+	Capital exports $19 982				

Source: Statistics Canada, *Canada's Balance of International Payments, Fourth Quarter*, 1993.

$31 602 million dollars. See figure 16.10. Net errors and omissions totalled about $6981 million. Our unfavourable balance of payments was $598 million.

Exchange rates

An **exchange rate** is the price of one currency, such as the U.S. dollar, expressed in terms of another currency, such as the Canadian dollar.

You have probably seen notices in store windows telling you that the storeowner is willing to pay a certain premium on bills paid in U.S. dollars. If, for example, the premium on U.S. dollars is 30 percent and you pay your bill in a Canadian restaurant with a U.S. ten-dollar note, then the restaurant cashier regards this note as $10 + 30 percent of $10 = $10 + $3 = $13. If you only have a cup of coffee, you may come out of the restaurant with more dollars than when you went in!

If you visit another country, you will be obliged to change Canadian funds into the currency of that country. This involves knowing what currencies are worth in terms of Canadian dollars. Exchange rates continually fluctuate. If you check exchange rates in the business section of your daily newspaper on succeeding days, you are likely to see a number of small variations in the values of foreign currencies.

Flexible exchange rates

How are exchange rates determined? When the currencies of countries can be freely bought and sold on the foreign exchange market, the rate of exchange between two particular currencies is determined by the interplay of those two determinants we have met many times: the forces of supply and demand. By means of a supply and demand graph, let's see how exchange rates are determined.

From figure 16.11, we can see that the demand curve for British pounds is downward sloping. Why? As British pounds decline in value in comparison to Canadian dollars, it means that in Canada the price of imports from Britain will decline. Canadians will be encouraged to buy more British goods and services, and the demand for British pounds in Canada will increase.

Again, as we can see from figure 16.11, the supply of pounds slopes up to the right. As the price of pounds in terms of Canadian dollars rises, more Canadian products will be demanded by the British, and more pounds will be supplied.

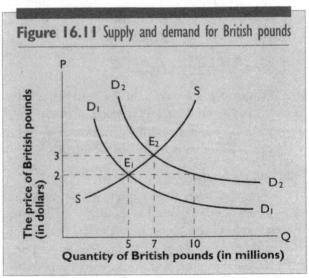

Figure 16.11 Supply and demand for British pounds

BUILDING YOUR SKILLS

Making foreign currency exchanges

If you decide to take a trip to Mexico or Jamaica or Barbados, one question you will almost certainly ask on some occasion is: "How much is it?" A reply such as, "It costs one Jamaican dollar" or "It is 1000 Mexican pesos" may not be very helpful unless you know how much the Jamaican dollar or Mexican peso is worth in terms of the Canadian dollar. In this exercise, we will learn to use a foreign exchange table.

Foreign exchange tables can be found in the business section of many local newspapers. In table 16.1, we have taken a few of the rates from a much more complete table. If you examine the table, you will see that it is divided into three columns: the name of the country; the name of the currency; and the last entitled Canadian dollar per unit. If we look at the first row, we read that the country is the United States, and the currency is the dollar. So far, no surprises! The last column tells us that there are 1.39 Canadian dollars for each one of the U.S. dollars. That means that $1 U.S. was worth $1.39 Canadian on the day the table was prepared. On the same day, one British pound was worth $2.10 Canadian, one German mark was worth $.84, and so on.

How to calculate the exchange

1. To change *our* money into *their* money, we *divide*.

   For example: what do we get when we change 10 Canadian dollars into British pounds?

   $$\$10 \text{ Canadian} = \frac{10}{2.16} = 4.63 \text{ British pounds}$$

2. To change *their* money into *our* money, we *multiply*.

   For example: what do we get when we change 10 German marks into Canadian dollars?

   $$10 \text{ marks} = 10 \times .84 = \$8.40 \text{ Canadian}$$

3. To change one foreign currency into another, we change the first money into Canadian dollars, then convert the Canadian dollars into the foreign currency. For example, suppose we wanted to change $10 U.S. into Indian rupees.

   $$\$10 \text{ U.S.} = 10 \times 1.39 = \$13.90 \text{ Canadian}$$

   $$\$13.90 = \frac{13.90}{0.05} = 278 \text{ Indian rupees}$$

Table 16.1 Foreign exchange

Mid-market rates at noon, June 2, 1994. Prepared by the Bank of Montreal Treasury Group.

Country	Currency	Cdn. $ per unit
U.S.	dollar	1.39
Britain	pound	2.10
Australia	dollar	1.03
Bahamas	dollar	1.39
Barbados	dollar	0.69
China	renminbi	0.16
France	franc	0.25
Hong Kong	dollar	0.18
India	rupee	0.05
Italy	lira	0.0009
Jamaica	dollar	0.05
Japan	yen	0.01
Mexico	peso	0.42
Portugal	escudo	0.008
Russia	ruble	0.0007
Germany	mark	0.84

Source: *Globe and Mail*, June 2, 1994.

Practise your skill

1. Change 100 Jamaican dollars into Canadian dollars.

2. Change 100 Canadian dollars into Hong Kong dollars.

3. Change 100 Russian rubles into Canadian dollars.

4. You are on holiday in Barbados and you would like to take a trip on a sailing ship until you reach Jamaica, where you'll make a stop. The cost of the trip is 350 Barbados dollars. How much will the trip cost you in Canadian dollars?

5. You are on holiday in Beijing, China at the Great Wall Hotel. The cost of the meal in their sixth-floor restaurant is 500 renminbi. How much will the meal cost you in Canadian dollars?

Big Mac attacks around the world

The Big Mac is sold in 68 countries around the world with only trivial changes in the recipe and the decor of the restaurants. The average cost of a Big Mac in four American cities is $2.30 (U.S.); in Japan, you have to fork out 370 yen. In London, a trip under the golden arch for a Big Mac costs 1.81 British pounds. A Big Mac on the fashionable Champs-Elysées among the outdoor cafés close to the Arc de Triomphe will set you back 18.5 French francs; down under, in the land of the kangaroo and the koala bear, $2.45 Australian. In Hong Kong, the Big Mac is a mere $9.20 (Hong Kong). By comparison, a Big Mac averages $2.86 (Canadian) in Canada.

Source: *The Economist*, April 9, 1994.

1. Where is it most expensive to have a "Big Mac attack"?

2. Where is it least expensive to have one of the famous attacks?

The intersection point of the supply and demand curves for pounds determines the dollar price or exchange rate for pounds. As we can see from the graph, when the demand for pounds is D_1D_1, the price or exchange rate for pounds is two dollars and the quantity demanded is five million pounds.

Suppose that the taste of Canadians changes so that there is a greater preference for British goods. The demand curve for pounds will shift from D_1D_1 to D_2D_2. The new exchange rate will be three dollars for the pound and seven million pounds will be demanded. Under a freely operating exchange system, shifts in supply and demand take place easily, without government intervention.

Fixed exchange rates

There are times when governments seek to fix exchange rates. Suppose that the Canadian government fixes or pegs the value of our dollar at two for each British pound. As long as the equilibrium of supply and demand for dollars is at two dollars, there is no problem. Suppose, however, that under a system of fixed exchange rates, there is a shift in the demand for British goods from D_1D_1 to D_2D_2. If the exchange rate is fixed at two dollars to the British pound, then there will be a supply of five million pounds and a demand for ten million pounds. There is, then, a shortage of pounds. How can the shortage be met? To meet it, the Canadian government can sell its reserves of other currencies for pounds or it can seek to borrow pounds from other countries. These two methods are, at best, only short-term solutions. If the shortage of pounds persists, then government may introduce controls on foreign exchange. All Canadian exporters may be obliged to sell their pounds to the government. The government, in turn, may ration pounds among importers. In this way, the shortage of pounds is met by controlling the demand.

Another way to meet the shortage is for the Canadian government to limit the demand for imports, and thus the demand for pounds, by imposing tariffs and quotas. Thus, the volume of imports would be diminished and with it, the demand for pounds. At the same time, the government can subsidize certain Canadian exports, making them more competitive in world markets and increasing their sales. Thus, the amount of foreign currency earned by their sale is increased.

As a last resort, a government can revalue its currency so that the new value comes closer to the equilibrium rate.

An assessment

Which of the two systems — fixed or fluctuating exchange rates — is better? The floating exchange rate system has the advantage of adjustments being made easily and automatically in accordance with fluctuations in supply and demand. On the other hand, the fixed exchange rate system has the advantage of the dollar value remaining stable. With a relatively stable dollar, importers and exporters know the price of goods well in advance. Thus, an element of uncertainty is removed from trade between nations.

Since 1945, Canada has had, at different times, both fixed and floating exchange rates. In the early 1970s we had a period of floating exchange rates. Since then, we have had a system of managed (or "dirty") floating rates in which the Bank of Canada intervenes in the foreign exchange market to smooth (or even to stop) changes in the value of the dollar by varying interest rates, and buying and selling Canadian dollars in foreign exchange markets.

Towards freer trade

Since 1945, there has been a trend towards freer international trade. Recognizing the advantages to be gained from increased international trade, many countries have moved to lessen trade barriers.

General Agreement on Trade and Tariffs (GATT)

The General Agreement on Trade and Tariffs (GATT) was signed by about ninety countries, including Canada and the United States. GATT is based on three main principles: equal nondiscriminatory treatment for all member nations; general reduction of tariffs; and the elimination of non-tariff barriers (e.g., quotas) to trade. GATT member nations meet periodically to renegotiate the Agreement.

Following the initiative of President Kennedy of the United States in the early 1960s, an agreement was reached in 1967 to cut existing tariffs by about one-third. This successful "Kennedy Round" was followed by another agreement among the nations in GATT (the "Tokyo Round") to cut tariffs by another third. A further round of negotiations, the eighth such series of talks, was proposed by U.S. President Ronald Reagan in 1985. Negotiations on this round got underway in 1986 at Purta Deleste in Uruguay — and are therefore called the "Uruguay Round." Its objectives were to cut not only tariffs but also non-tariff barriers (such as quotas) as well.

The Uruguay Round of negotiations was concluded successfully — to many people's surprise — in December 1993. The Agreement was scheduled to come into effect on January 1, 1995, after ratification by the 114 members of GATT. It provided for the establishment of a Multilateral Trade Organization to oversee the operation of the Agreement, and to act as a body for settling disputes and reviewing trade policy. The Uruguay Round extended GATT coverage in agriculture, textiles and clothing, services, and intellectual property rights.

For the first time, agriculture would be covered by GATT rules. Non-tariff barriers (such as quotas) would be converted to tariffs and export subsidies would be reduced. GATT rules were also extended to services such as telecommunications, transportation, and financial services. Finally, with regard to intellectual property rights, foreign owners of patents, copyrights, and trademarks were to be given the same treatment as domestic owners.

The European Union (EU)

Another development in the liberation of trade between nations has been the movement towards economic integration. The most striking example of this has been the formation of the European Union (EU), formerly called the European Community.

In 1958, the Union was established with six member nations: (West) Germany, France, Italy, Holland, Belgium, and Luxembourg. In 1973, it was expanded with the admission of the United Kingdom, Ireland, and Denmark. More recent additions have included Spain, Portugal, Greece, Austria, Finland, and Sweden. Other countries that have indicated an interest in joining the 15-member Union include Norway, Hungary, Poland, and the Czech Republic.

The European Union seeks the abolition of tariffs and quotas among the member nations. At the same time, it aims to establish a common system of tariffs on all imports from outside the EU. Eventually, labour and capital will be free to move anywhere within the Union.

On January 1, 1993, a single European market was established among the members of the EU. As a result, there would be — with certain exceptions — free movement of goods, services, capital, and persons throughout the member countries.

Since its formation, the European Union has made significant economic progress in raising its members' standards of living. But how much is due to its formation and how much to other factors is difficult to assess.

Freer trade between Canada and the United States and Mexico

As we have seen, the United States is the main market for our exports and our main supplier of imports. Developments that will provide us with access to the U.S. market are therefore of great importance to Canadians. Our access to this market has been improved by the GATT agreements mentioned earlier. Three developments in the economic relations between the two countries merit special consideration: the Automotive Agreement (the Auto Pact) of 1965; the Canada-U.S. Free Trade Agreement (FTA) of 1987; and the North American Free Trade Agreement (NAFTA) of 1994 between Canada, the United States, and Mexico.

The Auto Pact of 1965

Before 1965, there was a tariff on imported automobiles of about 15 percent. Because of the small size of the Canadian market and the large numbers of the models produced, Canada was unable to take full advantage of mass production. As a result, car prices in Canada were higher and workers' wages were lower. By the terms of the Automotive Agreement, all duties at the manufacturer's level on imports of cars and car parts were abolished. As a result, automobile plants in Canada were able to specialize in a limited number of models for the entire North American automobile market. Thus, costs fell and wages rose.

Canada-U.S. Free Trade Agreement, 1987

Free trade is international trade that takes place without the obstacles of tariffs or other barriers to the unhindered movement of goods and services between countries.

In the mid-1980s, Canada and the U.S. began a series of negotiations to see if they could reach a comprehensive free trade agreement. In early October 1987, after many months of tense negotiations, the two countries finally signed a Free Trade Agreement. Here is a summary of the main features of the FTA:

1. A binding mechanism will exist to settle trade disputes between the two countries. A panel of representatives from Canada and the United States will act as a final court of appeal to ensure the fair settlement of disputes.

2. There will be a complete elimination of all tariffs between the two countries by January 1, 1998. Some tariffs will end as soon as the Agreement goes into force. Others will be phased out over a five-year period, and the remainder over a ten-year period.

3. Canadian and U.S. service industries will be given the right to do business on either side of the border.

4. No export subsidies will be permitted on trade between Canada and the United States in agricultural products. Canada has agreed to increase its import quotas for poultry and eggs. Both countries have agreed to exempt each other from import restrictions on meat.

5. U.S. citizens and U.S.-controlled companies will receive the same treatment that Canadians receive in Canada. Canada will end the 25 percent foreign ownership restriction on Canadian-controlled financial institutions. The 10 percent limit on any one shareholder will be retained.

6. Canadian rules on foreign investment will be eased. Canada agrees to make permanent its policy of not restricting new U.S. investment, and agrees to limit the review of U.S. acquisitions of Canadian corporations.

7. The U.S. will be granted open access to the Canadian wine and liquor trade. The discriminatory practices of provincial liquor boards that favour Canadian or provincial wines and liquors will end.

8. Nondiscriminatory access of the U.S. to Canadian energy and secure markets for Canadian exports to the U.S. have been agreed on. Both sides agree to end restrictions on energy imports and exports.

Analyse the cartoon

RAESIDE Victoria Times-Colonist

Reprinted by permission of Adrian Raeside.

9. The production and Canadian content guarantees in the Auto Pact have been retained. Canadian subsidies in the form of favourable tariff treatment to encourage foreign car manufacturers to set up business in Canada are ended. The embargo on the import of used cars in Canada will be eliminated. Tariffs on tires, original equipment, and parts will be eliminated in ten years.

10. Cultural industries are largely exempt from the terms of the agreement on investment. Cultural industries include those engaged in book publishing, film, video, and audio production, and radio, television, cable, and satellite broadcasting.

From the Yukon to the Yucatan: The North American Free Trade Agreement

The ink was barely dry on the Free Trade Agreement (FTA) when the United States and Mexico began bilateral discussions on a free trade agreement. Later, Canada was invited to join the talks. Even though trade between Canada and Mexico is small, Canada formally entered the negotiations in February 1991 to preserve the gains made under the FTA. A tentative agreement was reached in 1992 and came into effect on January 1, 1994.

The FTA and NAFTA are separate agreements, but they have similar terms. The major terms include the following:

1. The gradual elimination of most tariffs between Canada and Mexico and Mexico and the United States over a ten-year period. In many cases, the tariff phase-out will be accomplished in a much shorter period, e.g., for such products as fertilizers, rail and industrial equipment, prefabricated housing, and auto parts.

2. Elimination of Mexican import licensing for goods.

3. Opening up of the Mexican market for U.S. and Canadian financial services companies: banks, securities firms, and insurance companies.

4. Liberalization of land transport — Canadian and U.S. truckers will be able to transport goods freely across the Mexican border after a six-year phase-in period.

5. Canada has retained exemptions for cultural industries and for health and social services.

6. Water in its natural state is not covered by NAFTA. Only when water is in the form of a commercial good — such as in bottles or tanks — will water exports be considered.

7. Canadian import quotas for eggs, poultry, and dairy products remain unaffected.

8. The dispute settlement mechanism in the FTA was extended to include Mexico.

9. A process for other countries in the Western Hemisphere to join the free trade alliance was established.

Characteristics of the NAFTA countries

Some of the main characteristics of the three NAFTA countries are given in table 16.2. Apart from the wide difference in size — the United States has about ten times the population and GDP of Canada — the two northern members of NAFTA have many common characteristics. Both had similar GDP per person in 1991. Both had roughly similar rates of economic growth and inflation in the period 1980-91; as well as a similar infant death rate, life expectancy, annual growth rates in population, and literacy rates. Income distribution was similar, although Canada had somewhat more equality than the United States.

Mexico, however, has a number of distinct differences from its two partners. Population is expected to grow by more than 60 percent, from 83 million — about three times Canada's 1991 population — to 136 million

Table 16.2 Characteristics of Mexico, Canada, and the United States

Population (millions)	Mexico	Canada	United States
mid-1991	83	27	253
2000 (est)	99	29	274
2025 (est)	136	34	319
GDP (millions of U.S. dollars), 1991	282 526	510 835	5 610 800
GNP per person, 1991	3030	20 440	22 240
Average annual growth rate in GNP per person, 1980-1991	−0.5	2.0	1.7
Inflation rate (average annual rate, 1980-1991)	66.5	4.3	4.2
Infant deaths (per 1000 live births), 1991	36	7	9
Life expectancy at birth	70	77	76
Average annual growth in population (percent)			
1970-80	2.9	1.2	1.0
1980-91	2.0	1.2	0.9
1991-2000	1.9	0.8	0.9
Adult illiteracy rate (percent)	13	less than 5	less than 5
Income distribution			
lowest 20%	4.1	5.7	4.7
second 20%	7.8	11.8	11.0
third 20%	12.3	17.7	17.4
fourth 20%	19.9	24.6	25.0
highest 20%	55.9	40.2	41.9

Source: The World Bank, *World Development Report 1993*, Oxford University Press.

by the year 2025. In the 1980s, Mexico's average GNP per person registered a decline; in Canada and the United States, the average GNP per person was positive. Mexico's rate of inflation in the 1980s was very high compared with that of Canada and the United States. Infant deaths per 1000 were much higher than in the two northern countries, while life expectancy was significantly lower. Income distribution was significantly less equal in Mexico than in the United States and Canada.

In the mid-1980s, in an attempt to revitalize its stagnant economy, Mexico undertook a program of economic liberalization. Average tariff rates were slashed from 25 to 10 percent. Many non-tariff barriers were eliminated. Mexico joined GATT. The privatization of state-owned industries began, and stiff rules on foreign investment were relaxed. The policy of promoting Mexican industry through the protection of high tariffs and quotas was revised. It was hoped that these policies would help revive the sagging Mexican economy.

Three perspectives on NAFTA

With about 363 million people and a total GDP of about $6¼ trillion (U.S.), NAFTA rivalled the smaller European Union with 326 million people and $5 trillion (U.S.) in 1991. Each of the three NAFTA countries has supporters and opponents of the Agreement. Let's examine the Agreement from the perspective of each country.

Canada

In Canada, the issue of free trade with Mexico produced a lot of debate. The Canadian Labour Congress argued that low wages in Mexico — about 7.5 times lower than those in Canada in 1993 —combined with Mexico's lax enforcement of its environmental protection laws with free trade between the two countries will result in Canadian jobs being lost to Mexico. Businesses, it is argued, will be attracted by the lower costs of production. Industries at risk are those which are labour-intensive, such as the manufacture of footwear, textiles, clothing, furniture, electronic components, and wood products.

Supporters of the Agreement argue that it is likely to have little immediate impact, since Canadian tariffs on Mexican products are low — averaging only 3 to 5 percent. Indeed, the amount of trade between the two countries is very small compared to their trade with the U.S. (See table 16.2.) They argue that Canada's participation in the Agreement was important to conserve the gains made in the FTA. For example, if Canada did not have a free trade agreement with Mexico but the United States did, then companies would tend to favour U.S. locations over Canadian ones because they would be able to sell in all three markets duty-free, whereas if they located in Canada they would only be able to sell in two markets duty-free. A study by a chartered accounting firm, Ernst and Young, suggested that several sectors should benefit from NAFTA. These included telecommunications, transportation equipment, biotechnology, financial services, information technology, and construction.

In telecommunications, for example, the Mexican telephone system has recently been privatized, but it can take several tries before a call is completed. Mexico averages only one telephone for fifteen residents — a fraction of the number in Canada and the United States. Thus, there's a large market for Canadian telecommunications equipment.

Similarly, most Mexicans don't have bank accounts and have never written a cheque. Canadians have one of the best networks of financial services in the world. Canadian financial institutions are therefore likely to play a part in helping Mexicans handle their money.

Mexico

The United States is Mexico's most important trading partner, taking 70 percent of Mexican exports and supplying 65 percent of Mexican imports. Merchandise exports accounted for about 18 percent of Mexican GDP. Before NAFTA, the average Mexican spent $450 U.S. on goods from its northern neighbour. Mexico is the United States' third most important trading partner (after Canada and Japan). The principal Mexican exports are petrochemicals, motor vehicles, engines and parts, plastics, parts for machinery, and oil. Mexico's principal imports before 1994 included gasoline, soybeans, grains, aircraft, motor vehicle assembly equipment, and computer equipment and parts.

Supporters of NAFTA point to the advantages they expect Mexico would enjoy from the Agreement. Mexico would gain assured access to its biggest market and, as tariffs decline, it would gain an advantage over its competitors (e.g., Brazil, Thailand, and South Korea) in the U.S. market. The existence of a large —and comparatively cheap — labour force and the world's richest free trade area will affect Canadian, U.S., Japanese, and other countries' investments. Thus, Mexico will be able to resume the economic growth of the four decades prior to 1980 and overcome stagnation and decline. Politically, too, it may give a new lease on life to Mexico's faltering but long-ruling party since the 1920s, the Institutional Revolutionary Party, which has never lost a national election.

However, the effects will not all be one-sided. Critics of the Agreement point to a number of disadvantages for Mexico. One fear of Mexicans (which many Canadians would understand) is the threat to their culture as a result of increased exposure to U.S. influence. Another is that U.S. investment will pour into the country and take over much of the economy. Thus, the unskilled, low-paying jobs will be performed by Mexicans, while the plum jobs will be held by Americans. Another fear — which in part led to the Chiapas uprising of the Zapatistas in southern Mexico in 1994 — is that the import of cheap grains from Canada and the U.S. will undercut the economic basis of the life of the peasant farmers, forcing their migration to the big cities. Many, too, wonder how well Mexican industry will manage. It has just begun to learn to walk after having been weaned from a diet of subsidies and protection by tariffs. Many wonder how well it will be able to compete in a race with U.S. industry.

The United States

For the United States, politics and economics are both important factors in the free trade negotiations. Some Americans believe that a free trade agreement with Mexico is a way of promoting the economic and political health of Mexico and improved relations between the two countries, thus helping ensure that the U.S. has a stable southern neighbour. In addition, a prosperous Mexico is one way of stemming the flow of illegal immigrants — estimated in the millions — into the United States.

Mexico, with a rapidly growing population, already the United States' third most important trading partner, has the potential of becoming even more important. The free trade agreement can open up the Mexican market further for those products in which the U.S. has a comparative advantage, e.g., capital equipment, household appliances, plastics, rubber, chemicals and many foodstuffs.

Many, however, are afraid that the laxer enforcement of weaker environmental protection laws and lower wage rates (about one-seventh of those in the U.S.) will cause many firms to leave the U.S. and set up business in Mexico. Thus, many jobs would be lost in labour-intensive industries, such as clothing, furniture, leather, glass, and aspects of the fruit and vegetable industries. Many U.S. industries have already migrated to the Mexican side of the 3000 km border. There, many U.S. border factories (called *maquiladoras*) have been established. Raw materials are imported duty-free by the *maquiladoras*. Products are exported to the U.S. with tariffs paid only on the value added to the products in Mexico.

The impact of NAFTA

The overall impact of NAFTA on Canada in the short term is likely to be fairly modest. As we have seen, the amount of trade between Canada and Mexico in 1993 was small and Canadian tariffs on imports from Mexico were low, averaging about 3 percent. In the long term, though, the Agreement should have a more substantial impact. If, as many expect, NAFTA provides a spur to economic growth in Mexico, then the country's importance as a trading partner for Canada should grow.

NAFTA may provide a model for an American Free Trade Area (AFTA). Already, some South American

Summary

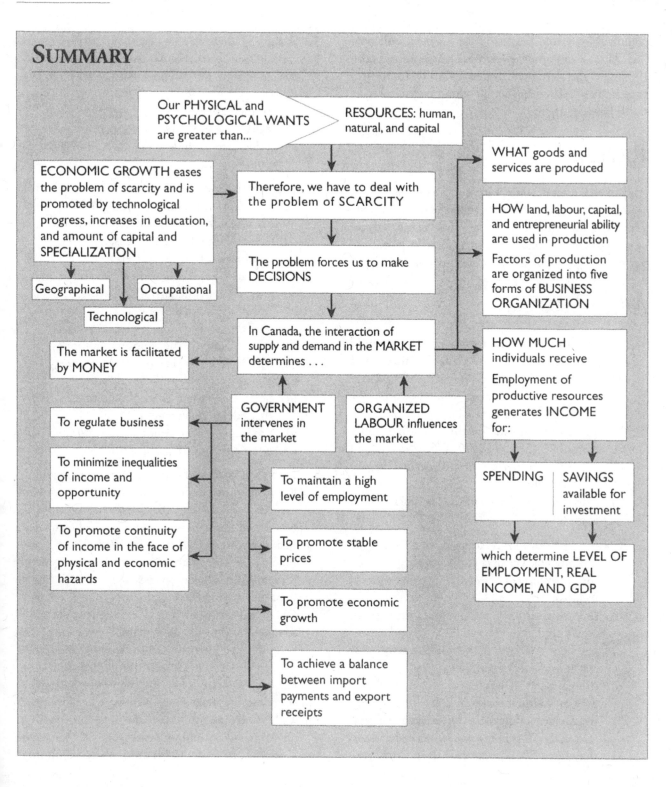

Our PHYSICAL and PSYCHOLOGICAL WANTS are greater than...

RESOURCES: human, natural, and capital

Therefore, we have to deal with the problem of SCARCITY

ECONOMIC GROWTH eases the problem of scarcity and is promoted by technological progress, increases in education, and amount of capital and SPECIALIZATION

Geographical

Occupational

Technological

The problem forces us to make DECISIONS

In Canada, the interaction of supply and demand in the MARKET determines . . .

The market is facilitated by MONEY

GOVERNMENT intervenes in the market

ORGANIZED LABOUR influences the market

To regulate business

To minimize inequalities of income and opportunity

To promote continuity of income in the face of physical and economic hazards

To maintain a high level of employment

To promote stable prices

To promote economic growth

To achieve a balance between import payments and export receipts

WHAT goods and services are produced

HOW land, labour, capital, and entrepreneurial ability are used in production

Factors of production are organized into five forms of BUSINESS ORGANIZATION

HOW MUCH individuals receive

Employment of productive resources generates INCOME for:

SPENDING | SAVINGS available for investment

which determine LEVEL OF EMPLOYMENT, REAL INCOME, AND GDP

countries — Chile heads the list — have indicated their interest in joining. Meanwhile, Argentina, Brazil, Paraguay, and Uruguay united in 1995 to form a group called "Mercosur," with the purpose of lowering tariffs between them.

REVIEW

Explain each term or concept in your own words with an example where appropriate: international trade, absolute advantage, comparative advantage, tariff, quota, balance of trade, balance of trade on current account, balance of payments, fixed exchange rates, flexible exchange rates.

APPLICATIONS

1. Assuming no other changes, what effects would the following have on the Canadian forest and forest-products industries? In each case, explain how you arrived at your conclusion.
   a) a recession in the United States
   b) an increase in value of the Canadian dollar from $.73 (U.S.) to $.90 (U.S.)
   c) a boom (or period of prosperity) in the United States
   d) a decline in the value of the Canadian dollar from $.90 (U.S.) to $.73 (U.S.)

2. Classify the following according to whether they are visible or invisible Canadian imports or exports.
   a) the expenditures of New Brunswick tourists in Japan
   b) the expenditures of Japanese tourists in Newfoundland
   c) payments by Canadian business people for travel on American airlines
   d) the payment of interest on bonds by Nova Scotian municipalities to U.S. bondholders
   e) the payment of dividends by Canadian subsidiaries in the West Indies to Quebec shareholders
   f) the sale of P.E.I. potatoes in New York.

3. Assuming no other changes and a floating exchange rate, what effect(s) would each of the following have on the exchange value of the Canadian dollar?
   a) an increase in Canadian exports
   b) a decrease in Canadian exports
   c) a decrease in the exchange value of the U.S. dollar

4. Suppose that over the last few years, Canada has been experiencing a balance of payments deficit. Which of the following would help reduce the deficit? Explain why in each case.
   a) a reduction in duty-free exemptions for Canadian tourists when they return to Canada
   b) a decrease in the airport departure tax
   c) the introduction of a departure tax for Canadian licensed vehicles at the border
   d) restrictions on the amount of money that can be taken or sent out of the country
   e) provision of subsidies to exports
   f) permission for increased energy exports by the federal government
   g) the imposition of quotas on imports
   h) a temporary increase in tariffs on imports

5. If you had noticed the license plates in the parking lots of shopping centres in many American towns and cities close to the U.S.-Canada border in 1991, you would have found an abundance of Canadian plates: many B.C. plates in Washington state; many Manitoba plates in North Dakota; many Ontario and Québec plates in New York State; many New Brunswick plates in Maine. Two-and-a-half years later, in June 1994, you would have found far fewer Canadian plates. Why? One of the reasons is the fluctuation in cross-border shopping.

   Same-day car trips to the United States — considered to be a key indicator of cross-border shopping — peaked at 5.3 million in November 1991. These cross-border excursions were draining an estimated $5 billion a year from the Canadian economy. By June 1994, cross-border shopping sprees had decreased steadily to a seasonally adjusted 3 million trips. Explain what effect (if any) each of the following had on cross-border shopping by Canadians.

a) Decline in the value of the Canadian dollar from 88 cents U.S. in November 1991 to 72 cents U.S. in June 1994.

b) Introduction of the GST in January 1991.

c) In central and eastern Canada, deep cuts in federal and provincial taxes on cigarettes in the spring of 1994 and increased taxes on cigarettes in the U.S.

d) Increased gasoline prices in the U.S.

e) Lower prices and better service by Canadian retailers.

6. As you read the following parable, contrast the people's attitude to Consolidated Alchemy Limited at first, with the attitude later, and suggest reasons for the difference in attitude.

The Rise and Fall of Consolidated Alchemy Limited

A Parable of the Twentieth Century

During the last quarter of the twentieth century, an adventurous entrepreneur bought a thousand hectares of the Great Dismal Swamp in coastal British Columbia. After draining the land and building a road and rail spur, the mysterious entrepreneur, Ms. T., built a 4 metre electrified fence around her entire property, posted guards at the gates, and allowed no one to enter except her own trusted employees. She advertised for workers, offering $20.00 per hour, and hired 5000 workers, all sworn to secrecy. Ms. T. announced that she had made several scientific discoveries and inventions which enabled her to transform coal, wheat, lumber, copper, iron ore, petroleum and other products into a variety of finished products, including textiles, automobiles, shoes, cameras, watches,

chemicals, and TV sets. Within a few months, vast quantities of materials were pouring into Ms. T.'s guarded compound from all parts of the country. A flood of low-priced industrial and consumer goods began to pour out of Ms. T.'s gates and into the nation's markets, where househusbands, housewives, and industrialists eagerly bought them at prices 20 to 30 percent below the competition. Ms. T.'s company, Consolidated Alchemy Limited (CAL), reported large profits, and was soon listed on the Vancouver, Toronto, and Montreal stock exchanges, where it became the favourite of investors.

Meantime, the nation hailed Ms. T. as a genius and benefactor of humanity, a woman whose inventions greatly increased the productivity of labour and improved the standard of living of the masses. She was favourably compared to both J. Armand Bombardier and Sir Frederick Banting.

It is true that grumbles were heard in some quarters. Several manufacturers of TV sets tried to prevent their dealers from stocking or servicing CAL sets; textile manufacturers tried to persuade Parliament to establish production quotas for each firm based on average output in the previous 50 years; a labour union picketed stores carrying CAL merchandise; and two provincial legislatures passed laws requiring that stores display "Buy central Canada" posters. None of these activities had much effect, however. Buyers could not resist the low CAL prices, and many communities were prospering because of their rapidly increasing sales to Consolidated Alchemy. Parliament resounded with speeches calling upon the people to accept the necessity for economic adjustment and urging the benefits of technological change.

As for coastal British Columbia, it was booming as never before. Schools, houses, and roads were constructed, the Great Dismal Swamp was drained and used for market gardens, its extraordinarily fertile land was selling for $6000 per hectare; employment expanded, and average wages rose to $30.00 per hour.

Then one Sunday morning, a small boy, vacationing with his family at a nearby seaside resort, tried out his new skin-diving equipment, penetrated Ms. T.'s underwater screen, and observed that Consolidated Alchemy's "factories" were nothing but warehouses and that its "secret technical process" was nothing but trade. Ms. T. was, in fact, a hoax; her firm was nothing but a giant import-export business. She bought vast quantities of materials from Canadian producers, loaded them under cover of night onto a fleet of ships, and carried them off to foreign markets where she exchanged them for the variety of goods that she sold throughout Canada at such low prices.

When the boy told what he had seen, newspapers and television picked up the story and within 24 hours, Ms. T. was denounced as a fraud, her operation was shut down, her thousands of high-paid workers were thrown out of work, and her company was bankrupt. Several MPs declared that the Canadian standard of living had been protected from a serious threat of competition from cheap foreign labour and urged higher expenditures for research in industrial technology.

a) What was the general attitude of people toward CAL at first? Why?

b) How did some people attempt to restrict its activities?

c) What was the general attitude of people to CAL after its true nature had been discovered? Why?

d) What arguments in favour of restraining imports are not really examined in the parable?

e) Does the parable provide a convincing argument for the abolition of restrictions on imports? Explain.

f) Are there any circumstances in which imports should be restricted? Explain.

ISSUE
Free trade with the United States and Mexico

Debate the following resolution: "Be it resolved that Mexico will gain most from the North American Free Trade Agreement."

Glossary

ABSOLUTE ADVANTAGE the ability of one person, region, or country to produce a good or a service at a cost lower than a competitor's. Brazil has an absolute advantage in the production of coffee over Canada. Manitoba has an absolute advantage in the production of wheat over Ontario.

ADVERTISING the means that producers use to inform consumers about the distinctive features of products, with the purpose of convincing consumers to buy their products.

ARBITRATION an arrangement in a dispute in which both labour and management agree to accept the decision(s) of a third party, or arbitrator. The arbitrator's decision is final and binding on both parties.

AUTOMATIC STABILIZERS changes in taxation and expenditures that occur automatically with changes in the levels of employment, income, and output. These changes have the effect of stabilizing the economy. Examples include unemployment insurance, welfare payments, and personal and corporate income taxes. For instance, unemployment insurance payments increase as unemployment increases and decrease as unemployment decreases. Unemployment insurance payments thus act to stabilize the economy automatically.

AUTOMATION the automatic and self-regulatory control by machines of the whole, or a part, of a process of production. The use of robots on automobile assembly lines is an example of automation.

BALANCE OF PAYMENTS the summary of all the visible, invisible, and capital transactions that have taken place between one country and the rest of the world over a period of time — usually a year. Included in the balance of payments calculations are visible and invisible imports and exports, and capital imports and exports.

BALANCE OF TRADE the difference between the value of merchandise (or visible) exports and the value of merchandise (or visible) imports. The balance of trade is favourable if the country exports more than it imports, and unfavourable if the country imports more than it exports.

BALANCE OF TRADE ON CURRENT ACCOUNT the difference between the money value of a country's visible and invisible exports and the value of its visible and invisible imports.

BANK OF CANADA Canada's central bank. The Bank of Canada plays a vital role in the economy through its control of the money supply and its influence on the value of the Canadian dollar in terms of other currencies.

BANK RATE the interest rate charged by the Bank of Canada on loans it makes to chartered banks. The bank rate influences the rates of interest that banks charge their customers.

BOND a written promise to pay a stated sum of money at some time in the future. Until that time, interest is paid on stated dates. The best known bonds in Canada are Canada Savings Bonds.

BOYCOTT a collective refusal by supporters of a union to buy or use goods or services supplied by a firm or an industry in which a labour dispute is taking place.

BRANCH BANKING SYSTEM a system with few banks, each with a large number of branches; contrasts with the unit banking system, e.g., that in the United States, where there are more than 15 000 separate banks. Canada has a branch banking system.

BUDGET a financial plan that shows expected income and expenditures, and indicates the anticipated surplus or deficit.

BUSINESS CYCLE the ups and downs of the economy that follow a cyclical pattern over the course of time. The economy moves through four phases: trough, recovery, peak, and recession. Government tries to manage the economy through fiscal and monetary measures to prevent large swings in the business cycle.

CAPITAL DEPRECIATION any decrease in the value of capital equipment (buildings and machinery) used in production.

CAPITAL RESOURCES goods that are used in the production of other goods or services. Factories, machines, and tools are, for example, capital goods.

CARTEL (or COMBINE) an organization of independent producers that enter into an agreement to fix output or prices. Such agreements are usually illegal. The best-known example of a cartel is the Organization of Petroleum Exporting Countries (OPEC).

CASH-RESERVE REQUIREMENT a means of control exercised by the Bank of Canada to influence the lending abilities of the commercial banks. The chartered banks are required to keep a minimum reserve (also called a fractional reserve) of a certain percentage against their deposit liabilities in the form of either Bank of Canada notes or deposits with the Bank of Canada.

CEILING (or MAXIMUM) PRICE the highest price that may be charged legally for a good or service. Rent controls are an example of a ceiling price.

CETERIS PARIBUS a term meaning "other things being equal."

CHARTERED BANKS financial institutions that make loans and accept deposits. Chartered banks are established by government charter and are regulated by Parliament. The Bank of Montreal and the Bank of Nova Scotia are two of the largest chartered banks in Canada.

CHEQUE an order to pay an individual or a group of individuals a particular amount of money from a chequing account.

CIRCULAR FLOW a graphic representation that traces the exchange of goods and services in the economy. The use of money in the economy results in a two-way circular flow — of goods and services in one direction and money in the other direction — between the public, business, government, and other countries.

CLOSED SHOP a business in which only union members are allowed to work.

COLLECTIVE AGREEMENT a contract negotiated by representatives of union and management that sets out points of agreement and that includes procedures to be followed in the event of a dispute over the terms of the contract.

COLLECTIVE BARGAINING the negotiation between representatives of workers and employer(s) with the purpose of establishing terms and conditions of employment that are acceptable to both sides.

COMBINATION the amalgamation of firms to lessen or eliminate competition among themselves. Canada has anti-combines legislation to curb the development of monopolistic practices.

COMBINE *See* CARTEL.

COMMAND ECONOMY an economy in which government, or some other central controlling body, provides the answers to the three major questions: what, why, and for whom. The Soviet Union had a largely command economy.

COMMON SHARES securities that corporations offer to the public, enabling the shareowner to become a part-owner of the corporation with the right to vote in the affairs of the corporation and a right to share in its distributed profits.

COMPARATIVE ADVANTAGE the ability of one person, region, or country to provide a good or a service relatively more cheaply than other goods or services.

CONCILIATION (MEDIATION) a situation in a dispute in which both labour and management agree to submit their proposals to a third party, known as a conciliator or mediator. The conciliator, or the conciliation board, attempts to bring the two sides to an agreement.

CONGLOMERATE an organization that is formed when companies in unrelated industries combine. Canadian Pacific Limited is one example. It is involved in rail, ship, and truck transportation; energy; forest products; real estate and hotel operations; telecommunications; industrial products; engineering and construction services; and waste management.

CONSUMER CREDIT the ability to acquire goods and services now in exchange for payments in the future. A credit card, for example, allows us to buy goods now in exchange for payments in the future.

CONSUMER PRICE INDEX (CPI) a measure of the general changes in market prices of a selected group of goods and services purchased by a typical urban family. This price index is computed each month by Statistics Canada. It is widely used to show the rate of inflation and helps to show whether there has been real growth in the economy. In 1990, the Consumer Price Index was estimated at 117.0.

CONSUMER SOVEREIGNTY the dominant role of the consumer in a market economy determining what, how, and for whom to produce.

CONSUMPTION that part of an individual's income that is spent on goods and services rather than saved.

CONTRACT a collective agreement reached by labour and management; the set of rules and regulations governing labour-management relations that results from the collective bargaining process. Contracts apply to a definite period of time.

COOPERATIVE a form of business organization that members control and in which they share in the profit; it benefits its owners through lower prices and/or distribution of surpluses at the end of the year. The shareholder (or member) of the co-operative has only one vote. In consumers' cooperatives, members buy from the cooperative; in producers' cooperatives, members sell to it. Cooperatives are especially important in the Maritime provinces, Québec, and the Prairie provinces.

CORPORATION a form of business organization that has a legal existence of its own, separate from those who created it or own it. Many big businesses in Canada, such as Canadian Pacific Railway and General Motors, are corporations.

COST OF LIVING ALLOWANCE (COLA) an allowance demanded by many labour unions as part of collective agreements. With COLAs, wages rise along with increases in the general level of prices (the cost of living).

COST-PUSH (or SELLERS') INFLATION occurs when wages or other costs rise and these increased costs are passed along in the form of higher prices. Costs are "pushed up" by rising prices. Cost-push inflation can occur when there is widespread unemployment and sluggish demand. Cost-push inflation was common in the 1970s and early 1980s. One of the causes was the massive increase in oil prices brought about by the actions of OPEC.

CRAFT UNION a union with a membership restricted to workers with a particular trade. The International Printing and Graphic Workers Union is a craft union.

CREDIT UNIONS savings and loan associations owned and operated by consumers with a common goal. Trade unions and professional associations are two groups that often establish credit unions.

CROWN CORPORATIONS federally or provincially owned corporations established to provide goods or services for the public; also known as "public enterprises"; Canada Post and Air Canada are two examples of federally owned Crown corporations. Hydro Québec and Ontario Hydro are examples of provincially owned Crown corporations.

CYCLICAL UNEMPLOYMENT a result of inadequate demand during the declining economic activity of the business cycle. The high rates of unemployment in Canada in the 1930s and the early 1980s are examples of cyclical unemployment.

DECISION LAG the time that passes between recognizing a problem and deciding what to do about it. Decision lags limit the effectiveness of government fiscal and monetary policies.

DEFICIT the result of expenditures exceeding revenues.

DEFLATION a decrease in the general level of prices over time. In periods of deflation, the purchasing power of money rises. The early 1930s are an example of a deflationary period.

DEMAND the quantities of a good or service that buyers are willing and able to buy at various prices in a particular period of time.

DEMAND CURVE a graphic representation of the quantities of a good or service that buyers are willing and able to purchase at various prices.

DEMAND DEPOSIT money withdrawn from a chequing account on demand.

DEMAND-PULL INFLATION inflation caused by excessive total spending or demand compared to the total amount of goods or services that can be produced in the economy. Demand "pulls up" prices. Demand-pull inflation is therefore often described as "too much money chasing too few goods." In the 1940s, following World War II, Canada experienced a period of demand-pull inflation.

DEMAND SCHEDULE a chart showing the relationship between the price of a product and the quantity demanded.

DEPRECIATION any decrease in the value of capital goods (such as machinery and vehicles) due to technology, to wear and tear, or to the passage of time. Depreciation is a business cost.

DEPRESSION a prolonged period of greatly reduced economic activity, with little investment, high unemployment, declining prices, and many business failures. A depression is more severe than a recession, and lasts for a longer period of time. The most famous depression — known as the Great Depression — occurred in the 1930s.

DIFFERENTIATED OLIGOPOLY a kind of market in which companies strive to make their products distinctive, or different from their competitors'. Examples of differentiated products include such items as automobiles, tires, and breakfast cereals.

DIRECT INVESTMENT investment that entails ownership or control of a corporation. Direct investment can be made to establish or take over a business already in existence. Much U.S. investment in Canada has been in the form of direct investment.

DIRECT TAX a tax that is levied on and directly paid by a person or corporation and that cannot be shifted to others. Federal and provincial income taxes and provincial sales taxes are examples of direct taxes.

DISCOURAGED WORKERS people who would like to work but who have stopped looking for employment because they believe there are no jobs for them.

DISCRETIONARY FISCAL POLICY when government acts to change its taxation and its expenditure policies deliberately to influence the levels of income, output, and employment.

In a period of recession, for example, government may cut taxes and increase spending to raise the levels of income, output, and employment.

DISTRIBUTION the way in which the four forms of income (rent, wages, interest, and profit) are allocated among productive factors (land, labour, capital, and entrepreneurial ability).

ECONOMIC EFFICIENCY the use of economic resources in a way to produce goods and services at the minimum cost.

ECONOMIC FREEDOM the freedom of choice for workers, for consumers, and for business people.

ECONOMIC GROWTH the increase over a period of time — usually a year — in a country's (or a region's) output of goods and services. Economic growth is usually measured by the annual rate of increase in the real Gross Domestic Product (GDP) per person.

ECONOMICS the study of human activity involved in using scarce resources to satisfy wants.

ELASTICITY OF DEMAND the responsiveness of the quantity demanded to a change in price. Luxury items (such as expensive automobiles) tend to have *elastic demand* (in other words, quantity demanded is responsive to changes in price); essential goods (such as bread and electrical energy) tend to have *inelastic demand* because consumers cannot readily avoid using them.

ELASTICITY OF SUPPLY the ability of suppliers to increase the amount of a particular product in response to increased demand over a given period of time.

EMBARGO a ban on, or prohibition against, the import or export of certain goods.

ENTREPRENEURS individuals who start their own business or who aggressively expand existing ones. They organize the other productive factors (land, labour, and capital) for the purpose of producing goods or services, and assume the risks involved in running the business.

EQUILIBRIUM (PRICE) the price at which the quantity demanded for a product is equal to the quantity supplied. Another term for equilibrium price is market-clearing price.

EQUITIES investments in those things that we can both see and touch. The most common forms of equity investments are in homes (real estate) and in the common stocks of corporations.

EUROPEAN UNION (EU) an economic integration of member nations into a single European market based on the free movement — with certain exceptions — of goods, services, capital, and persons throughout the member countries.

EXCHANGE RATE the price of one currency, expressed in terms of another.

EXPORTS goods and services that are produced in one country and are then shipped to or sold in another country. Wood pulp produced in Newfoundland, Labrador, or Québec and sold in the United States is a Canadian export.

EXTERNALITY a side effect of production or consumption that may be harmful or beneficial. Pollution of air or water, for example, is a harmful side effect of the production of pulp and paper.

FEDERAL PUBLIC (or NATIONAL) DEBT the total amount owed by the federal government, to Canadians and foreigners, in the form of government bonds. The debt is a result of federal government budget deficits (when expenditures were greater than revenues) in the past.

FISCAL POLICY changes in government taxing and spending for the purpose of bringing about changes in the economy. In periods of high unemployment, government may adopt an *expansionary fiscal policy* of tax cuts and/or increased government spending. In periods of high inflation, government may adopt a *contractionary fiscal policy* of spending cuts and/or increased taxes.

FLOOR PRICE the minimum price below which it is illegal to buy or sell a good or a service. The minimum wage is an example of a floor price.

FRACTIONAL RESERVE also called cash reserve; a minimum reserve of a certain percentage against a bank's deposit liabilities in the form of either Bank of Canada notes or deposits with the Bank of Canada.

FRANCHISE a license or privilege granted by a corporation (the franchiser) to another corporation or individual (the franchisee) to sell a particular product or service with an advertised trade name. Many Tim Hortons donut shops are franchises.

FREE TRADE international trade that takes place without the obstacles of tariffs or other barriers to the unhindered movement of goods and services between countries. In 1987, Canada and the United States signed the Free Trade Agreement (FTA). On January 1, 1994, the North American Free Trade Agreement (NAFTA) came into effect; it was signed by Canada, the United States, and Mexico.

FRICTIONAL UNEMPLOYMENT temporary unemployment due to the time required to change jobs.

FRINGE BENEFITS payments and services other than wages or salary that are provided by an employer. Fringe benefits include vacations with pay and pension plans.

FULL EMPLOYMENT an unemployment rate of between 6 and 7 percent. Generally, an economy is not functioning satisfactorily if more than 6 or 7 percent of the working population is unemployed.

GENERAL AGREEMENT ON TRADE AND TARIFFS (GATT) an agreement signed by about 90 countries, including Canada and the United States, based on three main principles: equal non-discriminatory treatment for all member nations; general reduction of tariffs; and the elimination of non-tariff barriers (e.g., quotas) to trade. GATT member nations meet periodically to renegotiate the Agreement.

GOODS all concrete, visible things that satisfy human wants, that can be touched, and that last a period of time. Goods include essentials such as bread, and non-essentials such as diamonds.

GOODS AND SERVICES TAX (GST) a tax introduced on January 1, 1991 that taxes goods (such as automobiles) as well as services (such as haircuts). Goods produced in Canada but which are to be exported are GST-free, while imports are subject to the full GST.

GROSS DOMESTIC PRODUCT (GDP) a measurement of the total value at market prices of all final goods and services produced in Canada, i.e., domestically, over a period of time (usually a year). It differs from GROSS NATIONAL PRODUCT (GNP) in that it includes the output of foreign-owned productive resources in Canada and excludes the output of Canadian-owned productive resources located outside Canada.

GROSS NATIONAL PRODUCT (GNP) a measurement of the total value at market prices of all final *Canadian-owned* goods and services — no matter where they may be produced — in a particular time period (usually a year). Real GNP is GNP adjusted to changes in the value of the dollar. In the past, GNP was a widely used indicator of the health of an economy. *See* GROSS DOMESTIC PRODUCT (GDP) above.

HIGH INCOME ECONOMIES those with a GNP per person of $7911 U.S. or more in 1991.

HOLDING COMPANY a company that is set up to own or hold a significant proportion of the shares of one or more other companies (e.g., 51 percent), and thus control the activities of these companies and eliminate competition; a form of combination.

HOMOGENEOUS OLIGOPOLY a kind of market in which the goods produced by competing companies are so similar as to be virtually identical. For example, steel of a particular kind and quality produced by one company is almost indistinguishable from that of another steel company.

HORIZONTAL COMBINATION a situation in which a company takes over another company of the same type, thus getting rid of a competitor and gaining a wider share of the market. In the late 1970s and early 1980s, the Hudson's Bay Company took over Zellers and Simpsons.

HUMAN RESOURCES the services provided by workers (manual as well as non-manual); the skills and efforts that people use in an economy or a firm to produce goods and services; often called labour. Human resources include the productive services of farmers and factory workers as well as those of scientists and architects.

HYPERINFLATION extremely high rates of inflation; that is, extremely high increases in the general level of prices over a period of time. In times of hyperinflation, the purchasing power of money decreases at a rapid rate. Germany in the early 1920s suffered from a period of hyperinflation.

IMPLEMENTATION LAG the time that passes between deciding what to do about a problem and implementing a solution. Implementation lags limit the effectiveness of government fiscal policies.

IMPORTS goods and services that are produced in one country but consumed in another. If the sugar you sprinkled on your cereal this morning was produced outside Canada, then it was a Canadian import.

INCOME INEQUALITY the unequal distribution of income among individuals. If the degree of inequality is large, the beneficial effects of a country's economic growth will not be felt by everyone.

INDIRECT TAX a tax that can be passed on to others. Tariffs on imported automobiles may be paid by an importer, who adds the cost of the tariff to the price of the car. It is the consumer who finally pays the cost of the tariff.

INDUSTRIAL UNION a union with a membership consisting of skilled and unskilled workers in a particular industry. The Canadian Auto Workers is an industrial union.

INFLATION the general increase in the prices of goods and services over a period of time. In inflationary periods, the purchasing power of money decreases. Inflation is generally recognized to be of two types: *demand-pull* and *cost-push* inflation. During the 1970s and early 1980s, Canada and many other countries experienced high levels of inflation.

INSURANCE a contract in which one party (the insurer) agrees to pay another (the insured) a sum of money in the event of a specific loss. Insurance protects against losses due to death, sickness, accident, and fire. In return, the insured makes payments (premiums) to the insurer. Term insurance is an example of life insurance.

INTEREST the price paid to a lender for the use of a sum of money over a period of time.

INTERNATIONAL UNION a union that has a membership based in more than one country. The International Brotherhood of Electrical Workers is an example of an international union.

INVESTMENT money that is spent by business people on capital goods such as machines and factories.

INVISIBLE TRADE the import or export of services, investment income of foreigners, and transfers; these parts of trade cannot be seen or touched.

LABOUR UNION a recognized (i.e., certified) organization of workers that negotiates matters of wages, working conditions, and benefits with employers. The Canadian Union of Public Employees and the United Steelworkers of America are two of the largest labour unions in Canada.

LAW OF DIMINISHING MARGINAL UTILITY the law stating that each additional unit of a good consumed at any given time yields less satisfaction than the one previously consumed.

LAW OF DOWNWARD-SLOPING DEMAND the law stating that when the price of a good is raised (and there are no other changes), less of it will be demanded. If a large amount of a good is put on the market (and there are no other changes), then it can only be sold at a lower price. If the price of a good is lowered (and there are no other changes), then the quantity demanded will increase.

LEGAL MONOPOLY a market situation that exists when government makes it illegal for more than one company to supply a good or a service. Many municipal transit systems have a legal monopoly on public transit in their area.

LIMITED LIABILITY the risk that is restricted to the amount invested in a company. Should the company go bankrupt, the liability of any one of the owners is limited to the extent of that owner's financial interest in the firm.

LOCKOUT the closing of a business by management in a dispute with labour. Management may lock out the workers if it does not want to meet the union's demands.

LOW INCOME ECONOMIES those with a GNP per person of less than $635 U.S. in 1991.

MACRO-ECONOMICS the study of the economy as a whole. A study of the overall level of consumption, investment, government spending, prices, and employment in an economy is an example of macro-economics.

MARKET any network that brings buyers and sellers into contact with one another so they can exchange goods and services. A market need not be located in a particular geographical location. The Montreal Stock Exchange is an example of a market for corporation shares.

MARKET CLEARING PRICE *See* EQUILIBRIUM (PRICE).

MARKET ECONOMY an economy in which the uncoordinated actions of buyers and sellers of goods, services, and resources direct the economic system.

MEDIATION *See* CONCILIATION.

MERGER the combining of the assets of two or more companies into a single company. Mergers are usually the result of one company taking over another company.

MICRO-ECONOMICS the study of the economic actions of individuals and groups of individuals, such as consumers, households, and businesses. The study of the demand, supply, and price of French fries in your school cafeteria is an example of micro-economics.

MIDDLE INCOME ECONOMIES those with a GNP per person of more than $635 U.S., but less than $7911 U.S. in 1991.

MINIMUM WAGE the lowest wage that an employer may pay a worker. Minimum wages are set by the federal and provincial governments for workers under their jurisdictions. In 1994, the provincial minimum wage ranged from $5.00 an hour (Alberta) to $6.70 an hour (Ontario) for employees aged 18 and over.

MIXED MARKET ECONOMY an economy in which decisions about the allocation of resources are determined partly by the actions of individuals buying and selling in the market and partly by government. Today, Canada and many other Western industrialized nations have mixed market economies. Also called a modified market economy.

MONETARY POLICY government policy to bring about changes in the money supply. The federal government, through its agent the Bank of Canada, controls the banking system by influencing interest rates and the money supply in order to achieve full employment and price stability. The Bank of Canada may pursue an *easy* (or *expansionary*) *money policy* by lowering interest rates, thereby increasing the demand for loans, or a *tight money policy* by raising interest rates, thereby decreasing the demand for loans.

MONETARY RULE legislation by which the money supply would increase by the same rates as the annual increase in potential GDP; a policy advocated by economist Milton Friedman.

MONEY anything that people are willing to accept as payment for goods or services. In the past, Canada's money has included beaver pelts, brass and copper tokens, and playing cards.

MONEY SUPPLY (M1) the total amount of currency in circulation, plus the total amount held in chequing accounts by individuals and businesses. Money has three principle uses: as a medium of exchange, as a measure of value, and as a store of value.

MONOPOLISTIC COMPETITION a market situation in which there are many sellers providing a similar but not identical good or service. Examples include the markets for fast food and haircuts.

MONOPOLY a market situation in which there is only one producer of a good or service and many buyers. Local telephone service, for example, is usually supplied by one producer.

MORAL SUASION a means by which the governor of the Bank of Canada tries to persuade the chartered banks to vary their lending policies in the best interests of the country.

MORTGAGE money borrowed from a financial institution such as a bank or trust company that is used to buy a home.

MULTIPLIER EFFECT the magnification of a change in expenditure or a change in the tax level to larger changes in output and income. If government increases its public works expenditures by $1 million, this will have the effect of generating income that is a multiple of the $1 million.

MUTUAL FUND an investment in the stock market in which a large number of small investors get the same advantages as large investors: diversification (the spreading of risk) and professional management. There are five different kinds of mutual funds: equity funds, bond funds, mortgage funds, money market funds, and balanced funds.

NATIONAL INCOME the total earnings received by owners of the factors of production in a given period.

NATIONAL UNION a union with a membership base within a single country. The Canadian Union of Postal Workers is an example of a national union.

NATURAL MONOPOLY a market situation in which there is only one producer of a good or service and many buyers. The provision of electrical service is a natural monopoly.

NATURAL RESOURCES also called "land"; all the resources that occur in nature that have value and may be used in production. These resources include minerals, forests, water, and fish. Natural resources are considered by economists to be one of the factors of production.

OLIGOPOLY a market situation in which a few firms supply most of the goods and/or services. A few large oil companies, for example, supply most of the gasoline that we use.

OPEN MARKET OPERATIONS the buying and selling of federal government bonds by the Bank of Canada to control the money supply.

OPEN SHOP a business in which some workers belong to a union while others do not.

OPPORTUNITY COST the benefit lost in taking one course of action rather than another. If you decide to do your homework rather than watch TV, then the opportunity cost of the homework is the opportunity lost of enjoying TV.

ORGANIZATION OF PETROLEUM EXPORTING COUNTRIES (OPEC) an international cartel of oil exporting countries. The cartel raised the world price of oil many times during the 1970s; these increases fuelled inflation in the economies of countries dependent on oil imports.

PARTNERSHIP a business organization in which two or more individuals enter a business as owners, and share the profits and losses. Partnerships, like sole proprietorships, are common in agriculture; medical, dental, and legal professions; construction; repair work; and the restaurant business.

PERFECT COMPETITION a market in which uniform goods are bought and sold, and where prices are generally known; where there is competition between many buyers and sellers, and where no group of buyers or sellers attempts to fix prices. One example of a perfectly competitive market is a stock exchange.

PERSONAL INCOME the amount of money (from interest, wages, profits, and/or rent) received by an individual in a given period of time.

PHYSICAL WANTS the wants or needs that are necessary to sustain human life. Such wants include the need for air, water, food, clothing, and shelter.

PREFERRED SHARES stock issued by a corporation that shows ownership of the company; this stock has a preference over common stocks in the payment of dividends, and, in the event of the corporation's bankruptcy, in the distribution of the corporation's assets.

PRICE the exchange value of a good or service expressed in dollars and cents.

PRIMARY INDUSTRIES productive activity that is close to the land: farming, mining, fishing, forestry, and oil drilling; these industries produce staple products of grain, iron ore, wood pulp, oil, and fish.

PRIVATE PROPERTY the right of individuals and corporations to own not only consumer goods, such as shoes and televisions, but also goods used in production, such as factories and machines.

PRODUCTION any activity that serves to satisfy human wants. Thus, economists consider not only the manufacture of automobiles or the growing of crops to be production, but also the services supplied by teachers, surgeons, secretaries, and ballet dancers. Production involves the combining of economic resources (land, labour, capital, and entrepreneurial ability) to produce goods and services to meet our needs.

PRODUCTIVE RESOURCES labour or human resources (that is, workers of all kinds); natural resources or land (including forests, soil, and minerals); capital resources (such as tools, factories, and machines), and the entrepreneur (or self-employed business owner). All four resources are combined in production.

PRODUCTIVITY the output per person employed.

PROFIT the amount that is left over after all the costs have been met from the income of a business.

PROGRESSIVE TAXES taxes that progress or increase, along with the amount earned. The higher our income, the more we pay both in dollar terms and proportionately. As income increases, the percentage taken in tax also increases. Federal and provincial income taxes are examples of progressive taxes.

PROPORTIONAL TAXES the tax rate remains unchanged as income increases.

PROTECTIVE TARIFFS taxes imposed on imported goods in order to raise prices and thus restrict the amount sold. A protective tariff may be specific (that is, of a certain amount per unit), or ad valorem (that is, varying directly with the cost of the item).

PSYCHOLOGICAL WANTS the wants for those things that are not essential to sustain human life. They include wants for exotic food, fashionable clothing, and an air-conditioned home.

PUBLIC DEBT the debt incurred when government borrows money because tax receipts are not enough to meet government expenditures.

PUBLIC ENTERPRISE a form of business organization, also known as a Crown corporation, that is publicly owned and provides essential services. In Canada, the Canadian Broadcasting Corporation and Canadian National Railway are public enterprises.

PUBLIC GOOD a good or service that people cannot be prevented from consuming, no matter who pays for it. It is therefore usually provided by government. Police and military protection are examples of public goods.

PURE COMMAND ECONOMY an economy in which government, or some other central controlling body, provides the answers to the three major questions: what, how, and for whom (goods and services will be produced).

PURE COMPETITION a market situation in which there are many buyers and many sellers, with no seller or buyer being able to influence price. The stock market and some markets for agricultural goods are examples of pure (or perfect) competition.

PURE TRADITIONAL ECONOMY an economy in which the custom or tradition of the society provides the answers to the three major questions: what, how, and for whom (goods and services will be produced).

QUOTA a barrier imposed by government to restrict the amount of imports entering a country. Like tariffs, quotas protect domestic industry; unlike tariffs, quotas raise no revenue for government. In the past, Canada has imposed quotas on imported textiles and shoes.

RECESSION a period of the business cycle in which the Gross Domestic Product declines for at least two consecutive three-month periods. Canada experienced a recession in 1981-83, and in 1990-92.

RECOGNITION LAG the time that passes between the onset of a problem and the recognition of the nature of the problem. Recognition lags limit the effectiveness of government fiscal and monetary policies.

REGISTERED RETIREMENT SAVINGS PLAN (RRSP) a way to earn income for old age; every dollar contributed to an RRSP is deductible from taxable income. The income earned inside the RRSP is protected from taxes as long as it stays in the RRSP.

REGRESSIVE TAX as income increases, the percentage paid in tax regresses or declines. Provincial sales taxes and local property taxes are examples of regressive taxes.

RENT the payment made to the owners of a natural resource (land) for the use of that natural resource.

RESOURCES those things used to produce goods and services. These include human resources, the skills and efforts people use in organizing production; capital resources, such as factories and machinery; and natural resources, such as land and forests.

ROTATING STRIKE a strike in which workers in one location go out on strike for one day, to be followed by the workers in another location going out on another day, and so on.

SAVINGS that part of current income that is not spent.

SCARCITY the fundamental fact of economic life: there is a limited amount of resources that can be used to produce a limited amount of goods and services to meet relatively unlimited human wants.

SCHEDULE 1 BANKS large banks in which no individual can own more than 10 percent of the shares, and no group of foreign (except U.S.) investors can own more than 25 percent of the shares. There are six major schedule 1 banks in Canada.

SCHEDULE 2 BANKS small banks whose total assets are only a fraction of the big six schedule 1 banks. Most of Canada's 59 Schedule 2 banks are subsidiaries of foreign banks.

SEASONAL UNEMPLOYMENT the loss of jobs due to changes in the climate and other seasonal conditions. Lumbering, fishing, and retailing are examples of industries that experience seasonal unemployment.

SECONDARY INDUSTRIES productive activity that is involved in manufacturing staple products (grain, ore, wood pulp, oil, and fish) into finished goods.

SECURITIES instruments used by corporations to raise funds for business purposes. Securities are of three types: bonds, preferred shares, and common shares. Bonds represent loans to the corporation; the bondholder is the corporation's creditor. Preferred shares, as a rule, entitle the holder to a fixed rate of dividend. Common shares represent part ownership

in the corporation; common shareholders vote in the affairs of the corporation and share in the distributed profits.

SELF-INTEREST the pursuit of one's own advantage; the major motivating force in the pure market economy.

SERVICES all items that satisfy human wants, that cannot be touched, and that are consumed at the time of their production. A car tune-up is an example of a service.

SHIFTS IN DEMAND shifts that occur when there is a change in the quantity of a product demanded for reasons other than a change in price. For example, shifts in demand can result from changes in people's incomes or tastes.

SHIFTS IN SUPPLY shifts that occur when there is a change in the quantity supplied for reasons other than a change in price. For example, shifts in supply can occur with changes in the price of raw materials or productive resources.

SOLE PROPRIETORSHIP a form of business organization in which one person owns and operates the business. The majority of businesses in Canada are of this type. Sole proprietorships are common in agriculture; the medical, dental, and legal professions; construction, and the restaurant business.

STAGFLATION a situation that exists when a high level of unemployment (or *stag*nation) and a high level of in*flation* occur at the same time. Canada experienced stagflation in the 1970s and early 1980s.

STANDARD OF LIVING the quantity and variety of goods and services available in a country or society, including food, clothing, housing, education, and recreation.

STOCK EXCHANGE an organized market where listed stocks can be bought and sold. The Montreal, Vancouver, and Toronto Stock Exchanges are Canadian examples.

STRIKE withholding of labour services by members of a labour union.

STRUCTURAL UNEMPLOYMENT the loss of jobs due to long-term changes in consumer demand, the decline in natural resources, the development of new technologies, and shifts in trade between nations. For example, with the new technology of car building, blacksmiths were replaced by auto mechanics.

SUBSIDIES money paid by government to protect certain industries — e.g., defence and infant industries — from competition; an alternative to protective tariffs.

SUPPLY the quantities of a good or service that sellers are willing and able to sell at various prices in a particular period of time.

SUPPLY CURVE a graphic representation of the quantities of a good or service that sellers are willing and able to sell at various prices.

SUPPLY SCHEDULE a chart showing the relationship between product price and quantity supplied.

TARIFFS taxes levied on imported goods by government. A form of indirect taxation, tariffs may be imposed for the purpose of raising revenue for government or of protecting domestic industry. There are tariffs on automobiles imported from Japan and Germany to protect domestic industries.

TAXES obligatory payments made by individuals and corporations to government. Taxes may be direct or indirect. *Direct taxes* are paid by the person who is being taxed. These include income tax and provincial sales taxes. *Indirect taxes* can be passed on to other people. Consumers often pay taxes that manufacturers pass along in the cost of their products. Other examples of indirect taxes are federal excise taxes.

TECHNOLOGY the body of knowledge that can be applied to the production of goods and services. It includes the development of new products, new ways of organizing production, and new machines.

TERM INSURANCE a type of insurance that provides protection for a specified period of time.

TERTIARY INDUSTRIES the vital link between the producer and the consumer; these industries include transportation, marketing, and repair services.

TIME-SERIES GRAPH one of the most useful graphs in economics; represents time (e.g., weeks, months, or years) on the horizontal axis, and the variable (e.g., stock market prices or unemployment) on the vertical axis.

TRADITIONAL ECONOMY an economy in which the custom or tradition of the society provides the answers to the three major questions: what, how, and for whom (goods and services will be produced). Europe in the Middle Ages was largely a traditional economy.

TRANSFER PAYMENTS payments by one level of government to another level of government or to an individual or business. A good or service is not provided in return for the payment. Family allowances, pensions, and payments to provincial governments are examples of federal transfer payments.

UNDERGROUND ECONOMY economic activity that is not reported to Revenue Canada. It includes legal activities and illegal activities (such as the narcotics trade).

UNEMPLOYED those over age fifteen who are temporarily laid off, and those who are without work and who are actively seeking employment.

UNEMPLOYMENT RATE the percentage of members of the total labour force who are unemployed. In January 1995, the unemployment rate in Canada was 9.7 percent.

UNIT BANKING SYSTEM a system in which there are a large number of separate banks; contrasts with the branch banking system.

UNITARY ELASTICITY OF DEMAND a change in price brings about an exactly proportionate change in quantity demanded.

VELOCITY OF CIRCULATION the speed at which money circulates in an economy; the average number of times the money is spent. Changes in the velocity of circulation arise out of the decisions of consumers who decide how much of their incomes to spend and how much to save.

VERTICAL COMBINATION (or INTEGRATION) the control by a company of the various stages of production. A steel company, for example, controls the various stages in the production of steel from the mining of raw materials to the manufacture of finished steel products.

VISIBLE TRADE merchandise trade involving the import and export of visible, tangible goods.

WAGES regular payments to an employee for labour services. Wages are set by the hour, week, month, or year, or according to the amount of labour produced.

WAGE AND PRICE CONTROLS/GUIDELINES policies aimed at restraining inflation by holding wage and price increases below a specific level. The policies may be compulsory, in which case they are called controls, or voluntary, in which case they are called guidelines.

WANTS the need or desire for goods and/or services. Goods are visible and touchable, such as bread, computers, and clothes, while services are invisible and untouchable, such as airplane trips, rock concerts, and a lesson in economics.

WORK-TO-RULE a practice whereby workers obey to the letter all the laws and rules that relate to their work — thus bringing about a production slowdown.

BIBLIOGRAPHY

General

Baumol, William J., Alan S. Blinder, and William M. Scarth. *Economics: Principles and Policy.* 3rd Canadian edition. Toronto: Harcourt Brace Jovanovich, 1991.

Blomqvist, Ake, Paul Wonnacott, and Ronald Wonnacott. *Economics.* 3rd Canadian edition. Toronto: McGraw-Hill Ryerson, 1990.

Fellows, Michael C., et al. *Economics in a Canadian Setting.* New York: HarperCollins College Publishers, 1993.

Heilbroner, Robert, and Lester Thurow. *Economics Explained: Everything You Need to Know About How the Economy Works and Where It's Going.* New York: Simon and Schuster, 1994.

Hird, H. Richard. *Working with Economics: A Canadian Framework.* 3rd edition. Toronto: Collier Macmillan, 1991.

James, Elijah M. *Economics, a Problem-Solving Approach.* 2nd edition. Toronto: Prentice-Hall, 1991.

Luciani, Patrick. *What Canadians Believe, But Shouldn't About Their Economy.* Don Mills: Addison-Wesley, 1993.

Lyons, Brian. *Canadian Macro-economics: Problems and Policies.* 3rd edition. Toronto: Prentice-Hall, 1991.

McConnell, Campbell, R., and William Henry Pope. *Economics.* 5th Canadian edition. Toronto: McGraw-Hill Ryerson, 1990.

Parkin, Michael and Robin Bade. *Economics: Canada in the Global Environment.* Don Mills: Addison-Wesley, 1991.

Samuelson, Paul, and Anthony Scott. *Economics.* 6th edition. Toronto: McGraw-Hill Ryerson, 1988.

Stager, David. *Economic Analysis and Canadian Policy.* 7th edition. Toronto: Butterworths, 1992.

Thexton, James D. *Economics: A Canadian Perspective.* Toronto: Oxford University Press, 1992.

Vogt, Roy, Beverly J. Cameron, and Edwin G. Dolan. *Understanding the Canadian Economy.* 4th edition. Toronto: Dryden, 1993.

Reference

Dictionaries

Bannock, Graham, R.E. Baxter, and Evan Davis. *The Penguin Dictionary of Economics.* 5th edition. London: Penguin, 1992.

Crane, David. *The Canadian Dictionary of Business and Economics.* 2nd edition. Toronto: Stoddart, 1993.

Statistics

Statistical information before 1983

Urquhart, M.C., and K.A.H. Buckley. *Historical Statistics of Canada.* 2nd edition. Ottawa: Statistics Canada, 1983.

Recent statistical information

Bank of Canada. *Bank of Canada Review.* Ottawa: Bank of Canada, monthly and quarterly.

Statistics Canada. *Canadian Economic Observer.* Ottawa: Statistics Canada, monthly.

_____. *Canadian Economic Observer: Historical Statistical Supplement.* Ottawa: Statistics Canada, annually.

_____. *Perspectives Canada.* Ottawa: Statistics Canada, annually.

_____. *Canada Yearbook.* Ottawa: Statistics Canada, annually.

_____. World Bank. *World Development Report.* New York: Oxford University Press, annually.

Recent economic developments

Canadian News Facts.

Financial Post Corporation Service Cards. Index of Publicly-Held Canadian Companies. Toronto: Financial Post.

The following newspapers:
Financial Post
Financial Times
The Globe and Mail
Local daily newspaper(s)
The following periodicals:
The Economist
Maclean's
Canadian Business
Fortune
Profit

Scarcity and Decision Making

Heyne, Paul. *The Economic Way of Thinking.* 6th edition. New York: Macmillan, 1991.

Kennedy, Peter, and Gary Dorosh. *Dateline Canada: Understanding Economics through Press Reports.* 4th edition. Toronto: Prentice-Hall, 1990.

Robinson, Marshall A. *An Introduction to Economic Reasoning.* New York: Anchor Books, 1980.

National Decision Making

Barber, William J. *A History of Economic Thought.* Harmondsworth: Penguin, 1991.

Friedman, Milton. *Capitalism and Freedom.* Chicago: University of Chicago Press, 1982.

Galbraith, John Kenneth. *The Age of Uncertainty.* Boston: Houghton-Mifflin, 1977.

Heilbroner, Robert L. *The Worldly Philosophers.* 6th edition. New York: Simon and Schuster, 1986.

Helburn, Suzanne Wiggins. *Economics in Society: Communist Economics.* Toronto: Addison-Wesley, 1977.

Nove, Alec. *An Economic History of the U.S.S.R. 1917-1991.* New and final edition. Harmondsworth: Penguin, 1992.

Shmeley, Nikolai, and Vladimir Popov. *The Turning Point: Revitalizing the Soviet Economy.* New York: Doubleday, 1989.

Productive Resources

Economic Statistics: A Workbook. Toronto: Canadian Foundation for Economic Education, 1980.

Garrod, Stan. *Economics in Society: Canadian Case Studies.* Don Mills: Addison-Wesley, 1984.

Income Outcomes. Program 1. Getting It Together (Circular Flow). Computer Software. Bloomington, Indiana: Agency for Instructional Television, 1986.

Using Ratios and Graphics in Financial Reporting. Toronto: The Canadian Institute of Chartered Accountants, 1993.

The Entrepreneur

Bliss, Michael. *Northern Enterprise: Five Centuries of Canadian Business.* Toronto: McClelland and Stewart, 1987.

Bodell, Richard W. et al. *Entrepreneurship.* Toronto: Harcourt, 1991.

De Jordy, Herve. *On Your Own: Successful Entrepreneurship in the 90s.* Toronto: McGraw-Hill Ryerson, 1990.

Gould, Allan. *The New Entrepreneurs: 80 Canadian Success Stories.* Toronto: Seal Books, 1987.

Jennings, William E. *Entrepreneurship: A Primer for Canadians.* Toronto: Canadian Foundation for Economic Education, 1985.

Kao, Raymond. *Entrepreneurship and Enterprise Development.* Toronto: Holt, Rinehart and Winston, 1989.

Kretchman, M. Lily et al. *Entrepreneurship: Creating a Venture.* Toronto: John Wiley and Sons, 1990.

Kuriloff, Arthur H., and John M. Hemphill, Jr. *Starting and Managing the Small Business.* Toronto: McGraw-Hill Ryerson, 1983.

White, Jerry S. *The Art and Science of Small Business Management.* Markham: Penguin, 1989.

Business Organization and Finance

Bliss, Michael. *Northern Enterprise: Five Centuries of Canadian Business.* Toronto: McClelland and Stewart, 1987.

Financial Post Corporation Service Cards. Index of Publicly-Held Canadian Companies. Toronto: Financial Post.

Fuhrman, Peter H. *Business in the Canadian Environment.* 3rd edition. Scarborough: Prentice-Hall, 1989.

How to Read Financial Statements. Toronto: The Canadian Securities Institute, 1985.

Macpherson, Ian. *Each for All: A History of the Co-operative Movement in Canada.* Toronto: McClelland and Stewart, 1979.

Starke, Frederick A. et al. *Introduction to Canadian Business.* Scarborough: Allyn and Bacon Inc., 1990.

Using Ratios and Graphics in Financial Reporting. Toronto: The Canadian Institute of Chartered Accountants, 1993.

Demand, Supply, and Markets

Friedman, Milton, and Rose Friedman. *Free to Choose.* New York: Harcourt, Brace, Jovanovich, 1990.

Income Outcomes. Program Four. Balancing Act. Market Analytics I. Computer Software. Bloomington, Indiana: Agency for Instructional Television, 1986.

Income Outcomes. Program Five. What Might Happen. Market Analytics II. Computer Software. Bloomington, Indiana: Agency for Instructional Television, 1986.

Stager, David. *Economic Analysis and Canadian Policy.* 7th edition (Chapters 3 and 4). Toronto: Butterworths, 1992.

Monopoly and Oligopoly

Francis, Diane. *Controlling Interest: Who Owns Canada?* Toronto: Seal, 1987.

Galbraith, John Kenneth. *The New Industrial State.* Boston: Houghton-Mifflin, 1967.

Green, Christopher. *Canadian Industrial Organization and Policy.* Toronto: McGraw-Hill Ryerson, 1980.

Hamilton, Adrian, ed. *Oil: The Price of Power.* London: Michael Joseph/Rainbird, 1986.

Thexton, James D. *Economics: A Canadian Perspective* (Chapters 9 and 10). Toronto: Oxford, 1992.

Distribution

Armstrong, Pat and Hugh Armstrong. *The Double Ghetto: Canadian Women and Their Segregated Work.* Toronto: McClelland and Stewart, 1993.

Phillips, Paul. *Regional Disparities.* Toronto: James Lorimer, 1982.

Phillips, Paul, and Erin Phillips. *Women and Work.* Revised edition. Toronto: James Lorimer, 1993.

Smith, Larry. *Canada's Charitable Economy: Its Role and Contribution.* Toronto: Canadian Foundation for Economic Education, 1992.

Thexton, James D. *Economics: A Canadian Perspective* (Chapters 12-14). Toronto: Oxford, 1992.

Labour Unions

Abella, Irving, ed. *On Strike: Six Key Labour Struggles In Canada (1919-1949).* Toronto: James Lorimer, 1975.

Bercuson, David Jay. *Confrontation at Winnipeg: Labour, Industrial Relations, and the General Strike.* Revised edition. Montreal: McGill-Queen's University Press, 1990.

Kehoe, Frank, and Maurice Archer. *Canadian Industrial Relations.* 6th edition. Oakville, Ontario: Twentieth-Century Labour Publications, 1991.

Leblanc, Ronald C. *Values, Value Clarification and Economic Understanding.* Toronto: Canadian Foundation for Economic Education, 1986.

Morton, Desmond, with Terry Copp. *Working People: An Illustrated History of the Canadian Labour Movement.* Revised edition. Toronto: Summerhill, 1984.

Consumption and Savings

Canadian Consumer.

Consumer Report.

Chilton, David. *The Wealthy Barber.* Toronto: Stoddart, 1994.

Hagstrom, Robert G. Jr. *The Warren Buffett Way.* Toronto: John Wiley and Sons, 1994.

Income Outcomes. Program Three. Bank on It. Saving, Investment, and Banking: Financial Intermediaries. Computer Software. Bloomington, Indiana: Agency for Instructional Television, 1986.

Pape, Gordon. *1995 Buyer's Guide to Mutual Funds.* Toronto: Prentice-Hall, 1994.

_____. *1995 Buyer's Guide to RRSPs.* Toronto: Prentice-Hall, 1994.

Protect Yourself.

Rabbior, Gary. *Money and Youth.* Toronto: Canadian Foundation for Economic Education, 1987.

Snyder, J. Christopher, and Brian E. Anderson, eds. *It's Your Money.* 6th edition. Toronto: Stoddart, 1989.

Government Expenditures and Revenues

Department of Finance, Canada. *Goods and Services Tax: A Summary.* Ottawa, 1990.

Friedman, Milton, and Rose Friedman. *Free to Choose.* New York: Harcourt, Brace, Jovanovich, 1990.

Minister of Supply and Services. *Current Year Estimates. Part 1: The Government Expenditure Plan.* Minister of Supply and Services, Canada.

Rabbior, Gary. "An Overview of the Goods and Services Tax." *Economic Bulletin #3.* Toronto: Canadian Foundation for Economic Education, 1990.

Strick, J.C. *Canadian Public Finance.* 4th edition. Toronto: Holt, Rinehart, and Winston, 1991.

Walker, Michael A. *Focus on Flat-rate Tax Proposals.* Vancouver: The Fraser Institute, 1983.

Money and Banking

Binhammer, H.H. *Money, Banking, and the Canadian Financial System.* 6th edition. Toronto: Nelson, 1993.

Galbraith, John Kenneth. *Money. Whence It Came, Where It Went.* Boston: Houghton-Mifflin, 1975.

Income Outcomes. Program Two. Bank on It. Saving, Investment, and Banking: Financial Intermediaries. Computer Software. Bloomington, Indiana: Agency for Instructional Television, 1986.

Morgan, E. Victor. *A History of Money.* Harmondsworth: Penguin, 1965.

Rabbior, Gary. *Money and Monetary Policy in Canada.* Toronto: Canadian Foundation for Economic Education, 1994.

Unemployment

Berton, Pierre. *The Great Depression 1929-1939.* Toronto: McClelland and Stewart, 1990.

Galbraith, John Kenneth. *The Age of Uncertainty.* Boston: Houghton-Mifflin, 1977.

Grant, John. *A Handbook of Economic Indicators.* Toronto: University of Toronto Press, 1992.

Income Outcomes. Macropol. Macro-economic Policy. Computer Software. Bloomington, Indiana: Agency for Instructional Television, 1986.

Rabbior, Gary. *The "Macro" Economy: An Introduction to How It Works.* Toronto: Canadian Foundation for Economic Education, 1989.

Safarian, A.E. *The Canadian Economy in the Great Depression.* Toronto: McClelland and Stewart, 1970.

Inflation

Rabbior, Gary. *The "Macro" Economy: An Introduction to How It Works.* Toronto: Canadian Foundation for Economic Education, 1989.

_____. *Money and Monetary Policy in Canada.* Toronto: Canadian Foundation for Economic Education, 1994.

Rotstein, Abraham. *Rebuilding From Within: Remedies for Canada's Ailing Economy.* Toronto: James Lorimer, 1984.

Economic Growth and Productivity

Beck, Nuala. *Shifting Gears: Thriving in the New Economy.* Toronto: HarperCollins, 1993.

Cohen, Dian and Guy Stanley. *No Small Change: Success in Canada's New Economy.* Toronto: Macmillan, 1993.

Currie, Stephanie. *International Economic Development. What Path? What Future?* Toronto: Canadian Foundation for Economic Education, 1990.

Easterbrook, W.J., and Hugh G.J. Aitken. *Canadian Economic History.* Toronto: University of Toronto Press, 1988.

Howard, Ross, and Michael Perly. *Poisoned Skies: Who'll Stop Acid Rain?* Toronto: Stoddart, 1991.

Income Outcomes. Program Two. Economic Growth. Pursuit, Sources, and Economic Growth. Computer Software. Bloomington, Indiana: Agency for Instructional Television, 1986.

Income Outcomes. Program Six. Who Pays? Who Gains? Government Role in Economic Growth. Computer Software. Bloomington, Indiana: Agency for Instructional Television, 1986.

Marr, William L., and Donald G. Paterson. *Canada: An Economic History.* Toronto: Gage, 1980.

Schumacher, E.F. *Small is Beautiful.* London: Abacus, 1973.

Todaro, Michael P. *Economic Development in the Third World.* 4th edition. New York: Longman, 1989.

World Bank. *World Development Report.* New York: Oxford University Press, annually.

The World Resources Institute. *World Resources 1992-93.* New York: Oxford University Press, 1992.

International Trade

Barlow, Maude. *Parcel of Rogues: How Free Trade Is Failing Canada.* Revised edition. Toronto: Key Porter, 1991.

Currie, Stephanie. *International Economic Development. What Path? What Future?* Toronto: Canadian Foundation for Economic Education, 1990.

Income Outcomes. Program Eight. Trade It. International Trade. Computer Software. Bloomington, Indiana: Agency for Instructional Television, 1986.

Rabbior, Gary. *The Bridges Project: A Teaching Resource Kit.* Toronto: Canadian Foundation for Economic Education, 1993.

_____. *The Canadian Economy: Adjusting to Global Change.* Toronto: Canadian Foundation for Economic Education, 1990.

_____. *Export Canada: Opportunities and Challenges in the World Economy.* Toronto: Canadian Foundation for Economic Education, 1984.

White, Randall. *Fur Trade to Free Trade.* Toronto: Dundurn Press, 1988.

INDEX

CREDITS AND SOURCES

vi (1) © MacDonald Photography/Unicorn Stock Photos; vi (2), 1 (4, 6), 10 (2), 37 (6), 80 (1), 138 (4), 139 (5, 7), 182 (2), 198 (3) (Courtesy of Bank of Montreal), 199 (5), 246-47, 267 (3), 329 (6) Dick Hemingway: Photographs; vi (3) © Steve Bourgeois/Unicorn Stock Photos; 1 (5) © Martin R. Jones/Unicorn Stock Photos; 7-8 Gary Lautens, "A bitter pill for Rich Marvin," *Toronto Star*, 19 February 1974. Reprinted by permission of Jackie Lautens; 10 (1) © Fred Jordan/Unicorn Stock Photos; 10 (3), 138 (3) Winston Fraser/Ivy Images; 10 (4), 111 (4), 139 (6) Ivy Images; 11 (5) © Tom McCarthy/Unicorn Stock Photos; 11 (6) Courtesy of Canada Post Corporation, 1994 — In Business to Serve; 11 (7) © Jeff Greenberg/Unicorn Stock Photos; 12, 34 *Maclean's Magazine*, Maclean Hunter Ltd., 4 January 1993 and 4 January 1994; 26 (cartoon), 119 (article), 163 (table 8.2), 191-92 ("The Future of the Unions"), 250-51 (article), 286 (Issue), 304 (figure 14.9), 326 (Issue 1) Reprinted with permission - The Toronto Star Syndicate; 27 Roy Peterson, *Vancouver Sun*; 30 Copyright © Knight Ridder Newspapers. Reprinted with permission - The Toronto Star Syndicate; 32, 33 (l) Courtesy of the J. Armand Bombardier Museum; 33 (tr, b), 34 Bombardier Inc.; 36, 37 (5) Industry, Science and Technology photos; 37 (7) Garth Roberts/Ivy Images; 38 *The United States Tennis Association Yearbook*, 1994; 41 From *Canadian Economic Observer, Historical Statistical Supplement*, 1990-91 and November 1994, Statistics Canada, Catalogue 11-210. Reproduced by authority of the Minister of Industry, 1995; 42 From *Canada Yearbook 1994*, Statistics Canada. Reproduced by authority of the Minister of Industry, 1995; 47 From *Canadian Economic Observer, Historical Statistical Supplement*, 1992-93 and November 1994, Statistics Canada, Catalogue 11-210. Reproduced by authority of the Minister of Industry, 1995; 48 Copyright © United Nations, 1991; 49 (figures 3.20, 3.21) From *Canadian Social Trends*, Autumn 1993, Statistics Canada, Catalogue 11-008E. Reproduced by authority of the Minister of Industry, 1995; 50 From *Canadian Economic Observer, Historical Statistical Supplement*, 1993-94 and Nov. 1994, Statistics Canada, Catalogue 11-210. Reproduced by authority of the Minister of Industry, 1995; 51 From *Canadian Social Trends*, Summer 1993, Statistics Canada, Catalogue 11-008E. Reproduced by authority of the Minister of Industry, 1995; 58 (figures 3.31, 3.32) From *The Labour Force*, October 1994, Statistics Canada, Catalogue 71-001. Reproduced by authority of the Minister of Industry, 1995; 59 From *Canadian Economic Observer*, 1992-93 and August 1994, Statistics Canada, Catalogue 11-010. Reproduced by authority of the Minister of Industry, 1995; 60 (1) Courtesy of Lick's Burger & Ice Cream Shops; 60 (2) Photo Courtesy of Daniel Wexler; 61 (3) Ceiling Doctor, Inc. Text adapted from Gordon Donaldson, "Vaulting

ambition," *Canadian Business*, January 1989, and "The Platinum 200: Reaching For the Top," *Income Opportunities*, February 1995; 62, 63, 64, 72, 78, 91, 96, 104, 105, 152 ("Why gasoline prices move so crazily"), 194-96, 214, 244 (figure 11.7), 345 (table 16.1) Reprinted by permission of The Globe and Mail; 68 Reprinted with permission. From *Entrepreneurship in the U.S. Economy*, copyright © 1994. National Council on Economic Education, New York, N.Y. All rights reserved; 69, 70 Courtesy of The Venture Centre; 71 (tl) Tim Hortons; 71 (cl) Mark's Work Wearhouse; 71 (bl) Courtesy Century 21; 71 (tr) Alimentation Couche-Tard Inc.; 71 (cr) Stuart McCall/North Light; 71 (br) P.S. Atlantic Limited; 80 (2) © Dick Young/Unicorn Stock Photos; 80 (3) Alcan Aluminium Ltd.; 81 (4) Photo Courtesy of VIA Rail Canada; 81 (5) Courtesy of Alberta Wheat Pool; 81 (6) Courtesy of VanCity Credit Union Chinatown branch; 88 Reprinted by permission from *Canadian Business Magazine*, June 1993; 93 McGraw-Hill Ryerson Limited; 96 Sources: I.P. Sharp and Associates; The Globe and Mail; 110 (1) © A. Gurmankin/Unicorn Stock Photos; 110 (2) © Arni Katz/Unicorn Stock Photos; 110 (3) © Aneal Vohra/Unicorn Stock Photos; 111 (5) Photo Courtesy of Kitchener Farmers' Market, Kitchener, Ontario; 111 (6), 138 (2) Bourse de Montréal; 133 Schwadron. Cartoonists & Writers Syndicate; 138 (1) Courtesy of St. Jacobs Country Tourism; 140 © 1987 King Features Syndicate. World rights reserved. Reprinted with special permission of King Features Syndicate; 146 Adapted from *Calura*, 1991, Statistics Canada, Catalogue 61-220 (previously 61-210). Reproduced by authority of the Minister of Industry, 1995; 151 Henry G. Manne, "The Parable of the Parking Lots," *Economics*, McGraw-Hill Ryerson Limited; 154 Joint Council on Economic Education; 155 *The Financial Post*, 6 July 1993; *Source:* International Coffee Organization; 162 *Canadian Labour Law Reports*, CCH Canadian Limited, 1994; 163 ADAM © 1991 UNIVERSAL PRESS SYNDICATE. Reprinted with permission. All rights reserved; 163-64 *The Financial Post*, 29 April 1993; 163 Statistics Canada, 1991 census. Excerpted from *Toronto Star*, 2 May 1993; 169, 170 (figures 8.7, 8.8) From *Canadian Economic Observer, Historical Statistical Supplement*, 1992-93, Statistics Canada, Catalogue 11-210. Reproduced by authority of the Minister of Industry, 1995; 171 (table 8.3), 172, 174, 176 From *Income Distribution by Size in Canada*, 1992, Statistics Canada, Catalogue 13-207. Reproduced by authority of the Minister of Industry, 1995; 171 (figure 8.10) From *Family Incomes*, 1992, Statistics Canada, Catalogue 13-208. Reproduced by authority of the Minister of Industry, 1995; 178 CALVIN AND HOBBES © 1993 Watterson. Dist. by UNIVERSAL PRESS SYNDICATE. Reprinted with permission. All rights reserved; 178 From *Family Incomes*, 1985, Statistics Canada, Catalogue 13-208. Reproduced by authority of the Minister of Industry, 1995; 182

(1) McCord Museum of Canadian History, Notman Photographic Archives; 182 (3) Provincial Archives of Manitoba/N12299; 183 (4) Craig Robertson/Canada Wide; 183 (5) Wallace/Canapress; 185 (6) Gunn/Canapress; 185, 187, 189 Reproduced with permission of the Minister of Supply and Services, 1995; 198 (1) Veronica Milne/ Canada Wide; 198 (2) Ken Kerr/Canada Wide; 199 (4) Royce Bair/ Unicorn Stock Photos; 199 (6) © MacDonald Photography/Unicorn Stock Photos; 203 HERMAN © 1987 Jim Unger. Reprinted with permission of Universal Press Syndicate. All rights reserved; 204 From *Family Expenditures in Canada*, 1990, Statistics Canada, Catalogue 62-555. Reproduced by authority of the Minister of Industry, 1995; 207-209 Robert E. Pierce; 217 Source: 1993 Life Insurance Tables, Stone & Cox Limited; 218 The Toronto Stock Exchange, *1993 Shareholders Study*; 219 Royal Trust Corporation of Canada; 222-23 Source: *The Economist*, 17 October 1992; 223 REUTERS/ BETTMANN; 224 (1) Calgary Parks and Recreation; 224 (2) Shott/ House of Commons; 224 (3) Courtesy Government of P.E.I., Audio Visual Services; 225 (4) Courtesy of the Canadian Forces; 225 (5) Vancouver Trade and Convention Centre; 225 (6) National Research Council of Canada; 226 Adaptation of "Government business in the bathrooms of the nation" from *The Canadian Political System* by Richard J. Van Loon and Michael S. Whittington (McGraw-Hill Ryerson, 1981). Reprinted by permission of McGraw-Hill Ryerson; 230 (table 11.1), 340 (figure 16.5) From *Canadian Economic Observer*, April 1994, Statistics Canada, Catalogue 11-010. Reproduced by authority of the Minister of Industry, 1995; 230 Reprinted from April 1993 Budget (1993-94 projections) by permission of Finance Canada; 231 Sources: Government of Canada, *Public Accounts*, 1992-93, and Ministry of Supply and Services, *The Budget Plan*, 1994; 235 Source: Revenue Canada, *1993 Tax Guide*; 235, 237 Merle Tingley, Ting Cartoons; 236 Reprinted from *Public Accounts 1992-93* and *The Budget 1993*, Supply and Services Canada. Reproduced with the permission of the Minister of Supply and Services Canada, 1995; 238 *The Financial Post*, 27 July 1994; 240 Toronto Dominion Bank, Department of Economic Research. As at August 1994; 244 Source: *Maclean's Magazine*, Maclean Hunter Publishing Ltd., 21 February 1994; 247 (brochure) Courtesy of Canada Trust; 251 (figure 12.1), 293 (figure 14.5), 313 (table 15.1) Reprinted from *Bank of Canada Review* by permission; 252 © Field Enterprises Inc. 1974. By permission of Johnny Hart and Creators Syndicate, Inc.; 254 Excerpt from "The Economic Organization of a POW Camp" by R.A. Radford is reprinted from *Economica*, London School of Economics and Political Science, Vol. XII, No. 48, November 1945, by permission of Blackwell Publishers; 257 Source: *Corpus Almanac and Canadian Sourcebook*; 266 (1) Joe Sohm/Chromosohm 1990/ Unicorn Stock Photos; 266 (2) General Motors of Canada Ltd., Vintage Vehicle Services Inc., 267 (4) Glenbow Archives, Calgary, Alberta, NC-6-12955e; 269 From *Canadian Economic Observer*, 1992-1993 and July 1994, Statistics Canada, Catalogue 11-010. Reproduced by authority of the Minister of Industry, 1995; 270 Human Resources Development Canada; 270 From *Canadian Economic Observer*, 1992-1993 and March 1994, Statistics Canada, Catalogue 11-010. Reproduced by authority of the Minister of Industry, 1995; 272 Len Norris from the *Vancouver Sun*; 273 From *The Labour Force*, October 1994, Statistics Canada, Catalogue 71-001, and *Canadian Economic Observer*, 1992-93 and July 1994, Statistics Canada, Catalogue 11-010. Reproduced by authority of the Minister of Industry, 1995; 283 Reprinted by permission of Newspaper Enterprise Association; 288 (Coca-Cola ad; bicycle ad), 289 (movie ad) Metropolitan Toronto Reference Library; 288 (vegetable store) City of Toronto Archives/SC-244-339; 289 ("ladies' bicycle jerseys") The Eaton Collection at the Archives of Ontario; 293 From *The Consumer Price Index*, March 1994, Statistics Canada, Catalogue 62-001. Reproduced by authority of the Minister of Industry, 1995; 293 From *Canadian Economic Observer*, 1992-93, Statistics Canada, Catalogue 11-010. Reproduced by authority of the Minister of Industry, 1995; 305 *The Financial Post*, 5 March 1993; 306 Gallup Canada, January 1994; 308 (1a) Maritime Museum of the Atlantic; 308 (1b) Courtesy of Canada Steamship Lines Inc., 308 (2a) Photo courtesy of GM of Canada; 309 (3a) MT&T; 309 (3b) Marvin Moore, Photographer/MT&T; 309 (2b) Photo/Courtesy of GM of Canada; 313 From *Canadian Economic Observer, Historical Statistical Supplement*, 1990-91 and April 1994, Statistics Canada, Catalogue 11-210. Reproduced by authority of the Minister of Industry, 1995; 317-319 Adapted from an article by Deborah Jones from *Report on Business*, March 1994, by permission of the author; 319 Courtesy of the Government of Nova Scotia, photo by Robinson/Campbell & Associates, Halifax; 321 *Toronto Sun*, 30 September 1973; 322-24 From *World Resources 1990-91* by the World Resources Institute. Copyright © 1991 by the World Resources Institute. Reprinted by permission of Oxford University Press, Inc.; 325 From *World Resources 1992-93* by the World Resources Institute. Copyright © 1992 by the World Resources Institute. Reprinted by permission of Oxford University Press, Inc.; 328 (1) Courtesy of Canada Steamship Lines Inc.; 328 (2) California Artichoke Advisory Board; 328 (3) British Tourist Authority, 111 Avenue Road, Toronto, ON; 328 (4) AECL Candu; 329 (5a and b) Whistler Resort Association; 333-36 Adapted from "A Parable of Advantage," *The Financial Post*, 28 June 1980; 341 (figure 16.6), 342 (figure 16.7), 343 (figures 16.8, 16.9), 344 (figure 16.10) From *Canada's Balance of International Payments, Fourth Quarter*, 1993, Statistics Canada, Catalogue 67-001. Reproduced by authority of the Minister of Industry, 1995; 346 Source: *The Economist*, 9 April 1994; 349 Reprinted by permission of Adrian Raeside; 350 From *World Development Report 1993* by the World Bank. Copyright © 1993 by The International Bank for Reconstruction and Development/The World Bank. Reprinted by permission of Oxford University Press, Inc.